RACECHANGES

RACE AND AMERICAN CULTURE

Arnold Rampersad and Shelley Fisher Fishkin
General Editors

Love and Theft
Blackface Minstrelsy and the American Working Class
Eric Lott

The Dialect of Modernism
Race, Language, and Twentieth-Century Literature
Michael North

Bordering on the Body
The Racial Matrix of Modern Fiction and Culture
Laura Doyle

"Who Set You Flowin'?"
The African American Migration Narrative
Farah Jasmine Griffin

"Doers of the Word"
African-American Women Speakers and Writers
in the North (1830–1880)
Carla L. Peterson

Race, Rape, and Lynching
The Red Record of American Literature, 1890–1912
Sandra Gunning

Scenes of Subjection
Saidiya V. Hartman

Racechanges
White Skin, Black Face in American Culture
Susan Gubar

RACECHANGES

White Skin,
Black Face
in American Culture

SUSAN GUBAR

New York   Oxford

OXFORD UNIVERSITY PRESS

1997

Oxford University Press

Oxford   New York
Athens   Auckland   Bangkok   Bogotá   Bombay
Buenos Aires   Calcutta   Cape Town   Dar es Salaam
Delhi   Florence   Hong Kong   Istanbul   Karachi
Kuala Lumpur   Madras   Madrid   Melbourne
Mexico City   Nairobi   Paris   Singapore
Taipei   Tokyo   Toronto

and associated companies in
Berlin   Ibadan

Published by Oxford University Press, Inc.,
198 Madison Avenue, New York, New York 10016

Oxford is a registered trademark of Oxford University Press

Library of Congress Cataloging-in-Publication Data
Gubar, Susan, 1944–
Racechanges: white skin, black face in American culture /
Susan Gubar.
p.   cm. — (Race and American culture)
Includes bibliographical references and index.
ISBN 0-19-511002-1
1. Afro-Americans in popular culture.   2. Blackface entertainers—
United States—History—20th century.   3. Arts, Modern—20th
century—United States.   I. Title.   II. Series.
NX652.A37G83   1997   305.8'00973—DC20   96-28151

1 3 5 7 9 8 6 4 2
Printed in the United States of America
on acid free paper

For Donald Gray

CONTENTS

ILLUSTRATIONS

CHAPTER 7

COLOR INSERT (following page 168)
Eve, *Time* magazine cover girl
Robert Colescott, *Eat Dem Taters*
Robert Colescott, *George Washington Carver Crossing the Delaware*
Robert Colescott, *Shirley Temple Black and Bill Robinson White*
Robert Colescott, *Les demoiselles d'Alabama: Vestidas*
Robert Colescott, *Knowledge of the Past Is the Key to the Future*
(St. Sebastian)

PREFACE

After a dignified WASP medievalist from an Ivy League university confided in an airport bar that her eminent husband spoke "black talk" to their dog, I began to expect white people to respond to a description of my project with some kind of confession about the prominence of clandestine racial parodies in their own lives. An Irish-Catholic college administrator exhibited his perfected Stepin Fetchit shuffle; an Italian physician whispered his secret black nickname, intoning it à la Kingfish; a Jewish friend from college expressed delight that her dark complexion and kinky hair led Parisians to fete her (since her looks had only incited wary glances in the segregated neighborhood of her native Bronx); still another Jewish friend explained how bewildered (even abandoned) she felt when her sister—who socialized only with the black friends of her African-American husband—began identifying herself as a person of color and echoing the street cadences of the Harlem neighbors among whom she resided. "Zi Zigga ZUMbah ZUMbah ZUMbah, / Zi Zigga ZUMbah ZUMbah ZAY!": After months spent writing about the centrality of cross-racial mimicry in twentieth-century culture, I found myself less shocked, more bemused at a wedding reception when an ersatz "Zulu Warrior Chant," presumably taught to the paterfamilias of a Southern family by General Patton during the Second World War, was performed, accompanied by rhythmic hand-clapping and foot-stomping, by all his sons, sons-in-law, and grandsons.

That white people often engage in silly, sexy, sleazy, and sometimes sinister cross-racial masquerades was made manifest by impersonations that were often rendered within my extended family as well. White kids who went to inner-city schools on the East Coast did not necessarily get a better education than those who went to lily-white, small-town midwestern schools in the heart of Hoosier heaven except in one area, or so it seemed to me, comparing the extensive multiracial experiences of my friends' children with the more limited ones of my own.

> Ugh! Ungowah!
> Your Momma needs a shower,
> Your Daddy needs a shave!

> I said it,
> I meant it,
> I'm here to represent it.

Imitating the black kids in their New York City school, two honorary nieces performed their quasi-rap, quasi-cheer—"My back is breakin' / My belt's too tight / My booty's shakin' from left to right"—with an exuberant hilarity that came in part from the transgressive pleasure they savored in violating their own staunch convictions about its political incorrectness.

At a young age, after all, the girls had been brought up by their liberal parents—cherished friends of mine—to respect the right of African Americans to represent themselves. Yet they nevertheless reveled in a performance more savvy but just as ideologically suspect as my older daughter's frequent endearment to me at moments of parting: "I loves ya, honey," Molly would belt out, "but you'ze de WRONG color." She had taken in my stories about a childhood friend named Theresa who used to joke about my being the only white kid on the block and had made Theresa's language part of what in Molly's post-college days she now calls her own "idioverse." Having seen "blacks" mostly in movies like *Holiday Inn* (which features Bing Crosby dancing in blackface on Lincoln's birthday), Molly at the age of five or six felt pretty sure that Lincoln had been the first African-American President of these United States. Who said it, who meant it, who is here to represent it for people of color?

The answer, as everybody knows, is that whites have said what it meant to be black and have represented African Americans throughout the nineteenth and twentieth centuries. Although there has been a great deal of much needed scholarship documenting the history of black thinkers and artists lecturing, writing, and performing so as to demonstrate the intellectual and aesthetic acumen of the race not only to white audiences and readers but also to black ones, the humanity and the subjectivity of African Americans have often been staged by white people performing blackness. That whites have hardly produced flattering pictures of their black contemporaries has, of course, contributed to embarassment and anger over such portrayals. Simultaneously figured and disfigured, African Americans who were symbolically presented may have felt their race effectively erased in aesthetic productions—photographic, filmic, poetic, fictional—that always teetered on the edge of grotesque stereotyping and appropriation.

As the common determination to remain anonymous of the WASP scholar, the Irish administrator, the Jewish physician, the Southern paterfamilias, and the two adolescents indicates and as my opening anecdotes are meant to imply, my own interest in the ways and means by which—as well as the reasons why—white people imitate African Americans has been piqued by white people's determination to keep such exhibitions secret because of our shared belief that they are (or would be considered) wrong, unethical, degrading to real black people. What appears striking about those scenes of cross-racial impersonation, it seems to me, is the great divide between the highly censored, staid propriety with which people of conscience speak publicly about race and the private expression of far more disrespectful, indecorous attitudes felt to be vaguely shameful or shocking, a gap quite conscious and common in many white people's lives. Although the American imagination has repeatedly returned to figures attempting to cross the color line, although the recent appearance of newsletters and magazines entitled *New People* and *INTERRACE* attests to a growing population of biracial people, the pressures to separate black from white remain extensive.

The racial mutations and metamorphoses discussed in the pages to come have little to do with actual changes in melanin and sometimes have even less to do with real African Americans. Instead, they illuminate the psychology of whites who have evolved through a series of oppositional identities predicated on black Others. The "black" in the chapters that follow—not always or even usually an African-American human being—operates as a generic commodity constructed by the white imagination for white people. The pertinacity of our vocabulary of a racial duality of whiteness versus blackness—though it flies in the face of multiple ethnicities as well as clear visual evidence of a spectrum of shades and hues of complexion—reflects Manichean ideologies that have profoundly shaped aesthetic achievements in the twentieth century, ideologies that inform the manifold racial impersonations that I call "racechanges" and that I trace through the pages of this book.

As I worked on this project during this last decade of the twentieth century, many items in the news convinced me of its timeliness. Michael Jackson's infamous lightening of his skin was only the most obvious evidence of the ongoing evolution of passing traditions (rooted in Euro-American overvaluations of whiteness). Similarly, Ted Danson's shocking use of blackface at a Friars' Club roast was only the most conspicuous testimony of lasting taboos against minstrelsy (founded on Euro-American devaluations of blackness). When Susan Smith's description of the "black man" who stole her car and her two babies (strapped into the back seat) resulted in a composite drawing of the suspect, detectives began to surmise that she had performed a racechange so as to conceal her own crime by exploiting prevailing stereotypes about black criminality: "If you took off the stocking cap and narrowed his lips," police thought about the sketch, "he looked an awful lot like Smith's estranged husband, David" (*Newsweek*, Nov. 14, 1994, p. 28). According to many white TV addicts, O. J. Simpson entered his trial "as a fellow white man and grew darker as the proceedings went on" (*Time*, Oct. 16, 1995, p. 43).

In popular as well as elite art forms, too, racial masquerade and racechange appeared to play a crucial role for white men and women. Although the percentage of African-American undergraduates in college populations decreased throughout the last decade, many white kids displayed fashions from the ghetto, proof positive of the phenomenon Cornel West calls "the Afro-Americanization of white youth" (121): Some self-proclaimed "whiggers" sported cornrows, dreadlocks, or shaved scalps featuring razored designs; others flaunted baggy jeans, baseball hats worn backwards, or clunky, unlaced basketball shoes. During the same period that the movie *Soul Man* (1986) depicted a white student obtaining entrance into Harvard's Law School by impersonating a black and thus gaining affirmative action support, a group of musicians calling themselves Young Black Teenagers consisted of white rappers claiming affinities with black culture. On the USA cable channel weeknights, the syndication *Quantum Leap* featured a central character bounding into the bodies of oppressed people, with one episode showing the white hero becoming a black man at a segregated Southern lunch counter; in another he turns into an African American involved in an interracial romance during the Watts riot. The popular television series *Northern Exposure* included several episodes in which white Chris dreams his black brother Bernard's dreams, a signal of their interlaced subjectivities.

In 1993, two phenomena (that I contextualize in my introductory chapter) dramatically underscored the importance of cross-racial patterns of imagery. *Time* magazine featured a cover devoted to "The New Face of America," a computer-created portrait of a "new Eve" whose racial and ethnic features reflected the Anglo-Saxon, Middle Eastern, African, Asian, Southern European, and Hispanic countenances used to produce the composite image. At the same time, the Fox channel broadcast to some twenty-seven countries Michael Jackson's music video "Black or White," in which a white boy uses the heavy metal music his father dislikes to blast pater into an Africa peopled by tribesmen who metamorphose into Balinese and Native American dancers. Using the same Morph 2.0 computer program the editors of *Time* employed, Jackson next filmed a sequence of faces—black and white, female and male, Asian and Native American—blending into one another.

A couple of years later in a different riff on race, black actors on both sides of the Atlantic starred in *Hot Mikado*, a swing adaptation of Gilbert and Sullivan's 1885 use of ersatz Japanese characters to satirize the foibles of the British. Toward the end of 1995, Colin Powell's daughter, Linda Powell, performed in Douglas Turner Ward's play *Day of Absence* (1965), a satire about race relations with an all-black cast in "a reverse minstrel show done in white-face" (29), while the denouement of the movie *Devil in a Blue Dress* unmasked its light-skinned *femme fatale* as an African-American passer, and John Travolta starred with Harry Belafonte in *White Man's Burden*, Demond Nakano's film about an America populated by a wealthy black elite and an angry, dispossessed white underclass. At the time this manuscript was being read by its editor at Oxford University Press, ads started appearing for a movie called *A Family Affair*, in which Robert Duvall discovers that he has a black brother, James Earl Jones. On the day the copyeditor phoned to say she had finished her work on this manuscript, *The New Yorker* published Henry Louis Gates, Jr.'s article "White like Me" about "Anatole Broyard [who] wanted to be a writer, not a black writer. So he chose to live a lie rather than be trapped by the truth." As one acquaintance put it about the brilliant reviewer and memoirist, "He was black when he got into the subway in Brooklyn, but as soon as he got out at West Fourth Street he became white" (66–67).

To what extent, I wondered, were such racechanges motivated by multiple fantasies, propelled by various dynamics of desire. What were the motives, where did the pleasures reside in the psychology of racechange? Opinions about even one instance of cross-racial impersonation could vary quite sharply. About Anatole

Broyard, for instance, some felt he was simply "anti-black," while others saw him as a master of "self-creation" (74). Although the "whiggers" sought liberation from the numbing decorum of middle-class white suburbia, the central character in *Quantum Leap* aspired to some sort of identification with the injustly oppressed Other, as did the producers of *Day of Absence, Devil in a Blue Dress, White Man's Burden,* and *A Family Affair.* Derogation clearly impelled Susan Smith and the creator of *Soul Man;* however, Chris and Bernard on *Northern Exposure* seemed to represent the wish of whites for a utopian cross-racial union or mutuality. Michael Jackson's video ends with the rubric "Prejudice is ignorance," and *Time* magazine's racially mixed, computerized cover girl was put together to dramatize what the editors called "the impact of multiethnic marriage, which has increased dramatically in the U.S. during the last wave of immigration."

Yet despite such purportedly libertarian purposes, the networks censored footage of Jackson smashing store windows while *Time*'s cover girl sent the libertarian theorist Donna Haraway into "a dyspeptic attack of political correctness" at diversity paradoxically transfigured into a numbing, "utter homogenity" (364). Perhaps her chagrin is best explained by a Dutch couple surprised to discover that in vitro fertilization had given them one light- and one dark-skinned baby because a technician unwittingly reused a pipette that still contained some sperm from a Caribbean donor. Wilma and Willem Stuart—dismayed because "Brown people have a smaller chance to get a decent job in our society. They can't get a bank loan like white people"—questioned the possibility of the enlightened multi-ethnicity glamorized by morphed computer images: "Every time the right-wingers and racists in Parliament open their mouths," the non-biological father of the darker child admitted, "I am frightened" (*Newsweek,* July 3, 1995, p. 38).

When I began thinking about the historical and aesthetic precursors of such startlingly diverse racial permutations, the most stimulating critic addressing the issue of white psychology vis-à-vis blacks was Toni Morrison, whose pioneering *Playing in the Dark* concluded with an analysis of Ernest Hemingway's *Garden of Eden,* specifically a passage in which Hemingway's blond-haired heroine attempts to transform herself into an "African girl." Curiously, in the second volume of *No Man's Land: The Place of the Woman Writer in the Twentieth Century,* Sandra Gilbert and I had discussed Hemingway's novel in terms of sexual transmutations, entirely ignoring the experiments of its heroine on the color line. While it may seem like a simple step to move from a project that included a book entitled *Sexchanges* to one called *Racechanges*—both investigations into the transgressing of boundaries, the liminal spaces between categories—I had blinded myself in *Sexchanges* to even the most flagrant performance of racechange.

Why? Was the subject of transracial crossing more taboo than that of transvestism or transsexuality? Not only has the blatant racism of minstrelsy (quite reasonably) made white impersonations of blacks seem shameful, it has also (less sensibly) spilled over to discourage scholarship about its ongoing impact on American culture. Just as inhibiting, various intransigent categories at work in contemporary cultural criticism (as it is practiced in the academy) would deem such an investigation if not unthinkable then suspect. Women (and only women) are supposed to write feminist criticism, while blacks (and only blacks) are supposed to produce works in African-American studies and only lesbians or gay men are supposed to publish in queer theory. In captious article after article published in scholarly journals, hyper-conscientious academics attack approaches inattentive to the differences between multiply hyphenated subjectivities (or subject positions), arguing that such undertakings should not ignore nor privilege nor metaphorize race, class, gender, and sexual orientation. So who was entitled to write—or who would dare claim to be entitled to write—about autobiographers born Jewish who identified themselves as black or straight, middle-class authors in thrall to working-class, homosexual fantasies, or interracial lines of aesthetic influence between men and women of letters? Ironically, though, the boundaries of area studies and their methodologies have begun to be policed more rigidly at a time when many other scholars have become fascinated, on the one hand, with the elasticity or permeability of categories of race and gender and sexual preference and, on the other, with the transgressive or liminal aesthetic experiments produced throughout our cultural history.

Besides dealing with transracial performances usually considered unacceptable or indefensible, this study explores the creative endeavors of men as well as women, of blacks as well as whites—not in an effort to elide differences between them but rather to engage such differences. To some scholarly readers, therefore, my speculations may seem grounded in subjects too diverse, while to others they will seem undertheorized. I took both these risks quite consciously in an effort to enliven my topic for that phantom of desire haunting all writers, the figure Virginia Woolf called "the common reader." I therefore attempted to avoid the aridity of academic jargon, to substitute in its stead wherever possible the allure of visual treatments of the trope of racechange. Rather than seeking to romanticize racial masquerades that indubitably discount African-American subjectivity, I want my study to illuminate the powerful attraction of black people and their culture within the white imagination as well as the imaginative centrality of the color line for African-American artists. Film analyses, literary interpretation, and cultural studies in this context document white insecurity as well as status anxiety, a subject that will increase in importance when more whites realize that they (we) constitute each year a smaller percentage of the world population.

What does it mean, though, that white fascination with black culture comes at a time when the lives of many African-American men and women are so imperiled? At the present moment, sociologists cite harrowing statistics documenting this society's fatal effects on its black citizens: Blacks, who make up about 12 percent of the U.S. population, are overrepresented in prisons (some 45 percent of inmates) and as victims of crime (approximately 50 percent of murder victims), but underrepresented in colleges (receiving only about 5 percent of awarded bachelor's degrees); three times as likely to be unemployed as whites, African-Americans are nearly four times as likely to live in poverty. Although it will always be tricky to turn attention away from such injustice and onto those who may benefit from it, a focus on whites understandably engages the issue of white remorse about racial inequality, which turns out to be a more significant motive in twentieth-century aesthetic productions than many critics have realized.

As Shelby Steele explains about the historical advantage white Americans know they have derived from the subjugation of blacks, "racial guilt simply accompanies the condition of being white in America" (81). I suspect, too, that such shame will continue to play a major role in our contemporary society, where suicide and black-on-black homicide vie as the leading causes of death for young black men. Statistics confirming equally dire conditions in earnings, life expectancy, and imprisonment appear in a book entitled *Young, Black, and Male in America*, whose subtitle—*An Endangered Species*—cannot be dismissed as Draconian. The so-called "Million Man March" took place the week after a Washington-based Sentencing Project broke the news that one out of three black men aged 20 to 29 was in jail, paroled, or on probation. That the mid-nineties has witnessed the publication of *The Bell Curve*, with its biologizing of racially defined mental capacity, as well as legislative assaults against affirmative action, attests to a growing backlash among whites about the ethnic diversity the culture increasingly exhibits. (Significantly, one paperback response to *The Bell Curve* features a racechanged cover image composed of a biracial male face with African features prominent in the lower half and European features in the upper half, an iconography that extends a long tradition of identifying the European with the mind, the African with the mouth).

Thanks to a generation of brilliant African-American critics—thinkers like Henry Louis Gates, Jr., bell hooks, Toni Morrison, Michele Wallace, and Patricia J. Williams—these issues have entered the work of literary scholarship with a nuanced but deeply ethical sophistication upon which I hope to draw and to which I am profoundly indebted. I have also been influenced by Leslie Fiedler's insight in *Waiting for the End* about Americans. "Born theoretically white, we are permitted to pass our childhood as imaginary Indians, our adolescence as imaginary Negroes, and only then are expected to settle down to being what we really are: white once more" (*Waiting*, 134). While I was writing this book, the related work of Michael Awkward, Diana Fuss, Eric Lott, Michael North, and Michael Rogin appeared in print and shaped my thinking. Of course, though, as my subtitle and the pages following attest, my greatest intellectual debt is to Frantz Fanon, whose *Black Skin, White Masks* continues to serve as a source of inspiration for scholars studying the guilt-ridden psychologies of racism.

Although Fanon consistently universalizes the masculine perspective, his application of psychoanalytic concepts to the construction of racial subjectivity has encouraged critics to study race and gender as reciprocal, interactive categories. Elizabeth Abel's "Black Writing, White Reading: Race and the Politics of Feminist Interpretation," Anthony Gerard Barthelemy's *Black Face Maligned Race: The Representation of Blacks in English Drama from Shakespeare to Southerne*, Gail Ching-Liang Low's "White Skins/Black Masks: The Pleasures and Politics of Imperialism," David Roediger's "White Skins, Black Masks: Minstrelsy and White Working Class Formation before the Civil War," Michael Rogin's *Black-*

face, White Noise: Jewish Immigrants in the Hollywood Melting Pot, and Kaja Silverman's "White Skin, Brown Masks: The Double Mimesis; or With Lawrence in Arabia" all attest to Fanon's far-reaching influence and elaborate the chiasmus of his title. Evoking Fanon's rhetorical parallelism enables these studies to other whiteness, to race it, to denaturalize those dominant ideologies that make whiteness virtually invisible. Similarly, for me racechange became a trope that made whiteness as startlingly visible as blackness has historically been. In addition, Diana Fuss's comment that the comma in Fanon's title "allows simultaneously for an essentialist and a constructionist reading" foregrounds my own effort to question the association of race with biology while at the same time recognizing the ways in which racial categories have hinged on skin color (*Essentially Speaking*, 75).

What I set out to study about whites is a psychology of entitlement but also of guilt that men and women display quite differently in racial masquerades, with white men almost exclusively playing blacks on stage and screen, and white women of letters more focused on the relationship between race, sexuality, lineage, and reproduction. That I have not followed a reversal of Fanon's formula to subtitle this project "White Skin, Black Masks" means that I want to draw attention to a blurring of boundaries involved in racial masquerades: When white people portray African Americans, they embody (and displace) them. The phrase "Black Face" is meant to invoke the history of burnt cork in minstrelsy, vaudeville, and film, but also the transfiguring effect of the staging of blackness on white subjectivity. Put simply, it is not nearly as easy to take off a black face as it is to remove a black mask.

I also hope that this study might extend recent insight into the indebtedness of mainstream American culture to African-American people, a case made most assiduously by Ann Douglas, George Hutchinson, and Eric Sundquist, who argue that we can only represent American literature by integrating the canon so as to comprehend the dialectic between white and black works of art. From this perspective, black productions can hardly be ghettoized from white. Andrew Ross, citing some examples before the commerce between white rock 'n' roll and black rhythm and blues, calls hybrid cultural productions "miscegenated" and describes "Elvis's rockabilly hair, greased up with Royal Crown Pomade to emulate the black 'process' of straightening and curling, itself a black attempt to look 'white'" (68). What does it mean, then, that on the Oprah Winfrey show, a young black singer named L. D. Shore gained fame as "the Black Elvis," an African American imitating a white man imitating black singers? Or, for that matter, that one of the finest performers of Klezmer music—folktunes from the Polish-Jewish *shtetl*—is the African-American entertainer Don Byron?

Because of Michelle Shocked's recognition of the crossover dynamic at work in her own performances, the white singer, seeking to call attention to the "real 'roots'" of her tunes, initially wanted to present her record *Arkansas Traveler* (1991) with a coverphoto of herself "wearing blackface." Deciding against any image that might provide grist for hatemongers, she nevertheless explained in her album notes that "'blacking up' should be done correctly" in "a context of true respect for the cultures we ape." No wonder that Marlon T. Riggs asks, "What is, after all, the 'black' in black pop culture?" As Riggs goes on to speculate,

> how do Marky Mark and Vanilla Ice and Charley Pride and Living Colour fit within our frames of reference? That is, the first two kinda sound black but ain't, and the last two are black but don't sound like it, if you know what I mean. So—I mean this seriously—what is the marker of blackness in our pop culture? (104)

Unlike Ross and Riggs, I will be focusing primarily on the pre-seventies decades of the twentieth century and I will be dealing not with music but instead with films, poetry, fiction, painting, photography, and journalism; nevertheless, I raise comparable issues about the markers of whiteness and blackness in our high culture. For though, according to Stuart Hall, "there's nothing that global postmodernism loves better than a certain kind of difference" (23), I hope to show that turn-of-the-century movie makers, modernist poets, and midcentury novelists and journalists as well as contemporary photographers and painters also savored what Hall calls "a touch of ethnicity, a taste of the exotic, . . . 'a bit of the other'" (23).

At certain times and within certain genres, we shall see that the fascination of white artists with difference makes no difference at all, based (as it is) on consuming (cannibalizing) the Other. Tasting a bit of the Other becomes nothing but a sound bite. At other moments and within some milieus, however, it may provide a fleeting glimpse into what we (as individuals and as citizens of the United States) have to gain culturally from the risky Whitmanesque enterprise of trying to contain (without confining) multitudes. Although the Other often collapses into the self-same because of a kind of societal absorption or cultural assimilation, sometimes it provides the opportunity to unravel bounded definitions of the self, opening the self up to its own alarming alterity, moving us as spectators or readers toward (a possibly dystopic, possibly utopian) transracial consciousness. The performance artist Anna Deavere Smith, who plays the roles of Lubavitcher women as well as Haitian men, Korean store owners as well as El Salvadorian revolutionaries in *Fires in the Mirror* (1993) and *Twilight* (1994), has explained that she created her "documentary theater" so that "the reenactment, or the reiteration of a person's words" would "teach [her] about that person" (*Fires*, xxvi). Using the language and cadences of people she had interviewed about their reactions to racial conflicts in the Crown Heights neighborhood of Brooklyn and Los Angeles, Deavere Smith attempts to make the "frame of reference for the other . . . *be* the other," to learn "about the other by being the other" (xxvii).

In the process of writing, I have learned about the Other from many others, generous friends and colleagues who provided intellectual stimulation and intriguing suggestions: Richard Bauman, Linda Charnes, Eva Cherniavsky, Shehira Davezac, Linda David, Dyan Elliott, Jonathan Elmer, Alice Falk, Mary Favret, Tom Foster, Reginald Gibbons, Geoffrey Hartman, James Justice, Walter Kalaidjian, Tricia Lootens, Herb Marks, Portia K. Maultsby, Andrew Miller, Carolyn Mitchell, Andrea Most, Betty Rose Nagel, James Naremore, Cornelia Nixon, Gene Rice, Alvin Rosenfeld, Chris Sindt, Werner Sollors, Jan Sorby, Jayne Spencer, Paul

Strohm, and Susan Suleiman. I profited, too, from working with a group of smart graduate students: Louise Bernard, Kelly Burns, Kyeong-Hee Choi, Radiclani Clytus, Laura Dawkins, Christian Fahlen, Elena Glasberg, Melissa Valiska Gregory, Jonathan Hillman, Joan Hope, Renata Kobetts, Lori Landay, Mary Lane, Susan Moke, Betsy Oster, Liedeke Plate, Marguerite Rippy, Maia Saj Schmidt, Naoko Sugiyama, Abigail Sutton, Beth Sutton-Ramspeck, Robert Richardson, Ashley Tidey, Natasha Vaubel, and Ellen Weinauer.

The Lilly Library and the Black Film Center Archives, both at Indiana University; the Indianapolis Art Museum; and the Beinecke Rare Book Library provided indispensable research help, as did Peter Gordon, chief Curator of the San Jose Museum of Art; Mary Corliss and Terry Geesken at the Museum of Modern Art in New York; Paul Cox in the Picture Library, National Portrait Gallery, London; Dott. Giovanni Scichilone at the Museo di Villa Giulia in Rome; Richard Barrios at Photo-Fest; John Wessel at the Wessel O'Connor Gallery; and Ron Jagger of the Phyllis Kind Gallery. For a grant that made it possible for me to devote myself full-time to this project for an entire academic year, I am exceptionally grateful to the National Endowment of the Humanities. To helpful administrators at Indiana University—Kenneth Gros Louis, George Walker, Morton Lowengrub, and Kenneth Johnston—I give thanks for professional support. The encouragement of Diana Finch at the Ellen Levine Agency and the excellent editing of T. Susan Chang at Oxford University Press buoyed me up when I worried about the sensitivity of the subjects I was broaching.

With respect to those readers kind enough to comment so attentively and extensively on sections of this manuscript—Elizabeth Abel, Judith Kegan Gardiner, Sandra M. Gilbert, Ray Hedin, Carolyn Heilbrun, Eric Lott, Nancy K. Miller, Toni Morrison, Michael Rogin, Judith Roof, and Robyn Wiegman—I can only express my gratitude for the time and thought you so generously gave to me as well as my hope that the final product has profited from your insightful suggestions. Along with the late Elliot Gilbert, Sandra taught me what I knew about critical writing when I began this work, and I will always remain dazzled by her unfailing wit, her staunch intellectual integrity. Especially to Nancy, whose poise and humor were a constant source of inspiration, I owe my pleasure in the revising of this text.

On the home front, the outstanding research assistance I received from Katharine Ings went far beyond the usual checking of notes and shlepping of books to include scholarly sleuth work and critical discoveries. Aided by Rahul Mehta and Joellyn Ausanka at Oxford University Press, Anna Meek's help with the manuscript was exemplary. On a daily basis, I gained immeasurably from my dear friend Mary Jo Weaver, whose fortitude and kindness encouraged me "to boldly go" on this first solo flight. The amiable companionship of Julie Gray and Beau cheered me on, as did the downtown savvy of Susannah Gray and John Lyons. In addition, the unflagging energies of my mother, Luise David, turned her into an indefatigable source of information and inspiration. About Molly (now known as Marah) and Simone Gubar, I can only marvel: Their contribution took the form of enlivening ideas and stimulating texts as well as salutary reminders of the limits of my thinking. With their intelligence and good sense, they serve as a beacon for their sometimes misguided but always appreciative mother.

Finally, I dedicate this book to Donald Gray, whose brilliant editorial skills and cultural insights continually enliven and challenge my speculations. His curiosity and wisdom about the interplay among aesthetics, history, and ethics have taught me how to think, even as they have made him an inspiring model. Eccentric though it may seem, this book is my way of saying thank you for "The hourly kindness, the days' common speech, / The habitual content of each with each."

RACECHANGES

[T]he problem of the Twentieth Century is the problem of the color-line.
—W.E.B. Du Bois

One evening an actor asked me to write a play for an all-black cast. But what exactly is a black? First of all, what's his color?
—Jean Genet

What one's imagination makes of other people is dictated, of course, by the laws of one's own personality and it is one of the ironies of black-white relations that, by means of what the white man imagines the black man to be, the black man is enabled to know who the white man is.
—James Baldwin

Black slavery enriched the country's creative possibilities. For in that construction of blackness and enslavement could be found not only the not-free but also, with the dramatic polarity created by skin color, the projection of the not-me. The result was a playground for the imagination. What rose up out of collective needs to allay internal fears and to rationalize external exploitation was an American Africanism—a fabricated brew of darkness, otherness, alarm, and desire that is uniquely American. (There also exists, of course, a European Africanism with a counterpart in colonial literature.)
—Toni Morrison

To his white European patients, [Frantz] Fanon is ineluctably black—"the Negro doctor." To his black Algerian patients, Fanon is white: a French-educated, upper-middle-class professional who cannot speak the language.
—Diana Fuss

ADVENTURES IN
THE SKIN TRADE

[H]ow difficult it sometimes is to know where the black begins and the white ends.
—Booker T. Washington

[N]ot only must the black man be black; he must be black in relation to the white man. Some critics will take it on themselves to remind us that this proposition has a converse. I say that this is false. The black man has no ontological resistance in the eyes of the white man.
—Frantz Fanon

Can human beings (and the cultures they create) be defined as either black or white? Or are most human beings (and the cultures they create) both black and white? These are the questions that seem to be posed by fascinating artifacts about race which survive from ancient times in the form of Janiform vases depicting the heads of Europeans and Africans. Dating back to 510 B.C., the two faces on one such Italian urn embody a study in racial contrast which is constructed by juxtaposing, feature by feature, a white and a black woman (Fig. 1.1). Seen in profile, hair, nose, lips, chin, jewelry (or its absence), and neck suggest that racial difference—not merely skin deep—dictates physiognomy, perhaps even psychology. Antithetical, the abutting heads seem to set the women at odds, for each looks out from her own perspective in a direction that dooms her never to see the other. Hardly a melting pot, the vessel portrays the races as distinct, separate, unamalgamated. Yet the burden of the ornamented pail shared by the two heads signifies a commonality eerily echoed by the two handles that come into view when the artifact is presented in either frontal position (Figs. 1.2 and 1.3). The white face now hides the black, the black the white. Somewhat like two sides of one coin, the dual faces constitute one head, one being, whose mysteriously doubled features speak to the complementarity of Western and African images of womanly beauty, of domestic supportiveness, or even of the biological capacity of the female to contain life as well as life-giving fluids. In this context, the salient, silent form of the urn communicates a teasing truth about racial comingling, fusing, intermixing.

As in Keats's famous "Ode on a Grecian Urn," the vase from ancient Tar-

Figure 1.1 Janiform Vase (510 B.C.), Museo di
Villa Giulia, Rome. Courtesy of Archeologica per
L'Etruria Meridonale.

Figure 1.2 White Face of Janiform Vase   **Figure 1.3** Black Face of Janiform Vase

quinia—or what we see as contemporary viewers looking at the vase—could be said to tell us all we know and all we need to know,[1] in this case about the contradictory disposition of racial representation in Western art. On the one hand, European and American artists have stressed the rigid boundaries separating race from race, while, on the other, they have documented racial interconnectedness and mutuality. Similarly, the two epigraphs for this chapter juxtapose the view (of Frantz Fanon) that race constitutes a rigid bifurcation with the belief (of Booker T. Washington) that race needs to be understood as a graduated spectrum. Imagining race—a category that has promulgated stories about civilization and nation, about family and identity—spawns an absorption with purity and pollution, integrity and hybridity, unity and plurality, sameness and difference. Throughout modern times, artists in virtually all media have meditated on racial relationships using multifaceted figures composed of ethnic comparisons, contrasts, and metamorphoses.

Though certainly conceptualizations of race have not remained static since the creation of the Janiform pail in ancient times, reading the vase now demonstrates how configurations of corporeal traits contributed to a black/white divide that paradoxically provoked in people on each side of it various transgressive maneuvers, much as has the arranging of the world into male and female.[2] Indeed, to Simone de Beauvoir, a thinker as obsessed with the inequality consigned to the Other as Fanon and Washington were, the urn might suggest "deep similarities between the situation of woman and that of the Negro," though it also implicitly challenges the all-too-common assumption that "woman" is white, "Negro" male (xxiii). Just as numerous sexual narratives were used to justify or explain the subjection of women, by the end of the nineteenth century stories about civilization and nation, about family and identity generated by racial imaginings exploited ideas about purity and pollution, integrity and hybridity, unity and plurality, sameness and difference that contributed to the subordination of whole populations.[3] By the twentieth century, when images of transvestism, androgyny, hermaphroditism, and transsexuality multiplied to negotiate the gender gap, what I am calling racechange had become a crucial trope of high and low, elite and popular culture, one that allowed artists from widely divergent ideological backgrounds to meditate on racial privilege and privation as well as on the disequilibrium of race as a category.

Racechange: The term is meant to suggest the traversing of race boundaries, racial imitation or impersonation, cross-racial mimicry or mutability, white posing as black or black passing as white, pan-racial mutuality. Over the past several decades, Americans have been repeatedly informed by psychologists and sociologists that the classification of peoples into Asians, blacks, Hispanics, and whites has no basis in science or biology, but such "folk taxonomies" persist, indicating how many individuals have not really been able to internalize such a proposition.[4] Racechange provides artists in diverse media a way of thinking about racial parameters. Just as the Tarquinian urn can be said to stress the rigid borders separating the races as well as the easy commerce between them, representations of racechange test the boundaries between racially defined identities, functioning paradoxically to reinforce and to challenge the Manichean meanings Western societies give to color. To begin with its most ambivalent and thus benign twentieth-century manifestation, racechange may be best viewed outside the American context that will elsewhere take precedence in this chapter and this book, specifically through a glance at the work of two Continental visual artists. For the experimental photographs and photomontages of Man Ray and Hannah Höch exemplify the instability and centrality of racechanging iconography in the modern period, and they do so by continuing to meditate on the relationship "between the situation of woman and that of the Negro."

During the first half of the twentieth century, Man Ray returned to the Janiform design to depict the juxtaposition of black and white faces because this aesthetic form could sustain doubleness, based, as it was, on the idea of the two-faced god Janus, a deity who stood at (and for) portals. A modernist riff on the Tarquinian urn, Man Ray's *Noire et blanche* (Black and white) series of images (1926)—with its juxtaposition of Anglo and African, light and dark forms of beauty—simultaneously postulates and traverses a gulf between African and European races and cultures. In the most distinctive of the photographs with this title, the illuminated, pale skin of Man Ray's model (Kiki de Montparnasse) can be read as an either/or statement about race since it contrasts with the dark, obdurate stone of the black head she holds with her hand (Fig. 1.4). Whereas the living face has all the marks of European urbanity—the flapper's tight cap of lacquered hair as well as her penciled brows and lashes, powdered lids, lipstick bow-mouth, and hint of an earring—the sculpted mask displays its African difference: With its symmetrically designed hair or helmet, its almost nonexistent mouth, and its half-opened, half-closed eyes, this artifact appears markedly less realistic, more stylized than the photograph Ray takes of it. An *objet*, the dark talis hints that, as Fanon speculates, black subjectivity has no ontological reality for whites. Thus, Kiki possesses the fetish—her hand exhibits it—because the picture counterpoints *Noire* with *blanche*, savage with civilized, black with white, the fad of *negritude* during the twenties with the art of photography which enabled modernist artists to appropriate or assimilate the crafts of alien and presumably primitive cultures.

But of course this photograph (as well as the others Man Ray produced on this theme) also emphasizes the *et* of his title, the both/and of race, suggesting the interchangeability or fungibility of model and mask. Light and dark heads alike cast shadows on the surface upon which they rest. Given Kiki's closed eyelids, both are blind, the objects rather than the subjects of the gaze. If anything, the stone head contains more agency than the person since its verticality appears to decapitate her. Though Kiki presumably has the superior consciousness of humanity, she is horizontal, as if asleep or dead, while the upright mask appears paradoxically more alert. In addition, Kiki's make-up, hairdo, and modeling mean she is just as constructed as the African icon, just as "framed" by Man Ray's "shot." Indeed, consenting to her erotic objectification, she endorses a colonization as complete as that of the exotic object. Nor, given his pseudonym, could this photographer be unself-conscious about man's (voyeuristic) rays. Or so Kiki's prone face—"made up" like a Japanese mask—suggests, since it looks like a rare shelved artifact.

Figure 1.4 Man Ray, *Noire et blanche* (Black and white, 1926), gelatin-silver print, 6¾ × 8⅞ in. Copyright © Man Ray Trust-ADAGP/ARS, 1997.

From this perspective, the hand of Kiki represents less an act of ownership than an indication of bonding or camaraderie, a touching connection that links two fetishized objects of otherness, the beauty of blackness *and* of white femininity killed into art.

The negative version of *Noire et blanche*—switching lights and darks—graphically emphasizes the photographer's accord with Booker T. Washington's point that it is sometimes "difficult . . . to know where the black begins and the white ends" (267): Here the now illuminated mask is foregrounded, as if it might be slipped over Kiki's face (Fig. 1.5).[5] As in several other "solarizations" Man Ray produced, the effect is spectral, even apocalyptic. The inanimate object gains animation while the presence of the living model is reduced to a ghostly absence. Hannah Höch, a friend of Man Ray's and a theorist of cultural hybridity, extended his experimental variations on the Janus form which reinforce even as they challenge normative racial polarization. In *Entführung* (Abduction, 1925), Höch cut out a photograph of a roughly carved African animal statue on which several figures sit, placed it on a larger base, and substituted a New Womanly face for one of the primitive heads; eclipsing the original Other, an image of the self—the modern profile—stands out with startling whiteness, positioned backward on the sculpted body of an African female (Fig. 1.6). Paradoxically, then, the native travelers are facing forward, while the amazed modernist looks backward (as indeed Höch does) to a primitive past

Figure 1.5   Man Ray, *Noire et blanche* (1926), negative version. Copyright © Man Ray Trust-ADAGP/ARS, 1997.

she seeks to excavate even as she criticizes how her contemporaries—artists and anthropologists—have reconstructed it. Despite modernist quests for an Ur-mythology grounded in the physicality of ancient, exotic cultures, Höch's New Woman remains a self divided, cut off from the body, a talking head.

Many of Höch's other collages in her Ethnographic Museum series mix so-called primitive sculptures of dark materials given traditionally African shapes with photographed white body parts. Framed within their frames by sculptural bases, pedestals, or platforms, Höch's discordant montages display "the arbitrariness of all canons of beauty, both familiar and exotic," as Maud Lavin puts it (166). According to Lavin, Höch's "humanistic linking of the subjecthood of Western and tribal peoples through montaging body parts" enabled her to consider the uncanny relationship between women commercialized as commodity fetishes, exhibited as mannequins, and primitives commercialized as ethnographic fetishes, exhibited as freaks (167–68). *Denkmall II: Eitelkeit* (Monument II: Vanity, 1926) features the legs of a naked, posturing white woman attached to what looks like an ancient black, androgynous fetish (Fig. 1.7); *Mutter* (1930) creates a number of facial plains in a cubist portrait that reveals the interplay of multicultural forms that seem to muffle or suppress subjectivity; *Fremde Schönheit I* (Strange Beauty, 1929) presents a seductively posed nude topped by a wrinkled (looming but possibly shrunken) head whose eyes look magnified through the oversized spectacles that underscore the viewer's own act of voyeurism. In all these works the juxta-

Figure 1.6 *(Above)* Hannah Höch, *Entführung* (Abduction, 1925), collage, 19.5 × 20 cm. Copyright © 1997 Artists Rights Society (ARS), New York/VG Bild-Kunst, Bonn; courtesy of Kupferstichkabinett Staatliche Museum Preussiche Kulturbesitz, Berlin.

Figure 1.7 Hannah Höch, *Denkmall II: Eitelkeit* (Monument II: Vanity, 1926), collage, 25.8 × 16.7 cm. Copyright © 1997 Artists Rights Society (ARS), New York/VG Bild-Kunst, Bonn; courtesy of Rossner-Hoch, Backnang, Germany.

positions between human and other-worldly body parts, symbolic and realistic corporeal configurations, combine to create sometimes funny, sometimes grotesque
aliens. Using biracial imagery to meditate on the mind-body problem, Höch sought
to confront the difficulty of knowing "where the black begins and the white ends,"
even as she studied the appropriation of the primitive that marks the ways in which
race is codified when the African blatantly lacks "ontological resistance" or interiority.

If ambivalence distinguishes the Janiform design as well as its namesake, the
Roman god of portals, Janus, whose doorways stand as entrances or exits, contradiction resides in the character of the racechanger, a shape-shifter who took center stage in the modern cultural arena. "I want to be your African girl," croons the
blond-haired heroine of Ernest Hemingway's *Garden of Eden* (begun in the
1940s), explaining to her white lover the tanning process she has utilized to dark-
en her skin. The experimental photographs of Man Ray and Hannah Höch may
seem far removed from Hemingway's cross-racial impersonator or from Vachel
Lindsay exploiting purportedly black rhythms to recite his popular poem "The
Congo" (1914) or from the reincarnation of the dead, white Patrick Swayze in the
living, black body of Whoopi Goldberg in the movie *Ghost* (1990); however, the
shifty iconography of racechange has enabled artists working in diverse media and
with quite different purposes to traverse racial boundaries and question racial presuppositions. The "trick" of racial metamorphosis participates in the illicit, the liminal, the transgressive, the outré, the comic, or the camp. Not simply mimetic,
racechange is an extravagant aesthetic construction that functions self-reflexively
to comment on representation in general, racial representation in particular. To the
extent that racechange engages issues of representation, it illuminates the power
issues at stake in the representation of race.

In the chapters to come, the permutations of racechange provide a means to measure altering societal attitudes toward race and representation. Of course racial
crossover and ventriloquism have long been recognized in music, especially in the
history of popular music. One thinks immediately of what Andrew Ross calls "miscegenated" musical productions generated by the interaction of white performers
and African-American traditions—Benny Goodman's swing, Elvis Presley's rock
'n' roll, or Vanilla Ice's rap—as well as those created by black artists (say, Charley
Pride and Living Color) whose productions "don't sound" black to an astute lis-
tener like Marlon T. Riggs, who is led to ask, "What is the marker of blackness in
our pop culture?" (Ross, 68; Riggs, 104). Julie Dash's movie *Illusions* (1983) emphasizes the cross-racial dynamics at work in the music industry by presenting a
behind-the-scenes view of a black singer's voice dubbed onto footage of a white,
lip-synching actress. But what about the other, earlier aesthetic forms racechange
often took? More specifically, how did the legacy of slavery and discrimination in
the history of the United States shape the patterns racechange acquired among Man
Ray's and Hannah Höch's American contemporaries?

The pages that follow spotlight white actors sporting burnt cork in pioneering
twentieth-century films; black artists investigating the origins of color in literature
and the visual arts; white poets exploiting black vernacular to speak as if from an

African-American subjectivity, as well as white patrons representing themselves through the language of the Harlem Renaissance writers they supported; white journalists blackening their faces in political pranks; and novelists, essayists, and painters envisioning sexually deviant whites as queerly colored or imagining parents of one race giving birth to babies who look like they belong to another. These are the phenomena I will use to identify the centrality of racechange in twentieth-century literature and art. As in the Tarquinian vase, the Man Ray photographs, and the Hannah Höch photomontages, racechanging imagery deploys sexual iconography to create a host of provocative connections and tensions between conceptions of race and those of gender. In any case, however, such figures are hardly the ones that first come to mind when the subject of racial impersonation is addressed.

On the one hand, the most notorious and arguably the most influential instance of racechange—one that still remains taboo because of its overt racism—appeared on the nineteenth-century minstrel stage, where white actors ridiculed African Americans. On the other hand, the most morally acceptable representation of racechange—indeed, the only one that has received extensive attention from literary scholars—surfaced in so-called "passing" novels, in which African-American characters masqueraded as white so as to assimilate into mainstream culture.[6] I begin with such black figures transforming themselves into whites because, as the writers to be discussed in this chapter demonstrate, this type of racechange functions as *the* crucial subscript of a supremacist society. Even before the passing novels of the Harlem Renaissance, black-to-white racechange played a decisive role in American culture. That we sympathize with light-skinned blacks passing as white to gain their rights and responsibilities and that we revile white people masquerading as black to mock African-American culture: This asymmetry clearly speaks to the devaluation of blackness, the overprivileging of whiteness in European and American culture.[7]

Yet regardless of which race engages in the charade and with what motive, twentieth-century performances of racechange depend on the two factors this introduction seeks to establish: first, the ways in which a culture that systematically devalues blackness and establishes whiteness as the norm effectively endorses, even enforces, black-to-white racechange; second, that historically such racial metamorphoses nevertheless (and paradoxically) constituted a crucial tactic used by civil libertarian activists and artists as a means of disentangling the category of race from skin color. In a society that teaches "If you're white, you're right" but "if you're black, get back," adventures in the skin trade often involve politically progressive blacks and whites trading places: blacks to gain the privileges of whites, whites to dramatize the privations of blacks, and both to unmask the arbitrariness of the system that accords those privileges. What, then, of the modernist ambiguities Man Ray and Hannah Höch achieved in photomontages which recapture the teasing equivocations of the Janiform urn? What, too, of the label of prejudice that has firmly (and rightly) attached itself in contemporary times to minstrelsy?

Although racism necessarily influences American thinking about racechange, just as it has contaminated the reputation of racechange, we will see the ways in which even—and perhaps especially—in the context of racism, racial imperson-

ation can operate as a saving strategy, one that enabled African Americans' survival and fueled their satire. Indeed, this chapter attempts to demonstrate that
artists from Claude McKay to Adrienne Kennedy depict African-American characters effectively instructed by American society that they will be inducted into it
as full citizens with complete personhood only if (in the words of George Schuyler's
title) they manage to be "black no more." In addition, writers from Charles Chesnutt to Virginia Woolf suggest that whites can understand the effect of this lesson
on African Americans only if they temporarily become "black like me" (to adopt
the phrase John Howard Griffin borrowed from Langston Hughes to entitle a best-
seller about Griffin's venture across the color line). This liberal traffic across the
color line makes us appreciate why and how throughout the twentieth century
white impersonations of blackness functioned paradoxically both as a deeply conservative (even racist) as well as a shockingly radical (sometimes anarchic) mode
of cultural production, one that has played a complicated role in film, fiction, poetry, painting, and photography.

If You're White, You're Right

A racechange imperative—from black to white—lurks in the very subordination
of blackness to whiteness at the center of racist ideology, whether it appears in the
British context of colonialism or the American of slavery. Consider, for example,
the beginning of Blake's famous poem "The Little Black Boy" (1789):

> My mother bore me in the southern wild,
> And I am black, but O! my soul is white;
> White as an angel is the English child,
> But I am black as if bereav'd of light. (ll. 1–4)

The word "but," which clusters around the word "black," repeatedly implies that
Blake's speaker experiences his race as a catastrophe, his complexion grievously
at odds with his soul's color. Because Blake's boy is taught by his mother that his
dark body and sun-burnt face are like a "cloud" or a "shady grove" in which he
can learn to bear God's light and heat, His love and goodness, the black speaker
concludes about the paradise he will ultimately share with a white boy, "I'll stand
and stroke his silver hair, / And be like him, and he will then love me" (ll. 27, 28).
Not only is skin colored "black" embodied (unlike the soul), it also signifies absence of light (unlike whiteness, which is imagined as the totality of light).[8]

More recently, Caryl Churchill's play *Cloud 9* (1984) dramatized the schizophrenia of Blake's speaker by casting a white actor to play the role of a colonized
black servant. In the first act devoted to displaying the farcical ideologies of English imperialism in Africa, Churchill's Joshua sounds strikingly similar to "The
Little Black Boy":

> My skin is black but oh my soul is white.
> I hate my tribe. My master is my light.
> I only live for him. As you can see,
> What white men want is what I want to be. (4)

Alienated from their native religions, their families, their own interests and bodies, Blake's "Little Black Boy" and Churchill's Joshua exhibit the psychological damage Fanon diagnosed in his classic book *Black Skin, White Masks* (1952), specifically his view that the colonized man of color thinks about himself, "There is no help for it: I am a white man. For unconsciously I distrust what is black in me, that is, the whole of my being" (191). A crisis of "corporeal reconfiguration" is inflicted on people of color, who are subjected to the "mirror" of an idealized whiteness that makes blackness horrific (Silverman, 27, 29).

"And be like him, and he will then love me"; "What white men want is what I want to be": Heaven for the black boy or man means obtaining the love of his white peer which is in turn predicated on the eradication of difference, the appearance of resemblance. Within the context of slavery, of course, such a resemblance could become a crucial means of survival. William and Ellen Craft's *Running a Thousand Miles for Freedom* (1860) describes the only possible solution to the horror of slavery as an escape route made possible by Ellen Craft's looking "almost white" (2). Disguised as an invalid gentleman, Ellen could be accompanied by her dark-skinned husband when she played the role of master to his slave. In case either her illiteracy or her smooth countenance might betray her, Ellen Craft bound up her right hand in a sling and wore a handkerchief over her cheeks. Although free Negroes existed in the South, William Craft explains, "every coloured person's complexion is *prima facie* evidence of his being a slave; and the lowest villain in the country, should he be a white man, has the legal power to arrest, and question, in the most inquisitorial and insulting manner, any coloured person, male or female" (36).

As if William Craft understood the allure of Ellen's race- and sexchange, he reproduced a picture of her as the frontispiece of his escape narrative, explaining that he managed to obtain his mother's freedom in part by selling the engraving of his disguised wife (Fig. 1.8). With her top hat, cravat, spectacles, and short hair, Ellen in the portrait does not wear the poultice that she used to hide the smoothness of her face, and, therefore, as Ellen Weinauer has pointed out, the engraving displays not really Craft's "wife in the disguise in which she escapes" (*Running*, 12) but, instead, an enigmatic, indeterminate figure—quasi-performer, quasi-performed—contesting the stability of gendered and racial categories of identity (50, 52). And certainly the allure of this creature is sustained as long as the (truly feminine) Ellen Craft plays the role of the (fictionally masculine) master, for she seems attractively emboldened, even spiritually strengthened, though she weeps and swoons when she dons feminine garb and declines back into the position of the childish, invalid wife (79). Even when only impersonated, whiteness (like maleness) confers power as well as privilege, whereas blackness (like femaleness) conveys subordination as well as dependency. Paradoxically, then, in the condition of slavery Ellen Craft gained the status of becoming her husband's "master," while his joyous arrival at a state of "freedom" inaugurated her feminized confinement.

In the clarity with which it presented whiteness as a symbol of personal autonomy, *Running a Thousand Miles for Freedom* establishes black-to-white racechange as a bid for freedom, one that would be made again by Homer Plessy at the

Figure 1.8 Engraving of Ellen Craft. First published in the *London Illustrated News* (19 April 1851), and used as frontispiece of William and Ellen Craft, *Running a Thousand Miles for Freedom* (1860).

end of the nineteenth century when he challenged Louisiana's segregated railroad car law by using his light complexion to gain access to the whites-only car and then announcing himself a Negro. Plessy's contention against Jim Crow seating—that his being only one-eighth Negro and able to pass entitled him to ride in seats reserved for whites—was rejected by the Supreme Court. Although the Court's landmark decision in favor of "a separate-but-equal doctrine" in *Plessy v. Ferguson* (1896) legalized segregation, Plessy had used impersonation to undercut the notion that skin color could simply be conflated with racial identity.[9] Because a figure like Plessy was able to pass for white, he could choose to be black; nevertheless, it is still the case that because he was not able to decide to be white, Plessy could only pretend to be white.[10] In other words, culture or social context shapes racial identity without completely replacing biological definitions of race.

Walter White, a prominent spokesperson for the National Association for the Advancement of Colored People (NAACP) during the 1930s and 1940s, anticipated this point in his autobiography, *A Man Called White* (1948), which begins with the following two, incongruent sentences: "I am a Negro. My skin is white, my eyes are blue, my hair is blond" (3). For White, "There is magic in a white skin; there is tragedy, loneliness, exile, in a black skin" (3). Yet, imbued with the conviction that he can only pretend to be white, the paradoxically named White chooses to be black, tracing his claimed cultural identity back to an incident in his thirteenth year when he and his father were saved from attack during the 1906 race riot in Atlanta because of their light complexions. At the very moment, they fully comprehended the depth of their alienation from white society; for the same reason that they were assured safety—that is, their skin color—father and son could only stand and watch "a lame Negro bootblack" clubbed to death on the street (9). When it later looked like the mob was making for his family's house and his father handed him a gun, White explains, he knew that

> I was a Negro, a human being with an invisible pigmentation which marked me a person to be hunted, hanged, abused, discriminated against, kept in poverty and ignorance, in order that those whose skin was white would have readily at hand a proof of their superiority, a proof patent and inclusive, accessible to the moron and the idiot as well as to the wise man and the genius. No matter how low a white man fell, he could always hold fast to the smug conviction that he was superior to two-thirds of the world's population, for those two-thirds were not white. (11)

The fact that Walter White felt the need to explain why he did not take advantage of his light complexion and renounce his allegiance to the Negro community marks the power of the condition the contemporary novelist Charles Johnson has called "epidermalized Being" (*Oxherding Tale*, 52).

Whereas Walter White chose to be black and refused to pretend to be white, both Ellen Craft and Homer Plessy utilized a mode of masquerading that resembles the tactics of central characters in turn-of-the-century and twentieth-century passing novels whose costumes of disguise demonstrate the fluidity of racial categories no longer connected to skin color. The slave mother of Mark Twain's *The Tragedy of Pudd'nhead Wilson* (1894), for instance, saves her light-skinned infant from being sold down the river by placing him in the elegant baby clothes and cradle of her master's son, while divesting the legitimate heir of his necklace and putting him in her own child's unpainted pine cradle. Similarly, Jessie Redmon Fauset's *Plum Bun* (1928) features a fair-skinned heroine who simply changes her name and her neighborhood so as to pass herself off as white because whites "had power and the badge of that power was whiteness" (73). After Fauset's central character determines to get "acquainted with life in her own way without restrictions or restraint," she understands herself to be "young, she was temporarily independent, she was intelligent, she was white" (88).

Although such passing novels did contain subversive readings of whiteness, at least in part their authors used racechange to analyze the dynamics of racial envy and more specifically black women's adoption of white-defined standards of beauty. From Zora Neale Hurston's Mrs. Turner (in *Their Eyes Were Watching God* (1937)), who believes "We oughta lighten up de race" (135), to Toni Morrison's Pecola Breedlove (in *The Bluest Eye* (1970)), who drinks milk out of a Shirley Temple cup so as magically to gain storybook blue eyes, a female longing for racechange reflects the self-hatred bred by a racist society. In a photograph entitled *Mirror, Mirror* (1986–87), the contemporary artist Carrie Mae Weems comments on such socially induced self-loathing by presenting a black woman asking

Figure 1.9   Carrie Mae Weems, *Mirror, Mirror* (1986–87), silver print, 20 × 16 in. Copyright Carrie Mae Weems; courtesy of PPOW, NY.

her mirror "who's the finest of them all?" and being told, "Snow White, you black bitch, and don't you forget it!!!" (Fig. 1.9). To be sure, because the wicked queen in the mirror looks more directly at the viewer than at the African-American girl, the evil stepmother may reflect the values of (the white) viewer more than those of the girl; and because the African-American girl looks aside, clutching the mirror as if in the next minute to shatter it, the Snow White tale may not be able to effect its damaging ends.[11] Yet the debilitating split image of "Snow White" and "the black bitch" illuminates and is in turned illuminated by a comment of Lorraine O'Grady's that uncannily serves to contrast Weems's photograph to the ancient urn from Tarquinia:

> The female body in the West is not a unitary sign. Rather, like a coin, it has an obverse and a reverse: on the one side, it is white; on the other, not-white or, prototypically,

black. The two bodies cannot be separated, nor can one body be understood in isolation from the other in the West's metaphoric construction of "woman." White is what woman is; not-white (and the stereotypes not-white gathers in) is what she had better not be. (14)

Claude McKay's short story "Near-White" (1932) dramatizes the ways in which the breach between "Snow White" and the "black bitch" depends less on biology, more on ideology; less on visible signs of skin pigmentation, more on Manichean and transcendent ideas of whiteness versus blackness. Light-complexioned Angie Dove goes in search of romance and adventure in downtown Manhattan, much to the chagrin of her family in Harlem. Passing as white comes easily because "no tangible thing separated her from the respectable white audience down below, her features being whiter and more regular than many persons' who moved boldly and freely in the privileged circles of the Great Majority" (76). Since she displays no visible trace of "the stigmata of Africa" (86), she meets and eventually falls in love with a young man convinced that she is "the nicest, whitest little girl in the world" (99). Herself persuaded that "Prejudice is not stronger than love" (98), Angie determines to tell him the truth about her racial identity but is stopped after asking him to speculate about how he would feel if he found out he had been unwittingly involved with a quadroon or octoroon girl: "Me! I'd sooner love a toad!" (102).

This Jazz-age Cinderella—dancing nightly with a beau from whom she must escape at the close of the evening so as to keep her origins a secret—discovers that her kisses will never transform the Prince who (if he knew the truth) would consider her as repulsive as a toad. An anti-fairy tale, "Near-White" elaborates upon the passionate maxim of its heroine's mother: Speaking as one of the "light-colored ones," she asserts, "We hate [whites] more because we are *not* black" (95–97). What "near-whites" understand is the fictiveness of an oppressive system that generates the greatest hatred against "light-colored ones," a hatred based on fears about category confusion: Whites are "never sure about us, they can't place us" (96). "So close . . . and yet so far" from whites, "near-whites" prove that the color bar, though invisible, is nevertheless insurmountable. McKay strikes the point home by inundating the tale with references to Manhattan's melting pot society. The story begins with a song sensation launched by some "Yank or Yid" (72); continues with references to fashionable Spanish cabarets, German beer gardens, Arabian cafés run by Armenians, dance halls called the Pyramid; and concludes with Prince Charming assuring his doubtful date, "I'd love you if you were even Chinese!" (about which she muses, "Chinese! That was the lowest thing he could imagine" (101)). Yanks, Yids, Spaniards, Arabians, Armenians, Egyptians, and "even" Chinese have apparently managed to become "white," while whiter-than-white Angie remains as far away as "near-white."

The threat implicitly posed by Angie Dove on the marriage market is clearly related to her gender, since an unwitting husband could stand convicted of miscegenation, deemed a crime in many states until the 1957 decision in *Loving v. Virginia*. To be sure, the racial ambiguity of the "near-white" can be disturbing in male as well as female characters, or so William Faulkner's *Light in August* (1932) indicates. For the entire white community finds the "parchmentcolored" (304) Joe Christmas particularly dangerous since he cannot be categorized: "He never acted like either a nigger or a white man. That was it. That was what made the folks so mad" (386). However, women's role in reproduction caused female racial ambiguity to appear more sinister to those anxious about preserving the purity of a white patrilineage. Despite its liberal intentions, Jerome Kern and Oscar Hammerstein's *Show Boat* (originally produced on Broadway in 1927, made into a film in 1936, and revived in 1946 and 1994) inadvertently instructed audiences on the degradation a racechange from white to black entails for a sexually active (potentially reproductive) woman. The revelation that the light-skinned singer Julie is a "Negro" effectively makes her dispensable in the plot. First, after she and her white boyfriend Steve evade the charge of miscegenation by his cutting her hand and sucking her blood to prove he has more than "one drop" of "Negro blood" himself, the pair leave the showboat (on which they had been performing). Second, when she surfaces in the next act, Julie—abandoned by Steve and doomed to alcoholism—sacrifices a nightclub engagement so as to procure a job for the musical's white heroine and then disappears not only from respectable society but from any of the other characters' concern, an unnoticed casualty in the white community's happily-ever-after. As soon as her color is established, in other words, the beautiful and noble Julie suffers a series of catastrophes that ensure not only her demotion in the plot but the white heroine's promotion to center stage.

Given the entanglement of narratives like *Plum Bun*, "Near-White," and *Show Boat* with normative (white-defined) definitions of female attractiveness, it seems appropriate that the most extravagant racechange narrative to emerge from the Harlem Renaissance begins with a black man enthralled by a white woman. The hero of George Schuyler's freewheeling satire *Black No More* (1931) falls in love with a racist white woman whom he manages to marry only by turning himself white. And given the ways in which passing narratives conflate whiteness with life, blackness with life-in-death, it seems fitting that *Black No More* views the demise of blackness as the only viable solution for African Americans. As its title indicates, this tongue-in-cheek fantasy about a scientific method of triggering a "racial metamorphosis" (14) takes supremacist ideology to its logical conclusion by asking its readers to understand that freedom in America is predicated not only on whiteness but on the eradication of blacks. In a 1949 essay entitled "Has Science Conquered the Color Line?" Schuyler's distinguished contemporary Walter White outlined a similar point:

> Suppose the skin of every Negro in America was suddenly to turn white. What would happen to all the notions about Negroes, the idols on which are built race prejudice and race hatred? Would not Negroes then be judged individually on their ability, energy, honesty, cleanliness as are whites? (37)[12]

According to Schuyler, too, the only way for African Americans to achieve individuality, to avoid being viewed as racially representative, is through a color conversion. Schuyler further suggests that a hegemonic racechange script shapes American aesthetic values and political doctrines. Convincing blacks to believe in the superiority of the culture and characteristics of whites, this scenario effectively functions as a form of genocide, threatening to annihilate all African Americans.

To dramatize this idea, Schuyler centers attention on one black do-gooder, a Dr. Junius Crookman, whose studies of vitiligo—a disorder in skin pigmentation—lead him to perfect a method "of artificially inducing and stimulating this nervous disease at will" so as to "solve the American race problem" (27). Only three solutions remain available to African Americans facing that problem— " 'To either get out, get white or get along'" (27)—but most cannot or will not get out and many only barely get along. Determining therefore to get blacks white, Dr. Crookman places the thousands of interested customers he instantly attracts into "a cross between a dentist's chair and an electric chair" (34) so as to give them "the open sesame of a pork-colored skin" (35), even though it cannot yet be genetically transferred to their offspring. A "Race Man," the good doctor is convinced that "if there were no Negroes, there could be no Negro problem" (54).

Huge electric signs represent the commercialization of racechange in this economically astute novel:

> A black face was depicted at the lower end of the arrow while at the top shone a white face to which the arrow was pointed. First would appear the outlines of the arrow; then, BLACK-NO-MORE would flash on and off. Following that the black face would appear at the bottom and beginning at the lower end the long arrow with its lettering would appear progressively until its tip was reached, when the white face at the top would blazon forth. After that the sign would flash off and on and the process would be repeated. (43–44)

Because of the success of Dr. Crookman's business, hair-straightening parlors and whitening chemical concerns go bankrupt, but so do the various leaders of the black intellectual establishment—Santop Licorice of the once-flourishing Back-To-African Society (Marcus Garvey) and Dr. Shakespeare Agamemnon Beard, founder of the National Social Equality League (W.E.B. Du Bois)—since the citizens who once supported them are quickly disappearing. Ironically, then, the supposedly libertarian black intelligentsia, what Du Bois called the "talented tenth," oppose the Black-No-More entrepeneurs' plan for "chromatic emancipation" (87) as fervently as do the Klannish Knights of Nordica, whose members dread unwitting racial intermarriage and miscegenation.

When once-black Max Disher turned white Matthew Fisher joins the Knights of Nordica and marries its founder's daughter, he gains leadership through black-baiting for capitalists: Poor white workers are kept so busy worrying about "Negro blood" (130) and "white nigger" (128) labor competition that they forget to organize. Convinced that even a fiction about the "presence of the Negro as an under class" can continue to keep white workers underpaid and yet nonunionized, Matthew preaches racial supremacy, although "practically all the Negroes [left] are white" (158). But his success feels fragile because of his dread at his wife's producing a dark son, a fear that evaporates when a series of political maneuvers expose the racially mixed descent of the Democratic party and of the Knights of Nordica's leaders, who admit, "We're all niggers now" (193). Not only does

Matthew's racist wife believe her own ancestry may have caused the color of her baby, she also begins to use artifical methods to make herself look darker because in Schuyler's brave new world racism takes an odd twist. When it is discovered that "the new Caucasians were from two to three shades lighter than the old Caucasians" (218) (in other words, that "the blacks were whiter than the whites" (219)), prejudice against exceedingly pale people erupts and the marketing of face powders named "*L'Afrique*" as well as the wearing of "Egyptienne Stain," "Zulu Tan," or just plain charcoal (222) come into vogue.

As in the case of Matthew's wife, the Democratic antagonists of Dr. Crookman's Black-No-More enterprise discover how dangerous it is to be white no more when it is revealed that their own families derive from mixed racial inheritances. After two luckless Democrats try to escape Washington incognito by wearing blackface, they land amid "the most truly Fundamentalist of all the Christian sects in the United States" (203), whose preacher has asked for a sign from God consisting of "a nigger for his congregation to lynch" (208). The townfolk therefore greet the two blackfaced strangers with joy: "Niggers! Praise God! The Sign! Lynch 'em!" (213). Saved after they manage to reveal their pale skins, the doomed duo are next exposed as "damned Demmycratic candidates [who] is niggers" (215) and so their adventure ends with them stripped, their ears and genitals cut off, their bodies ignited on a pyre, their flesh roasted, and then their skeletons ransacked for souvenirs.

Schuyler's mordant indictment of Americans' virulent racism found disturbing confirmation in the fate of the daughter he and his white wife enthusiastically raised as an exemplar of "hybrid vigor" who would break down racial barriers. Some thirty years after the publication of *Black No More* and the birth of Philippa Schuyler, the talented, biracial pianist passed as the white Felipa Monterro not only to gain acceptance in the segregated world of classical music but also because, as she herself put it, "I will be accepted as a person not as a strange curiosity" and because being called "a Negro" would bring a "taint" and thus "30 more miserable years" (Talalay, 224). If the contemporary reviewer and memoirist Anatole Broyard passed in order "to be a writer, not a black writer," his racial imposture also hints that whiteness remains "the default position" for individuality, whereas blackness continues to be attached to the concept of race, of a race type, and thus to racial prejudice (Gates, "White," 66, 75).

"It don't matter if you're black or white," Michael Jackson has sung to popular acclaim at the end of the twentieth century; however, his own reaction to vitiligo adds proof to the continued timeliness of *Black No More*'s satire. Instead of darkening white blotches, as most patients do, Jackson whitened and westernized all of his features. Writing in the early fifties, Frantz Fanon described actual scientific schemes strikingly similar to those employed by Michael Jackson and by Schuyler's fictive Dr. Crookman:

> For several years certain laboratories have been trying to produce a serum for "denegrification"; with all the earnestness in the world, laboratories have sterilized their test tubes, checked their scales, and embarked on researches that might make it possible for the miserable Negro to whiten himself and thus to throw off the burden of that corporeal malediction. (111)

Set in the colonized locales Fanon studied, Julia Blackburn's novel *The Book of Colour* (1995) includes a reminiscence about a father who took on the work of "denegrification" every night when he washed his son's face "with a mixture of peroxide and the juice of a lemon" because the boy had "'been out in the sun, that is why your skin is too dark'" (8–9). Recently, when a black woman, married to an Italian, had a white woman's egg implanted in her womb so their offspring would be "spared the misery of racism," the science of "denegrification" horrified the legal theorist Patricia J. Williams, causing her to imagine black women serving as surrogate mothers and making more efficient the production of racially profitable white babies. As if bringing home the renewed relevance of Schuyler's narrative, Williams views this scenario as "nothing less than the transformation of the social difficulty of being black into an actual birth defect, an undesirable trait that technology can help eliminate" (*Rooster's Egg*, 241).

Back in the nineteenth century, illustrations of countless European and American soap commercials sold cleanliness as godliness by portraying blacks (often toddlers) attempting a racechange by trying to wipe away the dirt and grime of blackness, as did many pictures in children's books (Fig. 1.10). The critic Anne McClintock has argued about Victorian Pears' Soap ads that the purification of the physical body becomes a metaphor for the rejuvenation of the body politic. In the first frame of the bathing scene displayed on one such advertisement, the magic of soap promises to "regenerate the Family of Man by washing from the skin the very stigma of racial and class degeneration"; however, the second frame—in which the bathed child's body has undergone a lightening but his face has not—demonstrates that the white boy as an agent of historical progress cannot completely induct his "lesser brother" into the civilities of the European Enlightenment: "In the Victorian mirror," McClintock explains, "the black child witnesses his predetermined destiny of imperial metamorphosis but remains a passive racial hybrid, part black, part white, brought to the brink of civilization" (213) but never fully inducted or assimilated into it.

At the beginning of the twentieth century in middle America, Madame C. J. Walker (neé *Breedlove*) established her multi-million-dollar fortune by selling lightening creams that could be used on the body as well as the face and straightening solutions for the hair. Elsewhere, Fanon calls such "denegrification" methods a kind of "lactification" whereby whitening the race saves it from "falling back into the pit of niggerhood" (47), a process not unrelated to Pecola *Breedlove*'s great thirst for milk in *The Bluest Eye*. The brilliant photograph of Whoopi Goldberg taken by Annie Leibovitz shows the actress immersed in a tub of milk and thereby jokes about the grotesque imperatives/impossibilities of "lactification" (Fig. 1.11). Again, and in a manner as risible as Schuyler's narrative, the connection is made between racechange and death, for whiteness will only prevail when Whoopi's entire body—her legs, arms, face, and especially her nose and mouth—will be submerged beneath its surface. Is she grinning or grimacing, waving or drowning in her milk bath?

No wonder that Langston Hughes produced a brief but pointed satire of narratives in which characters seek to pass themselves off as white so as to gain social

Figure 1.10 Pears' Soap Advertisement of the Victorian Period. Courtesy of Unilever.

Figure 1.11 Annie Leibovitz, *Whoopi Goldberg*. Copyright © 1986 Annie Leibovitz/Contact Press Images.

acceptance and status. In "Limitations of Life" (1938), a parody of the very successful passing novel *Imitation of Life* (1933) by Fannie Hurst as well as its popular movie renditions, Hughes criticizes those conventions simply by transposing them. According to Hughes, the conventional passer of, say, Hurst's novel—a white wannabe—reinscribes the devaluation of blackness articulated by characters from Blake's "Little Black Boy" to Churchill's Joshua. What would happen if white people felt so ugly and worthless, so dependent on blacks for approval and financial success that they either dedicated themselves to serving blacks or attempted to transform themselves into blacks? What if the overvaluation of whiteness that causes blacks to pass as white were replaced by a privileging of blackness that motivated whites to try to turn black?[13]

In Hurst's popular tear-jerker, a large black woman named Delilah works as a domestic for a white woman and together they successfully market the pancakes Delilah makes; but in the process this twentieth-century mammy loses the affections of her very light-complexioned daughter who—somewhat like McKay's Angie Dove—seeks to pass as white and therefore will not recognize her mother until "too late": that is, Delilah's (ornate) funeral.[14] *The Bluest Eye* underlines the connection between Hurst's portrait of the passer and a racially marked ideal of (white) beauty when one of Morrison's characters confuses the name of the novel's heroine, Pecola, with the movie protagonist, Peola, the "mulatto girl [who] hates her mother 'cause she is black and ugly but then cries at the funeral" (67). Attempting to uncover the absurd racial assumptions of this maternal melodrama, Langston Hughes simply reverses racial markers. For Hughes, an imitation of whites leads to an imitation life for blacks that can only be understood as a limitation. He counters that limitation by switching the tables and producing a spoof that takes off on the image of a white Aunt Jemima on the box of pancake flour in Mammy Weaver's kitchen.

Wealthy Mammy Weaver (carrying a Metropolitan Opera program and speaking "perfect English with Oxford accent") is greeted in her elegant Harlem residence by blond Audette Aubert (Claudette Colbert played the passer in one of the movies), who falls all over herself in grateful servitude: "Mammy Weavers, ah been waitin' up for you-all. Ah thought you might like some nice hot pancakes before you-all went to bed" (656). Although Mammy, who has just come from the Mimo Club (where she dined on lobster à la Newburg), declines, she lets Audette rub her feet and sympathizes with the plight of her fair daughter who has been "lyin' out in de backyard in de sun all day long tannin' herself, ever day, tryin' so hard to be colored." When Audette is asked what she wants in exchange for all of her services—as nurse, cook, housekeeper, mother surrogate—this ideal domestic refuses a day off or a nice home of her own. Instead, all she wants "is a grand funeral when I die." What makes Delilah so very loveable in Hurst's *Imitation of Life*—a selflessness bordering on masochism in her service to whites—appears ludicrous when the races are switched around.[15] What makes Delilah's daughter a prototypical tragic mulatto—the contradiction between her "lowly" origins (the black mother) and her "high" aspirations (the white world)—seems equally absurd when played out through a character who seeks to pass as black.

Whereas Hughes's sketch uses humor, Adrienne Kennedy's experimental one-act play *Funnyhouse of a Negro* (1964) exploits surrealism to uncover the murderous logic of Western culture's racechange imperative. Its central character, Negro-Sarah, is haunted by ghostly white avatars of herself like the Duchess of Hapsburg and Queen Victoria Regina, surrogates who wish to be told "of a royal world where everything and everyone is white and there are no unfortunate black ones" because they "know" that "black is evil and has been from the beginning" (5). Wearing identical alabaster masks, both begin the play with "frizzy hair, unmistakably Negro kinky hair" (6), and both suffer the humiliation of alopecia. Negro-Sarah's original wish "not to be" and her ultimate fate as a suicide find their analogue in the baldness of her alter egos, for the falling out of wild kinky hair symbolizes the infantilization of black people (bald like babies), the castration of black people (shorn like Samson of power), the violation of black people (the rape of their locks), the disease of black people (suffering hair loss due to illness), and the premature decrepitude of black people (aging before their time).

If You're Black, Get Back

While some black characters seek to become white so as to gain privileges ("If you're white, you're right"), other white characters are turned black so they will understand and sympathize with the plight of those who are told "if you're black, get back." Just as Hughes's Audette Aubert exhibits the psychological masochism of the prototypically black mammy, just as Schuyler's fable concluded with white politicians suffering the fate (of lynching) more usually accorded blacks, a number of reform-minded writers attempted to educate whites about what Fanon called the "corporeal malediction" of color by presenting narratives of white-to-black racechanges that place racists in black people's shoes and thereby teach them that race matters most unfairly. Although the switch seems like a reversal—whites turning black instead of blacks turning white—it sometimes attests to the very same values, of whiteness and rightness, blackness and backness. An early and late example of this type of racechange—a story in Charles W. Chesnutt's *The Conjure Woman* (1899) and an episode in the musical comedy *Finian's Rainbow* (1947)—can stand here for liberal efforts to promote a kind of racial negative capability that would attenuate the virulence and violence of white supremacists. Yet, as in Schuyler's novel, blackness can remain anathema in this tradition, especially when it is inflicted as a punishment fitting the crimes of inhumane whites. Only when the boundaries separating black and white are perceived as demonstrably permeable does racial mutability lead to the undermining of race itself as a category.

Chesnutt's "Mars Jeems's Nightmare" is a tale told in dialect by the ex-slave Julius about a plantation owner whose cruelty leads one slave to consult "Aun' Penny, de free-nigger cunjuh 'oman" (76), who pounds up roots to be stirred into the master's okra soup. The next morning Master Jeems goes away on business, after describing to his overseer Master Johnson how his "niggers is gittin' monst'us triflin' en lazy en keerless" and advising his second-in-command "ter make a reco'd dat 'll show w'at kinder oberseah you is" (79). Naturally, Johnson takes this as a hint to overwork and underfeed the slaves. Predictably too, when a brash new slave is bought and brought to the house, Johnson responds to his backtalk and ineptitude by chaining, starving, beating, and finally selling him down river. Aunt Peggy is horrified to learn "'bout dis noo nigger bein' sol' 'erway" (87) and manages to get a conjured sweet potato to him just in time. The very next day, a transformed, repentant Master Jeems appears. Having suffered the "nightmare" of being the "noo nigger," he awakens a "noo man" (98), firing Johnson and making work bearable, play possible for his lucky slaves.

Though it may be difficult to determine how the spelling of "noo" marks a different pronunciation of the word "new," clearly it is meant to stand for a visible mark of the difference vernacular makes. The frame tale—written in standard English—clarifies the elderly ex-slave-narrator's moral. At the beginning of Chesnutt's story, the white couple who find Julius's grandson careless, lazy, and untrustworthy fire the boy; after hearing about Master Jeems's nightmare, the wife decides to give the grandson another chance. Imagining the horror of Jeems's change from free master to abused slave makes it possible to think about the human subjectivity of blacks not only for the wife in the frame tale but also by extension for Chesnutt's white readers as well. Exactly this boon born of racechange occurs in *Finian's Rainbow*, where the racism of Senator Billboard Rawkins—played in the 1968 movie by Keenan Wynn—is punished when he is turned black and forced to experience the humiliations daily suffered by African Americans (Fig. 1.12).

Figure 1.12   David Wayne and Keenan Wynn in *Finian's Rainbow* (1968). Courtesy of Museum of Modern Art Film Stills Archive.

Initially the bigoted master of an anachronistic Southern plantation, white Senator Rawkins had himself enforced a grotesque racechange upon his servants, one that turned proud African Americans into fawning darkies. When college-educated Howard took a job with the Senator, for example, the dark-skinned young man was taught how to act like a servile "boy." A white staff member set himself up as a role model—a kind of imitation Negro—for the new domestic by giving "a quick course in Southern-julep-serving, based on the minstrel tradition of Dixie shuffle and exaggerated accent": "Yousah julep, suh, Mr. Rawkins, suh, all frosted and minty—yawk, yawk!" Since a white man models black masculinity for an African American, racechange here, as elsewhere, questions authenticity, sincerity, and integrity, implying there is no single or stable racial identity. A black person is instructed to imitate a white counterfeiting blacks who are mimicking . . . . (A comparably vertiginous moment occurs in Douglas Sirk's version of *Imitation of Life* (1959) when a white actress pretending to be a light-skinned mulatto copies whites simulating blacks.)[16] In a fitting plot reversal, then, *Finian's Rainbow* manufactures a whimsical wish (magically implemented by a leprechaun) that triggers an epidermal metamorphosis, forcing the Senator to experience the vulnerability, injustice, and fear inflicted on blacks until he eventually manages to find happiness by joining a nomadic barbershop quartet. After the rapacious, mendacious Senator is subjected to the insults of discriminatory attitudes he had himself touted, he becomes a "better person," one who comprehends the injustice and arbitrariness of white supremacy.

As in Chesnutt's "Mars Jeems's Nightmare" and *Finian's Rainbow*, a racechanging script operates pedagogically to raise white consciousness about American racism in Melvin Van Peebles's movie *Watermelon Man* (1970). Here a white insurance salesman insensitive to racial injustice is played by (a heavily made-up) Godfrey Cambridge, who wakes up one night to the shocking realization that he has undergone a racial metamorphosis that proves to be longer and more disorienting than the "nightmare" he initially takes it to be. After various attempts at lightening his complexion fail—including milk baths that produce frames anticipating Annie Leibovitz's photo of Whoopi Goldberg (Fig. 1.13)—Cambridge suffers the indignities some African Americans commonly experience in everyday existence. Instead of his daily run for the bus being taken as a ritual sporting event, it immediately elicits the assumption of his criminality from neighbors and law enforcement officials alike. Because of his skin color, the Job-like Cambridge loses his children, his wife, his house, his job. At the end of the film, rage against injust persecution drives him to a mysterious room—a health club? a martial arts studio? a storeroom for janitors?—where he is last seen with a group of chanting black men brandishing mops and brooms in a quasi-African war ritual.

Precisely the advancing of racial consciousness that prompted Van Peebles's satire motivated the racechanges of two white journalists inspired by the civil rights movement. When in 1959 John Howard Griffin—and, later, following his example, Grace Halsell—traveled through the South as an African American, he was attempting to understand the nature of racial prejudice in this country: "How else except by becoming a Negro could a white man hope to learn the truth?" (7).

Figure 1.13   Godfrey Cambridge in *Watermelon Man* (1970). Courtesy of Photofest.

In *Black Like Me* (1961), one of the first and most commercially successful instances of so-called "new" journalism, Griffin recounted his use of a treatment developed for victims of vitiligo and of a skin stain to effect a transformation that seemed to "imprison" him in the dark "flesh of an utter stranger, an unsympathetic one with whom I felt no kinship" (15), a process presumably more effective than the burnt cork that hardly disguises white James Whitmore in the 1964 movie version of *Black Like Me* (Fig. 1.14). At times experiencing the invisibility of black citizens (too unimportant to be noticed), at times the hypervisibility of black citizens (too out of place to go unnoticed), Griffin became horrified, on the one hand, by the fact that "the Negro is part of the black mass, the white is always the individual" (48) and, on the other, by the racist "hate stare" (52), a look of passionate but eerily "unreasonable contempt" (87).

After Griffin returned to his white identity so as to publicize his findings, he was hung in effigy by anonymous members of his community: "a dummy, half black, half white, with [his] name on it and a yellow streak painted down its back, was hanging from the wire" (149). Later named a "lynching" (150), this ritual sacrifice implies that befriending African Americans subjects the white liberal to their fate. Of course the death and disappearance of a number of white civil rights activists in the sixties—most famously Michael Schwerner—drove home this point. Toni Morrison's *Beloved* (1987) makes a similar claim about white abolitionists during Civil War times: The egalitarian Edward Bodwin is termed a "bleached nigger" and his face is "shoe-blackened" by his proslavery enemies (260). About his own "experiment" in blackness, Griffin believed that according to most people "because I was a Negro for six weeks, I remained partly Negro or perhaps essentially Negro" (156). This perception helps explain both the strength and the weakness of *Black Like Me*'s journalistic experiment. For Griffin grounds his social critique on his evolving distrust of his own white privileges and of the depravity of vicious white stereotyping of African Americans; but the extraordinary popularity of a book that became a staple in junior high and high school classrooms depended upon Griffin's assumption that he could speak for black people and the persistence of white readers in assuming black people incapable of elaborating upon their own experiences (Wald, 154).

Grace Halsell—a White House staff writer during the Johnson administration—describes in *Soul Sister* (1969) a meeting she arranged with Griffin before her own journey, first to Harlem and later through Mississippi, as a black woman. At the time, in the spring of 1968, Griffin had undergone surgery because "certain bones were disappearing" which the doctors replaced with steel (21). Jokingly categorized as "a work of art" by his surgeon, Griffin did not attribute the disintegration of his bones to the doses of trimethyl psoralen or the exposure to ultraviolet rays he used for his racechange. Nor does Grace Halsell, who follows this same procedure to darken her skin. Yet after his death, a number of obituaries implied that Griffin had been slowly killed by the process he had undertaken to "pass over"

Figure 1.14 James Whitmore in *Black Like Me* (1964). Courtesy of Photofest.

(Griffin, 12), a phrase that associates passing with passing over from life to death or passing out. Perhaps rumors of Griffin's death-due-to-passing reflect a widespread belief that, as Isaac Julien has put it, "crossing racial lines usually results in punishment" (263), or, indeed, that it *should* result in punishment.

Certainly, before and after their passing episodes, both Griffin and Halsell suffered from a kind of racial schizophrenia. Like Halsell, who describes herself as "two persons" or a being "cast in a twin, paradoxical role of oppressor and oppressed," Griffin experienced himself as "two personalities, two sets of eyes, two bodies" containing "a single human heart in conflict with itself" (Halsell, 220–21). At least in part, their self-division derives from a conviction that "self-segrega[tion] . . . pains and cripples the white American . . . even more than the black American" (Halsell, 221). (Fanon also believed that "the Negro enslaved by his inferiority, the white man enslaved by his superiority alike behave in accordance with a neurotic orientation" (60)). Both Griffin and Halsell gain not only sympathy or understanding but a sense of community, profound societal insights, and a conviction of moral self-worth when "turned" black. Similarly, white Senator Rawkins in *Finian's Rainbow* was selfish, conniving, and cutthroat; however, black Rawkins gains in sympathy and love for his fellow creatures. Plus, he's got rhythm. (It was precisely the musicality of black communities that led Alan Lomax to put on blackface so he could accompany Zora Neale Hurston—the two thereby evading white authorities, not fooling African Americans—to collect material for the Music Division of the Library of Congress.[17]) When blackness is valued as intrinsically worthwhile or superior, racechange from white to black can be re-envisioned as a way to transform not only the individual conscience or consciousness but also our conceptualization of the major icons, myths, and institutions of European and American culture.

Rather than replicating a conventional system of representation that Others blacks, a number of artists and thinkers use cross-racial strategies to underline African cultural centrality in Western civilization. Countee Cullen's "The Black Christ" (1929) performs a racechange on Jesus, as do many paintings of the Harlem Renaissance in which the blackness of Jesus bespeaks his spiritual grace under inexplicable but murderous oppression.[18] From Jean-Paul Sartre's *Black Orpheus* (1963) to Angela Carter's *Black Venus* (1985), from Martin Bernal's *Black Athena* (1987, 1991) to China Galland's *Longing for Darkness: Tara and the Black Madonna* (1990), twentieth-century critical and creative speculations reinvent Western legends in such a way as to restructure our ideas about race and culture. The most ambitious of these—*Black Athena*—argues that Greek civilization resulted from Afroasiastic influences so that, for instance, the city name of Athens as well as the divinity Athena derive from Egyptian and Semitic sources. Rooted in black experience but reinvented by racist historians who wished to attribute the glory that was Greece to European or Aryan colonization, Western civilization itself, according to Bernal's widely acclaimed book, underwent an extraordinary whitewashing, a racechange from black to white.[19]

If the major myths of Europeans and Americans could be imagined as black stories, so might the founding narratives of popular culture. A number of modern musical productions have used racechange to ask, what differences does color make? Transforming *Carmen*'s cigarette factory and enthralling toreador in nineteenth-century Seville to a parachute factory and seductive fighter in twentieth-century America, *Carmen Jones* (1943, 1954 film) follows Bizet's script closely enough to suggest that the logic of erotic thralldom will work itself out inexorably on the lives of men and women, regardless of racial, geographic, or historical factors.[20] Just as Gilbert and Sullivan's *Mikado* (1885) had utilized racechange to spoof the English in the guise of the Japanese, two adaptions—entitled *The Swing Mikado* (1923) and *The Hot Mikado* (1939)—employed African-American performers to blast all notions of racial stereotyping, as did the the 1995 production mounted by David H. Bell, first for Washington, D.C.'s, Ford's Theatre and then for London's Queen's Theatre: blacks lampooning Brits playing Asians. When Frank Baum's *The Wonderful Wizard of Oz* (1900) and the Judy Garland film version surfaced on Broadway as *The Wiz* (1975), an all-black musical hit, some critics viewed Dorothy's trip from Kansas to the Emerald City as a metaphor for the great migration, the Wicked Witch of the West as a slave-mistress, the Emerald City as a superhip Harlem, and the Wiz himself as a hustling Sly Stone or Walt Frazier (Rollins). The use of black singers in the leading male roles of Peter Sellars' production of *Don Giovanni* (1991) engaged audiences in examining their preconceptions about race and promiscuity. Such exuberant transformations of white scripts redefine the color line that W.E.B. Du Bois saw as the central problem of the twentieth century as an inspiring opportunity for aesthetic innovation.

More focused on the unacknowledged creative contributions of African Americans to literary history, Shelley Fisher Fishkin's *Was Huck Black?* (1993) asks whether the model for Huck Finn's voice was a black child and thereby draws attention to the cross-racial lines of influence that Eric Sundquist sees at work in many of the most classic of nineteenth-century American texts, that Ann Douglas and George Hutchinson trace in the most modernist of twentieth-century American texts. For several decades, such speculations about hidden black roots have fueled discussions, for example, about artists like Beethoven, Alexander Pushkin, and Alexander Dumas. In a curious, three-volume meditation on *Sex and Race* (1944), the provocative cultural enquirer J. A. Rogers reproduced a painting of Beethoven as well as descriptions of his "swarthy" complexion and "flat broad nose" to argue that "there is not a single shred of evidence to support the belief that he was a white man neither from those who knew him nor from his biographers" (III: 306; Fig. 1.15). In more recent times, in a chapter of *White Man Listen!* (1957) devoted to "The Literature of the Negro in the United States," Richard Wright first claims that Pushkin and Dumas were "Negro" and then that, because they were fully integrated into their respective cultures, "no matter what the color of their skins, they were not really Negroes. One was a Russian, the other was a Frenchman" (75). Wright shows how arbitrary the color line is, how easily it can be abrogated.

Although an antithetical concern for recovering hidden racial roots may motivate the genealogist seeking to map her own family tree, this sort of a quest can also result in a conviction about the unreliability, permeability, or fictiveness of

Figure 1.15 Portrait of Beethoven
in J. A. Rogers, *Sex and Race*
(1944).

racial labels. In "Passing for White, Passing for Black," the conceptual artist Adrian Piper describes any search into the ancestral past as "full of guesswork, false
leads, blank spots and mysteries. For just as white Americans are largely ignorant
of their African—usually maternal—ancestry, we blacks are often ignorant of our
European—usually paternal—ancestry" (228). Such ignorance, at times (but certainly not always) an offshoot of the sexual exploitation of female slaves by white
masters, may be more common than usually supposed. According to some geneti-
cists, 95 percent of "white" Americans have varying degrees of black heritage and
75 percent of all "African" Americans have at least one white ancestor. In other
words, concludes another genealogist named Shirlee Taylor Haizlip, "many Americans are not who they think they are; hundreds of thousands of white people in
America are not 'white'" (15). For Piper, castigated as a "paleface" (216) by visibly black and white acquaintances alike, as for Haizlip, what happened in their
families "calls into question the concept of color as a means of self-definition"
(Haizlip, 15).

If "you look white, act white, live white, vacation white, go to school white,
marry white and die white," perhaps race is "simply a matter of context," concludes Haizlip, while Piper wonders "whether the very idea of racial classification
is a viable one," whether the concept of race might soon become "obsolete"
(247).[21] A comparable argument for disentangling definitions of race from skin
color is mounted by two contemporary scholars who also point to cases of mistaken racial identity. In 1982, a light-skinned plaintiff named Susie Guillory
Phipps, who lived her life believing she was white, failed in her law suit against

the Louisiana Bureau of Vita Record; the bureau refused to change the racial classification on her birth certificate from black to white. Michael Omi and Howard Winant conclude that the case "illustrates the inadequacy of claims that race is a mere matter of variations in human physiognomy, that it is simply a matter of skin color" (54). If this is so, then racial folk taxonomies based on complexion may soon become antiquated.[22] Unlike Homer Plessy and Walter White, who subscribed to the idea that they could only pretend to be white (because of the one-drop rule), the lawsuit of Phipps as well as the speculations of Haizlip and Piper intimate that the dangerous concept of race itself might be detonated when color no longer codes it. The indeterminacy of racial categories, breaking down either/or approaches to difference, would generate an appreciation of pan-ethnic, transracial persons of unclassifiable colors, fitting citizens of a syncretic society.

A technological analogue to such transgressive imaginings about racial mutability or pigment mutations beyond the confines of racial categories, the new computer program Morph (for metaMORPHosis) mixes features in such a way as to produce a picture of, say, Queen Elizabeth as a woman of color (Fig. 1.16).[23] The regal symbol of an empire upon which the sun would not set in the nineteenth century is melded through the magic of modern science with the physiognomy of those colonized. Similarly, like a number of United Colors of Benetton ads, the computer-generated, multicultural picture of Eve that appeared on the cover of *Time* magazine to illustrate America's "New Face" in the 1990s stressed the enticing glamor of ethnic diversity. The image produced by combining the features of Anglo-Saxons (15%), Middle Easterners (17.5%), Africans (17.5%), Asians (7.5%), Southern Europeans (35%), and Hispanics (7.5%) led one staff member to fall in love: "It really breaks my heart that she doesn't exist," exclaimed a journalist enthralled by this cybergenetic, multi-ethnic offspring (see color insert and Fig. 1.17).[24] Just as the chart of the 49 progeny produced from various combina-

Figure 1.16 *The Morphing of Queen Elizabeth* (1994), courtesy of COLORS magazine (Issue #4 Race).

Figure 1.17   *Rebirth of a Nation* in *Time* magazine (Special Issue, Fall 1993). Courtesy of
Time magazine.

tions of seven ethnicities is titled *Rebirth of a Nation* so as to establish itself as
a retort to the racism of a founding film like *The Birth of a Nation*, the *Time* magazine cover seems to be subscribing to the moral conveyed not only by the morphed sequence of ethnic dancers in Michael Jackson's music video "Black or
White" (1993) and the morphed Asian, Native-American, male, female, African-
American, and Euro-American faces that conclude it but also by its take-home
message: "Prejudice is ignorance."

Endeavoring to prove the speciousness of disabling racial pigeonholes, political pranksters had imagined such racial transformations long before they could be
seen on a T.V. or computer screen. The earliest manifestation of Virginia Woolf's
contempt for patriotism and militarism found expression in a racial masquerade
that signaled her alienation from British imperialism. The so-called "*Dreadnought
hoax*" occurred in 1910 when Woolf (then Virginia Stephen), her brother Adrian,
and several of their friends dressed up as the emperor of Abyssinia and his en-
tourage for an official inspection of one of the most famous ships in the British
fleet (Fig. 1.18). The group was given a full tour of HMS *Dreadnought* and offered
a twenty-one-gun salute as well as a Guard of Honour for their inspection. In native garb and blackface, Woolf the Abyssinian dignitary makes a mockery not only
of a preeminent symbol of British military superiority but also of the rites and rituals of imperial etiquette, the pious inanities of ambassadorial amenities. Clearly
the bold impudence of this send-up expresses the racial privilege of a group of intellectuals convinced of their right to take a holiday from whiteness so as to thumb
their noses at even the highest authorities. Aware of the whiteness beneath the disguise, Woolf and her friends probably relished, on the one hand, the excitement of
their hidden identities as British citizens and, on the other, the exhibition of the ex-

Figure 1.18 *The Emperor of Abyssinia and His Suite*, from the *Daily Mirror* (Wednesday,
February 16, 1910). Standing, left to right: Guy Ridly, Horace de Vere Cole, Adrian Stephen,
Duncan Grant. Seated, left to right: Virginia Stephen, Anthony Buxton.

oticized natives they enacted.[25] Still, presenting herself as the Other, the youthful writer established the anti-establishment sympathies that would fuel her subsequent pacifism and feminism.[26]

Anarchic or antic, the racechanger breaks taboos and pays the price with societal censure, as Woolf did, or with psychological self-division, as Griffin and Halsell did. However, what Griffin conceded in an afterword to his book—"The day was past when black people wanted any advice from white men" (177)—suggests that even the most high-minded, idealistic motivations will not save white impersonators of blackness from violating, appropriating, or compromising black subjectivity in a way that will inevitably rebound against the ethical integrity of whites, a point Dick Gregory makes in a racechanging parody of *Black Like Me* (Fig. 1.19). If *White Like You* is "the story of a Mississippi sharecropper who painted himself white and moved to Arizona" (wearing his patchwork overalls and toting watermelons), then perhaps *Black Like Me* presented just as blatant a counterfeit—even a stereotype—of African-American men.

Using the same title but skewed differently, Eddie Murphy's "White Like You" sketch for *Saturday Night Live* (1989) shows a made-up Murphy penetrating be-

Figure 1.19 *White Like You*, from Dick Gregory, *What's Happening?* (Dutton 1965), photographs by Jerry Yulsman. Courtesy of Dick Gregory.

hind the facades erected before black people to understand that whites bond with each other, support each other, acclaim each other as if they were members of a club or a conspiracy. For example, the whitefaced Murphy boards a bus on which only one visibly black passenger sits surrounded by silent commuters ignoring each other; as soon as the black gets off, all the whites turn to each other and begin partying, leading Murphy to speculate that all his friends should resort to cosmetics as well. One of Langston Hughes's short sketches, "Who's Passing for Who?" (1952), is equally sardonic, though in his case about the uncertainty and indeterminacy racial masquerades spawn and also the asymmetrical racial values that make passing morally acceptable only for blacks, never for whites. Whether or not whites pretend to be black in order to learn more about the mores and morals of African-American communities, according to Hughes, the counterfeit is a cheat that robs black people of their dignity and their right to privacy.

In a Harlem club, Hughes describes how he and his friends encountered some white people visiting from Iowa. When a brown-skinned man knocks down a blond woman, the red-haired man from Iowa gets up to protect her; however, he stops when he is informed "she's colored" (31). Hughes's companions are horrified that the Iowa man wouldn't defend a woman from a brute, "no matter what race she may be" (32), and banish him from the cabaret. After some speculation that the abused woman might have been "just passing for colored" and a discussion of several passing novels by Harlem Renaissance writers, the remaining white couple explain that they have "just been *passing* for white for the last fifteen years" (33) so as to make more money. "All at once," Hughes explains, "we dropped our professionally selfconscious 'Negro' manners . . . and kidded freely like colored folks do when there are no white folks around" (33). At the end of the episode, as they are getting into a cab, the tourists explain that they are really white: "We just thought we'd kid you by passing for colored a little while—just as you said Negroes sometimes pass for white." Not knowing which way he and his friends have been fooled, Hughes ends on an uneasy note:

> Were they really white—passing for colored? Or colored—passing for white?
> Whatever race they were, they had had too much fun at our expense—even if they did pay for the drinks.

Who is conned by whom and for what purpose? Hughes implies that it is one thing for blacks to impersonate whites, quite another for whites to masquerade as blacks. He feels exploited, his culture invaded and spied upon, his authenticity at risk. And of course he is addressing a taboo still very much with us. Eddie Murphy elicits laughs when he uses the satiric tradition of racechange to impersonate Mr. Rogers in his parodic "Mr. Robinson's Neighborhood." Asking little boy and girl viewers if they know the meaning of two important words in the 'hood, he pulls on his cardigan, laces his shoes, faces the camera, and earnestly mouths the phrase "Eviction Notice." Even when Eddie Murphy puts on white make-up, it only signals a kind of antic clownishness, as in the photograph of Dick Gregory;[27] however, the minstrel in blackface remains a taboo emblem of reactionary white supremacy whose shock value was seriously underestimated recently by a companion of Whoopi Goldberg. Despite the imprimatur of Goldberg and the anything-goes atmosphere of a Friars Club roast, the actor Ted Danson could not get away with a Jolsonesque appearance in blackface that caused talk show host Montel Williams to view the event as a rally for the KKK and that led New York City Mayor David Dinkins to protest jokes "way over the line" (*Times*, Oct. 12, 1993).[28]

Perhaps the title of Fanon's classic attack on racism, *Black Skin, White Masks*, explains this asymmetry by suggesting that black-skinned people have to wear white masks. "[N]ot only must the black man be black," Fanon claimed; "he must be black in relation to the white man." And to those who would argue that this proposition has a converse, Fanon replied emphatically, "this is false. The black man has no ontological resistance in the eyes of the white man" (110). Despite Fanon's characteristic erasure of the black woman, he astutely maps in racial terms the difference that clusters around the issue of volition or agency. Ellen Craft needed to pass in order to obtain her freedom, whereas Virginia Woolf did so in a puckish prank; McKay's and Schuyler's characters can obtain life and latitude only by being black no more, while Hughes's Harlem tourists are motivated merely by a titillating voyeurism. In other words, racial impersonation and masquerading are a destiny imposed on colonized black people who *must* wear the white mask—of customs and values, of norms and languages, of aesthetic standards and religious ideologies—created and enforced by an alien civilization. "We wear the mask that grins and lies, / It hides our cheeks and shades our eyes,—": Paul Laurence Dunbar's poem speaks for the heroine of Jessie Fauset's *There Is Confusion* (1924), who can dance the part of America on a Broadway stage only if she wears a white mask, and for the black actors of Jean Genet's *The Blacks* (1960), whose imposed white masks hardly conceal but effectively intensify their racial rage.

A sardonic photograph that illuminates the title of James Clifford's *The Predicament of Culture: Twentieth-Century Ethnography, Literature, and Art* (1988) can serve here to summarize Fanon's, Dunbar's, Fauset's, and Genet's point. "*White Man*" (1982), which the author originally placed between the introduction and the first chapter, now graces the cover of the paperback edition (Fig. 1.20). Herbert M. Cole's picture displays a black man sardonically masquerading as a white man. The dark hands of the marginalized Nigerian hold a pencil and notebook to record African customs. The covered face of the subject—strikingly similar to the draped and thus blinded heads of René Magritte's portrait of a kiss joining two curtained, faceless lovers in *Les amants* (*The Lovers*) (1928)—has rendered Cole's subject invisible, silenced, even criminalized in his concealment. Astride a kerchief tied around the black man's brow rides the white man's head, a kind of amiably arrogant figurehead or hood ornament featuring the power of the white man's implacable gaze under a Doctor-Livingston-I-Presume hat. Like Fanon, this black-turned-white racechanger might think about himself, "There is no help for it: I am a white man. For unconsciously I distrust what is black in me, that is, the whole of my being" (191).

At the same time, however, the impersonator uses his face-change ironically as a weapon or retaliation against his colonization. Clearly the Doctor-Livingston observer-recorder is a satiric portrait of The Anthropologist whose geographical

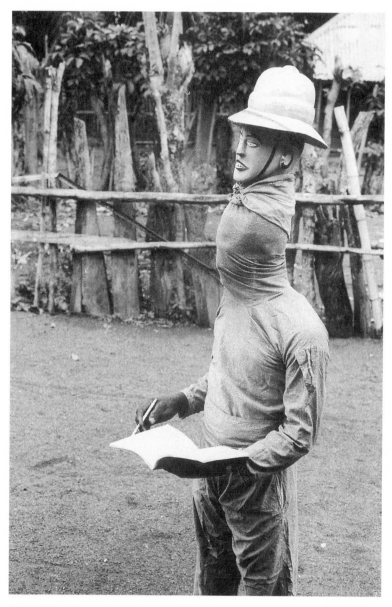

Figure 1.20 Herbert M. Cole, *White Man*, photograph of Onyeocha, a performer at Igbo masquerades, south-east Nigeria (1982). Courtesy of Herbert M. Cole and UCLA Museum of Cultural History.

and authorial incursions name and colonize the "exotic" or "native" or "primitive" Other. The hierarchical connection between the white explorer-author and the muffled black head reflects a relationship of dominance that entombs black reality even as it inscribes it. Bearing the white man as his burden, the black man is effaced by the colonizer, though it is possible to see a retaliation at work here, for whiteness appears impaled on the stake of the black body. The very concept "white man" depends on the subordinated black body, a point that helps illuminate the extraordinary importance of racial impersonation in the evolution of Western art produced by and for whites. Not an image of complementarity like the Janiform vase, Cole's picture captures a profoundly ambiguous and unstable imbalance buttressed throughout several centuries of global history: the black man elevating himself to the white man he mocks; the white man dependent on the black man he surmounts.

The Ethics of Racechange

What does it mean for the white scholar to enter into the intellectual marketplace of the skin trade? Is the critic of racechange—like The Anthropologist—guilty of silencing black subjects or is she an apologist for white co-optation of black culture? As the Igbo masquerade hints, the predicament of Western culture consists in its appropriation not only of black physical bodies but also of muffled black presences. The ambivalent twoness of the Janiform vase is hierarchized here, the black subordinated to the white. Certainly, too, the white-to-black racechanges to be analyzed in the subsequent chapters of this book contributed to the silencing and objectification of black people. Even though, as the preceding sections of this introduction attempted to show, a "white skin, black face" scenario could work toward libertarian ends, most people today would agree with John Howard Griffin and Langston Hughes that the time for racial impostures has passed. Yet because we have become a society more aware of how insulting such impersonations can be, the time for studying racial imitations has now begun.

For if the concept of whiteness depends—as Cole's image suggests it does—on the appropriation of black beings, then perhaps one of the predicaments of white culture has resided in its blindness about its dependency on represented (and thus effaced) black bodies. Although taboos against white impersonations of blackness need to be understood, they should not stop us from appreciating the extent to which twentieth-century Western culture is indebted to African and African-American tropes, images, mimicries, and masks. "The Negro is comparison" (211), Fanon argues elsewhere in *Black Skin, White Masks*, again insisting that this comparison is one inflicted only on black consciousness; however, we shall see that at certain moments the white person must be white in relation to the black, that the "Negro is comparison" for whites, even if (perhaps especially when) blacks have no ontological resistance in the eyes of whites.[29]

One of Fanon's most interesting interpreters, Homi Bhabha, puts it this way:

The representative figure of [colonial] perversion . . . is the image of post-Enlightenment man tethered to, *not* confronted by, his dark reflection, the shadow of colonized man, that splits his presence, distorts his outline, breaches his boundaries, repeats his action at a distance, disturbs and divides the very time of his being. (44)

The staging of the ambivalence of the colonizer cannot be conflated with the performance of the ambivalence of the colonized; however, the recurrence of racechange allows us to see the extent to which Euro-Americans remained tethered to a dark reflection that splits and distorts their being. Although impersonation has functioned as a fate imposed upon or a strategy adopted by the disempowered, it has also operated as a means or method of disempowering others, of Othering others.[30] Indeed, the long history of racechange demonstrates that no single effect, no simple ideology can be said to emanate from a trope that embodies the slipperiness of metamorphosis in its adoptions or adaptions as well as in its historical evolution.

Hemingway's darkening heroine in *The Garden of Eden* (who tries to transform herself into an "African girl") is the character deployed by Toni Morrison to conclude her brilliant critical book, *Playing in the Dark* (1992), a summons for critics to study the uses to which dark and light images have been put by the white imagination. Responses to Morrison's call, the chapters that follow set out to understand the psychological, aesthetic, and ethical dimensions of cross-racial mimicry and imagery in the American canon. Yet, from antiquity to present times, Western culture's fascination with racial imitation, transformation, and mutability has gone unnoted because of embarrassment at what we have rightly been taught to view as racist activity and because of generalized discomfort over images that invoke while breaching conventional boundaries.[31] On the one hand, cross-racial masquerades rely upon strategies of commodification that have historically been used by whites to subordinate people of color; and, on the other hand, they disturb not only those who wish to police the parameters of racial categories (keeping black and white in strictly segregated separate spheres) but also those who wish to eradicate altogether the demarcations of racial categories (draining the very terms "black" and "white" of efficacy). In short, such racechanges have remained largely invisible because characters like Hemingway's blond African could trace their genealogical ancestry back to the minstrel and because of a recent theoretical emphasis on the fictionality of all racial categories.

To take this last matter first, a study of cross-racial impersonation may appear vexed from the perspective of current critical efforts to underscore the diversity of ethnicities and the social construction of race, for recent scholarship has tended to view stable racial categories as essentialist or biologistic, smacking (in other words) of the racism that put racial vocabularies into place during the Enlightenment.[32] At least in part to consolidate the so-called rainbow coalition of multi-hued people, "color" has recently made a comeback in popular as well as critical parlance, returning after "colored" gave way to "Negro," "Negro" to "black," "black" to "Afro-American," and "Afro-American" to "African American." Henry Louis Gates's "personal statement" for his Yale application nicely captures the rapidity of changing fashions of nomenclature: "My grandfather was colored, my father was Negro, and I am black," explained the now prominent spokesperson for

"Afro-American Studies" (in an account included in his recent memoir, significantly entitled *Colored People* (201)).

How can we write or speak about "black" and "white," proponents of the rainbow coalition might ask, in the context of Egyptian, Armenian, Sri Lankan, or Jamaican ethnicities? Some time ago, Joel Williamson expressed it this way: "There are, essentially, no such things as 'black' people or 'white' people" (522). As Robyn Wiegman—speculating about racial categories rendered "real" through "naturalizing" descriptions of the body—puts it, "making the African 'black' reduces the racial meanings attached to flesh to a binary structure of vision," thus imprisoning African Americans in a "prisonhouse of epidermal inferiority" (4, 11).[33] Given the empirical unreality of black and white, don't many of us feel the way the autobiographical writer Jane Lazarre does when she experiences herself as either "colorless" or "multicolored, some combination outside the known spectrum with no name to hold [us] down"? (*Worlds*, xiv). "Color" may be in vogue because it rejects the lure of ethnic absolutism, accepting in its stead (an also now fashionable) hybridity or plurality.

However, I do not restrict myself to the more stylish of these words because I seek to consider the imaginative prevalence black-and-white racial polarities have attained in modern culture. Curiously, an obsession with "racial purity" or "racial authenticity" has characterized not only right-wing fascist rhetoric in the twentieth century but also left-wing civil rights politics. Although such biologically and nationally based concepts of racial difference have been dubbed essentialist by contemporary theorists,[34] recent descriptions of the social construction of race sometimes seem too facile, or so a growing number of sophisticated interlocutors in the conversation about racial politics have begun to realize.[35] As Diana Fuss has argued, race—"a variable and flexible term"—may work "as a political concept" even when it is known to be "a biological fiction" (*Essentially Speaking*, 91). Neither an illusion nor a fact, race operates in a manner similar to gender—as a complex of meanings transformed by political frameworks.[36] Though race may be a fiction, in other words, it remains what Wallace Stevens called a Supreme Fiction that has exploited the corporeal body to put in place, sustain, and justify powerful systems of inequality. In both political and aesthetic realms, an iconography of ethnic absolutism has been abrogated and sustained by cross-racial intermixing, creolization, and impersonation. Drawing on a growing corpus of work on the racial significance of whiteness, I use the terms "black" and "white" throughout this book to accentuate the persistent power these categories have continued to exert, a power that speaks to the recalcitrance of the Western imagination, its recondite refusal to heed demythologists of racial definitions.[37] One major way the African was "made" black, in other words, was achieved through a series of racechanges undertaken by performers and artists who established whiteness as an escape from "the prisonhouse of epidermal inferiority" (Wiegman, 11).

But if the language of this study proves dated, what could be more anachronistic or retrograde than one of its primary subjects: whites masquerading as blacks? The second inhibition related to this study, then, pertains to the historical origins of whites' impersonations of blacks. The first channel white masquerades of blackness took, minstrelsy founded American entertainment by turning African Americans into figures of fun. No wonder that one of the most brilliant scholars of racial impersonation has claimed that almost any approach to this subject remains suspect: "To attack blackface (who would now defend it?)," Michael Rogin has speculated, "may simply be another way of putting it on" ("Blackface, White Noise," 438). What seems particularly ghastly about minstrelsy, of course, is that this white impersonation of blackness refuses black people intellectual agency or cognitive capacity.

In a 1992 radio interview about the importance of representation, Paule Marshall explained, "Once you see yourself truthfully depicted, you have a sense of your right to be in the world" (Funderburg, 9). Conversely, many racechange performances teach a cruel lesson to black audiences. When you repeatedly see yourself falsely depicted, you have no sense of your right to be in the world, or, indeed, you gain a conviction that you cannot, do not, should not exist. At its most sinister, in blackface performances, racechange taught precisely this lesson, for the white actor in burnt cork obsessively erased black subjectivity in a guilty reenactment of the murderous dynamics at work in a racist society. Yet simply to ignore cross-racial masquerades because they are psychologically damaging is, on the one hand, to miss an opportunity to examine one of the most pervasive and influential modes of racism in Western culture and, on the other, to lose the chance of understanding the different ideological work done by racial representation. As ethically disturbing as they are, such white masquerades of blackness nevertheless have had a checkered past that clarifies not only the dynamics of racial stereotyping and the psychology of racism but also the creative impact of race on the Anglo-American imagination.

Paradoxically, modernist racechange—so often subversive in its intent, so often avant-garde in its setting—finds its historical roots in exceptionally popular and virulently racist entertainments undertaken primarily by and for white men. In the commercially successful and technologically innovative movies featuring blackface actors that are analyzed in the second chapter of this book, minstrel and vaudeville traditions produce a gratingly abrasive compound of aesthetically fascinating but ethical repulsive scripts. The remaining pages of *Racechanges*—attending to the tendency of male artists to approach the subject through dramatic forms of impersonation while women of letters for the most part remain more absorbed by issues of lineage and inheritance—recount various artistic efforts of twentieth-century artists to grapple with the Othering blackface symbolically inflicted on African Americans. Like Man Ray and Hannah Höch, the African-American artists discussed in Chapter 3 attempted (in different ways and with varying degrees of success) to right the wrong of white privilege in the 1920s, in the case of the Harlem Renaissance thinkers by creating myths of racial origin that explained (without justifying) the historical fact of white supremacy. In Chapter 4, I discuss their white contemporaries, modernists who used black talk as back talk, exploiting cross-racial ventriloquism to establish—and then question—their identification with what had been rendered Other by their own culture.

The last two chapters concentrate more explicitly on the interactive influences of race and gender in racechange scripts. Especially in the period after World War II, I argue in Chapter 5, white men and women of letters pathologized and eroticized the black man—on whom was projected a criminalized yet alluring form of masculinism. Because white men and women of letters oscillated between wanting to become and wishing to have such a figure, their work tends to link the blurring of racial borderlines with the transgressive collapsing of homosexual and heterosexual categories. At the same time, as the last chapter demonstrates, birth stories about new breeds composed of mixed races enabled a host of writers to focus on mothers of one race giving birth to babies that look like they belong to another so as to see what the racechanged baby's reception might tell us about the possibilities of a post-racist society. That my meditations on the libertarian potentiality of racechange consistently encountered discouragingly recalcitrant scripts made it necessary to append the final chapter, a postscript in which I speculate that—despite its contributions to racist totalizing—racechange continues to hold out an aesthetic possibility of bridging the gap between blacks and whites.

What does it mean that racechange informs the most retrograde and the most revolutionary—the most conventional and the most experimental—works of art in the twentieth century? Whether as a manifestation of guilt, a form of pleasure, or a kind of guilty pleasure, white privilege plays itself out through almost obsessive racial masquerading. That the minstrel tradition established the parameters of racechange in America, a tradition shockingly incompatible with the benign impartiality of the Tarquinian urn and its equivocal faces, suggests the impossibility of collapsing the aesthetically pleasurable into the ethically acceptable or of associating racial impersonation with any monolithic ideological design—or, for that matter, of defining racism itself as a monochromatic phenomenon. Given what Homi Bhabha calls "the *ambivalence* of mimicry" (86), we need to understand white masquerades as a mockery of and menace to the Other, as an assertion of difference, but also a form of competition, as an admission of resemblance, a gesture of identification or solidarity, even a mode of self-mockery. Or so the centrality of Jews in the history of racechange—as performers and writers—will illustrate. For, just as Simone de Beauvoir began *The Second Sex* not only by comparing "the situation of woman and that of the Negro"—"the eternal feminine" with the "black soul"—but also by likening both with the situation of "the Jew" and "the Jewish character" (xxiii), racechanging conventions enabled artists from manifold traditions to relate nuanced comparative stories about various modes and gradations of Othering.

America's first national theater, first talking pictures, first radio shows, and first "new" journalism as well as Europe's first experimental literature, painting, and photography: All were marked by various forms of cross-racial performance, most frequently whites masquerading as Africans or African Americans. Historically, white *posing* counters black *passing*. Often, in other words, the white poser flagrantly exhibits the artifice of the performance, its theatrical falsity, while the black passer seeks to screen or camouflage signs of a discrepancy between hidden identity and outer appearance. Unlike the "passing" tradition, in which African Americans attempted to produce mimetically realistic replicas of Euro-Americans, whites posing as blacks often emphasized the spurious or ersatz caricature they created. Like the complicated motives of minstrelsy described by Eric Lott, nineteenth-century extravaganzas that both mock and celebrate the power of blacks, racial impersonations in the twentieth century stage white ambivalence about African Americans and their culture. The critic Susan Willis has speculated that "blackface is a metaphor for the commodity" (189) and we will see that black-face in the movies, blackface on the black faces of African-American Broadway entertainers, and various aesthetic transmutations of blackface flirt with even as they defend against the black Other, who becomes a kind of commodity fetish for white people.[38] To the fetishized, the process can only be perplexing, posing problems for real human beings harnessed to or assimilated into weirdly evocative images and stereotypes. However, for those whites shopping not only in low but also in high cultural markets, the shifting, shifty images of the fetish adorn the closet where the self slips on, tries out, purchases, or discards the outrageous costumes of its various incarnations. Unlike black people, who often had to adopt white masks to gain their rights and privileges, white people have chosen various modalities of racial impersonation, which in the course of the century have evolved from mockery to mimicry to an emphasis on inter-racial mutuality and mutability— not replacing mockery with mimicry or mimicry with mutuality but eventually playing out all three modes. More specifically, *Racechanges* traces an evolution from the mean mockery of blackface in the movies through the adulatory mimicry of the ersatz primitivism found in modernist verse and fiction, from the confused erotics of black envy during the post-World War II period to the loving emphasis on inter-racial mutuality at work in contemporary narratives of the mixed child.

   That white artists continue to be fascinated with the permeable boundaries of racial markers means that their work documents their indebtedness to African-American culture. A consideration of white appropriation of black images therefore uncovers the extent to which mainstream American culture, no longer Anglo-American, has moved in the course of this century to becoming not only indebted to black aesthetic forms and traditions but itself profoundly African American.[39] Such a fusion holds out the promise of future reciprocity and respect, in the place of past thievery and scorn. A post-racist society cannot possibly come into being until Americans comprehend how the dualism of "black" versus "white" has operated to hide the cross-racial dynamics of our interwoven cultural pasts. To some extent, as we have seen, *COLORS'* computerized photo of a black Queen Elizabeth, Michael Jackson's morphed multi-ethnic sequence of faces in his instantaneously popular 1993 music video, and *Time*'s computerized portrait of a cybergenetic Eve dramatize racial merging as well as the reconfiguration of ideas about race. Indeed, a wish to celebrate a multi-ethnic diversity that would facilitate the "Rebirth of a Nation" informs all these "Morphies," whose eyes and lips, skin and hair represent 50–50 combinations of the physical characteristics of their African or Asian, Hispanic or Anglo-Saxon progenitors. Despite the recycling of such tried and tired terms as "Queen of the Empire" and "Eve," morphing postulates a visual elasticity beyond racial dualism, encouraging viewers to consider the ramifica-

tions of appreciating color divested of the category of race. The electronic melding of images produces perceivably new, transracial beings that resist old racial
categories.

It would be wrong to conclude this first chapter on such an optimistic note,
however. For even at its most utopian, racechange often fails to dislodge psychological and aesthetic structures generated by what Winthrop Jordan's title calls the
prevailing arrangement of *White Over Black*. Although Michael Jackson overtly
advertised his music video "Black or White" as an attack on prejudice, network
officials objected to the violence of its conclusion and therefore cut footage of the
superstar taking a crowbar and smashing car and store windows (bearing fascist
and racist graffiti). And as sagacious a thinker as Donna Haraway found herself
plummeted into "a dyspeptic attack of political correctness" upon gazing on the
Time cover bearing the new Eve's face (364). Judging "the sense of utter homogeneity that emanates from *Time*'s matrix of diversity" nothing but "numbing,"
Haraway protests against its "evacuation of histories of domination and resistance," equates it with "the replicants for sale" in the futuristic movie *Blade Run-
ner* (1989), and argues that this Eve "ensures the difference of no difference in the
human family" (366). By emphasizing especially in its African and Hispanic faces
blended or moderated skin tones as well as mostly Caucasian features, the genealogy of *Time*'s cybernetic cover girl hints that her creators eschew extremes
as unattractive. Similarly, Patricia J. Williams looked at the depiction of Queen
Elizabeth as a black woman (and other Benetton ads in which "the Pope becomes
Chinese, Arnold Schwartzenegger becomes 'a negro'") to wonder at "this sifting
through the jumbled jewelry box of cultural assets, selected body parts, and just
the right accessories": Do such assemblages signify "the whole self" or the dis-
embodiment of "No one"? (*Rooster's Egg*, 242–43).

Probably the most brilliant painter to exploit racechange, Robert Colescott,
would endorse Haraway's and Williams's skepticism, for he proves just how far
off the promised end of a post-racist society remains in his two most satiric works:
Eat Dem Taters (1975) and *George Washington Carver Crossing the Delaware:
Page from an American History Textbook* (1975). The first of these, a racechanged
version of Van Gogh's *The Potato Eaters* (1885), hints at theft by reminding us of
what one critic calls "the already Negroid features of the down-trodden peasants"
in the original (Sims, 4, see color insert). Not simply a picture of the parallel oppressions of black sharecroppers and European peasants, Colescott's painting
proves that the exploitation of the European peasant received its due in the dignified portrait produced by Van Gogh; however, American blacks suffer the added
indignity of a representation that scornfully presents them happily embracing their
impoverishment. The characters seated around the table in *Eat Dem Taters* look
less like African Americans, more like white minstrels' depictions of African
Americans. Similarly, in *George Washington Carver Crossing the Delaware: Page
from an American History Textbook* (see color insert), the cook and the banjo player, the fisherman and the drunkard, and the wench displaying her bare bottom recall the characters of minstrelsy.

While Emanuel Leutze's original, *Washington Crossing the Delaware* (1851), testifies to the historic liberation of America by its first national leader, Colescott's parody takes one of the few black men to enter the history books—George Washington Carver—and places him in a ship of fools; that is, among the African Americans more often taught to whites: "the menial workers—Stepin Fetchits, Aunt Jemimas, boot blacks," in Colescott's words (Sims, 4). With its river so allusive of freedom and its cottony ice flows, the contemporary parody of *Washington Crossing the Delaware* contrasts the myth of freedom established by the founding fathers with the reality of slavery, even as it slyly hints that minstrelsy's version of African Americans provided the founding origins of American culture. Taken together, both of Colescott's racechanged paintings address African-American impoverishment as poverty and as the deprivation inflicted by degrading representations. At the same time, Colescott points a finger at the aesthetic past, reminding us that black figures have been marginalized and exploited as symbols or caricatures in the great masterpieces of Western civilization. Through the use of comic book images and parodic narration, post-modernist or in-your-face arrogation becomes a way of subverting earlier, clandestine appropriations of the African-American body, but it also provides a vehicle for placing African-American figures at the very center of the history of Western art and of American culture.

Yet what would happen if we approached Colescott's canvases without knowledge of his racial identity? Wouldn't they appear to be deeply unethical in their stereotyping of African Americans? This is precisely the question racechanging productions often pose as well as the query Henry Louis Gates, Jr., encourages us to ask in his provocative essay on "'Authenticity,' or the Lesson of *Little Tree*," which starts off with the irony that the best-selling *Education of Little Tree* was touted and taught in Native American literature courses as a true story composed by the grandson of Cherokees until it was discovered that the pseudonym Forrest Carter hid one Asa Earl Carter, a Ku Klux Klan terrorist and author of Governor George Wallace's famous speech "Segregation now . . . Segregation tomorrow . . . Segregation forever." From white abolitionists who composed ersatz slave narratives to the many male novelists who wrote not only about but through the consciousness of their heroines, authorly interlopers have refused to heed any border patrols in the realm of the imagination. "Ethnic transvestism" is the clever phrase coined by Werner Sollors to describe the "many fake ethnic writers, from the times of Henry Harland, who published 'Jewish' novels under the pen name Sidney Luska, to the recent case of Daniel James, who wrote 'Chicano' stories under the assumed name Danny Santiago and fooled critics for a while" (*Beyond Ethnicity*, 252).[40]

Is it true that the genuine, authentic, sincere experience of, say, an ethnic group can be expressed only by one of its own or are we too often entrapped by what Nancy K. Miller calls "as-a" criticism (20); and if we expect artists and scholars to confine themselves "as a black" to black writing or "as a lesbian" to lesbian writing, aren't we just putting into place another form of segregation now, tomorrow, and forever? Besides, what would such a protestation mean and to what extent could it deliver? The folklorist Roger Abrahams has shown, after all, that so-called "authenticating stories"—in which writers like Joel Chandler Harris, Lafcadio Hearn, Mark Twain, and George Washington Cable "make righteous claims to have learned major portions of their repertoires from specific black performers"— constituted just one more formulaic "way of establishing one's credentials as a ver- nacular artist, whether on the minstrel stage, the lecturer's platform, or the written page" (142–43). Like these, most authenticating maneuvers remain qualified strategies that can never completely certify legitimacy, for creative artists—even those telling stories from their own social repertoires—never fully possess or con- tain their creations;[41] even with the best intentions, they must invent characters and locales more or less than themselves and their places of origin. What the artists engaged in the conventions of racechange do is spotlight the discrepancy between creator and creation, performer and repertoire, usually by making obvious the white person behind the black persona, for example, or, more paradoxically, the black face behind the black mask. We do read Colescott's painting differently once we interpret it in terms of the racial identity he espouses, and that very difference is a mark of how vertiginously disabling racist iconography remains: The African- American artist who mocks grotesque caricatures of blacks finds himself replicat- ing the most pernicious white representations.

If, as Richard Dyer has argued, "the invisibility of whiteness colonises other norms—class, gender, heterosexuality, nationality"—and if it "also masks white- ness as itself a category" (46), racechanges like those performed by Colescott make whiteness visible. (In Colescott's framework, it makes us see the canvases of Van Gogh and Leutze in a new way.) Finally, then, I have decided to close this introductory chapter with several images that help us envision the respect so fla- grantly, pointedly violated in Colescott's paintings (as well as to instate a contrast to the Janiform faces looking in opposite directions at the start of this book and to illustrate an ongoing fascination with racechanging iconography). Consider, then, the images of racial interdependence developed by a striking series of portraits in which white and black faces are presented in parallel—rather than oppositional— poses.

One version of Man Ray's *Noire et blanche* makes the mirroring between mod- el and mask quite explicit. The upright Kiki looks toward (leans into) the mask as if seeking her own alter self, the uncanny and unknown originatory psyche she al- ways glimpses at the corner of her eye but can never fully comprehend (Fig. 1.21). Because Kiki's hand and cheek now embrace and encircle the mask, the two fig- ures appear in the position of doubles, a twinning that eludes hierarchized racial and sexual categories. Two portraits that bring the homoerotic more explicitly into play through inter-racial doubling are Charles Cullen's "Tableau" (1927) and Robert Mapplethorpe's "Ken Moody and Robert Sherman" (1984), for the male profiles seem not really like two versions of one self so much as like two lovers in an intimate coupling (Figs. 1.22 and 23).

The visual emphasis on sameness—in positioning, in gender—infuses the racial contrasts here with a tantalizing tension so that blackness and whiteness perform the function of (hetero)sexualizing the couple. Its campy stars and rising sun, its swooning white man fondled and framed by his black partner, make Cullen's draw-

Figure 1.21 Man Ray, *Noire et blanche* (1926), vertical pose. Copyright © Man Ray Trust-ADAGP/ARS, 1997.

ing presage a glitzy new day, a show time of theatrically demonstrable, rapturous strutting. Mapplethorpe's more thrilling, more somber photograph meditates on the serious intent shared by its subjects' hauntingly interlaced subjectivities, an intensity of vision that highlights their vulnerability as the object of our gaze. As if the photographer were meditating on Fanon's belief that "European civilization is

Figure 1.22 Charles Cullen, *Tableau* (1927). Copyright © Armistad Research Center, Tulane University, New Orleans, administered by Thompson and Thompson, New York.

Figure 1.23 Robert Mapplethorpe, *Ken Moody and Robert Sherman* (1984), platinum print. Collection of Aaron and Barbara Levine. Copyright © 1984, The Estate of Robert Mapplethorpe/courtesy A+C Anthology.

characterized by the presence . . . [of] the Negro who slumbers in every white man" (187), the models' bald skulls make them seem universal, representative of a splitting in the psyche, for the open-eyed white man appears like a protector of his more vulnerable, sleeping black companion.

Less erotic but just as resistant to hierarchical valences are the curious post-modern totem poles next to the major highway that connects Bloomington, Indi-

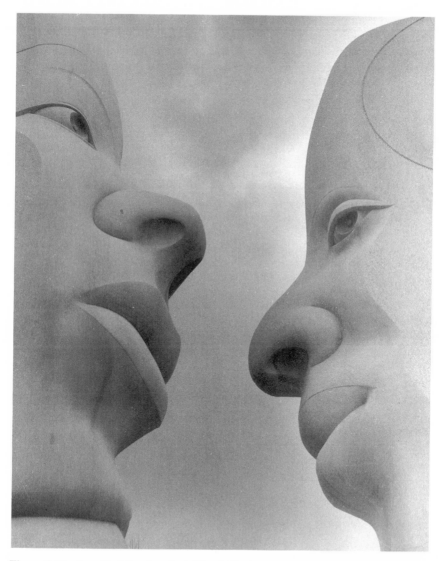

Figure 1.24 Jean-Paul Darriau, *Red, Blond, Black, and Olive* (1980), 14-foot limestone sculpture commissioned by Mayor Frank McClosky of Bloomington, Indiana. Photo by Kevin Hutchinson; courtesy of Jean-Paul Darriau.

ana, to the state capital: two limestone columns or pillars, riffs on Janiform emblems of racechange. Here racially marked faces—neither antithetical (positioned
in opposite directions) nor parallel (looking in the same direction)—peer at each
other. Jean-Paul Darriau's sculpture *Red, Blond, Black, and Olive* (1980) displays
Native American, Caucasian, African, and Asian profiles, each head (of course)
sharing the same beige-gray colors of the stone quarried in this region of the country, each here absorbed in an act of attention toward the other (Fig. 1.24). "The
proximity of the Other is the face's meaning," the ethical philosopher Levinas has
rather mysteriously mused. Attempting to capture the defenseless vulnerability
and exposure of the face, Darriau's sculpture seems to illuminate Levinas's point:
"The face before me summons me, calls for me, begs for me, as if the invisible
death that must be faced by the Other, pure otherness, separated, in some way, from
any whole, were my business" (82, 83).

The racechanges to be examined in this book do make commercially profitable
business out of the Other, but they can also make the Other the ethical business of
whites. At their most clarifying, racial masquerades illuminate manifold factors
within the psyche and the society that converge to construct Otherness, powerful
forces which, as Ursula Le Guin has observed, fatally conspire to impoverish our
moral being:

> If you deny any affinity with another person or kind of person, if you declare it to be
> wholly different from yourself—as men have done to women, and class has done to
> class, and nation has done to nation—you may hate it, or deify it; but in either case
> you have denied its spiritual equality, and its human reality. You have made it into a
> thing, to which the only possible relationship is a power relationship. And thus you
> have fatally impoverished your own reality. You have, in fact, alienated yourself. (99)

Yet the odd paradox of this study consists of the puzzling (even disquieting) in-
consistency that exactly what has depleted and challenged our ethical integrity has
enriched our cultural inheritance. Just as paradoxically, we shall see that claims of
sameness can be quite as destructive as those of difference. To revise Le Guin, "if
you [affirm an] affinity with another person or kind of person, if you declare it to
be wholly [the same as] yourself," you may also have "denied its spiritual equality, and its human reality." The pages that follow testify to the dialectical collisions
and collusions between morality and Western megalomania played out in the arena of racial metamorphosis.[42]

2

SPIRIT-MURDER
AT THE MOVIES

Blackface Lynchings

The disaster of the man of color lies in the fact that he was enslaved.

The disaster and the inhumanity of the white man lie in the fact that somewhere he has killed man.

—Frantz Fanon

The return of the dead is a sign of a disturbance in the symbolic rite, in the process of symbolization; the dead return as collectors of some unpaid symbolic debt.

—Slavoj Žižek

A still from Irving Berlin's *Holiday Inn* (1942) encapsulates the point of this chapter, even as it provides a reminder of the longevity of blackface as America's favorite form of racechange (Fig. 2.1). Wearing burnt cork, Crosby here dances the part of (a now "African-American") President Lincoln with his companion appearing as a parodic pickaninny complete with cornrows, pinafore, and pantaloons. As is often the case late in its history, the use of blackface has presumably only been justified by the need for a disguise: In an earlier scene, a jealously possessive Crosby broke out the "bootblacking" so as to hide his attractive dancing partner from his rival, Fred Astaire. But as also often happens, an excess of meaning attends the assumption of burnt cork, in this instance after the blond-haired dancer bemoans the make-up as a "punishment" visited upon her for dreaming about "how pretty" she would look at the Inn on the occasion of Lincoln's birthday. Not at all a mimetically realistic disguise, her racechange contrasts black skin with white wig to make her look like a singular anomaly.

Shades of the prisonhouse of American history close upon the subsequent production number (which is supposed to parallel Fred Astaire's firecracker hoofing on the Fourth of July in the same movie). For Crosby's part-plantation minstrel, part-Lincoln struts a dance of emancipation to celebrate the liberation presumably effected by the Civil War. But the very assertion of black freedom supposedly in-

Figure 2.1 Bing Crosby and Marjorie Reynolds in *Holiday Inn* (1942). Courtesy of Museum of Modern Art Film Stills Archive.

augurated by President Lincoln is undercut by the grinning, singing, prancing Tom and Topsy and by the chorus crooned in the kitchen by the stereotypical Mammy—"Who was it set the darkie free?"—and answered by the chirping black children in her abundant lap: "Abraham! Abraham!" As the etiology of blackface and the genealogy of the blackface actor will demonstrate, racechanges shaped by the early movies constitute a cosmetic approach to white compunction about the abuses of slavery as well as the failures of Reconstruction. During the period when the nonwhite, Africanlike presence Toni Morrison calls "the Africanist persona" (*Playing in the Dark*, 6) became highly charged, on the one hand, with exotic and criminally deviant valences and, on the other, with clownish and childlike ones, blackface illuminates the longterm effects of slavery and in particular white people's efforts to repeat, rationalize, camouflage, confess, or repair the grievous injury inflicted on blacks by international and national forms of subjugation.

"Everyone seems to think that the Negro is easily imitated when nothing is further from the truth," Zora Neale Hurston once mused about would-be white racechangers. "Without exception," she continued, "I wonder why the black-face comedians *are* black-face; it is a puzzle—good comedians, but darn poor niggers" ("Characteristics," 186). As she herself intimates, the answer to this question had less to do with realism and more to do with white psychology. Hurston's good-humored protest addresses the "puzzle" of motivation and in particular the "puzzle" of white people's cross-racial performances to which Ralph Ellison returned in his analysis of "the Negro as national scapegoat." According to Ellison, even seemingly fun-loving portrayals of African Americans stage what he called "a ritual of exorcism." The "joke" a racechanging actor shares with his audience in minstrel and vaudeville halls constitutes a "yoke" for those caricatured, as Robert Colescott's paintings of grotesquely stereotyped black figures slyly illustrated in the last chapter ("Change the Joke," 49, 48).

When taken together, Hurston's and Ellison's reactions hint that racial impersonation serves a unique function for white people, not so much mimetic as punitive or purgative: a way of replaying the subordination of black people as well as exonerating it. If, as Frantz Fanon has commented in *Black Skin, White Masks*, the psychology of blacks differs from that of whites, then throughout the twentieth century blacks continue to suffer from their past enslavement while whites remain haunted by the killing fields of their history: "The disaster and inhumanity of the white man lie in the fact that somewhere he has killed man." Whereas cultural imperialism causes people with black skin to internalize white-defined standards or to don white masks, the minstrel tradition and its offshoots on stage and screen uncover a psychological mechanism that motivates people with white skin to assume the coloration of those they have colonized.

Although the picture of the Janiform vase which appears in the opening pages of this book represents the ambivalent doubleness of racial contrasts, holding out the promise that cross-racial iconography could function as an emancipatory force in history, a far more malevolent mode of racechange became extraordinarily popular in the nineteenth-century minstrel show, and it was this blackface performance of racechange that shaped the film industry when it emerged at the beginning of the twentieth century. Despite the common assumption that minstrelsy declined at the turn of the century, it profoundly influenced America's first movies and musicals, raising questions about the degree to which these apparently new and innovative genres contained and sustained conventional structures of oppression. Not only did minstrel shows play an important role in the social fabric of many small towns in America; not only did minstrelsy continue to appear in large city productions into the 1990s; it also influenced many art forms not generally associated with it.[1]

The surprising importance of blackface on stage and screen, I will argue in this chapter, arises from the dynamics of white guilt generated by the racially inflected psychological patterns so brilliantly captured by Fanon's contrast between the "disaster" troubling "the man of color," who inherits a history of enslaving systems that annihilated his personhood as well as his genealogy, and the quite different "disaster" haunting "the white man," who confronts the culpability of his own lethal past. Fanon's dramatic formulation of the white man's guilty consciousness that "somewhere he has killed" can be extended by linking it to Patricia J. Williams's analysis of what she calls "the spirit murder" of twentieth-century racism. Williams's *The Alchemy of Race and Rights* introduces this concept in a meditation on the case of a black civil rights worker stabbed thirty-nine times, an act she views as "not merely" body murder but as "spirit murder" (73). In her legal "diary," Williams wonders "what it was that would not die, what could not be killed by the fourth, fifth, or even tenth knife blow; what sort of thing would not die with the body but lived on in the mind of the murderer?" (72).

Within the conceptual framework provided by Fanon and Williams, the exceptional popularity of blackface suggests that it functioned as one method of repeatedly obliterating the black body, substituting in its stead not only the white body but also the white man's parodic imitation-black-body. Could it be, in other words, that the tenacity with which performers and audiences clung to blackface is not unrelated to what motivated the spirit-murder of the civil rights worker who was stabbed thirty-nine times: "What the murderer was trying to kill was a part of his own mind's image, a part of himself and not a real other" (72). Williams's phrase rings true with respect to the creation of the "darkie" played by so many white men on stage and screen. For besides displacing the body of an actual black person, white actors' performances replaced that body with a projection of the white mind, namely a knavish or foolish character clearly accountable for (culpable of) past wrongs. Thus, what blackface entertainers attempted to annihilate was white responsibility for a past injurious to African Americans, "the symbolic debt" they owed the dead (to use the language of Slavoj Žižek).

An act/art that came into being during slavery and reached its peak of popularity during its turbulent aftermath, blackface provides insight into the culpable mental condition of a genocidal society. "Why do the dead return?" asks Žižek in his study of contemporary horror films, and he answers, *"because they were not properly buried"* (23). If, as my second epigraph warns, the not-properly-buried dead come back "as collectors of some unpaid debt," perhaps blackface performances, which justify white oppression of blacks (by making African Americans look so evil or so foolish that they must be the guilty party), dramatize a horrific return of the displaced black body—now paradoxically borne on and reborn in the white body. Such a return or mimetic mirroring provides evidence of white consternation about the transparency of the lie blaming African Americans for their own suppression. In Žižek's terms, whites who have refused to pay their debt or admit their liability to the (African-American) dead continue to be haunted by them. Uncannily, as we shall see, this haunting took the form of a reenactment that encased the white actor inside the black's role as scapegoat. After the Emancipation, blackface performers effectively colluded in what Trudier Harris considers the work of lynching, namely "to keep Blacks contained politically and socially" (19). If lynching staged a spectacle that sought to discipline its black audience while it communalized whites by "territorializing the black body" (Wiegman, 13), we will see that blackface stages a comparable scenario. No wonder, then, that lynching played a prominent role in early Hollywood films which were promoted through gruesome advertising copy: "Hear His Moans and Groans, Price One Cent."[2]

Paradoxically, even in nonviolent movies the blackface performer who effectively attempted to avoid accountability for racial injustice bore the burden of the Undead in/on his own body. Thus, this historically important form of racial impersonation constitutes not only a crime of spirit-murder, not only a justification for that crime as well as a displacement of responsibility for it, but also an odd reprisal or punishment, at times, curiously, a reparation or mode of mourning. For we shall see that even as the blackface performer metaphorically sacrificed a black character, he himself enacted the role of scapegoat, much as had his precursors on the minstrel stage. This chapter will explore the crucial role blackface played in two foundational movies in America's film industry—the first blockbuster and the first talkie—before turning back to the historical roots of blackface on the minstrel stage and then forward to its later evolution in Hollywood. To the extent that blackface proliferated a series of white lies about the subjection of African Americans in American culture, it whitewashed past and present injustices. That it did so within movies depending upon repetitive symbolic lynchings of the black male body attests to the centrality in early film scripts of camouflaged scenes of racial subordination. The phrase "repetitive lynchings" sounds like a case of overkill and is meant to because, as Virginia Woolf once put it in a different context, "it is far harder to kill a phantom than a reality" (240) and the fictitious nature of this celluloid black specter kept it alive, creeping back to haunt the white imagination.[3] Only in later modes of racechange did the victims of racism begin to receive the equivalent of a decent burial in aesthetic productions that attempt to recapture an equanimity comparable to that of the Tarquinian urn and in so doing confront the trauma of the innocent suffering of African Americans in order to absorb that scandal into the nation's historical memory.

The Birth of a Nation's Movie Industry

Two seemingly antithetical uses of blackface in two of the most important movies produced in this country at the start of its rich cinematic history illuminate the centrality of racial impersonation in American cultural history. The first film masterpiece, *The Birth of a Nation* (1915), and the first talkie, *The Jazz Singer* (1927), used blackface in apparently opposed ways, the former featuring the blackface actor as criminal, the latter as clown. In addition, though audiences today may find Jolson's film suspiciously patronizing about African Americans, *The Jazz Singer* presented itself as a liberal contrast in matters of racial ideology to the overt racism of *The Birth of a Nation*. While Griffith portrayed blackface characters as sexual predators out to destroy the nation by polluting white womanhood, Warner Brothers produced a blackface entertainer seeking to please white America by crooning to his "Mammy." Whereas Griffith followed his source, the novels of Thomas Dixon, to depict most of his black characters as looming bucks menacing weakened whites, Jolson on bended knee signified a tried and true, tamed Uncle Tom. Yet ultimately, the criminality and the clownishness of the stage Negro in both films operated as a form of character assassination or spirit-murder that provided a bizarre justification or penance for the lynchings all too common in this same period of time.

Most of the portraits of African Americans in Griffith's still shockingly racist film corroborate the assertion of its second intertitle that (in a characteristically disingenuous euphemism) "the *bringing* of the African to America planted the first *seeds* of disunion" (emphasis mine). Quite a bit later in the film a would-be rapist (acted by Walter Long in blackface) attempts to sow such seeds. *The Birth of a*

Figure 2.2 Walter Long as Gus in
The Birth of a Nation (1915). Cour-
tesy of Museum of Modern Art Film
Stills Archive.

Nation's Gus pursues the innocent, youthful, white Flora Cameron (Mae Marsh)
in a pine forest, stalking her as camera shots shift rapidly back and forth between
her spontaneous, joyful wanderings in the woods and his prowling chase. Carrying a water bucket instead of a basket, the frolicking girl prancing off the beaten
track plays Little Red Riding Hood to his Big Bad Wolf. According to Griffith's
biographer, Walter Long was instructed to run doubled-over with a sort of "ani-
malistic scuttle" and to gargle with a bottle of hydrogen peroxide so as to create
the effect of foaming at the mouth (Schickel, 232, Fig. 2.2).[4]

After Flora hurls herself suicidally down a precipice in the forest rather than
submit to Gus's bestial pursuit—"For her who had learned the stern lesson of hon-
or we should not grieve that she found sweeter the *opal gates of death*" (Title
1093)—her brother recovers and cradles her broken body. Soon, too, this para-

digmatic Southern hero, the Little Colonel of the Cameron family, finds "inspiration" watching white children under a sheet frightening (predictably terrified) pickaninnies at play and so decides to organize the mighty Ku Klux Klan whose white knights will redeem the honor of good girls like Flora by revenging themselves against the bestial black rapist and whose final ride-to-the-rescue would allow Griffith to film on a grand scale. "Instead of saving one poor little Nell of the Plains," he explained, "this ride would be to save a nation" (Schickel, 213).[5]

And, of course, in his sexual criminality Gus typifies the other blackface characters from whom the nation must be saved, two of whom are attached to the Northern senator Austin Stoneman, the deluded antagonist of the pastoral South, here typified by the Cameron family. With melodramatic symmetry, Pennsylvanian Stonemans and South Carolinian Camerons visit, befriend, and fall in love with each other before the Civil War; after its outbreak, however, the brothers of one family will murder the brothers or be rescued by the sisters of the other family, as Union and Confederate armies clash on the battlefields of the war. Based upon Thaddeus Stevens, the Pennsylvanian Republican deeply committed to racial equality in the Congress, Stoneman represents those misguided Northerners whose commitment to the liberation of the slaves inflates blacks with insolence and threatens to undermine the stability of the nation. Both Stoneman's mulatto mistress, Lydia Brown, and his mulatto henchman, the amazingly named Silas Lynch, act like lascivious predators whose hideously dominant sexuality affects and reflects their overweening political ambition.

Austin Stoneman's decision to commit himself to the radical Republican cause is first influenced by his housekeeper-mistress, who wishes to ferment rebelliousness in Southern blacks after the Civil War. We initially see Lydia Brown aspiring to social equality while presiding over the events in Stoneman's Northern residence, specifically a visit from Charles Sumner, who puts her in her place as a housekeeper by refusing to behave as if she were the mistress of the house. As soon as Sumner departs, Lydia falls into a paroxysm of rage, furious at the social slight and apparently determined to exploit this or any other incident to strengthen her hold over Stoneman. Ranting and raving, ripping her own clothing, repeatedly spitting and collapsing, she seems like a classic hysteric or madwoman, but it soon becomes clear that she will use her torn dress to pin blame on the unsuspecting Sumner, casting suspicion on him in Stoneman's eyes even as she fawns, caresses, and flatters her unsuspecting master (Fig. 2.3). The chapter of *The Clansman* (1905) devoted to Lydia is entitled "The First Lady of the Land" because Dixon wished to emphasize how this "sinister," "catlike," "sphinx" would "cast a shadow across the history of a great nation," becoming as Stoneman's consort "the arbiter of its social life," her self-serving, mendacious "ethics the limit of its moral laws" (94).

But in the movie Stoneman is blinded even more effectively by his other mulatto companion, the evocatively named Lynch who seeks (with Stoneman's approbation and the furtive glee of Lydia) to gain national leadership. Played by George Siegmann in blackface, Lynch looks like a cross between Orson Welles and Dan Ackroyd, puffing up as he gains political power and becomes Lieutenant

Figure 2.3   Ralph Lewis as Austin Stoneman with Mary Alden as Lydia Brown in *The Birth of a Nation*. Courtesy of Museum of Modern Art Film Stills Archive.

Governor of South Carolina. A leader of the black party, Lynch along with his co-horts manages to pervert democracy in America—we are shown black people stuffing the ballot box, disenfranchising whites, and murdering other black citizens who refuse to toe the black party's line—and it soon becomes clear why Lynch has his name. In the weird, topsy-turvy world of *Birth of a Nation*, African Americans themselves are presented as the guilty lynchers, turning their adversaries into "the helpless white minority." And so through the coalition of "negroes and carpetbaggers," Lynch rules a black-dominated state house of representatives whose rowdy black members pontificate while chomping on peanuts or joints of meat, downing both with intermittent swills of liquor. When a (predictable and presumably unnerving) bill for intermarriage is passed, it become apparent that the traitorous Lynch wants to marry not just any old white woman but Stoneman's own beautiful daughter, Elsie (presumably a fitting punishment for a Northerner made to understand that his egalitarian platform inevitably rests upon miscegenation, which in turn means the loss of racial "purity").

Richard Schickel argues about the portrayals of Gus, Lydia Brown, and Lynch that Griffith's decision to use make-up which "cannot and does not fully transform" his white actors into Negroes mitigates the film's racism. "He must have been aware that if a white man was playing a black man there was no way to disguise that fact" (233). And to the modern viewer, the blackface performances do seem parodically stereotypical, obviously designed to inspire the effect Thomas Dixon wanted, "to create a feeling of abhorrence in white people, especially white women against colored men" (Geduld, 98–99). At least in part, then, the black-faced actors look like what they are, namely (nasty) white people's (nasty) idea of blacks. However, part of the film's eerie effect derives from the use of "real" black extras: cavorting slaves on the antebellum plantation, carousing Northern soldiers disrespectfully bullying whites off the streets. At times, too, it is difficult to tell if blackface is being used: for example, in the case of those trusty and true family servants, the Camerons' loyal, loving Mammy and Uncle Tom. And the nefarious mulattos of the Stoneman residence can appear oddly light-skinned in some versions of the film, with Lydia Brown looking less like the nineteenth-century trag-ic mulatto and more like the nineteenth-century exotic Jewess. In the context of this potential confusion, the white masks of the Klan provide clarification, setting in order the chaos that threatens to contaminate Aryan culture.[6]

That misrule achieves a climax toward the close of the film when the screen is filled with multiple images of white men tarred and feathered, white husbands beaten with rifles by black soldiers, white citizens delivered from jail into the howling rage of the mob. A representative white father, the patriarch of the exem-plary Southern Cameron family—miraculously still alive, despite the deaths of two of his sons in the Civil War and the suicide of his little Flora—is forced to take shelter in a wooden shack. The once and future master of a magnificent ancestral mansion cowers in a log cabin after having been arrested by Lynch and paraded in chains before his former slaves for the crime of possessing a Klan outfit; rescued by "loyal black souls," he owes his escape to the Mammy and Uncle Tom of his household and to the two Union veterans who share their refuge. As one intertitle puts it, "The former enemies of North and South are united again in common de-fence of their Aryan birthright." But united where, if not inside what looks suspi-ciously like an Uncle Tom's cabin? Within the brave new world ruled by Lynch's law, Griffith suggests, the slave quarters will confine white gentlemen regardless of their regional or political loyalties, reducing their families to hostages and chat-tel—unless, that is, they are rescued by the Klan.

Indeed, just as earlier in the film Elsie Stoneman went to President Lincoln to obtain a pardon for her true love (the young Cameron son) during the war, it be-comes clear that Lynch has taken Lincoln's place when she petitions the Lieutenant Governor to free the Camerons from their cabin and is subjected to the lewd in-dignities of his lust (Fig. 2.4).[7] Unlike Griffith's gentle Lincoln, however, Lynch heeds not Elsie's plea for clemency. With Elsie locked up and cowering in Lynch's office, a title informs us that he proposes to "build a Black Empire and you as a Queen shall sit by my side." While the camera cuts back and forth between a hor-rified Elsie pounding at or flinging herself against the door and the Clansmen gal-loping along tree-shaded roads, another title explains that "Lynch, drunk with wine and power, orders his henchmen to hurry preparations for a forced marriage." The camera lovingly returns over and over again to an image of the vulnerable Lillian Gish imprisoned, gagged, and bound, all swooning purity and terror in her white

Figure 2.4   George Siegmann as Silas Lynch and Lillian Gish as Elsie Stoneman in *The Birth of a Nation*. Courtesy of Photofest.

flowing dress, threatened by a black fist, fainting in a dishevelled, fragile heap of grace under pressure.[8]

Exactly why Mr. Lynch insists on continuing to behave in this bullying manner remains beyond rational comprehension, except to justify Griffith's narrative conclusion.[9] If the first section of *The Birth of a Nation* closes with the senseless violence between North and South during the Civil War, the second part ends with the morally justified—even divinely sanctioned—violence of whites against blacks in a veritable race war. To vindicate the victimized Flora, to save the endangered Elsie, to rescue the captured patriarch of the Camerons—in other words, to reestablish traditional definitions of white femininity and masculinity—Gus, Lydia, Lynch, and indeed all black people must be destroyed. Given the use of scenes clearly marked as "Historical Facsimiles" (Sherman's march to the sea, the assassination of President Lincoln) as well as the periodic enactment of historic tableaux (all of which are touted as documentary in their accuracy), the film's claims to veracity easily spill over to camouflage pernicious racial ideology as pious race truth.[10] Rapid cutting after the Klan's "trial," "conviction," and murder of Gus—with shorter and shorter shots of the Camerons' cabin surrounded by black troups and Elsie Stoneman gagged in Lynch's study—emphasizes the compensatory solution to what one critic calls the "paranoid fantasies of white sexual inadequacy" that fuel this melodrama (Cripps, 51).

Thus, when white robes float over the moonlit roads of South Carolina at the end of the show to rescue Mr. Cameron from the slave cabin and Elsie Stoneman from the lustful Lynch, white crowds in cities all across America cheered what amounts to a Christian crusade for law and order. The rousing orchestration (teetering on the edge of Wagner's "Ride of the Valkyries") and the massive number of horses and riders involved, as well as the heroic, heraldic camera angles, transform this Nordic trek from a chase-to-the-rescue into an apocalyptic conflagration. A contrast to the tragic internecine destruction of the Civil War, the military mission of the Klan evokes cowboys come to slay the heathen Indians; the sheriff's posse about to reclaim a frontier town-gone-wrong; Arthurian knights out to win the tournament, protect the grail, man the round table, and assure the purity and honor of their ladies. As in the last illustration in Dixon's novel, though, the Clansman cum cowboy-sheriff-knight retains the moral stature of crusader (Figs. 2.5 and 2.6). It seems appropriate that one of Griffith's actor-riders was the soon-to-become famous director of westerns John Ford and that this was the first movie to be shown at the White House, dubbed (by President Wilson) "history written in lightning" (to which he added, "And my only regret is that it is all true" (Schickel, 268–70)).

History as whitening but also as a kind of electrocution. With night-riders in white sheets featured on posters—crosses emblazoned on each breast, hooded like their horses—with one publicity ploy involving hired horsemen, garbed in Klan robes, galloping through city streets, Griffith's film saved the endangered white femininity of Elsie Stoneman and the equally imperiled white masculinity of Cameron *père* through an Oedipal solution that issued a death sentence to black people, especially black men. Fearful white male insufficiency—the murder of Lincoln as well as the jeopardized paternity of all the other white men in the melodrama—threatens the continuity of the White House, of patriarchal genealogy itself. In opposition to the upstart pseudo-son Lynch and his Black Empire stand the true heirs apparent of the Invisible Empire, wearing their phallic hats, wielding their potent swords, and as spectral, invincible, and unified in their galumphing columns as any Lacanian would want. What accompanies the destruction of the criminalized bodies of Gus and Lynch, then, is an epithalamium: The wedding of the Cameron and Stoneman families reunifies South with North to deliver the birth of one nation under God, indivisible. With the dead Gus dumped on Lynch's doorstep, with Lynch himself in the hands of the Clan, Stoneman and Cameron descendants can unite in sexual unions to save the national Union from "Africanization."[11]

Like love and marriage, blackface and white hood seem to go together in Griffith's film. Two odd moments late in the movie explain why. First, at one point we are informed that blackfaced white actors on screen represent not African Americans but white spies using disguise to infiltrate the hegemonic black party so as to uncover its stratagems. Second, after the little Colonel as Clansman comes to res-

Figure 2.5 "The Fiery Cross of Old Scotland's Hills!" from Thomas Dixon, *The Clansman* (1905).

Figure 2.6 [*Below*] Gus captured by the Klan in *The Birth of a Nation*. Courtesy of Museum of Modern Art Film Stills Archive.

cue Elsie Stoneman, he finds it necessary to assure her of his identity by raising his hood so she can see his face. Taken together, the scenes remind viewers of the potential for racial confusion. Indeed, blackface itself might be considered a symbolic defense against such (inevitable) complications. Since it may be impossible to "tell" if a person is actually of black descent—especially in the context of the "one drop rule" (defining a person with just one "drop" of "black" blood as racially Other)—complexion is neither an infallible nor a stable index of race, while blackface assures audiences that difference is visible, always encoded in the same way, skin-deep. Also, given the evil roles played by the characters of African-American descent in Griffith's narrative, perhaps blacks are so polluting that they ought not to come into contact with white actors at all; maybe "that kind" of in-humanity should be represented only through surrogates, like the totemic symbols or fetishes used to stand for and ward off evil spirits in exorcist rituals.

From this perspective, blackface insures the 100 percent certifiable purity of an all-white cast/community of film actors and makers, unsullied by the threat of miscegenation against which they preach. And indeed, though a few African-American leads and some black extras were employed in the making of his movies, Griffith explicitly forbad any "black blood" in actors who touched white actress-es, rejected players who had skin blemishes on their faces, and experimented with what he called "hazy photography," placing a white sheet beneath the actor's feet while a bright light would illuminate the body from above, thus, in his words, "eras[ing] imperfections" (May, 83, 76). That Lydia Brown just disappears from the film while Gus and Lynch must be destroyed so as to redeem the honor of Flo-ra Cameron and Elsie Stoneman indicates that the real problem for Griffith, a man who late in his life claimed to have loved only one person, his father, is the black man and the threat he poses to the white patriarch as well as his lineage.[12] When the Klan victory ensuring the lynching of Gus and Lynch is followed by *Birth of a Nation*'s concluding images of a surrealistic Mars turning before our eyes into Christ-the-Clansman, we are meant to understand that the Prince of War will meta-morphose into the Prince of Peace only when race war has brought victory to the white son, whose resurrection (erection) requires the sacrificed (castrated) black body.

The birth of the American nation and of its film industry is predicated upon the death of African Americans. Indeed, blackface marks that hope, the time when the only blacks will really be whites, whose blackness can be washed off like a cos-metic or paint. As warpaint, then, blackface constitutes a white declaration of war on blacks. Just as important, using blackface to portray the evil of blacks meant turning the victims into the perpetrators of racial violence, the lynched into the lynchers or the disenfranchised domestic servant into the "First Lady of the Land." Since the transparency of the lie underlines white culpability, blackface discloses the crime it was meant to conceal. Yet John Hope Franklin has pointed out—by explaining that William J. Simmons decided to realize his plans to revive the Klan when the film opened in Atlanta—that *"Birth of a Nation* was the midwife in the rebirth of the most vicious terrorist organization in the history of the United States"* (431). Understandably, critics at the time of the film's release decried it as a "spiritual assassination" (Hackett, 163), for blackface in Griffith's film attempted to move African Americans from slavery to servitude by whitewashing American history.

The Atonement of the Jazz-Jew

While African Americans threaten the death of the American nation in Griffith's film, African Americans seem to epitomize America in *The Jazz Singer*, for Jolson as Jakie Rabinowitz manages to assimilate—to transform himself into Jack Robin, to extricate his fate from the control of his father, Cantor Rabinowitz, and to win the shiksa he loves—by defying his father's pious injunctions and appearing on stage wearing burnt cork.[13] Primarily blackface operates mimetically in *The Birth of a Nation*, marking a (supposedly) realistic difference between the races; however, in *The Jazz Singer* burnt cork is merely theatrical make-up. Whereas the former film preaches racial hatred, moreover, the latter counsels racial respect not only between gentiles and Jews but also between the cultures of whites and blacks.

The leering, lusty blackfaced Gus, Lydia, and Lynch must be tramped under the crusading hooves of Christ and his Clansmen; yet the meek and mild blackfaced Jolson on bended knee, with arms outstretched, looks somehow childlike, submissive, sorrowful, even Christlike. As Michael Rogin points out, though, the apparent opposition between *Birth*'s attack on miscegenation and *Jazz*'s promotion of inter-racial marriage hides the ways in which the latter "facilitates the union of Gentile and Jew, not white and black" ("Blackface," 420). Taking this point one step further, I want to claim that both films participate in a common task that illuminates the link between travesties of American justice and of African-American culture.[14] If *The Birth of a Nation* impersonates black men so as to justify their lynching, *The Jazz Singer* represents black masculinity also to unman, in this case by substituting infantilized "boy" for aggressive "buck" and thereby reenacting spirit-murder in its own, albeit different register. Yet if *The Birth of a Nation* uses blackface to effect a kind of spiritual assassination, *The Jazz Singer* remains haunted by the need to atone for that crime. Together, both films explain the popularity of the blackface performer who could dramatize for white audiences contradictory responses to the shame of a supremacist society.

"Orchard Street would have had some difficulty in recognizing Jakie Rabinowitz of Beth-El choir under the burnt cork of Jack Robin": so reads Title 49 of *The Jazz Singer* right after the first planned close-up of Jack Robin in blackface, applauding in the wings as he watches his girlfriend and patron Mary Dale complete her dance routine on stage (Carringer, 80). In the scene that follows (which was played in whiteface), Mary tells a doting but shy Jack about a new theatrical engagement that will launch her career, and although he congratulates her, he silently suffers because of their impending separation. From this point on, Jack's stage self becomes associated with his secondary position: his thralldom to Mary as well as his tormented contrition about his professional aspirations. The pattern of Mary's authority and Jack's admiring but dumb acquiescence recurs when they meet again, this time not in Chicago but in New York. An indebted Jack gets his

Figure 2.7   Al Jolson as Jack Robin with May McAvoy as Mary Dale in *The Jazz Singer* (1927). Courtesy of Museum of Modern Art Film Stills Archive.

break on Broadway because of Mary, and she is the one who invites him to the dinner that will eventuate in their engagement. Repeatedly, bashful Jack the impoverished ingenue gratefully admits to plucky Mary the established celebrity that he owes whatever success he will achieve to her patronage. Throughout their courtship, then, Mary's New Womanly determination and autonomy contrast with the hesitations and dependency of Jack. Unlike the blackface which hypermasculinizes in *The Birth of a Nation*, in *The Jazz Singer* burnt cork contributes to the already ongoing infantilization of its central character (Fig. 2.7).

Before and after he darkens his countenance, tears repeatedly course down Jack's cheeks, one sign of an effeminacy long attributed to the loyal, pious, long-suffering Uncle Tom.[15] As a young boy, Jakie cowers before and sobs after a beating inflicted by his orthodox father who has hauled him out of a bar and punished him for singing "raggy" songs.[16] He runs away, but not before taking tearful leave of his mother's portrait. Weeping is also part of his singing style: When he sings "jazz," there is said to be a "tear" in his voice; when his father advises a young boy to chant "with a sigh—like you are crying out to your God," he remembers how Jakie "had a voice like a angel." At the climax of Jack's bathetic self-displays, his most melodramatic self-division, the film introduces a scene in which Jack smears on blackface. Backstage for the last rehearsal of his first Broadway show and only hours before Yom Kippur, he completes the make-up by donning a wig of cropped wool; although he promises Mary to do his best for the show, the background music launches into a schmaltzy version of "I'd walk a million miles for one of your smiles, my Mammy."

Seated at his make-up mirror, a remorseful Jack envisions his father in the synagogue and hears the strains of "Kol Nidre." The putting on of blackface occurs when Jack seems most in need of parental approval, narcissistically watching himself being surveyed, passive with respect to Mary, and anxious about his professional aspirations. Although he agrees with Mary that his career must come first, the songs of his people are "tearing at [his] heart," rendering him vulnerable when his mother and Yudelson the Kibitzer (a synagogue *macher*) enter to make their plea. Embracing his mother (who sighs, "Jack, this isn't you"), the blackened Jack looks to Yudelson like Jack's "shadow" (originally in Alfred A. Cohn's film script his "nigger"). Papa is dying at home, we are told by a weeping Mama; sunset and Yom Kippur only two hours away! Who will sing the prayers? (Fig. 2.8).

Wiping his eyes, pulling away from his mother, Jack dons shirt and jacket, moves on stage and sings (to the disgust of the original story-writer) a number about mother-love which elicits Mama's emotional admission that her boy belongs in show business or (as she puts it) "to the world":

> Mother, I wandered away,
> breaking your heart.
> Now I'm grown up,
> Mother of mine.
> When friends all doubt me,
> I still have you,
> Somehow you're just the same.
> Mother divine,
> With your arms around me,
> I know I'm not to blame . . . .

After being congratulated at the rehearsal—"Wonderful, Jack! You were actually crying!"—Jolson wipes a hand across his weeping eyes, leaving a streak on his face. Though he glimpses in the enthusiastic reaction of the cast an impending professional triumph, the realization that his mother has left the theater and that his father is close to death casts him down. The camera zooms in and fades out as he sits alone in his dressing room, removes his wig, and lets his blackened, inconsolable face drop into his hands (Fig. 2.9). The next scene plays out Jack's self-division in whiteface an hour or so later within the patriarchal death chamber.

Again, Jack's eyes are "streaming" and his shoulders "shaking convulsively with suppressed sobs" (128). Kneeling by his father's bedside, Jack is joined by Mary and the show's backer, both of whom worry that he will "queer" himself on Broadway if, instead of opening, he gives into his mother's request to sing "Kol Nidre" at the synagogue adjoining the cantor's apartment. As Mama lights the Sabbath lights and Jack worries that he hasn't sung in the temple since a child, Yudelson promises him, "What a little boy learns, he never forgets." Jack's divided loyalties are represented by Mama and Yudelson the Kibitzer on one side of the screen,

Figure 2.8 Al Jolson as Jack with Mama (Eugenie Besserer) in *The Jazz Singer*. Courtesy of Museum of Modern Art Film Stills Archive.

the backer and Mary on the other. Synagogue or stage? Skullcap and prayer shawl or blackface and wig? "Kol Nidre" or "Mammy"? Jewish orthodoxy and separatism or assimilation into mainstream American culture and intermarriage? The familial duties of childhood or the personal ambitions of maturity? The traditions of the past or the innovations of the future? Obviously, the black and white faces of Jack emphasize his self-division, his divided loyalties, his sense of doubleness or duplicity.

In the scene of Oedipal resolution that the screen treatment used as its conclusion, we see Cantor Rabinowitz dying, Mama weeping by the bed ("we have our son again"), and Mary listening too as the camera cuts next door to Jolson in rabbinical robes at the altar. Jack's chanting of the most plaintive passages of the "Kol Nidre" elicits Mary's judgment that "It's his last time in [the synogogue]. He *has* to come back to us." What was supposed to be the final shot shows Jack sorrowfully praying and visited by the spectral appearance of the (now dead) cantor whose misty form blesses the son and then disappears. The young man has managed to take on his father's roles and robes, an act of contrite, filial submission that will free him to defy paternal injunction in a brave new future world of Jewish assimilation. By dutifully relinquishing his Broadway opening night, Jack makes amends for his parricidal rebellion against Cantor Rabinowitz and thus the dead but propitiated father blesses his rebellious but penitent son.

Figure 2.9   Al Jolson, partially unmasked, in *The Jazz Singer*. Courtesy of Museum of Modern Art Film Stills Archive.

The movie caps this planned ending with Jack appearing on stage at the Winter Garden in blackface, and again Oedipal victory is emphasized, as Mary radiates approval from the wings and Mama beams from the audience. If on Yom Kippur Jack atones for his betrayal of his Jewish origins, in the next and last scene he reaps its benefits, doing what Jolson's audiences expected him to do. In the process of filming Jolson's racial impersonation in "My Mammy," moreover, *The Jazz Singer* demonstrates how this type of racechange effectively colludes in the sort of spirit-murder performed in Griffith's *The Birth of a Nation* even as it proves the persistence of minstrelsy on the vaudeville stage and the movie screen. "My heart strings travel around Al-a-bammie": Jolson's Uncle Tom typifies the nostalgic slave returning to happy-go-lucky plantation times. Just as earlier Jolson's blackface was associated with his feminization, it is conflated now with the boy-child arrested in a pre-Oedipal moment of maternal bonding. Both of the songs Jolson sings in blackface are focused on the mother, indicating that staged blackface signifies a protected arena in which men can be boys.

Jolson in burnt cork is "a-comin'" to the smiles of his "Mother O'Mine" or his "Mammy" (Fig. 2.10). His outstretched arms, his pleading on bended knee, his passionate declaration of loyalty and love, his whitened and widened mouth, his effort to gain the approval of his mother and girlfriend: All these unman as effectively as hypermasculinization and castration do in Griffith's film.[17] As in Jack's first song in *Coffee Dans*, "Dirty Hands, Dirty Face" (about a part-devilish, part-angelic little boy), blackface provides white men a playful and temporary make-believe place to regress to an infantilized or effeminized bonding with (phantom) black boys or with a lost pre-Oedipal boyhood. At one and the same time Huck Finn and Jim, Jack corroborates Leslie Fiedler's point that Americans are "Born theoretically white" but permitted to pass their "adolescence as imaginary Negroes" (*Waiting for the End*, 134), even as Jack's two faces prove Yudelson correct: The blackened entertainer is the white performer's "nigger."

Therefore, the Jolson who had already made his reputation as a blackface belter and the Jack Robin based on that historic Jolson are masculinized by the feminized part of the slave their art masters. The final scene of *The Jazz Singer* confers upon Jack his mother's approbation, his girlfriend's adoration, and his own status as a successful white male adult. While the represented darkie is infantalized, the representing ventriloquist is empowered (only white boys have Mammies, after all) and allowed to win the girl who symbolizes the American success story by first posing, then defusing the visual threat of Mama or Mary coupling with a black man (only white men relinquish their Mammies for white Mommy-surrogates). As Rogin argues, the Warner Brothers production thus holds out the promise that acceptance of interfaith marriages between Jews and Christians can ward off inter-racial marriages between blacks and whites.

Figure 2.10 Al Jolson in the final scene of *The Jazz Singer*. Courtesy of Photofest.

But if burnt cork flirts with boyishness as well as miscegenation, *The Jazz Singer* also asks, what is the relationship between Jews, black mimicry, and African Americans? Oddly, blackface here seems to stage a mourning over precisely the injust spirit-murder it repeatedly enacts. An anti-semitic review written by Aldous Huxley picks up on the idea of mother love to examine the connection between the Jewish and jazzy faces of Jolson. According to Huxley, "dark and polished young Hebrews, whose souls were in those mournfully sagging, seasickishly undulating melodies of mother love," created characteristically "Jewish contributions to modern popular music" (Huxley, 58). Here the often-noted absence of "real" jazz from *The Jazz Singer* signifies the presence of the Jew-as-Jazz, the Jew-as-black. Not only such blackface Jewish stars as Sophie Tucker, Eddie Cantor, George Jessel, and Jolson himself but also Jewish "swing" composers and musicians like George Gershwin, Irving Berlin, Jerome Kern, and Benny Goodman forged links between the cultures of "dark Hebrews" and blacks. What Ann Douglas calls "Black art in whiteface" may or may not have been generated by the commonality she claims between Jewish and African-American music; however, the success of white blackface performers did coincide with the years of black exile from musical theater (354, 358, 362).

Despite the displacement of blacks by Jews, various intertitles and speeches in *The Jazz Singer* create analogues between Jewish and black cultures. The very first title before the long shot of New York's East Side ghetto explains that its daily life throbs to "the rhythm of music that is older than civilization." Raphaelson, the author of the original story, believed that jazz, with its "rhythm of frenzy staggering against a symphonic background," must be understood "principally [as] prayer" (23). But if jazz is a kind of secularization of prayer, the movie portrays prayer as a type of worldly performance: In Chicago, Jack sees a billboard that attracts him to a concert of Cantor Rosenblatt singing sacred songs on stage. When explaining to his father the importance of his career, then, Jack argues that his songs mean "as much to *my* audience" as his father's prayers mean to his synagogue's congregation. Though Jack's new "religion" consists of the belief that "the show must go on," he fervently affirms about his vaudeville sound, "There's something in my heart—maybe it's the call of the ages—the cry of my race." Finally, when Mary overhears his chanting of the "Kol Nidre," she dubs him "a jazz singer—singing to his God."

Curiously, *The Jazz Singer*'s narrative about Jewish assimilation addresses questions of passing more rigorously than does the racial impersonation at its end. After all, Jakie Rabinowitz has to change his name, his clothes, his hair, his accent so as to distinguish himself from his paternal origins. As a Jewish Mama's boy, Jakie lives out in his life the infantilization of the stereotypical black boy. Guilt over selling out his family and its history, over what kinds of betrayals and compromises the American success story entails, about defying the paternal law ("Stop" is the only word Cantor Rabinowitz actually can be heard to speak in the Vitaphone medium), about replacing the Jewish mother with the *shiksa*, Jewish guilt—the gift that keeps on giving—drips from this melodramatic plot, splashing over in its typical excess onto the plight of the black who is not as free as the Jew to make all these profitable compromises of assimilation. For clearly Jack's success depends on the privileges of his white skin, his ability to "pass" as a gentile.

Of course Jewish assimilation itself involves remorse over the betrayal of one's roots as well as the white lies entailed in masquerades of passing. Jews certainly knew that such an assimilation/impersonation gained immigrants (including but not exclusively Jewish ones) acceptance by virtue of their proving themselves to be not-black. What better way for a "dark" Hebrew to employ in demonstrating his not-blackness than by putting on blackface as a spectacularly theatrical act? "The price the white man paid for his ticket [for passage from the Old to the New World] was to become white": James Baldwin's point infuses the end of *The Jazz Singer* where racechange enables the Warner Brothers' American hero to wash himself white by siphoning off Otherness from the Hebrew to the African. To revise those historic first words spoken in this premier talkie ("Wait a minute. You ain't heard nothin' yet!"), you ain't seen nothing yet; you thought those guys with beards and prayer shawls in the synagogue looked *verkocktah*, but wait a minute; at least they're not *schvartzehs*! If the African American is dramatized as Otherness incarnate, then surely the Jew who plays him becomes less Other, more centrally human. In *The Jew's Body*, Sander Gilman makes the point with this question: "Does black-face make everyone who puts it on white?" (238). To be white in *The Jazz Singer* is to need to define oneself as neither orthodox Jew nor black. As in *The Birth of a Nation*, ultimately the American certifies his identity by proving himself not African-American.

Uncannily, though, in blackface Jolson looks like he is doing penance for the fact that ethnic acceptance and integration into American society are attained by stereotyping or scapegoating black people. Perhaps the poignancy of Jack's portrait in blackface depends on an inescapable consternation about one ethnic group rising at the expense of another as well as the more obvious icongraphy of the funnyman facade hiding a bleeding heart. Does *The Jazz Singer* focus from beginning to end on Yom Kippur because this holiday originated in the substitution of a scapegoat for a human sacrifice? That the film counterparts rabbinic ceremonies on Yom Kippur with blackface performances on Broadway raises this question, if only on a visceral level. "May all the people of Israel be forgiven including all the strangers who live in their midst, for all people are at fault": The words of the "Kol Nidre" prayer make explicit the moral urgency of mourning over past misdeeds so as to gain absolution. Penitential like the ashes of Ash Wednesday or the sackcloth and ashes of Nineveh, burnt cork evokes the dust of the grave, reparation for past losses and lapses, all of which find analogues in a soundtrack that returns not only to "Kol Nidre" but also to "Yahrzeit," the prayer for the dead. For if blackface signifies the death of Otherness (the cantor is dead, long live the entertainer!; Mama is displaced, long live the shiksa!), it reminds us that the Jew, standing in the place of the stigmatized African American, suffers the scapegoated Other's fate even as he inflicts a violence on the absent Other, a point to which a publicity poster for the movie testifies (Fig. 2.11).

As Rogin points out about this famous image, "Black holes in space fragment, stand in for, and render invisible the broken-up, absent black body" ("Blackface,"

Figure 2.11   Publicity Poster of "Warner Bros. Supreme Triumph." Courtesy of Museum of Modern Art Film Stills Archive.

429). It is possible to view the character presented here as falling back into a pit of darkness, the hands outstretched and reaching for help. From this vantage, the eyes look terrified, the mouth less the all-too-familiar racist grin so much as gaping open in anguish or in a scream of terror. Grasping at air, the hands reach out, but the body vanishes into the background. Like the Undead or living dead who Žižek describes "as sufferers, pursuing their victims with an awkward persistence, colored by a kind of infinite sadness" (22–23), the melancholy Jack Robin seems "colored by a kind of infinite sadness."[18] Given the context of Yom Kippur, Jolson-in-blackface resembles a human (not a symbolic) sacrifice or the sacrifice effected by animalizing the scapegoated Other who evokes the figure Dorothy Sayers called "The Human Not Quite Human". One caption might be, "Don't shoot until you see the whites of their eyes."

Although Jewish anguish assuredly is not the point of the picture, it lies just beneath the surface of black exploitation, interfusing the image with ambiguity. If the enigmatically connected Jakie Rabinowitz, Jack Robin, and Al Jolson as blackfaced performers appear to suffer the torture they inflict on the black male body, such a mirroring finds shocking confirmation in another poster from a later age (Fig. 2.12), for its central image proves the elasticity of racist suppositions. With an earring that recalls the gypsies and homosexuals endangered in Nazi Germany as well as the more overt Jewish star, the part-bug, part-Jiminy Cricket figure sneakily peers out of the shadows. The prominent star and saxophone attribute the decadence of jazz to the contaminating collaborations of subhuman Jews and blacks; if *The Jazz Singer* had tried to assimilate its Jewish hero into mainstream society by stressing the distance between the (white) performer and the (black) performed, the Nazi poster collapsed the two back into one. In the "Degenerate Art Exhibit" that toured the Third Reich, the image of the "Jazz-Jew" demonstrates that the division of labor meant to be executed by blackface never could successfully divide the dark Hebrew from the African or, for that matter, the white from the black.

The Anatomy of Blackface

Together, *The Birth of a Nation* and *The Jazz Singer* use blackface to put into circulation dramatically contradictory attitudes toward color. In particular, burnt cork articulates two jostling propositions made by whites about blacks, a syntax which contributes to supremacist ideology: "We can be (like) them" versus "They need not exist." The actors who played the parts of, say, Gus, Lynch, and Jack use their white bodies to take on the aura of the not-there black body of the Other, simultaneously erasing and reproducing, slaying and resurrecting him. As Philippe Lacoue-Labarthe, following René Girard, has explained, "the origin of desire is mimesis—mimetism—and no desire is ever forged that does not at once desire the death or disappearance of the model or 'exemplary' personage that gave rise to it" (102). Similarly, "*every* identification involves a degree of symbolic violence," Diana Fuss argues, because identification—like representation—entails the "process of killing off the other in fantasy in order to usurp the other's place" (*Identification Papers*, 9). Racial mimesis of the Hollywood variety engages white impersonators in a love-hate relationship, for the wish to represent the absent black body intersects with the desire not only to replace it but also to obliterate it with a surrogate that is debased as well as debasing.

Blackface in both films presents the black as (eventually, inevitably) castrated, lacking, wounded, feminized, a mark of meaning and not a maker of meaning, an object on display for the visual gratification of whites, a construction of white ac-

Figure 2.12   *Entartete Musik*, Adolf Hitler's 1938 poster for the Nazi exhibition of "degenerate" art. Los Angeles County Museum of Art, The Robert Gore Rivkind Center for German Expressionist Studies, purchased with funds provided by Anna Bing Arnold, Museum Associates Acquisition Fund, and deaccession funds.

tors for white audiences, a nonbeing. Within the darkened movie theater, with its screen filled with shadows and lights, blackface allowed white audiences to enjoy looking at a black person without having actually to see one; it allowed them to assure themselves about the inferiority of (especially) black men by re-enacting the devaluation or disavowing it. If, as one historian has argued, "Minstrelsy is negrophobia staged as negrophilia, or vice versa, depending on the respective weight of the fear or attraction" (Ostendorf, 81), the hypermasculinized buck of *Birth of a Nation* and the undermasculinized boy of *The Jazz Singer* sustain minstrel conventions, setting both negrophobia and negrophilia in the context of the Oedipal dilemma with its attendant anxieties about successful maturation into white manhood. Whether darkness signifies endings or beginnings, death or birth, lynching or infantilization, the rampant sexuality exorcised in Griffith's film counterpoints the childlike innocence exhibited on stage in the Warner Brothers production.

In addition, both *The Birth of a Nation* and *The Jazz Singer* frame the blackfaced man and the white woman as the paradigmatic couple which must be shot— that is, posed in order to be deposed or disposed of—as it is in many less famous movies (like, for example, *Kid Millions* with Eddie Cantor (1934, Fig. 2.13)). The breaking of racial taboos can be enjoyed even as the righting of racial order will (predictably, certainly) be established. But the blackfaced man/white woman couple—be it Gus and Flora Cameron, Lynch and Elsie Stoneman, or Jack Robin and Mary Dale—also theatricalizes precisely the sexual paranoia that helped establish Jim Crow laws and that was used to justify lynchings at the end of the nineteenth century and the beginning of the twentieth. Perhaps for this reason *The Birth of a Nation* and *The Jazz Singer* can be used to establish an uncanny connection between lynching, on the one hand, and, on the other, the popular traditions of minstrelsy as well as its Hollywood manifestations. Looking backward to Victo-

Figure 2.13 Eddie Cantor in *Kid Millions* (1934). Courtesy of Photofest.

rian minstrelsy and forward to the continued use of blackface in later twentieth-century movies, *The Birth of a Nation* and *The Jazz Singer* remain pivotal texts for understanding the curious mirroring between public performances of torture inflicted on the black body and the staging of punitive blackface representations.

Although most historians of minstrelsy date its demise with the turn of the century, the history of blackface in modern movies continues traditions that date back to Civil War times in America, to the Renaissance in Europe. Fittingly, then, the period in our history associated with "Jim Crow legislation"—that is, the end of the nineteenth century and the first half of the twentieth century when segregation was legal in this country—derives its name from the early Negro minstrel performance of "Daddy" Rice who, some time between 1828 and 1831, became a hit impersonating a rheumatic slave entertainer:

> First on de heel tap, den on de toe,
> Ebery time I wheel about I jump Jim Crow.
> Wheel about and turn about and do jis so,
> And ebery time I wheel about I jump Jim Crow. (Wittke, 26)

That the legal doctrine of separate but equal took its name from minstrelsy may or may not intimate public awareness about segregation as a farcical form of equality. However, from today's perspective, that tenet enacts a kind of unconscious repetition of the minstrel's insulting portrait of the less-than-equal darky.

One often cited pun from early minstrelsy indicates that white performers were not unaware of the economic incentive for their mimetic violence: The question "Why is we niggas like a slave ship on de Coast of Africa?" is answered with the rejoinder, "Because we both make money by taking off the negroes" (Roediger, 119). The modicum of truth in this joke consists of understanding the take-off of slavery and that of cross-racial parody as replicating forms of commodification for commercial exploitation. If we place Ralph Ellison's view of "the Negro as national scapegoat" in the context of such economic use, blackface performances justify and reenact racial exploitation. Add to this idea Philippe Lacoue-Labarthe's and René Girard's theories about a mimetic process that diverts violence onto symbolic objects so as to restore harmony to the society, and blackface becomes the secular rite by which a surrogate (black) victim is hung in effigy by the white community, thus deflecting violence's objectives away from that community.

In this next section, before returning to Hollywood's use of blackface, I want briefly to anatomize the various ways in which blackface performances can be considered a symbolic rite of scapegoating, the flip side of lynching: burnt cork instead of charred flesh, the grin and the grimace of pain, bulging eye balls, and twitching limbs or stiffness of body parts. For blacking up in even seemingly benevolent movies can be interpreted not only as a historical continuation of Victorian minstrelsy but also as an uncanny enactment of a punitive supremacist ideology.[19]

Historians disagree over the number of people lynched in America during the turn of the century. Whether one counts 3,724 people lynched in the United States from 1889 through 1930 (Raper, 1) or 4,951 between 1882 and 1927 (Harris, 7), the notion of representational violence remains grotesquely pertinent. The connection between the physical violence of lynching and the mimetic violence of blackface is probably best encapsulated in the July 5, 1943, issue of *Life* magazine that features stills from the nostalgic "bio-pic" movie *Dixie* (1943), in which Bing Crosby played minstrel man Dan Emmett, as well as photographs of African Americans beaten by white mobs in the worst race riot since 1919: 31 dead, more than 600 injured, and 1800 arrested (Figs. 2.14–2.16). Through mimetic mimicry, the gothic effects of scapegoating inflicted on the Other are played out on the body of the white impersonator, turning blackface not simply into a justification for ideologies perpetuating segregation or supremacy but paradoxically also into a symbolic form of punishment, a compulsive admission of guilt, the figurative payment of a debt to the dead.

Burnt Cork/Charred Flesh

Whether as warpaint or penitential ashes, burnt cork draws attention to its own artifice, just as it did in Victorian times when advertisements pictured dignified, aristocratic-looking white performers (dressed in formal evening attire) counterpointed by images of the strumming and strutting Zip Coons they impersonated in a kind of temporary slumming. Once again, a nineteenth-century joke emphasizes the nonmimetic effrontery of blackface as well as the ways in which such artifice constituted not only a brief installment of symbolic death or mourning but also a flirtation with feminization. "Why am I like a young widow?" a minstrel-comic would ask and then answer, "Because I do not stay long in black" (Toll, 40).

"With white face," a *London Illustrated News* explained about minstrelsy, "the whole affair would be intolerable. It is the ebony that gives the due and needful color to the monstrosities [and] the breaches of decorum" (Wittke, 54). Although blackface in film frequently attends narratives of disguise or camouflage, cosmetically darkened skin is as often conflated with mud or grease or coal as with make-up; it is smeared on like tar, soot, dirt, or feces, enabling the wearer to regress back to what one critic calls "the height of polymorphous perversity" through "infantile play with excrement or dirt" (Roediger, 118). Its color sometimes called "ebony," sometimes "mahogany," sometimes "chocolate," the complexion of the face links the performer to commodity objects. At times associated with bootblack, metaphorically burnt cork turns the top of the body (the head) into the toe, consciousness into physicality, human skin into animal hide or leather.[20]

In Fannie Hurst's short story "The Smudge" (1922), about a woman who uses burnt cork to play the role of "buxom negro" maids on Broadway but who also manufacturers "Brown Cold Cream—Guaranteed Color-fast—Mulatto, Medium, Chocolate," the make-up transforms her into "a black crocodile" on stage, a stark contrast to the lead actress's "fair" narcissus and to her own "fair" daughter (146, 157). Yet "For everything fair" that her daughter possesses, the blackfaced mother "had brownly paid" (147). Hurst's tale revolves around the mother's "dark secret" (149), a secret about an illegitimate affair or an illegitimacy in racial origin conflated with the "brown mud" she wears, as well as the mother's dread that the mud will "smudge" and thereby pollute her daughter (151). As Rogin puts it, "Dirt

Figure 2.14 *Life* magazine photo of "Buck and Wing" (June 15, 1943). Courtesy of *Life* magazine.

Figure 2.15 *Life* magazine photo of Bing Crosby playing Dan Emmett in *Dixie*. Courtesy of *Life* magazine.

Figure 2.16 *Life* magazine photo of "a fear-crazed Negro boy" rescued by soldier from a Detroit mob. Courtesy of *Life* magazine.

was the magical, transforming substance in blackface carnivalesque (particularly transgressive for the blackface Jew, since the term *ham actor* originated from the use of ham fat to wipe off burnt cork)" ("'Democracy,'" 7). The opposite of purity and chastity, blackface signals not only the degradation of physicalization but (as it seems in the picture of Bing Crosby playing Dan Emmett in *Dixie*) also the penalty or penance of being covered over with mud, of being buried alive.

Just as linked to the base and the physical, the minstrel's Renaissance ancestor—the trickster-servant harlequin—often appeared in *commedia dell'arte* shows wearing a rough, bushy, or hirsute half-mask or carrying a phallus to link him to the satyr (Nicoll, 69; Gates, 61). Like the harlequin's dark mask, the black head of the minstrel sits atop an alien trunk (the contrast between head and body often marked by huge ties, bows, or collars), a signature of a kind of physical decapitation/castration. According to some critics, the harlequin's role became so stylized that he simply pointed to one of the black patches on his suit to become invisible (Gates, *Figures in Black*, 51). If the blackened body part looks like absence imposed (through burial or eradication or a process of petrifying or putrefying),[21] burnt cork on the face means a brain-dead minstrel who becomes all body. Blackface destroys the human subject on stage, replacing it with the black Other as corporeal object whose insignificance makes him invisible (like a pet, a servant, a child, a corpse) or hypervisible (like a pet, a servant, a child, a corpse). In popular skits performed in civic centers and town halls, hypervisible performers were sometimes called "unbleached American citizens" while invisible members of the cast were described as "so dark that they cannot be seen."[22]

The Grin/The Grimace of Pain

According to Carl Wittke, minstrel performers exercised great care in fixing their distended mouths, "for there was a rather widely accepted superstition among them that they would be unable to work properly in their acts unless this part of their make-up was perfect" (141). Red or white in outline, the large lips of the blackface performer connect him to the clown and, like the clown, he mocks language, reducing it to the physical either through dance, mime, gesture, instrumentation (horn, banjo, tambourine, bones) or by fracturing sense into highflown nonsense, pretentious malapropisms, and ungrammatical repetitions that emphasize its mere materiality. The "cork black, white-lipped, white gloved and 'derby'd'" minstrels in Leonard Bernstein and Alan Jay Lerner's musical *1600 Pennsylvania Avenue* (1976) engage in the prattling patter of bombastic incomprehensibility, their pretentiousness always destined to plummet them into nonsense:

UNCLE SAM: Well, Mr. Greenback, one must be pholocifical.
MR. GREENBACK: You mean lisophosical.
UNCLE SAM: I mean sifopholical. (369)

Accompanying the linguistic mistakes of the fool, the smile of the black man, according to Fanon, signals "Service with a smile, every time"; the grin "'as we see it—as we make it—always means a *gift*,'" he explains, quoting another thinker on the subject (Fanon, 49). The large lips of the minstrel—which Mark Twain described as "thickened and lengthened with bright red paint to such a degree that their mouths resemble slices cut in a ripe watermelon"—functioned historically to placate white guilt about slavery (*Autobiography*, 61): Look how happy those darkies are; they are not forcibly owned but give themselves freely as a gift to their masters! Sardonically or stereotypically, Gertrude Stein referred to "the wide, abandoned laughter that makes the warm broad glow of negro sunshine" throughout her most famous portrait of black life, "Melanctha" (1909, 340).

Later in his book, Fanon describes himself as "battered down by tom-toms, cannibalism, intellectual deficiency," but claims "above all else" to have been bludgeoned by "'Sho' good eatin'" (112). What the stage Negro craves are "lip-smacking," "mouth-watering" pork, chicken, and watermelon. Yet, as Fanon's comments about cannibalism and eating imply, smiling lips also represent white fear of black retaliation, white dread of being gobbled up by black people. An early minstrel song entitled "Gal from the South" typifies the conflation of oral and sexual appetites:

> One morning massa goin' away,
> He went to git his coat,
> But neither hat nor coat was there,
> For she had swallowed both;
> He took her to a tailor shop,
> To have her mouth made small,
> The lady took in one long breath,
> And swallowed tailor and all. (Lott, 26)

Large lips above the neck signify large lips below, placing minstrel performers—all (of course) male—under the sign of the engulfing, cannibalistic female, a form of temporary license the comedienne Martha Raye could tap in a film like *College Holiday* (1936; Fig. 2.17).[23]

Insatiable like that of an infant or an animal or a woman, the large mouth threatens to engorge what it cannot possibly digest. A blackface performer in Melville's *Confidence-Man* (1857) illustrates the ways in which the grin of the minstrel mimes the tortured grimace of the body in pain. A white man impersonates a "grotesque negro cripple" with his head thrown back and his mouth open—"at once target and purse"—to catch coins in "a strange sort of pitch-penny game"; "nearly always he grinned, and only once or twice did he wince" (16). Greedy like an animal, this human piggy bank symbolizes the black impersonator as repository of/for racial commodification. According to the French theorist Bataille, "human life is still bestially concentrated in the mouth" (59). Though the gaping mouth which signifies gross appetites can cannibalize just about anything (tailors, coins, watermelon), what it gives out is the false coin of malapropisms, pomposities, non sequiturs. Target and purse are, of course, exactly what the blackface performer makes of the African American.

Figure 2.17   Martha Raye in *College Holiday* (1936). Courtesy of Photofest.

Bulging Eyes

When Hurst's mother in burnt cork blackens her eyelids, the trick turns her "good gray eyes" into "popping whites" (158). Characteristic expressions of astonishment, stupidity, fear, or delight on the actor wearing burnt cork mimic a look as easily understood to stand for strangulation and terror. Rolling or bulging white eyes may appear frenzied at least in part because enormous collars, oversized suits, and huge shoes made the minstrel look like he was drowning in his borrowed togs, doomed by the black dandy's misbegotten efforts to dress up in (an inevitably tawdry) effort to ape "his betters." The patchquilt costume or one composed of the Harlequin's geometrical suit of dark and light triangles created a checkered effect, setting off the contrast between black skin and white eyes and emphasizing the contradictory, disabling tension of the minstrel's being.

Indeed, such eyes belie the grin, or so Flannery O'Connor's description in the short story "The Artificial Nigger" (1955) implies. A plaster figure of "a Negro sitting bent over on a low yellow brick fence" was obviously "meant to look happy because his mouth was stretched up at the corners but the chipped eye and the angle he was cocked at gave him a wild look of misery instead" (268). Like O'Connor's statue of a Negro—which exists, according to her white characters, because "They ain't got enough real ones here. They got to have an artificial one"— blacked-up actors could be viewed as figures reified into "artificial niggers"[24] whose abundance might have prompted Gertrude Stein's apparently unmotivated aside in *Tender Buttons* (1914): "needless are niggers" (494).

Twitching Limbs/Stiffness of Body Parts

Two nineteenth-century observers of minstrelsy stressed the odd energy that seemed to surge through the minstrel's body parts. A New York editor who witnessed "Daddy" Rice's acting of "our American Negro" found himself most impressed by "such a twitching-up of the arm and shoulder! It was *the* Negro, par excellence" (Wittke, 31). And Charles Dickens, visiting New York, watched the famous Juba who danced "with two left legs, two right legs, two wooden legs, two wire legs, two spring legs—all sorts of legs and no legs—" (91). Eric Lott has discussed the "stiffness and extension of arms and legs" (as well as "coattails, hanging prominently between characters' legs, and personae . . . often pictured with sticks or poles strategicaly placed near the groin") as annoucements of "unsuccessful sublimations of sexual desire" (*Love and Theft*, 117, 120). Lott persuasively emphasizes the ways in which the black phallic figure of minstrelsy hints at homosexual attraction, male identification, and male rivalry. Just as noteworthy are the ways in which this phallicism transforms the entertainer's leg or arm into a prosthesis, enacting the rigidity that is rigor mortis, the stiffness of death. Frenzied but jerky in motion, the black figure who looks like a wind-up toy or mechanical doll on stage grotesquely shudders his way through death throes or convulsions that recall bodies hung, burnt alive, or dismembered in lynching performances.

When taken together, the anarchic impropriety and licentiousness of the minstrel verify Nathan Irvin Huggins's point that this performer offered a respite from the self-sacrifice and self-restraint of America's aggressive achievement ethic, "creating a distance between white men's normative selves (what they had to be) and their natural selves (what they feared but were fascinated by)" (357). Enjoying a holiday from the work ethic, the white actor nevertheless punished himself (at least symbolically) for the forbidden pleasure he took in physicality and freedom. Just as the minstrels' gags about slaves gagged African Americans, Hollywood black-face was only one but a quite effective means of maintaining racial subordination long after the passage of the Thirteenth and Nineteenth Amendments, a method that paradoxically played out the suffering of the victim on the body of the victimizer.[25] A ritual of exorcism, blackface episodes within Hollywood movies often display a curious combination of bodily pain and pleasure, physical confinement and release, bringing into modern times what Lott calls "the dialectical flickering of racial insult and racial envy" that shaped nineteenth-century minstrel impersonations (18). Always, such scenes return to the tropes we have already seen as central in *The Birth of a Nation* and *The Jazz Singer*, illuminating what Lott (in the title of his book on minstrelsy) calls "love and theft," a dynamic in blackface movies that teeters on a love/hate axis.

In "The Artificial Nigger," O'Connor dramatizes the community/communal solidarity effected by that dynamic when a feuding white grandfather and his grandson are reunited through their discovery of the "plaster figure of a Negro." After the old man mutters, "They ain't got enough real ones here. They got to have an artificial one," he feels its effect as a "dissolving [of] differences [between whites], like an action of mercy" (269). Suffering the fate O'Connor elsewhere described as "clownishness and captivity,"[26] the lineaments and physical attributes of "the artificial nigger" on stage and screen scapegoated blacks to bring together whites, testified to white guilt about the process, and eerily visited a suitable punishment for that guilt on the white body of the performer. Nor are such rituals of scapegoating over and done with: In *A Trap for Fools* (1989), Amanda Cross (aka Carolyn Heilbrun) presented a villainous university administrator casting suspicion onto African-American faculty by blackening his face before committing his murders. Nor are they simply fictional: In October of 1993, two teenagers dressed in Ku Klux Klan costumes attended a Halloween party at Yosemite High School (in Oakhurst, California) with a friend in blackface—whom they pretended to lynch. They won prizes for their costumes, though the school's principal soon regretted his decision to allow them to attend.

That blackface performances justified and replicated white violence against the black body is a point made brilliantly at the turn of the century by the plot of Charles W. Chesnutt's novel *The Marrow of Tradition* (1901). The degenerate aristocrat Tom Delamere puts on the long blue coat with brass buttons and plaid trousers of his grandfather's faithful black servant, Sandy Campbell, first to imitate "the quaintness of the darky dialect and the darky wit," then to dance "a buck dance" before admiring Northern visitors (118). Later in the novel, Tom again dresses as Sandy to rob his own aunt, an act that results in Sandy's imprisonment for murder and his near lynching. "He is black, and therefore guilty," one character explains (199). But the "example" of burning Sandy "would be all the more powerful if we got the wrong one," another white reveals; "It would serve notice on the niggers that we shall hold the whole race responsible for the misdeeds of each individual" (182). Blackface served that notice as well.

Hollywood's "Artificial Nigger"

From a host of take-offs and sequels of *The Jazz Singer* to more experimental, contemporary films, American movies have continued to exploit blackface. To begin
with, *The Singing Fool* (1928), *Wonderbar* (1934), *A Song to Remember* (1945),
Rhapsody in Blue (1945), and *The Jolson Story* (1946) sustained a tradition to
which Danny Thomas (in 1952), Jerry Lewis (in 1959), and Neil Diamond (in
1980) returned in revisions of the original story.[27] From Moran and Mack in *Why
Bring That Up?* (1929) and Laurel and Hardy in *Pardon Us* (1931) to *The Dolly
Sisters* (1945) and *Somebody Loves Me* (1951), blackface played a prominent part
in comedy and in musical production numbers. More recently and satirically, Bri-
an De Palma directed *Hi, Mom!* (1970), in which Robert De Niro joins a theater
of cruelty troupe that stages an audience-participation play, "Be Black, Baby": After whitefaced black actors dab dark paint on the faces of the white spectators so
they can experience what it means to be black, members of the audience are then
beaten, robbed, and raped. But of course such a grotesque scene reflects contemporary discomfort with the convention of blacking up which—in its heyday during the thirties—produced a number of movies that repeatedly returned to justify,
reenact, or expiate the spiritual murder of American Americans and the eradication of their history.

Like Bing Crosby's burnt-cork number in *Holiday Inn*, Shirley Temple's use of
blackface in *The Littlest Rebel* (1935) illustrates the uncanny way in which Hollywood movies that exploit racechange obsessively dwell on the inheritance of the
Civil War, often to effect reversals that legitimized American slavery. After the
sound track opens the credits with "Dixie" and "Old Folks at Home," *The Littlest
Rebel* presents Shirley Temple as one cute little Virgie (Virginia? Virgin?), the
pampered only child of an aristocratic Southern family threatened first when the
father must ride off to join the Confederate Army and later when the territory surrounding their plantation is occupied by Union soldiers. Once the powerful Yan-
kees arrive, striking fear in blacks and whites alike, all scramble to hide food and
family treasures in a secret room that will also provide a hiding place for Shirley
T. and a pickaninny-companion. The net result of the subsequent blackface scenes
mark the true victims, villains, and heroes of the Civil War as white; African Americans just quake in terror as they watch on the sidelines, rooting for their genteel,
gentle masters and mistresses.

To begin with, Shirley Temple appears safe only when she can become (as unintimidating or insignificant as any) black (slave). Looking to beat the white Con-
federates, Union soldiers won't hurt slaves, one black actor explains, even as his
stereotypical cowardice shuffles him into a coat closet discovered by the Union
troops (though they leave him unharmed, a testimony to the fact that blacks have
nothing to fear but fear itself). Far more vulnerable but now wrapped in an Aunt
Jemima bandana, Shirley can temporarily survive because of the dark varnish furnished by "Bixby" shoe polish, a preserver of the spirit of "Dixie" that would send
those Northerners "away, away" (Fig. 2.18). But the true "white" character of that
spirit cannot so easily be hidden: When the officer in charge takes her for a slave,

Figure 2.18 Shirley Temple as Virgie in *The Littlest Rebel* (1935). Courtesy of Museum of Modern Art Film Stills Archive.

sits down, and orders her to remove his boots, her plucky revolt against his injust possession of her father's house takes the form of pushing him off the chair. Rebellion is a white affair, bred of the privilege that makes it impossible for Shirley to adopt the role of subservient slave. A scuffle between her and the toppled officer results in the smudging of her polish, revealing a white-and-black blotched face.

The phrase "littlest rebel" gets applied to Shirley by the much more humane, kindly Yankee high commander who arrives on the scene just in time to administer justice. In this version of the Southern experience, good white men put bad white men on the whipping post. In a revision of the lashing usually imposed on slaves, the beneficent Union officer in charge orders his offensive subordinate to be whipped until he bleeds. Further erasing the dye around her eyes, Shirley earns her title, proving her intrepidity at precisely the moment she is revealed as only a make-believe pickaninny, an "artificial nigger" (to use O'Connor's sardonic phrase). As in *The Birth of a Nation* and *Holiday Inn*, Lincoln himself eventually makes an appearance in *The Littlest Rebel*. Drawing Shirley T. onto his lap and murmuring "Tell me about it," Honest Abe turns shrink here, issuing a pardon (not only for her imprisoned father but also for her imprisoned father-surrogate, the good Yankee officer) that proves the Civil War was waged to free white men. An even more direct character assassination is performed on African Americans through the portrait of its best representative, the wonderful dancing partner and trusty servant Uncle Billy (played by Bill Robinson) For though he hides Shirley in the secret room, Uncle Billy leaves tell-tale signs that lead to her detection (a skirt hanging out of the door) and becomes so fearful of the Northern troops that he drops a pitcher, inadvertently drawing attention to the hiding place. As in *The Jazz Singer*, blacks are childish, fearful, vulnerable; they can be saved only by the protection and authority furnished by whites.

That even the brilliant Bill Robinson is implicated in the character assassination of *The Littlest Rebel* and the other movies he made as Shirley Temple's playmate may be the source of the pathos in Fred Astaire's tribute to him in "Bojangles of Harlem," his only blackface performance and the climax of *Swing Time* (1936). A visually astonishing moment occurs at the start of this production number when a gigantic black face metamorphoses into the soles of two huge feet and then splits apart (in what Arlene Croce calls "a bad moment of 'amputation'" (107)) as enormous trousered legs (described by Croce as "long . . . guard rails") are separated and hauled off by a chorus of beauties, revealing just at the crotch area none other than Fred Astaire in burnt cork (Figs. 2.19 and 2.20). Clearly invoking the minstrel phallicism of big black feet and stiff prosthetic legs, the scene seems to imply that Astaire feels he cannot fill the shoes of his major black precursor, and so *Swing Time* works off Griffith's vision of the African American as threateningly potent. Indeed, the plot surrounding the scene furnishes the reasons for white men's fear that they cannot fill the black man's pants.

Swing Time begins with a marriage (of convenience, not love) postponed when Astaire's fellow dancers take his trousers away to be cuffed; only cuffed trousers are the vogue, they explain after drawing them on an advertised pair of pants. It ends with a similar trick played on Astaire's rival for his true love, the band leader about to marry Ginger Rogers. This Latin lover relinquishes his trousers when Astaire convinces him they must be cuffed, realizes his mistake, and dons the pants of his black servant, but they fall down because they are way too big for him. White men (even those with Latin blood) find black men daunting sexual competitors, the movie seems to hint. Significantly, then, Astaire puts burnt cork on after Ginger Rogers and he have kissed, and her lipstick has left a striking mark near his mouth. Though the kiss itself cannot be seen—it takes place behind a convenient door—clearly the smudge of sex (lipstick) leads directly to the trace of race (blackface) and to a dance that manages to express sexual envy as well as aesthetic indebtedness or even belatedness.

As a form of homage, then, "Bojangles of Harlem" addresses feelings of rivalry and emulation; Bill Robinson becomes Fred Astaire's role model, but Astaire's efforts to dance with (enormous) shadowed legs projected on a wall behind him prove that he cannot anticipate nor imitate nor control their motions. (That Thomas Rice's most famous Jim Crow act was his "shadow dance," in which a child actor in blackface emulated his every move, places Astaire's performance squarely in the minstrel tradition.[28]) A tribute to Robinson that admits he was scaled down to dance with Shirley Temple, *Swing Time* equates blackness with carnival, hinting

Figure 2.19 Fred Astaire at start of "Bojangles of Harlem" number, *Swing Time* (1936). Courtesy of Museum of Modern Art Film Stills Archive.

Figure 2.20 Fred Astaire in "Bojangles of Harlem" number, *Swing Time*. Courtesy of Museum of Modern Art Film Stills Archive.

that only on holidays or honeymoons can white people enjoy the bodily joy and grace that imbue Bojangles even in shadow.

By containing blackface within either stock vaudevillean comedy or historical episodes that self-consciously capture the minstrelsy "of old," Hollywood managed to recycle the form. An example of the first type of recycling—the recasting of humorous minstrel strutting and stuttering—Freeman F. Gosden and Charles V. Correll's *Check and Double Check* (1930) displays the ignorant buffoonery of Amos 'n' Andy, partners in Harlem's Air Taxi Company, within a plot that allows the two blackface comics to bumble into rescuing the paternal inheritance of the endangered son of their beloved white benefactor back in the memorialized, cherished South (Fig. 2.21). An example of the second—the historicizing of a minstrel episode—the characters in search of a finale in *Babes in Arms* (1939)—including Judy Garland and Mickey Rooney—perform a blacked-up number singing "My Daddy Was a Minstrel Man" (Fig. 2.22) because they remain loyal to the past, much as they do in its sequel, *Babes on Broadway* (1941) or in Crosby's depiction of Dan Emmett in *Dixie*. *Swing Time* is unusual in its deployment of blackface within a framework that at least implicitly questions the uses to which white America had put black culture. The white entertainer feels dwarfed by his belatedness (in relation to Robinson as a precursor) and his inadequacy (vis-à-vis black artistry), or so Astaire's doomed efforts to keep up with the brilliant background dancing legs imply.

Figure 2.21   Freeman Gosden and Charles Correll as Amos 'n' Andy in *Check Double Check* (1930). Courtesy of Museum of Modern Art Film Stills Archive.

Figure 2.22   Judy Garland and Mickey Rooney in *Babes in Arms* (1939). Courtesy of Museum of Modern Art Film Stills Archive.

Although racist in other respects, the Marx brothers' movie *A Day at the Races* (1937) shares with *Swing Time* a use of blackface that attends to the racial remorse of a supremacist society. During a blatantly stereotypical musical interlude of prancing plantation darkies who are first held up as an object lesson of happy spontaneity, then led by a piping Harpo in a parade of "Gabriel," and finally depicted jitterbugging and blowing their horns to "All God's Children Got Rhythm," the black community exemplifies free-for-all antics (in accord with those of the anarchic Marx brothers themselves). When the bad guys show up (the law and the rich), Groucho and his two brothers hide beneath a wagon and use its axle grease to anoint their faces so as to escape detection. A number of curious ironies here and at the close of the movie draw attention to the guilt of an inequitable society. First, when the law arrives, the black folk scurry off, protesting their innocence but clearly assuming that they will be judged guilty of wrong-doing simply by virtue of the color of their skin. Second, when the Marx brothers in burnt cork finally manage to nail the bad guy in the barn, he is shown left in a stall with a bit in his mouth, a torture that recalls those practiced on slaves treated like horses or cattle. Third, at the end of the movie, the winning horse, High Hat, is identified as the Marx brothers' pick only after mud is wiped off the number he wears. "I haven't seen so much mud since the last election": Groucho's crack at dirty politics does not deflect from the visual point that High Hat will be denied his victory so long as he appears covered in black.

That people are what they pretend to be, that whites miming an Africanist presence will somehow undergo a moral racechange that blackens their character: This is the more typical point of burnt cork and the subject of *A Double Life* (1947), featuring Ronald Colman as the British actor (Tony) who gets caught up and confused by his theatrical role as the Moor in Shakespeare's *Othello* (Fig. 2.23). Although Shakespeare's drama attempted to reverse Renaissance stereotypes by presenting the white Iago as the villain who lures the innocent, dark-skinned hero into evil, *A Double Life* exploits blackface to reinforce the racist identification of blackness with madness and damnation. As in minstrel or vaudeville convention, it is

Figure 2.23   Ronald Colman as Othello in *A Double Life* (1947). Courtesy of Museum of Modern Art Film Stills Archive.

Figure 2.24 Bing Crosby and Marjorie Reynolds in *Dixie* (1943). Courtesy of Photofest.

the mouth that speaks of a voracious, destructive orality that would feed off and swallow the whole white world and in particular the world of white femininity. Seeing his own reflection in a window as the face of the black character he plays on stage, Tony becomes embroiled in a love-hate plot with two women: his classy ex-wife Brita (Signe Hasso) and the sexy waitress Pat Kroll (Shelley Winters). Jealous of Brita (who plays Desdemona to his Othello), he devises and practices a suffocating "kiss of death" in their final bedroom scene, but he actually perfects and uses it to murder her working-class surrogate, Pat.

Just as actors of nineteenth-century minstrel versions of *Othello* jumped Jim Crow between scenes, even those modern approaches to *Othello* that sought to celebrate diversity or Otherness tend to participate in the dynamics of spirit-murder implicit in the blackface tradition. When Laurence Olivier got ready for his part in *Othello* (1965), he explained the transformation blackening triggered within him as a kind of incorporation or even enslavement of the Other:

> Black all over my body, Max Factor 2880, then a lighter brown, then Negro No. 2, a stronger brown. Brown on black to give a rich mahogany. Then the great trick: that glorious half-yard of chiffon with which I polished myself all over until I shone . . . . I am, I . . . I am Othello . . . but Olivier is in charge. The actor is in control. The actor breathes into the nostrils of the character and the character comes to life. For this mo-

ment in my time, Othello is my character—he's mine. He belongs to no one else; he belongs to me. When I sigh, he sighs. When I laugh, he laughs. When I cry, he cries. (158–59)

Thus Othello becomes Olivier's monster, a slave to the actor's magisterial artistry. How paradoxical, as Timothy Murray has pointed out, that Olivier's make-up can be seen on screen rubbed off onto the fair face of his Desdemona whose smudged cheek puts the lie to precisely the constructing and effacing of difference that blackface undertakes (112). That same type of smudge appears on the cheek of Marjorie Reynolds, presumably smeared off the blackfaced Bing Crosby in *Dixie* (Fig. 2.24). Alive and well, harlequin continues to perform the role immortalized for him by Joseph Conrad in his modernist classic about race, *Heart of Darkness*, ushering us into the darkness at the heart of the white imagination.

3

MAKING WHITE, BECOMING BLACK

Myths of Racial Origin in the Harlem Renaissance

Can the Ethiopian change his skin
or the leopard his spots?
Then also you can do good
who are accustomed to do evil.
—Jeremiah 13:23

Whereas men affirm this colour was a Curse, I cannot make out the property
of that name, it neither seeming so to them, nor reasonably unto us; for they
take so much content therein, that they esteem deformity by other colours, describing the Devil, and terrible objects, White.
—Thomas Browne, *Pseudodoxia Epidemica*

Just a few years ago, two scholars at Kenyon College excavated evidence that the
Confederate anthem "Dixie Land," popularized by the white minstrel Dan Emmett
(who claimed authorship), was actually composed by two black musicians, Ben
and Lew Snowden.[1] The controversy typifies debates over scholarly evaluations
of minstrelsy as a popular art form tapping authentic African-American traditions
or as one reflecting the sexual repression and negrophobia of whites.[2] Could minstrelsy be effectively adopted and adapted by African-American artists or would
it prove inexorably debilitating, even demeaning to them? Though, as Houston
Baker has declared, "it is, first and foremost, the mastery of the minstrel mask by
blacks that constitutes a primary move in Afro-American discursive modernism"
(*Modernism and the Harlem Renaissance,* 17), the answer to both these questions
remains a resounding "yes" in the cultural achievements produced during the oddly named Harlem Renaissance; that is, in a period of astonishing productivity for
African-American artists, one that never remained bounded by Harlem and that
should not be considered a rebirth (re-naissance) because there simply was no earlier opportunity for comparable creativity.

What both positive answers reveal is the double bind behind the questions. To adopt minstrelsy is to collude in one's own fetishization; but to relinquish efforts to adapt it is to lose completely a cultural past appropriated by whites. The problem facing African-American writers, entertainers, and visual artists was further complicated by the way in which the minstrel played out the age-old philosophic conundrum of mind-body dualism by presenting the white mime as the mind, the mimicked black as the body. A parable about the dynamics of cultural imperialism, composed by the Nobel award-winning dramatist Wole Soyinka, is worth quoting at some length here since it racializes that dualism, exposing the difficulty it poses for African Americans.

Soyinka's allegory begins by reinventing Conrad's Kurtz in *Heart of Darkness* as Descartes "in his pith-helmet, engaged in the mission of piercing the jungle of the black pre-logical mentality with his intellectual canoe":

> As our Cartesian ghost introduces himself by scribbling on our black brother's—naturally—*tabula rasa* the famous proposition, "I think, therefore I am," we should not respond, as the negritudinists did, with "I feel, therefore I am," for that is to accept the arrogance of a philosophical certitude that has no foundation in the provable. . . . I cannot imagine that our "authentic black innocent" would ever have permitted himself to be manipulated into the false position of countering one pernicious Manicheism with another. He would sooner, I suspect, reduce our white explorer to syntactical prospositions by responding: "You think, therefore you are a thinker. You are one-who-thinks, white-creature-in-pith-helmet-in-African-jungle-who-thinks and, finally white-man-who-has-problems-believing-in-his-own-existence." (*Myth, Literature,* 138–39)

Like Descartes, the minstrel writes a sentence on the black body that excludes African Americans from rationality, reducing them instead to physicality, desire, animality, entertainment. According to Soyinka, "I feel, therefore I am"—the acceptance of the minstrel persona—remains an inadequate response to the Cartesian "I think, therefore I am" because this proposition perpetuates "Manicheism" and also because it is "unprovable." Countering the "negritudinists," the African thinker advises the colonized to focus attention back on the motives, needs, and anxieties of the colonizer.

Many participants in the Harlem Renaissance anticipated the tactic advocated by Soyinka. They trained their attention on the neurotic motivations of whites and in particular on their dread of nonbeing, their need to turn toward African Americans as if toward being itself so as to negate white nothingness with a something destined always to elude. If a Cartesian thinker-ghost had monopolized the word "thinking" for himself, the black (taken to be a) *tabula rasa* could comment sardonically on the motivation of the white thinker's fearful alienation from the physical or natural. Curiously, however, an appreciable number of African-American writers also embraced the negritudinist "I feel, therefore I am" and did so at least sometimes in a manner that evades the naiveté against which Soyinka warns. Through a kind of "black black impersonation," some artists performed white people's conceptions of the stage Negro with a defensive irony that called attention to the artifice of the role.[3] If the only revolt against the Cartesian's "I think, therefore I am" consisted in scribbling the antithetical word "feeling" on the body of the black *tabula rasa*, then that body could perform such a script so as to comment sardonically upon the artifice of the physical or natural as an adopted pose.

Regardless of this swerve from Soyinka, most of the participants in the Harlem Renaissance would have agreed with him about the perplexity of their situation within a culture that denied them the very authority they sought to attain as authors. Whether African-American artists debunked white colonizers or glamorized colonized blacks, they anticipated Soyinka's attempt to counter the destructive effects of white supremacist logic. Perhaps for this reason, namely the problem of their color, often they returned to myths of origin about the nature of race, stories that fall under the rubric of "ethnogenesis."[4] Not "Who am I?" but "Why am I?" and especially "Why am I black?" are questions that repeatedly motivate and shape their achievements. Throughout history, of course, originatory myths have been used to account for creation, sexual subordination, even the geographical location of nations; however, in the twentieth century, Western culture has been polka-dotted by stories about the origins of color, many of which attempt to explain not only the experiences but also the existence of African Americans.

Two miniatures of such moments, one at the beginning of modern times and one within contemporary memory, can be used to bracket this period and capture the sense of frustration black people attributed to their entrapment in an alien and alienating white society. First, in Mark Twain's *Pudd'nhead Wilson* (1898), the light-skinned son who discovers he has a slave mother and wishes he were dead asks,

> "Why were niggers *and* whites made? What crime did the uncreated first nigger commit that the curse of birth was decreed for him? And why is this awful difference made between white and black?" (44)

Second, in an example of the "American Negro's New Comedy Act" of the 1960s, the following exchange between an unemployed black man and God returns to a similar question:

> "Tell me, Lord, how come I'm so black?"
> "You're black so that you could withstand the hot rays of the sun in Africa."
> "Tell me, Lord, how come my hair is so nappy?"
> "Your hair is nappy so that you would not sweat under the hot sun in Africa."
> "Tell me, Lord, how come my legs are so long?"
> "Your legs are long so that you could escape from the wild animals in Africa."
> "Tell me, Lord, what the hell am I doing in Chicago?" (Boskin, 222)

Tragic or comic in tone, such narratives about color record a sense of bewilderment ("Why" or "Tell me, Lord") at the injustice of racial subordination (the "crime" or "curse of birth"), the inadequacy of explanatory ideologies ("this awful difference"), and feelings of dislocation ("what the hell am I doing . . . ?"). Although they are strikingly dissimilar, both the lament of the character authored by the white writer and the joke of the stand-up black comic function something like the naive child's response in "The Emperor's New Clothes," for they question the obvious: Why more than one type of skin color? Why the enslavement or subordination of one race to another? Radical though they are in this regard, however, both remain conventional in their addressing blackness—not whiteness—as the problem in need of a solution or rationalization. "Can the Ethiopian change his skin?" asks Jeremiah, not "Can the Israelite change his?"[5] Even when a seventeenth-century skeptic like Thomas Browne rejected the notion that "a mighty and considerable part of mankinde, should first acquire and still retain the glosse and tincture of blacknesse" because of a "curse of God" (274), he admitted that this logic prevailed among his contemporaries. Nor did he ask why a considerable part of mankind should first acquire the gloss of whiteness.

Blackness may still be conceptualized as the problem because, as Andrew Hacker puts it in *Two Nations: Black and White, Separate, Hostile, Unequal*, "being white has a worth" (31). Hacker illustrates the point with a markedly fantastic racechange fable he tells college students so as to gauge by their reactions the estimate they place on their own skin tones. They will be visited by an official who admits a mistake has been made; each of them was supposed "to have been born black":

> So at midnight tonight, you will become black. And this will mean not simply a darker skin, but the bodily and facial features associated with African ancestry. However, inside you will be the person you always were. Your knowledge and ideas will remain intact. . . . [B]eing born to the wrong parents was in no way your fault. Consequently, [the official's] organization is prepared to offer you some resonable recompense. (32)

When asked to name a sum of money appropriate for this compensation, many of Hacker's undergraduates felt "it would not be out of place to ask for $50 million or $1 million for each coming black year," leading him to state that in contemporary culture "to be white is to possess a gift whose value can be appreciated only after it has been taken away" (32).[6] A similar point is made by a visually savvy use of racechange imagery: Dick Gregory's self-portrait in whiteface entitled "Stop the world, I want to get on!" hints at the privileges in class and in confidence that accompany whiteness (Fig. 3.1). But why does whiteness constitute an asset, blackness a debit? How and when did it come about that whiteness was experienced as desirable, a blessing, blackness a dreaded curse?

Perhaps inevitably, the overvaluation of white over black in Western culture has meant that most etiological accounts of color take whiteness as a starting point or standard, blackness as a deviance or devolution. In addition, given recent critical speculations about the fictionality of race and the inadequacy of representing the spectrum of diverse colors through the simple binary of white and black, such myths of racial origin may seem reductive, even biologically essentialist. Yet this type of story enabled twentieth-century artists to meditate on the relationship between "Descartes" and the "jungle"—Euro-American and African civilizations—while illuminating the imaginative centrality of race in our cultural history. In particular, originatory narratives about race often exploit images of racial meta-

Figure 3.1 "Stop the world, I want to get on!," from Dick Gregory, *What's Happening?* (Dutton 1965), photographs by Jerry Yulsman. Courtesy of Dick Gregory.

morphosis: "Tonight, you will become black." While, as we have seen, blackface impersonations justified and even reenacted the subordination of African Americans, Ur-myths of racechange surfaced to interrogate, subvert, or topple racist stereotypes. During the Harlem Renaissance—from the teens through the early thirties—they even enabled some artists to wonder aloud, "Can the Israelite change his skin?" or to create an atmosphere in which some spectators might worry, "Lord, how come I'm so white?" Black modernists who deployed originatory fables of racechange to defamiliarize race relations sought to explain the inexplicable, to narrate the irrational, to confront and confound the "awful difference . . . between black and white."

Produced in the 1920s, the verse of Anne Spencer, the drawings of Richard Bruce Nugent, and the early dramatic work of Zora Neale Hurston can serve to establish a complex set of prevailing twentieth-century attitudes toward color, although these quite different achievements have gone largely ignored by cultural historians.[7] Taken together, the myths of ethnogenesis they fashion lay bare the structure of racial domination that infiltrates all manner of thinking and in so doing offers alternative ways of imagining the relationship of white to black. Anne Spencer's verse and Richard Bruce Nugent's prints stand for a newly militant effort among African-American artists to right the wrongs of history by reversing normative valuations of color: Some artists of the Harlem Renaissance accomplished this the way Spencer did, through a scathing vilification of whiteness, while others achieved it the way Nugent did, through the glorification (really the glamorization) of blackness. As if using the same logic as that of Soyinka, Spencer and Nugent analyze the Cartesian ghosts of Western culture that have framed the mind-body problem in racial terms. For Spencer and Nugent, black is the color of natural energy or primacy, while white is the color of unnatural entropy or belatedness. In other words, black being counters white nothingness, and both artists lay bare what the "white-man-who-has-problems-believing-in-his-own-existence" experiences during his encounters within "the jungle of the black," namely the insecurity that motivates cultural imperialism.

When placed alongside the achievements of their contemporaries, Spencer's critique of whiteness and Nugent's valoration of blackness link racial identity to performance. Whereas black characters imitating whites in passing narratives contributed to the deflation of whiteness, African-American entertainers imitating whites imitating blacks staged the valorization of blackness. Thus, two racechanging creatures emerge from Spencer's and Nugent's subversive approach to the etiological primacy of color: The former's angry account of the fall from a paradise of color hinges on the doomed "ex-coloured" character, while the latter's fanciful study of a colorful paradise regained deploys the resilient "re-colored" character. Noteworthy though the efforts of Spencer, Nugent, and some of their peers were, however, they pale when juxtaposed with Hurston's much more disturbing portrait of racechange. For, by drawing upon the most recalcitrant foundational narrative about color in Western civilization, Hurston dramatizes the impossibility of evading the negritudinist proposition, "I feel, therefore I am." In the process, she clarifies the ways in which hegemonic myths of originatory racechanges functioned historically to justify and even abet the subjugation of people of color by setting in place the political and spiritual systems that defined whiteness as an asset and a blessing, blackness as a debit and a curse.

Paradise Lost: Ex-Colored and Excoriated

What is the basic relationship of blackness to whiteness and why is it that black has been dominated by white? The first stanza of Anne Spencer's poem "White Things"—which appeared in a 1923 issue of *The Crisis*—strikingly disentangles preponderance from power, majority from might, in its meditation on these questions:

> Most things are colorful things—the sky, earth, and sea.
>   Black men are most men; but the white are free!
> White things are rare things; so rare, so rare
> They stole from out a silvered world—somewhere.
> Finding earth-plains fair plains, save greenly grassed,

They strewed white feathers of cowardice, as they passed;
   The golden stars with lances fine,
   The hills all red and darkened pine,
They blanched with their wand of power;
And turned the blood in a ruby rose
To a poor white poppy-flower. (ll. 1–11)

Beginning with black human beings, Spencer's poem subversively locates white-ness as an aberration. Most of the earth and its inhabitants are colored so where did the whites come from and why, asks the poet, is the white race "free"?

Unlike black men in Spencer's poem, whose color complements the green plains, golden stars, red hills, darkened pines, and ruby rose of nature, the white race appears unnatural: Whiteness is represented by "things," rather than beings, things which are "rare" and alien, as if from a "silvered" world elsewhere. Inter-lopers on the earth, the whites steal (creep out) into the world of sky, earth, and sea so as to steal (appropriate) it by steeling for warfare. Indeed, the first stanza ends with a cluster of images of destruction: "white feathers of cowardice," used throughout World War I to encourage men to volunteer for the front and almost certain death; the "wand of power" as a magical, magisterial phallus or weapon; the blood drained from the bleached, blanched "white poppy-flower." Rare, ex-pensive, silver white things have devolved by the end of the stanza to "poor" white things, for the "wand" of white power blanches or bleaches, leaching color from the earth.

In the second and final stanza of "White Things," the stealing of the whites moves beyond pilfering and pillaging to the systematic murdering of a lynch mob:

They pyred a race of black, black men,
And burned them to ashes white; then,
Laughing, a young one claimed a skull,
For the skull of a black is white, not dull,
   But a glistening awful thing
   Made, it seems, for this ghoul to swing
In the face of God with all his might,
And swear by the hell that sired him:
   "Man-maker, make white!" (ll. 12–20)

When the fire of the pyre changes black into white, life turns into death, burnt flesh and skin become ashes, heads revert to glistening skulls. In this nightmare con-clusion, a ghoulish "young one" swings such a skull "In the face of God" and de-mands that this deity "make" the world and its inhabitants "white" or, in James Weldon Johnson's term, "ex-coloured." Spencer concludes her poem, then, with a scene of lugubrious drollery reminiscent of the fates of Gus and Silas Lynch in *The Birth of a Nation*. Her ghastly Descartes/Kurtz responds to the jungle as a suitable setting for a scapegoating ritual from a theater of cruelty not unlike the lynchers dancing "round the dreadful thing in fiendish glee" at the end of Claude McKay's sonnet "The Lynching" (1920).

As a statement about the psychology of racism, Spencer's poem suggests that the marginalization of whites, their insecurity at being a minority, their guilt at appropriating a world in which they feel alien, their envy of a natural beauty not their own, all these factors combine to cause the murderous mastery of imperialist violence. Here whiteness resembles cowardice or fear and its reaction-formation, domination.[8] According to one of the very few critics who interpret Spencer's verse, "the mad desire of a minority race to destroy everything unlike itself" triggers acts of terrorism against African-American men and women (Honey, 9–10). Reversing normative ethical and spiritual valuations of color, Spencer hints that the white race should be associated with evil. For the "ghoul" who swears "by the hell that sired him" utters not a pious prayer but a daemonic curse that God "make white," and "white" rhymes here with "might." The only hope the poem holds out persists in the quotation marks of the last line which contain the possibility that the God who made (black) men (not white ghouls) is a deity of color who will refuse to hear or heed the deadly malediction.

A powerful protest poem, "White Things" illustrates exactly how extraordinary a cultural moment occurred during the Harlem Renaissance because this poem traverses normative stories about race. By starting with a "colorful" world peopled by "Black men," Spencer topples the usual view of beginnings offered by traditional myths of racial origin. Throughout classical and early modern times but most explicitly in Ovid's *Metamorphoses* (ca. 8 A.D.), dark complexions and not light were explained by the climate. Ovid's myth of racial origin recounts how Phaethon overcame the objections of his father, the sun god Phoebus, drove his father's chariot, suffered a panic attack, lost control, and scorched the universe: "It was then, as men think, that the peoples of Aethiopia became black-skinned, since the blood was drawn to the surface of their bodies by the heat" (77). In the wasteland context—Libya dries up into a desert, nymphs bewail lost pools of water, river banks catch fire, intense heat melts the sands, and "Great cracks yawn every where" (79)—black skin embodies the misrule resulting from a mere boy-mortal attempting a god's manly job. Even when color was not explicitly associated with catastrophe, race itself became identified with dark and not light epidermis, a premise that explains why Thomas Browne, who rejected all the prevailing racial expositions of his culture including that of climate, wondered not over the existence of whites but instead "Why some men, yea and they a mighty and considerable part of mankinde, should first acquire and still retain the glosse and tincture of blacknesse" (274). It is hard to imagine Soyinka's Descartes in his pith-helmet peering into the black pre-logical jungle and asking, "How come I'm so white?"

Unlike most earlier speculations, Spencer's poem operates under the radical assumption that black people are the "first" race in the sense that they are the originatory, natural people inhabiting a landscape of their own; the whites—Promethean and Satanic—are second-comers, sly and destructive thieves. She therefore attributes racism to white belatedness, the anxieties of whites about entering a world of green, gold, red, dark, and ruby rose colors, all of which are born and born alive, while whiteness is produced by and through death. At its most gruesome Spencer's poem implies that, though colors simply exist, whiteness must be manufactured out of sacrificed black bodies. If blacks turn white only in death, perhaps white men are dead men, ghoulish ghosts in a silvered world of Unbeing.

As so often in satiric portrayals of lynching, whites are the savages who engage in cannibalism, the human sacrifice of pyring a race. The poet therefore sees the advancing, colonizing culture of whiteness as one grotesquely committed to transforming black into white and in the process murdering nature, killing colorful lives into ashen, blanched things.

According to Spencer, then, white culture dedicates itself to genocidal race-change, reducing black heads to white skulls, for no other reason than the need of whites to assert dominion. As Trudier Harris has explained about the lynchings that occurred between 1880s and 1920s, this ritual remained "fixed in a mental perception of [whites] as superior to other human beings," not (as during ancient times) in the belief that a scapegoat was necessary to insure the survival of a society endangered by drought, pestilence, or famine (12). The theories of W.E.B. Du Bois add up to a similar point in his extension of the thinking of *Souls of Black Folk* (1903) to "The Souls of White Folk" (1910), for in the later piece Du Bois simply defines "whiteness [as] the ownership of the earth, forever and ever, Amen," a perverted "religion" that he describes as a transmutation of the accident of skin color into a register of superiority (339).

"Make white!": Racechange surfaces as the crucial imperative of Western culture, the mandate upon which all other prerogatives depend, one which the black poet deplores. In this respect, "White Things" epitomizes a critique of Western society sustained not only by Spencer's contemporary, George Schuyler (whose analysis of racechange as genocide in *Black No More* was discussed earlier), but also by Jean Toomer. In one of the short, imagistic poems he included in *Cane* (1923), Toomer linked America's racechange imperative "Make white!" to lynching. Through its grotesque personification of those who perpetrate racial violence, "Portrait in Georgia" hints that the hurt inflicted on victims boomerangs to damage the victimizers:

> Hair—braided chestnut,
>   coiled like a lyncher's rope,
> Eyes—fagots,
> Lips—old scars, or the first red blisters,
> Breath—the last sweet scent of cane,
> And her slim body, white as the ash
>   of black flesh after flame. (29)

Brilliantly collapsing several planes of meaning, Toomer presents a woman (with hair, eyes, lips, breath, and a slim body catalogued as in a love sonnet); an illness much like advanced stages of syphilis (scars, red blisters); and lynching (a coiled rope, fagots to fuel the flame).[9] The pathologized portrait of Georgia that emerges is a sexchanged personification of the character Anne Spencer called the "ghoul," here a murderous *femme fatale*. Like a syphilitic whore, this deathly dame demands the sacrifice of the black man who undergoes a racechange from black flesh into white ash because of a fiery consummation in "flame[s]" that invoke the hot passion of the miscegenation used to justify such scapegoating but also the whole burnt offering of the sacrificed body, which is the literal meaning of the word holocaust. To fall from the primacy of color into the hell of whiteness is to be excoriated, a word connoting condemnation that literally means being stripped of one's skin. In the shocking protests of Spencer and Toomer, whiteness emerges as simply the fantastic, destructive belief in superiority Du Bois had analyzed in "The Souls of White Folk." White ash is all that remains of black flesh after flame. For, as Walter Benn Michaels notes, "whiteness is produced by (rather than produces) the burning of black flesh" in a poem that turns out to be a "narrative of the origins of racial difference, a narrative in which white bodies are depicted as the consequence of violence against black bodies" (61–62).

Although novels about African-American characters trying to make themselves look white ultimately do contribute to the sort of critique of whiteness Anne Spencer, Jean Toomer, and W.E.B. Du Bois mounted, at first glance the passing genre appears to be quite conservative in its identification of whiteness with human dignity. After all, light-complexioned characters born in black families manage to escape the social stigma and professional restrictions placed on African Americans by pretending to be white. When the young boy of James Weldon Johnson's *The Autobiography of an Ex-Coloured Man* (1912) is shocked to discover from his darker mother that he is a "nigger," he knows that "she gave me a sword-thrust . . . which was years in healing" (19) because he experiences color as a "label of inferiority" (190). A similar wound of color pains the heroines of Jessie Fauset's *Plum Bun* and Nella Larsen's *Passing* (1929), both of whom reject this "label of inferiority" through white impersonation. From Charles W. Chesnutt's *The House Behind the Cedars* (1900) to the movies *Pinkie* (1949) and *Lost Boundaries* (1949), narratives about characters crossing the color line establish the material benefits accorded whites as a major plot motivation.

However, subsequently encased inside a hostile white culture, most passers are displayed feeling cut off from a nurturing black world. Making themselves white (though born black), they become "tragic mulattos," suffering a psychological and cultural splitting that reduces them to self-destructive liminality. Since whiteness ends up bringing them nothing but ontological insecurity, they ultimately experience their racechange as a kind of life-in-death, and thus endure exactly the doom analyzed by Spencer. Different as they seem from Spencer's poem, therefore, passing novels do contribute to the poet's satire on whitening as deadening when the passer loses a sense of social community, psychological coherence, and genealogical continuity. On this last count, the female imposter in particular suffers anxieties about those offspring she might produce whose skin tones could betray the secret she seeks to hide, and thus her counterfeit alienates her from the possibility of the life she contains within her. Her trajectory is one of homesickness: Beginning in a state of dis-ease at her confining black origins, she ends up after her traffic in an invalid white culture sick over her inability to return to those origins.

In this sense, the passer—neither black nor white—remains "ex-coloured." Since, as Michelle Cliff points out, "Passing demands a desire to become invisible. A ghost-life" (*Claiming an Identity*, 21), it brings into narrative the fragmentation and alienation so central to modernism. James Weldon Johnson's evocative term hints that cross-racial impersonation does not constitute a gain in whiteness

so much as a haunting estrangement from colorful origins. The ex-colored heroine of Larsen's *Passing*, imbued with longing "to see Negroes, to be with them
again, to talk with them, to hear them laugh" (200), typifies the ways in which the
assumption of a spurious white identity catapults the black central character into
a desire for a life-affirming reconnection to the African-American community. For
to be ex-colored is to be Xed out or canceled: The X in ex-colored marks the burial spot of the excoriated, excommunicated living dead who can be reanimated
only by a returning to color. Ultimately, the masquerade of whiteness undertaken
by the passers of James Weldon Johnson, Jessie Fauset, and Nella Larsen deflates
whiteness itself as a kind of masquerade because the passers comprehend exactly
the gratuitous privileges, the almost religious assumption of election, Du Bois associated with "The Souls of White Folk."

Only the most threatening circumstances would lead a character into the excoriated excommunication of the "ex-coloured." When James Weldon Johnson's
light-skinned boy grows up and decides to become "an ex-coloured man," it is at
least in part because he witnesses the type of lynching scene described by Anne
Spencer and Jean Toomer. Curiously, what he feels is horror not at the lynchers but
at the lynched. Smelling the stink of burnt flesh, he experiences a "great wave of
humiliation and shame . . . that I belonged to a race that could be so dealt with"
(188):

> it was not discouragement or fear or search for a larger field of action and opportuni-
> ty that was driving me out of the Negro race. I knew that it was shame, unbearable
> shame. Shame at being identified with a people that could with impunity be treated
> worse than animals. For certainly the law would restrain and punish the malicious
> burning alive of animals. (190–91)[10]

Another passing character in Fauset's *Plum Bun* experiences the same illogical revulsion: Having seen her innocent husband shot, his fingers and toes and ears cut
off by "Souvenir hunters," this woman believes blacks are "cursed, otherwise why
should we be so abused, so hounded?" (289–90). As if recycling a line about such
anxiety that appears in Robert Browning's dramatic monologue "'Childe Roland
to the Dark Tower Came,'" the characters of James Weldon Johnson and Fauset
suspect that they or their race "must be wicked to deserve such pain" (l. 84).

Behind the twentieth-century slandering of color, these passages and Spencer's
and Toomer's poems suggest, lurks the ignominious puzzle of victimization. Why
were black people "treated worse than animals," why have they been enslaved or
burnt alive by whites? Despite taboos of political solidarity that would censure
such speculations, Spencer, Toomer, Johnson, and Fauset hint at the repugnance
felt by some African Americans about the burden of their own history, a self-
loathing spawned by the suspicion that somehow black people "deserved" or "ac-
quiesced in" their fate, a dread that blackness has been inextricably contaminated
by the unbearable shame of innocent suffering. By daring to write about such
shame, of course, Spencer and Johnson reduce it to a sham, the scandal of a lying
culture that would cover up the even more ignominious puzzle of why whites vic-
timize blacks. What puts the lie to race shame, too, is the resourceful resiliency of

the passer dedicated to survival. Through inventive self-fashioning, the passer re-veals the deceitfulness of any script that would assign to blacks a sacrificial role.

Such tricky self-fashioning points to the last devaluation of whiteness to be dis-cussed here, one derived from the color blindness induced by assumptions of white privilege. In African-American literature of the Harlem Renaissance, as in the Crafts' slave narrative *Running a Thousand Miles for Freedom*, passing charac-ters, impersonators of whiteness, function like con artists who can move across the color line and return back again to tell their tale of trickery. Although their white companions are almost always duped, their knowing black relatives and friends watch the show with various degrees of relish, resentment, or remorse. At two points in *Passing*, Larsen's heroine meditates on the ease with which black peo-ple can fool whites. First, when she is herself passing, Irene thinks,

> White people were so stupid about such things for all that they usually asserted that they were able to tell; and by the most ridiculous means, finger-nails, palms of hands, shapes of ears, teeth, and other equally silly rot. They always took her for an Italian, a Spaniard, a Mexican, or a gipsy. Never, when she was alone, had they even remote-ly seemed to suspect that she was a Negro (150).

Skin, hair, fingernails, palms fail to register any visible evidence pertaining to race, making the category radically indeterminate. Destabilizing racial categories as well as the privileges founded upon them, the passing plot implies that "when 'race' is no longer visible, it is no longer intelligible" because (as Elaine Ginsberg puts it), "if 'white' can be 'black,' what is white?" (8).

Second, at a party where Irene's friend is passing, she explains to a white spec-tator that nobody can tell, "Not by looking," and then qualifies this assertion by explaining that especially white people cannot tell: "There are ways," she admits, "But they're not definite or tangible" and certainly not to the white gaze. In addi-tion, "It's easy for a Negro to 'pass' for white. But I don't think it would be so sim-ple for a white person to 'pass' for coloured" (206). In Fannie Hurst's novel *Imi-tation of Life*, as in the film versions of it (by John M. Stahl in 1934 and by Douglas Kirk in 1959), the light-complexioned Sarah Jane's imposture—a rebellion against her black mother's servile adherence to the role of mammy—goes undetected by whites unless she is exposed by her mother. (More recently, in Julie Dash's movie *Illusions,* a black singer whose voice is dubbed in for white women filmed lip-synching explains to the passer who is her producer, "They can't tell the way we can.") Why can blacks see racial truths that elude whites? Why do whites suffer a color blindness that makes the "ex-coloured" person unidentifiable?

Perhaps Soyinka's Descartes sees a blank slate in the jungle inhabitants because of a sightlessness linked to his propensity to project what he fears himself to be onto others. Larsen's plot corroborates her heroine's insights into the illogic of racial assumptions that allow "an Italian, a Spaniard, a Mexican, or a gipsy" to be labeled "white" by "fay" witnesses ignorant of the drama in which they are them-selves involved. White people, who assume what they see is white because they can imagine personhood only in terms of their own whiteness, suffer a lapse in imagination also evident in their inability to pass as black. "How can you tell who is black?" asks Judy Scales-Trent, a professor of law who has recently published *Notes of a White Black Woman* (1995), and she goes on to add that the stigma keeping gay people in the closet resemble those that keep African-Americans with white skin inside what we might call a racial closet (88–89). Still, the color blindness of whites who "Make white" inadvertently licenses the black tricksters' illicit acts, their mimetic mockery. For, as James Weldon Johnson put it, "the coloured people of this country know and understand the white people better than the white people know and understand them" (22). Like Anne Spencer and Jean Toomer (as well as the protagonists of numerous slave narratives before them), he believed that such understanding was a necessary survival skill.

Paradise Regained: Black Black Impersonation

Whereas Spencer's poem uses racechange in a myth of origin to protest against Western civilization's genocidal determination to "Make white!," Richard Bruce Nugent's four "Drawings for Mulattoes" can be interpreted as an etiological narrative about the interdependence of black and white in the evolution of American culture, for his pictures of racechange hold out the possibility of mutuality instead of domination, indeed of interracial creativity. If Spencer's poetry epitomizes the protest literature that delegitimized whiteness in the Harlem Renaissance, Nugent's drawings represent the ways in which many artists of the period theatricalized race not only to valorize blackness but also to undercut stable racial definitions, thereby linking the crucial concept of the newly glamorized New Negro with the newness of modernism. To return to Soyinka's formulation, although Spencer and the black impersonators of whiteness in passing novels protest against white anxiety about nonbeing, Nugent and the black impersonators of blackness so prevalent in the early twentieth-century entertainment industry dramatize the ways in which African Americans stage fullness of being.

Printed in Charles S. Johnson's collection *Ebony and Topaz* (1927), Nugent's prints can be read as a series about ethnogenesis that moves from depictions of the primitive to images of civilization, all of which emphasize the primacy of blackness as well as the aesthetic centrality of Africa in the evolution of twentieth-century Western culture. In opposition to George Santyana, who censured American culture for leaping from barbarism to decadence without the intervening stage of civilization, Nugent portrays Western civilization as an enticing amalgam of barbarism and decadence. Drawing number 1 locates itself in Africa, but because mannered forms similar to those of Aubrey Beardsley, Erté, and art deco seem to stylize this landscape, the very notion of the "primitive" or the "barbaric" is put in question (Fig. 3.2). Three naked figures—the central one caught in dance? in ritual? in oration?—are separated by vertical lines that might be the bark of trees but that simultaneously look like totem poles or abstract, baroque panels of geometrical design. In the beginning, according to Nugent (as according to Spencer), was the black race; from its community or its representative figure (captured in the three different frames) a sense of mobility and physical exuberance emerges that contrasts with the fixity of the next drawing.

Figure 3.2   Richard Bruce Nugent,
*Drawings for Mulattoes—Number
1.* Courtesy of Fisk University.

In drawing number 2, Nugent produces two images of racechange, one masculine and the other feminine (Fig. 3.3). The half-white, half-black woman in the bottom center of this picture—an ersatz, sexy Venus on the half-shell—may seem like
a version of the jungle dancers in the first drawing. But here she appears encased
inside the double-faced male head that, like the god Janus, looks both ways. And
the features of this two-faced head reverse normative racial markers, for the dark
face positioned next to palm trees has a Roman profile while the white face positioned next to industrialized beams has an African profile. Because the dancer has
been removed from the African landscape and repositioned inside a mysteriously
doubled patriarchal head, one could view this picture as a meditation on dislocation or exile. The African dancer almost looks as if she has been incorporated, internalized, or repressed inside the consciousness of the black-and-white male
psyche.

One telltale aspect of this gestalt complicates and enriches such a reading, namely the odd extension of the white face's lips which look weirdly exaggerated. When
we consider the exceptional importance of the lips in the portrayal of the minstrel—the grin of the blackfaced white performer who drew thick lines around a
mouth often held or painted or photographed as gaping wide open—Nugent's
drawing associates the idea of Africa with Western presence (the face on the left)
and the transmission of the African to the Western world with a stereotyping of the
black man (the face on the right). Can lips like these extended ones speak? Put another way, the drawing poses another question: Does the white man's burden consist of bearing the culpability for appropriating Africa (the profile on the left) and

displacing Africans not only from their homeland but also from a sense of authentic interiority (the profile on the right)? And does such guilt create a kind of neurotic self-division? In a picture that rings changes on the two faces of ancient Janiform vases, Richard Bruce Nugent seems to meditate on Du Bois's influential notion of "double consciousness":

> One ever feels his twoness—an American, a Negro; two souls, two thoughts, two un-reconciled strivings; two warring ideals in one dark body, whose dogged strength alone keeps it from being torn asunder. (Du Bois, *Souls of Black Folk*, 8–9)

Implicitly, too, Nugent asks, Who suffers double-consciousness, the black man, as Du Bois thought, or the white?[11]

The dancers of the first two pictures coalesce into the central focus of Number 3, another figure of racechange positioned against a background of stylized, black-and-white contrasts (Fig. 3.4). Nugent splices together the black naked dancer with the white flapper in her striped, two-piece outfit, complete with a high heel. The primitive energies of the jungle-dancer appear combined with the liberated sexuality of the New Woman. And again Nugent complicates any simple notion of twoness, for we are given the frontal portrait of the black-and-white performer except for her buttocks, skirt, and the back of her leg. Anatomically impossible, this creature thus emerges with various geometrical dimensions or planes on view in something like the manner of a cubist subject or a *Yellow Book* take on one of René Magritte's surrealistic creatures. Yet though we see "around" her, she remains mys-

Figure 3.3 Richard Bruce Nugent, *Drawings for Mulattoes—Number 2*. Courtesy of Fisk University.

Figure 3.4   Richard Bruce Nugent, *Drawings for Mulattoes—Number 3*. Courtesy of Fisk University.

teriously Other, a composite of African and Western, old and new impulses, a fitting citizen of the place Ann Douglas calls *Mongrel Manhattan*. The clothing
of the flapper and the breast of the African dancer appear to gender her female;
however, the position of the muscled black leg (as well as the droop of the breast)
seem almost satyr-like. As Walter Kalaidjian has pointed out, Nugent's "interracial images of the urban mulatto" recode "what was a conflicted figure of racial
'passing' and black 'double-consciousness' into a more subversive, cosmopolitan
sign" (68).

Exactly the hermaphroditic quality of this dancer is replicated in the black and
white chorus line at the bottom of the fourth and last drawing (Fig. 3.5). Wearing
high heels but as naked and exuberant and androgynous as the women in the first
drawing, these dancers again indicate that the Jazz Age offers the possibility of a
recovery of African origins. In the central forms here, racechange appears as a
playful reinterpretation of the traditional masks of tragedy and comedy. With a design reminiscent of the covers of sheet music, Nugent displays signs of the cabaret
(the treble clef, musical notes, the (stage?) door) and a jungle scene (trees, masks,
naked dancers), invoking song and dance numbers for jazz or blues nightclubs or
the Broadway shows of the twenties. In this world of commodified African artifacts, which is the mask, which the face? Is the New Woman only a facade, the veneer removed here to reveal the flesh-and-blood black woman? Or do these two
stylized images—neither tragic, nor comic, but highly reminiscent of Man Ray's
Noire et blanche photographs—signify the ways in which the (black or white) fem-

inine is put on display as an aesthetic spectacle? Linking gender with drama, the sequence also emphasizes the theatricality of race, the ways in which we are taught to impersonate ideas of color and its absence.

Taken as a whole, Nugent's series of prints questions whether the move from the African landscape to the Broadway stage or Harlem club is one of evolution or devolution, progress or decline and for whom. Perhaps the development is cyclical, a matter of the return in contemporary times of the far-away-and-long-ago repressed. Or is such a movement itself an illusion since Africa is "always already" represented through the lens of the downtown musical or uptown cabaret? What the diaspora means for artists like Richard Bruce Nugent is the impossibility of telling an etiological story about roots in an ancient Africa without at the same time inscribing the ways in which one's vision of the primitive must be filtered through a modernity marked by complete assimilation in American society. Any myth of

Figure 3.5 Richard Bruce Nugent, *Drawings for Mulattoes— Number 4*. Courtesy of Fisk University.

origins, Nugent suggests, must understand the African past as well as the more recent African-American slave past and the American present as several layers of
meaning on a palimpsest, each calling the authority and integrity of the other into
question.

Naked jungle dancers, sinuous flappers tapping the energies of ancient tribal
rhythms, masked entertainers singing the praises of antebellum times on the plantation: By the twenties, American culture here and in Paris had been saturated by
such images, often (as in Nugent's case) produced by black artists influenced by
white precursors, patrons, or audiences. If the devaluation of whiteness undertak-
en by the artists of the Harlem Renaissance frequently assumed the form of black
characters impersonating whites in passing novels, the glamorization of black origins associated with an urban and urbane cult of *negritude* led artists to adopt the
configuration of blacks impersonating whites impersonating blacks—a kind of
black black impersonation. Whereas the critique of whiteness helped form the "ex-
coloured" character who had fallen from the paradise of color, we shall see that
the romanticized staging of blackness helped shape what we might call the "re-
colored" figure who regains the paradise of origins by fusing the past with the present.

As early as the 1870s, Billy Kersands exhibited what one observer called a "co-
piousness of mouth and bredth of tongue that no white man could ever expect to
rival" (Toll, 254; Fig. 3.6). Filling his mouth with billiard balls or a coffee cup and
saucer, he was rumored to have quipped to Queen Victoria, "If God ever wanted
my mouth any bigger, he would have to move my ears" (M. Watkins, 114). His

Figure 3.6   Billy Kersands in *Cal-
lender's (Georgia) Minstrels*. Courtesy of the Billy Rose Theatre Collection, The New York Public
Library for the Performing Arts,
Astor, Lenox and Tilden Foundations.

Figure 3.7 Bert Williams in blackface. Courtesy of Frank Driggs Collection.

self-presentation clearly mirrors the caricatures produced by white minstrels in blackface. At the turn of the century, black entertainers like Bert Williams and George Walker continued to imitate white minstrels who had "blacked up" to mimic and mock the dialect, music, and dance of African Americans throughout the second half of the nineteenth century (Fig. 3.7). Advertised as "Two Real Coons," Williams and Walker presented the "strutting dandy" and the "shuffling darky" of minstrelsy (Alkire, 36–37). A comment by Walker captures the vertiginous interactions of white and black theatrical representations of African Americans. "My idea was always to *impersonate my race just as they are*," Walker explained, in a glitch of thinking which he went on to illuminate: "The colored man has never successfully *taken off* his own humorous characteristics, and the white impersonator often overdoes the matter" (emphasis mine; D. Gilbert, 284). Understandably enmeshed in such mimicries, the black entertainer Ernest ("The Unbleached American") Hogan remained haunted until the end of his successful career by the smash success of the "humorous" ditty he composed, "All Coons Look Alike to Me" (1890; Woll, 4).

Racist as the influence of minstrel productions was, the staging of race resulted in what Eric Lott calls its "carnivalizing" (226); white appropriation of African or slave cultural forms could be re-manufactured by the black performer in ways paradoxically both demeaning and empowering. During the twenties, the new phenomenon of Broadway musicals featuring black actors—*Shuffle Along* (1921), *Dixie to Broadway* (1924), *The Chocolate Dandies* (1924), *Africana* (1927), and *Blackbirds of 1928*—presented contemporary numbers (the cakewalk, the black bottom, the tango, the Charleston, the lindy hop) as if they were modifications of plantation or African choreography and thus ironically drew upon what Mark Twain in his autobiography praised as the "glad and stunning surprise" of the white-produced, white-performed "nigger show" (64).[12] So popular were these productions that "It's Getting Dark on Old Broadway," a song included in the *Ziegfeld Follies of 1922*, claimed that New York's theater district was undergoing a racechange; "the very famous dazzling White-Way night lights" were "growing dimmer" because the arts of America's premier northern urban center were shaped by those of the pre-industrial, rural south:

> Ev'ry cafe now has the dancing coon.
> Pretty choc'late babies
> Shake and shimmie ev'rywhere
> Real dark-town entertainers hold the stage,
> You must black up to be the latest rage.
>
> Yes, the great white way is white no more,
> It's just like a street on the Swanee shore. (Woll, 76)

Despite commercial success and exhilarating visibility, the first generation of black Broadway stars must have known that they were tapping widespread assumptions "that Negroes have . . . a special theatrical genius" (Huggins, 245) as well as minstrel and vaudeville stereotypes that found their way even into presumably jubulent production numbers like "It's Getting Dark on Old Broadway." Stories and pictures of the blackened black face of Bert Williams convey the weird series of travesties set in motion, but perhaps a photograph of Josephine Baker in blackface best captures the black performer's wry awareness of her entanglement in this process (Fig. 3.8). Cross-eyed and thus willfully blind to the spectacle she has made of herself, she derisively displays herself as an antic figure of foolish fun.[13] If the shuffling, grinning blackfaced minstrel ridiculed African Americans

Figure 3.8 Josephine Baker sporting blackface in *Chocolate Dandies* (1925). Courtesy of the Billy Rose Theatre Collection, The New York Public Library for the Performing Arts, Astor, Lenox and Tilden Foundations.

as lazy, superstitious, childish, or sexually loose, Baker's pose burlesques the mockers through self-mockery. And throughout her career, Baker sauced her sexy numbers with comically exaggerated, antic gestures that distanced her from the sexual frenzy she was putting on display.

That display, of course, was promoted by the more widely circulated pictures of Baker which attest to her ability to transform the supposed atavism, carnality, and exuberance of the stage Negro into a self-glamorizing iconography of *negritude*. A genius at generating striking advertisements, the woman Picasso called the "Nefertiti of now" inspired the architect Adolf Loos to design a house for her that conjures up "the stripes of an African zebra" and stimulated the architect Le Corbusier to honor her by "appearing at a costume ball in blackface and with a circle of feathers around his waist" (G. Watkins, 135). Whether posed with a leopard or slithering on her belly like a snake, whether naked on all fours like a monkey or dressed only in a skirt of dangling bananas, Baker presented herself with boyishly short, cropped hair and daringly exposed, fashionably small breasts as an oxymoronic icon of the newly primitive. Just as capable as Baker of turning the famed rhythms of Africans and African Americans into a vertiginous mobility, Valerie Snow, Florence Mills, Ethel Waters, Nina Mae McKinney, and the chorus lines of girls they danced with on stage or screen "wiggle[d] and shim[mied] in a fashion to outdo a congress of eels, and they [flung] their limbs about without stopping to make sure that they [were] fastened on" (quoted in Huggins, 289). To the delight of many observers, such choruses consisted of "every colour and combination that our race goes through," including "blonds and girls with blue eyes, grey eyes, right through to what they used to call cafe-au-lait to dark-skins" (O'Connor, 9).

Proving "for the first time [that] . . . black was beautiful," as Janet Flanner explained (xx), Baker typified the ways in which all these performers manipulated the iconography of the flapper-as-savage, welding it to the image of the dangerously alluring, exotic-erotic-neurotic *femme fatale*: As one book about her puts it, Baker became a cross between "the 'Douanier' Rousseau of the music-hall, a living Gauguin, [and] the 'Black Venus' of Baudelaire" (O'Connor, 119). To be sure, Baker's white peers in the pioneering schools of modern dance—Loie Fuller, Isadora Duncan, Martha Graham, and Ruth St. Dennis—also found themselves transformed into avatars of the *femme fatale*. But Baker's merging of the modern or the new with the primitive or African complements Nugent's picture of the flapper-as-satyr. Almost as successful at melding the past with the contemporary and just as determinedly oxymoronic, Florence Mills dressed as the spirit of Dixie (Fig. 3.9) and sang hilariously inappropriate but flamboyantly spirited songs about those good old plantation days gone by:

> On my pillow at night,
> I see fields of white
> And mammy's songs and stories, I recall.
> Dixie scenes all pass before me
> And I live my childhood it seems.
> At the close of each day
> Mister dream-man I pray
> Bring back my Dixie dreams. ("Dixie Dreams")[14]

As Phyllis Rose explains about Josephine Baker's prominence in the twenties, when American culture "turned a face to Europe, that face was black" (80), but America's facial racechange repeatedly depended upon black black impersonation. During the twenties, dancers and singers were only the most visible of black

Figure 3.9 Florence Mills in *Dixie to Broadway* (1924). Courtesy of the Schomburg Center for Research in Black Culture, The New York Public Library, Astor, Tilden, and Lenox Foundations.

artists subjected to but also drawing upon the kind of fetishization Baker and Mills sometimes seemed to encourage from fans. In the process and with varying degrees of irony, musicians and poets proposed genealogical links between the African-American present and the African-American or simply African past. Yet like Langston Hughes, most proponents of racial uplift were aware that Duke

Ellington and his Jungle Band, playing at the Kentucky or Cotton Clubs, could not be heard by ordinary Negro patrons unless they were rich like A'Lelia Walker or famous like Bojangles. Although many of the writers of the Harlem Renaissance sought to affirm their African origins and slave histories less sardonically, such attempts left them open to charges of regression, cultural nostalgia, or simply bad faith. Hughes's poem "Afro-American Fragment" (1930) admits about American blacks' relation to African roots that "Not even memories" survive "alive / Save those that history books create, / Save those that songs / Beat back into the blood—" (129). Countee Cullen, seeking to link himself to a cultural heritage elsewhere, could ask hopefully, "What is Africa to me?" However, Waring Cuney would implicitly answer "not much": About a Harlem girl who might be made aware of her beauty "If she could dance naked under palm trees / And see her image in the river," Cuney concluded, "But there are no palm trees / On the street, / And dish water gives back no images" (99).

Because black artists suffered from a sense of "always looking at [themselves] through the eyes of" whites, modern attempts to recover African-American slave culture or African roots could plummet black actors into the paradox of recycling a highly commodified primitivism eroticized and appropriated by whites and thus catering to prurient stereotypes. As in Virgil Thompson's opera based on Gertrude Stein's *Four Saints in Three Acts* (1934–35), for example, American blacks appeared as one more exotic or experimental sales pitch in performances composed for and by whites. In a 1936 production for the WPA's Negro Theatre Project that Orson Welles called a "Negro Version" but that has been come to be known as his "Voodoo" *Macbeth*, feudal Scots were transported to nineteenth-century Haiti and the three witches turned into voodoo priestesses attended by forty-three celebrants (McCloskey, 410). However, the news commentator Edward R. Murrow, objecting to the drums and chants that pulsed throughout the production, disparaged its "blackface attitude" (France, 70).

Despite her own unconscious racism, Gertrude Stein examined the relationship between such fetishization and racechange in a passage of *The Autobiography of Alice B. Toklas* (1933) that focuses on the other American Negro who was in vogue with Europeans during the twenties, Josephine Baker's male counterpart, Paul Robeson. The famous black singer—sent by Carl Van Vechten to Stein's salon—understands "american values and american life as only one in it but not of it could know them." In other words, like Stein herself Robeson gained insight into American culture by remaining aloof and alienated from it. However,

> as soon as any other person came into the room *he became definitely a negro*. Gertrude Stein did not like hearing him sing spirituals. They do not belong to you any more than anything else, so why claim them, she said. He did not answer. (224; emphasis mine)

Though Stein's subsequent contention that "the african is not primitive, he [*sic*] has a very ancient but a very narrow culture and there it remains" (224) partakes of the same placidly stupid condescension about racial "types" that can be found elsewhere in her work, her record of Robeson's racial metamorphosis hints at the complexity of his situation. When refusing to answer Stein's question, is the North-

ern born and trained artist politely acquiescent, mutely resistent, or really in accord with his hostess about the fictitiousness of his relationship to nineteenth-
century, Southern spirituals? Precisely such a question is raised if we contrast three
photographs that document Robeson's black black impersonations: one taken in
1919 in which the decorous Rutgers University undergraduate sports his Phi Beta
Kappa key, and the other two, shot during a summer vacation from Columbia Law
School, showing Robeson looking carnivalesque in harlequin or minstrel pants and
striking a bizarrely militant pose in ersatz African regalia for a production of the
review *Voodoo* (Figs. 3.10–3.12). The juxtaposition of such images makes
poignant Stein's subsequent diagnosis "that negroes were not suffering from persecution, they were suffering from nothingness," an analysis that begins to address
the ontological confusion which might accompany performances of blackness by
entertainers like Robeson.

Certainly Stein's testimonial that Robeson "became definitely a negro" links
racechange to self-consciousness, spectatorship, and performance. From Williams,
Walker, and Hogan to Baker and Robeson, black entertainers put on color with or
without the help of burnt cork. In the literature of the Harlem Renaissance, the possibility of becoming not "ex-coloured" but re-colored as "definitely a negro" finds
a fictive setting in bar scenes where what Claude McKay called "Jungle jazzing"
leads to a surrealistic racechange that presages a return to origins, a reverting to
"primitive joy" (*Banjo*, 58). After the heroine of Nella Larsen's *Quicksand* (1928)
feels "drugged" by the "extraordinary music, blown out, ripped out, beaten out"
in a Harlem cabaret, she returns to everyday consciousness with "a shameful certainty that not only had *she been in the jungle*, but that she had enjoyed it . . .
[though] *She wasn't, she told herself, a jungle creature*" (59; emphasis mine). Less
disgusted with herself but just as aware of "becoming definitely a negro," in "What
It Means to Be Colored Me" (1926) Zora Neale Hurston imagines herself sitting
in "The New World Cabaret with a white person, [and] *my color comes*." Jazz
causes her to "dance wildly inside myself; I yell within, I whoop; I shape my as-
segai above my head, I hurl it true to the mark *yeeeeooww*! I am in the jungle and
living in the jungle way" (154; first emphasis mine).

Hurston's savage sentiment—"I want to slaughter some thing—give pain, give
death to what, I do not know"—inevitably buttresses the idea that black people
have obtained only a "veneer [of what] we call civilization." Yet, as Barbara Johnson has pointed out, the folklorist—who was herself often castigated for telling
"lies" and "playing the darky"—maintains some degree of irony about this rever-
sion to type by describing her color not as a biological complexion but as a cos-
metic rainbow of hues: With her face "painted red and yellow" and her body
"painted blue," Hurston presents her coming and going color as an aesthetic phenomenon that could be manipulated, a form of black black impersonation (154).
Just as Baker established a seductive image out of the juxtaposition of herself as
New Woman/savage or jungle beast/flapper, Robeson and Hurston negotiated between cosmopolitan, continental sophistication and "becoming definitely a negro"
by letting "color come." One of Ann Douglas's contentions in *Terrible Honesty:
Mongrel Manhattan in the 1920s* establishes a context to understand that negotia-

Figure 3.10 Paul Robeson with Phi Beta Kappa Key, Rutgers University, 1919. From *The Whole World in His Hands: A Pictorial Biography of Paul Robeson* (Citadel Press 1981); courtesy of Paul Robeson, Jr.

Figure 3.11 (*Below, left*) Paul Robeson in *Voodoo* (London 1922). From *The Whole World in His Hands: A Pictorial Biography of Paul Robeson* (Citadel Press 1981); courtesy of Paul Robeson, Jr.

Figure 3.12 (*Below, right*) Paul Robeson in *Voodoo* (London 1922). From *The Whole World in His Hands: A Pictorial Biography of Paul Robeson* (Citadel Press 1981); courtesy of Paul Robeson, Jr.

tion: "If actual blacking up, Eddie Cantor-style, decreased in the 1920s, blacking up, speaking metaphorically, increased dramatically" (78). With all the performances of Baker, Robeson, and Hurston, as with Nugent's "Drawings for Mulattoes," the faintly disturbing effect of blacks blacking up derives from their teetering on the edge of the stereotypical and thereby drawing attention to what in another context Eric J. Sundquist calls "the painful entanglement between cultural self-determination and racist domination," an entanglement that requires complex "cultural negotation[s]" on the part of African Americans (449–50). How did Hurston feel when she could get seated at a restaurant with her traveling companion, Fannie Hurst, only when the white novelist introduced the aspiring black writer as "Princess Zora"? Or when the folklorist signed letters written to her patron "Your Pickanniny, Zora"?

Yet it is pointless to censure such negotiations because they remain inevitable, a sign of the interwoven strands—indeed, the indistinguishable fabric—of African-American and American cultures. At their most optimistic, moreover, the flapper-cum-savage (Baker) and the concert-singer-cum-slave (Robeson) sought to instruct America about the allure of "twoness": Unlike the analysis of Du Bois which presented the "dark body" (assumed to be male) "torn asunder," the art of Josephine Baker and Paul Robeson enacted the exciting energy of "twoness—an American, a Negro; two souls, two thoughts, two unreconciled strivings." Richard Bruce Nugent, together with Aaron Douglas, examined this same sense of twoness by producing red and blue murals on the walls of basement cabarets which functioned something like Escher prints. Under one light, an African past could be seen, but under another a modern cityscape would emerge (Wirth, 16). Also mapping this "twoness," Nugent's drawings in *Ebony and Topaz* picture it less as the "strife" or "warring" inside the schizophrenic black male psyche and more as a cultural condition of blacks and whites, men and women, and a condition of modernity that could enrich as well as test the limits of conventional categories.

From this perspective, it seems significant that Nugent's contribution to the landmark issue of *Fire!!*, the 1926 journal "devoted to Younger Negro Artists," consisted of what has been called "the first literary work on an openly homosexual theme to be published by an Afro-American writer" (Wirth, 16). A stream-of-consciousness story about a drug-induced fantasy, "Smoke, Lilies and Jade" centers on a man equally attracted to male and female lovers, convinced that "one *can* love two at the same time . . . ." (39).[15] Like Baker, who often appeared in public dressed in men's clothing, and like Florence Mills, who took the part of the groom on the Broadway stage, Nugent played with twoness by opting for "both/and" instead of "either/or" and celebrating the sexchanges of bisexuality. Nor was he unusual in this regard since, as Ann Douglas has pointed out, "most of the best-known black male writers in the New York scene were homosexual" (97). Still, loving two in the "Drawings for Mulattoes" mostly means loving the biracial contrasts created by the twoness of racechange. Interlaced or counterpointed, black and white exist in dizzying relationships that make either/or, better/worse thinking simply inadequate. Du Boisian "double consciousness"—so often taken as a sign of schizophrenic confinement—becomes transmuted into inclusive, nondichotomized artistry.

American society, Nugent and his peers suggest, had been so profoundly shaped by blacks as to have generated a culture of double consciousness for all of its citizens; every American's culture, in other words, is intrinsically "African American." A far more optimistic narrative about origins than Anne Spencer's, Nugent's series implies that the black race—uprooted and stereotyped though it has been—infuses Western culture with the inventions and energies of song, of dance, of theatricality or what these days is dubbed performativity. Indeed, Nugent's series intimates that race itself consists of performances and therefore participates in the mobility, the mutability, and the aestheticism of dance and drama. The Jazz Age foregrounds as most mutable, most mobile, most aesthetic the previously maligned "mulatto." No longer tragic, the mulatto whose color can come and go taps origins to emerge as a trope of racechange and the epitome of the archaic hybridity of the modern, the primitive audacity of the new.

Perpetual Exile: The Curse of Color

Yet the context in which Richard Bruce Nugent's drawings appeared somewhat qualifies this optimistic interpretation. Sandwiched between two articles—one on "Phantom Color Lines" and the other on "The Changing Status of the Mulatto"—the prints are integrated into the volume *Ebony and Topaz* through their title. But to the dismay of the author of "The Changing Status of the Mulatto," racists have attributed the "conspicuously successful" lives of mulattos to "a marked superiority rooting in the fact of a white ancestry and relationship" (107). Just as depressing, although the writer of "Phantom Color Lines" believes that African Americans can better their economic lot by admitting that "a large share of the Negro's failure to secure employment is his own fault," he admits that some white Northerners continue to justify job discrimination by invoking the persistent claim that "cold weather cannot be endured by sons of Ham from the torrid regions of the South" (102). Just how "changed" is the "status of the mulatto"? How "phantom" are "color lines"? In fact, how "New" is the "Negro"?

The passing allusion to Ham takes on prominence elsewhere in *Ebony and Topaz*, specifically in Zora Neale Hurston's contribution *The First One* (1927), a short play based on folkloric elaborations upon the biblical character of Ham and far less optimistic about race than her essay "How It Feels to Be Colored Me." Unlike Spencer and Nugent, who produced libertarian myths about the origin of color, Hurston neither delegitimized whites nor legitimized blacks. By tackling one of the most pervasive, pernicious legends of racial origin in Western culture, Hurston directly challenged the idea that black people in the twenties were experiencing a "Renaissance" or giving birth to a "New Negro" race. For, as in so many revisionary modernist texts by, say, James Joyce, T. S. Eliot, and H. D., *The First One* insists that the archaic stories which continue to exert their power over the twentieth-century imagination resist the efforts of artists to "make it new." In Hurston's case, that resistance complicates the attempts of activists as well and clarifies the recalcitrant structures of racism that continue to warp the lives of blacks and whites alike. From the severe point of view of Hurston's play, Spencer's defamation of white and Nugent's glamorization of black remain compensatory, belated, and doomed efforts to disentangle the black race from its secondariness. Despite Hurston's valiant struggle with the most influential and racist originatory myth of Western culture, we shall see that her revisionary play eventually re-assembles the ghastly contours of the age-old minstrel mask.

Though the Bible story of Ham's crime (of seeing Noah's nakedness), Noah's curse (against parental disrespect), and the subsequent punishment of Ham's son Canaan (when he is condemned to slavery) contains no mention of skin pigmentation at all, Hurston's drama about the first racechange draws on a long and complex history of biblical exegesis that exploited the narrative not only to explain the existence of people of color but also to justify their bondage. In the Ur-story, Shem, Ham, and Japheth—the sons of Noah who survived the flood in the ark—ultimately provide the generations who will people the entire world. According to the Bible, one day Noah became drunk and lay "uncovered in his tent," where Ham saw his nakedness and spoke about it to his brothers. After Shem and Japheth took a garment upon their shoulders, walked "backward and covered the nakedness of their father," Noah awakened and understood "what his youngest son had done" so he pronounced the famous sentences: "Curse be Canaan; a slave of slaves shall he be to his brothers" and "Blessed by the Lord my God be Shem; and let Canaan be his slave" (Genesis 10: 26–27). Even though color or complexion never appears in the Bible passage, even though Canaan (not Ham) is (inexplicably) cursed, the story very quickly found elaborators who used it to justify the slavery of Africans identified as Ham's descendants. Because "the view of Africa as a continent condemned to eternal servitude was eminently suited to a theological assessment of slavery," Jan Nederveen Pieterse has explained, the identification of Africa with Ham and with divinely ordained servitude "remained the most popular explanation of slavery" well into the nineteenth century (44).

While Anne Spencer's poem used racechange to protest the genocidal whitening of Western society, while Nugent's drawings employed it to imagine a new amalgam of ancient African and modern American cultures, Hurston's achievement was to make their projects seem utopian at best, specious at worst. For she hints that the twentieth-century imagination continues to identify people of color with Ham and with divinely sanctioned bondage. By beginning with a white race that makes black come into being as an affliction, Hurston grappled with an Ur-story about racechange that established the juridical justification of slavery as well as the ethical underpinnings behind twentieth-century ideologies of white supremacy. The Bible's sacralization of beginnings made ethnogenesis a particularly complicated problem for Hurston. Although she valiantly struggled to rescue the biblical myth from the bigoted uses to which it had been put by a long line of interpreters, ultimately the ubiquitous racism of that textual history resisted her efforts to make it new.

A one-act dramatic revision of Genesis 9:18–27, *The First One* elaborates on the biblical narrative, supplying new details and changing the meaning of others. On the third-year anniversary of their survival after the appearance of the rainbow covenant, Hurston's Noah and his wife and his sons (all married now) return to the

Valley of Ararat in order "to commemorate [their] delivery from the flood" (81). Immediately, Hurston's dialogue contrasts the temperaments of the two older brothers, Shem and Japheth, with that of the youngest, Ham. The former two clearly represent the work ethic—their days have been spent farming the fields and the vineyards, supplying meat for the offering, making the "dingy" robes they wear— while Ham, his wife (here called Eve), and their baby epitomize the ethos of play or artistry. Sporting white goat-skins, shiny green wreaths, and scarlet garlands, they bring flowers and music to the ritual, offering to "dance before Jehovah and sing joyfully upon the harp that [Ham] made of the thews of rams" (81).

Mrs. Shem and Mrs. Japheth—like Eve, they are entirely of Hurston's invention—put the plot in motion. Their jealousy of Noah's affection for the child of his old age stirs up dissension among the brothers. This, along with the naming of Ham's wife, makes *The First One* read like an echo of the garden of Eden story. As an interpreter of Genesis, then, Hurston emphasizes the ways in which the Noah-Ham story reiterates some of the same tropes as those in the account of the fall from paradise: the crime of (Eve's) disobedience or (Ham's) disrespect for authority and the subsequent punishment (exacted by God or Noah); the act of ingesting (Adam and Eve's eating the fruit or Noah's drinking the fruit of the vine), followed by (the first couple's or Ham's) seeing of nakedness and expulsion. After Hurston's Noah gets drunk, so as to drown out painful memories of the destruction wrecked by the flood, Mrs. Shem and Mrs. Japheth overhear the inebriated Ham laughing inside his father's tent and muttering as he emerges from it about "The old Ram" who "has had no spring for years" (84). As in the story of Eve's temptation of Adam, it is the women in Hurston's retelling who hatch the plot that brings disaster, goading their husbands to gain Noah's vineyards and flocks by reporting Ham's behavior to Noah, the self-proclaimed "Lord of the world" (82), who then acts like the God of the garden, cursing and casting out.

An enraged patriarch ("shall the lord of the Earth be mocked? Shall his nakedness be uncovered and he be shamed before his family?" (85)), Noah makes his proclamation without knowing the name of the perpetrator of the crime. First, Hustom's aged father pronounces a sentence about skin color that never appears in the Hebrew Bible: The scoffer "shall be accursed. His skin shall be black!" Next Noah adds the curse of slavery that does have a basis in Genesis: "He shall serve his brothers and they shall rule over him" (85). Departing from the biblical narrative completely, Hurston then portrays the immediate remorse of all concerned, their unsuccessful efforts to "unsay" or "Unspeak the Curse" (86). Finally, Ham—"horrified" and "stupefied" at the discovery that he is black—is brought his (now also) black child by Eve and the three of them are sent into exile by Noah: "Arise and go out from among us that we may see thy face no more, lest by lingering the curse of thy blackness come upon all my seed forever" (88). Disturbingly, in a number of respects Hurston's play appears more misogynist and racist than the original Genesis story, for *The First One* repeatedly conflates the color black with malediction and expulsion from the human (white) community, even as it blames this punishment on female ambition. The first racechange here constitutes a fall from the paradise of a whiteness so primordial that it remains invisible, unnamed, taken for granted, naturalized.

Just as significant, the biblical Noah curses not Ham but Ham's son, Canaan, who is to become "slave of slaves . . . to his brothers" (9: 25), while Hurston has Noah denounce the culprit directly and only by indirection his child (who also turns black). This last difference between the plot of Genesis and that of *The First One* points to the ways in which contradictions in the bibilical account are smoothed over or resolved by Hurston.[16] In addition, the ancient account does not even allude to complexion in general or to Africans in particular and thus in the Bible bondage remains unrelated to color. Indeed, because "the table of nations" (Genesis 10:1–32) implies that the entire human race—scattered all over the globe, different in its ethnicities and complexions—comes from the single family of Noah, the Bible can be said to embrace the idea of the essential unity of humankind. Yet by the time Hurston came to write *The First One*, the so-called "curse of Ham"—"the curse that never was," in Gene Rice's evocative phrase—functioned as a veritable lynchpin in the justification of American slavery at least in part because ancient commentaries set in place a racist account of the appearance of the first black human being and the first racechange. Only an understanding of these noxious elaborations upon the Ur-text can elucidate what would seem to be Hurston's apparent complicity in using the story to justify the expulsion of blacks from political power and spiritual primacy. What such a contextualization establishes, surprisingly, is how—within the confines of this noisome textual history—Hurston struggled to supply a potentially liberating counter-commentary, a midrash of her own.

How did Ham get his color? The name itself is "etymologically related to the word *hm*, 'warm,' 'hot' (from *hmm*, 'to become warm, hot'), or derived from the Egyptian Keme, 'the black land' (a name for ancient Egypt)" (*The Anchor Bible Dictionary*, III, 31). Because, as Ovid's tale in *Metamorphosis* illustrates, climatic causation had been used to explain a complexion thought to be burnt by the sun, Western commentators may have conflated heat and color. According to biblical ethnographic ideas, the descendants of Ham's sons—Cush (Ethiopians), Misraim (Egyptians), Put (Libyans), and Canaan (Canaanites)—occupied lands south and west of Israel. Early commentaries on the Bible often assume that Ham's "seeing" of Noah's nakedness must be read as a euphemism for some other, more heinous crime, thus linking the curse against Canaan to the outlawed sexual offenses attributed to the Canaanites in Leviticus (18: 24–30). In this way, sexual practices defined as the moral failure of the Canaanite people were used to justify the otherwise reprehensible notion that the (innocent) son Canaan is punished for the sins of his father, Ham.[17]

At least some of the conjectures about the actual crime committed by Ham led early thinkers in Talmudic, Midrashic, and other rabbinical sources (from the second to the fifth centuries A.D.) to transform the Noah-Ham-Canaan tale into a pernicious racechange narrative. Rabbinic commentaries on Genesis in Bereshith Rabbah link Ham's offense against Noah with castration and bestiality, conflating the evil of both acts with darkness:

> R. Huna said in R. Joseph's name: (Noah declared), "you have prevented me from
> begetting a fourth son, therefore I curse your fourth son." R. Huna also said in
> R. Joseph's name: "you have prevented me from doing something in the dark (co-
> habitation), therefore your seed will be ugly and dark-skinned." R. Hiyya said: "Ham
> and the dog copulated in the Ark, therefore Ham came forth black-skinned while the
> dog publicly exposes its copulation. . . . " (Midrash Rabbah-Genesis cited in Copher,
> 232)[18]

These interpretations, the source of many later ideological uses to which the Noah-
Ham-Canaan story was put, contain several crucial motifs: a justification of the
curse of Canaan in terms of an Oedipal struggle between a rivalrous Ham and the
father he renders impotent or castrated; an identification of dark skin with ugliness; the stigmatizing of black skin, now linked not only with bestiality but also
with bestial sexuality.

Other influential commentaries on Ham's seeing Noah unclothed conflate
voyeurism with the act of castrating, attributing both to dark-skinned people and
their supposed phallicism; the following passage, in which the speaker is Noah-
the-judge ruling against his son, is produced by Robert Graves and Raphael Patai
from various ancient sources:[19]

> "because you twisted your head around to see my nakedness, your grandchildren's
> hair shall be twisted into kinks, and their eyes red; again, because your lips jested at
> my misfortune, theirs shall swell; and because you neglected my nakedness, they shall
> go naked, and their male members shall be shamefully elongated." Men of this race
> are called Negroes; their forefather Canaan commanded them to love theft and forni-
> cation, to be banded together in hatred of their masters and never to tell the truth.
> (Graves and Patai, 121)

Hair "twisted," eyes "red," lips that "swell," the male member "shamefully elongated": The black (male) body appears to be a body in pain, a torture it is said to
earn by virtue of the crime of looking and laughing at Noah's nakedness and unmanning him. Dedicated to theft, fornication, hatred, and lies: The black (male)
mind is demonized as a mind of the damned. Early interpretations of the Genesis
story so besmirched the reputation of Ham that in one midrashic passage "sodomy
has been added to Ham's crimes" (Graves and Patai, 122). Said to have "defiled"
and "mutilated" his father, to have "preven[ted] procreation," to have committed
incest with either his father or his mother, Ham became the embodiment of the sexual evil attributed to black men throughout the Middle Ages and the Renaissance.[20]

Before and after 1773, when Phillis Wheatley, the first poet-slave of the New
World, wrote in "On Being Brought from Africa to America" (1773)—

> Some view that sable race with scornful eye:
> "Their colour is a diabolic dye."
> Remember, Christians, Negroes black as Cain
> May be refined and join the angelic strain (ll. 5–8)

—the "'diabolic dye'" of the mark God set on Cain had merged with that on Ham
and Canaan.[21] This, despite the fact that the mark in Genesis reflects God's efforts
to protect Cain during his wanderings. One century later, Joseph Smith—the au-

thor of the *Pearl of Great Price* (1851) and founder of the Mormon church—put into practice doctrines that supported slavery, forbade racial intermarriage, and denied the priesthood to blacks because he believed that "all the Canaanites were blackened, . . . they were the seed of Cain, and from them spring the Egyptians via Egyptus (a black Canaanite married to Ham), preserving a black race descended from both Cain and Ham" (Mellinkoff, 79).[22] Following this imaginative line of speculation, defenders of slavery like one John Fletcher of Louisiana could present Ham's sin as miscegenation: Ham had married into the race of Cain, whose skin had turned black because of his murdering of Abel (H. Seldon Smith, 131).

Predictably, then, the biblical narrative of Noah's curse became especially attractive to Americans seeking to justify slavery as a divinely inspired and sanctioned institution. If the natives of Canaan, polluted because of their purported sins of disrespect or castration or what were castigated as various modes of sexual perversion ranging from incest to sodomy, could be thought of as no longer meriting their own lands or as in need of Israel's superior ethical leadership, the blacks of the South could be contaminated by their genealogical relation to Ham or Canaan and thereby converted into the moral burden of their white masters. Although New World theologians disagreed about the relationship between Ham, Canaan, and African Americans, they nevertheless repeatedly invoked the Bible either to defend or attack the institution of slavery.[23] As Theodore Weld observed in his antislavery tract *The Bible Against Slavery* (4th edition 1838), the "prophecy of Noah is the *vade mecum* of slaveholders and they never venture abroad without it" (H. Sheldon Smith, 130).

Even the most arcane and bizarre theories about racial origins tended to return to the story of Noah's curse. One example will suffice here. Josiah Priest's *Slavery as It Relates to the Negro, or African Race* (1843) begins in what we would today consider a politically correct manner, but then quickly degenerates. Adam and his progeny were all born red until God mysteriously decided to make Japheth white and Ham black (Fig. 3.13). Alas, for the latter, the name "not only signified *black* in its literal sense, but pointed out the very disposition of his mind": Demonstrating his etymological inventiveness, Priest argues that Ham means "*heat* or *violence* (murder, war, butcheries, and even *cannibalism*)" as well as "deceit, dishonesty, treachery, low mindedness, and malice" (33). This ingenious scholar then finds the words "*cursed Ham*" in the Bible and claims that they mean "he had been *always* a bad person, even from childhood; for let it not be forgotten, that Ham, at the very time he did that act [of laughing at his father], was more than 100 years old" (79). Why God would have bothered to create "such a race thus low in the scale of human existence . . . is more than can be known by human research" (83) and must simply be accepted in terms of "one of the great facts of God's jurisprudence among men [which] appears to be the *judicial* appointment of the black race to slavery" (83–84).[24]

Whether or not Hurston read any of these texts, her culture was saturated with allusions to them. Actually, though pseudo-scientific explanations of racial difference at the turn of the century displaced theological ones, as recently as 1959 the author of a book about *The Bible and Race* explained that some people exploit "the

Figure 3.13   Josiah Priest, "The Family of Noah," in his *Slavery as It Relates to the Negro, or African Race* (1843).

curse of Canaan, frequently erroneously referred to as 'the curse of Ham,'" to argue that "the Negro, as a descendant of Ham, is destined by God to fill permanently a subservient place in society" (Maston, 105). As late as 1963, James Baldwin realized that, "according to many Christians, I was a descendant of Ham, who had been cursed, and that I was therefore predestined to be a slave. . . . my fate had been sealed forever, from the beginning of time" (*Fire Next Time*, 50).[25] Similarly, in his 1986 Nobel lecture, Wole Soyinka described "apartheid's mentality" as "The sons of Ham on the one hand, the descendants of Shem on the other. The once pronounced, utterly immutable curse" (12). Interpreting the myth of "the first one" as an injurious attack on African Americans (or a kind of forecast of "the last one"), the dramatist Suzan-Lori Parks brings in a character greeted as "HAM BONE HAM BONE" whose every other word is "SOLD" in her surrealistic play *The Death of the Last Black Man* (1992).

Although ultimately *The First One* does give off some such disturbing resonances, although it appears more misogynist and racist than the Bible, Hurston could be said to correct rabidly racist misreadings of Genesis. God does not pronounce the curse of color in *The First One*; as in the Bible, the sentence issues only from the mouth of a man. Thus, the oath loses divine sanction. More, the curse in Hurston's play comes from an intoxicated Noah who is suffering amnesia and a hangover. When woken up out of his drunken sleep after the cursing of Ham, a contrite Noah says, "I know of no curse" (86) and immediately joins the rest of the community in asking God to undo it. And as with the curse, so with the crime. Although biblical exegetes viewed Ham's crime of seeing the naked father not only as disrespect but also as a veiled allusion to a variety of sexual perversions, Hurston's Ham—as tipsy as his dad—simply talks to himself (more than to his brothers) when he emerges from Noah's tent and says, "Our Father has stripped himself, showing all his wrinkles. Ha! Ha! He's as no young goat in the spring" (84). Indeed, right after this speech, Ham passes out. Not especially respectful or modest in their motives, Shem and Japheth are propelled by wives who merely use the talk about "a father so mocked and shamed by his son" (84) to cover up the profit motive. In *The First One*, the acquisitive efforts of Mrs. Shem and Mrs. Japheth, the mainspring of the plot, turn attention to the relationship between paternity, private property, and slavery.[26]

For Hurston, then, the biblical narrative offers an opportunity to meditate on derision, the dishonoring of paternal authority, ownership, and bondage. Her play invites us to read the inauguration of an ethical justification for slavery as an Oedipal script set in a decidedly patriarchal framework. Just as Oedipus was guilty of murdering his father, Ham's crime consists of laughing at the phallus, a laughter in part motivated by the revelation that the young man is now ready to supersede his father. Though he is "as a young ram in the Spring" (83), Noah is "The old Ram" with "no spring for years" (84).[27] In his rebelliousness against the patriarch, Ham embodies a devotion to playfulness over and against work, a potentially anarchic and libidinal pleasure principle over and against a rigid, super-egoistic reality principle. The youngest of the three children, a favorite, and (in his singing as well as his dedication to honesty and pleasure) a bit of a fool, Ham functions as a truth-teller, somewhat like Shakespeare's Cordelia, with Mrs. Shem and Mrs. Japheth resembling Goneril and Regan. And, as in *King Lear*, in *The First One* the division of the father's goods among three offspring causes the rivalry between siblings that brings dissension and grief. If Ham plays the role of Oedipus, then, it is a Cordelia-like, fool-like Oedipus, a feminized "anti-Oedipus" who refuses to enter into a murderous rivalry with the father because he has no wish to become (like) the father.

As a statement about the psychology of bondage, Hurston's play suggests that paternal anxiety about potency as well as genealogical claims to legitimacy and property motivate racial subjugation. Laughing at the phallus is the outrage; disrespect for the father (even when the father has earned it) will be punished in the patrilineal, patri-centered ancient world. Slavery or white supremacy is the result of the law of the (insecure, out-of-control) father outraged and determined to assert authority and control over his family, his property, and his future. "Isn't laughter the first form of liberation from secular oppression?" Luce Irigaray has asked. *"Isn't the phallic tantamount to the seriousness of meaning?"* Like Irigaray, who speculates that women transcend "the sexual relation . . . 'first' in laughter" (163), Hurston imagines laughter as the irreverent crime of "the first one." As do Hélène Cixous and Julia Kristeva, Hurston presents laughter as the "volcanic" capacity to "break up the 'truth'" of a "phallogocentric order" (Cixous, 258) or as "what lifts inhibitions by breaking through prohibitions" (Kristeva, 224).

From this perspective, the black race derives from anti-patriarchal men—a fool or a youngest son or an anti-Oedipus—whose love of the sensual pleasures of

life—which include the arts of music and dance as well as the beauties of nature—
threatens the status quo and must therefore be repressed by a system that requires
conformity to the rules of an anxiously defensive white patriarch. From this perspective, too, Eve and Ham at the end of the play—dedicated to music, laughter,
and fun—function like precursors of Hurston's Janie and Tea Cake in *Their Eyes
Were Watching God*. For the outcast couple's Dionysian joyousness and playfulness contrast sharply with the gloom of the whites on stage, all of whom have been
traumatized by the horrors of the flood in the past and now by the mortifications
of the injust curse: Noah looking "tragically stern," his other offspring appearing
"ghastly," and his wife sobbing her dedication to a Jehovah who refuses to right
the wrong of Noah's rash oath (88). Exhausted and demoralized, the white family, visibly suffering guilt over the wrongful fate inflicted on the "first one," en-
dures the doleful spiritual consequences of its expulsion of Ham and his progeny
from the human community. Ironically, too, though Noah and his family ask Jehovah to set a rainbow in the heavens as a sign of redemption, though they hopefully ask each other "do ye see colors appear?" (87), Ham's appearance as a man
of color only repulses them.

Attractive as is such a reading of the subversiveness of *The First One*, it cannot
fully account for the effect of Hurston's early effort at revisionary mythmaking.
To be sure, Hurston's biographer, Robert Hemenway, interprets *The First One* as
a play "pok[ing] fun at all those who take seriously the biblical sanction for racial
segregation" (68) and he thereby suggests that the comedy contrasts Ham's innocent mirth with the materialism and cunning that do him wrong and do him in. A
drunken old man mistakenly curses a tipsy son: how silly a basis for proclaiming
a totalizing racial difference that would support slave systems. In the context of
the play's authorial signature (Hurston's fame today as a subversive, black-
affirming mythologist) or in the context of the play's African-American audience
(Hurston's own awareness of her readers' suspicions about the misuses to which
the Ham passage had been put), perhaps it can be understood as satiric. Unfortunately, however, such a reading too easily glosses over the ways in which *The First
One* falls into the unprovable, Manichean "negritudinist" position encapsulated by
Soyinka in the sentence "I feel, therefore I am." After all, Hurston emphasizes
Ham's dreamy inability to comprehend his state of expulsion at the end. Noah
prays, "If Jehovah keeps not the covenant this time, if he spares not my weakness,
then I pray that Ham's heart remains asleep forever" (87). And when the rainbow
fails to appear, it is clear that God will not undo the curse, so Eve says, "Let us go
before you awake and learn to despise your father and your God" (88).

At the end of the play, Ham goes off stage and the audience is left wondering
about a future awakening. Will the black race never confront the stigma of its fate,
will it simply accept the rash injuries of the white father and the white father's
God?[28] The happy-go-lucky Ham seems to submit with a grin to his injust exclusion from the human community. Indeed, after Hurston's Eve tells Ham, "Look at
thy hands, thy feet. Thou art cursed black by thy Father," Ham embarks on his exile in true minstrel style, strumming his harp and blithely singing. What are we to
make of the author's attitude toward her material? Has she subscribed to a view

that the black race is so damned, so execrated as to be cursed by color and also by unconsciousness, a dumb submission to malediction, a mollified "shucks but let's go make hay while the sun shines"?

In the nineteenth century, Ham did play a role in comic songs of minstrelsy like this one about the origins of the banjo:

> Now Ham, de only nigger dat was runnin' on de packet,
> Got lonesome in de barber ship, an' couldn't stan' de racket
> So for to amuse himself he steamed some wood and bent it
> An soon he had a banjo made, de first dat was invented.

Curiously, however, this song could be viewed as less racist than Hurston's script since the minstrel Ham is not made black for any sin but instead is excluded from Noah's community *because* of his color. And, as William Stowe and David Grimsted point out in their discussion of stump sermons about color transformation on the stage, other minstrel speeches subversively presented Adam, Eve, and their children as originally black; after an angry God seeks out the guilty Cain, in one of their examples, the murderer "got frightened, and he turned white; and dis de way de first white man cum upon dis earth! And if it had not been for dat dar nigger Cane, we'd nebber been trubbled wid de white trash 'pon de face of dis here circumlar globe" (92).

Paradoxically, if myths of racial origin on the minstrel stage could poke fun at the overvaluation of whiteness, one of the most famous artists of the Harlem Renaissance could buttress the devaluation of blackness. Deeply implicated in the racist ideologies permeating nineteenth-century uses of the Bible, *The First One* can be said to perpetuate ideas about the ugliness, the secondariness, and the carnality of black people. For, as in Countee Cullen's poem "The Shroud of Color" (1925), Ham could say, "My color shrouds me in, I am as dirt / Beneath my brother's heel" (26). Not only is color a source of horror, not only is it created and then castigated by a white community, but at his first entrance on stage and at his last exit, Ham sings, "I am as a young ram in the Spring / Or a young male goat" (83). Like the harlequin carrying his club, Hurston's Ham counters his social liminality by touting his sexual prowess. Besides this clearly compensatory overvaluation of the physical, what does it mean that the black race is defined by Hurston solely in male terms? Until the end of the play, Eve remains white; the only other racechange besides Ham's is his son's.

A white Eve (not a temptress but a real helpmate here), a black man, and a black child constitute the first family of the black diaspora at the end of the play. Although it might be nice to think that Hurston slyly suggests that "black" has historically been conceptualized in terms of the black man, her first bi-racial family endorses the erasure of the black woman even as it seems to submit to the credo, "I feel, therefore I am." To gloss over the ways in which Hurston's text is embroiled in the history of its Ur-text would be to lose the significance of a play like this being produced by one of the foremost artists of the Harlem Renaissance, a writer whose early and late works exhibit a deep commitment to the liberation efforts of black women and men. The pervasive racism of the culture that grudgingly contained and misnamed the Harlem Renaissance inexorably molded even its most crafty advocates.[29]

Later in her career, during the prolific and creative years she spent in the 1930s, Hurston produced several versions of another etiological story about race that also presented the genesis of color as an error. *Mules and Men* (1935) includes a tall tale told by one "Gold" about the day God decided to "give everybody they color" and "He send de angels, Rayfield and Gab'ull," because he was tired of waiting for the "niggers" to show up:

> They hunted all over Heben till dey found de colored folks. All stretched out sleep on de grass under de tree of life. So Rayfield woke 'em up and tole 'em God wanted 'em.
>
> They all jumped up and run on up to de th'one and they was so skeered they might miss sumpin' they begin to push and shove one 'nother, bumpin' against all de angels and turnin' over foot-stools. They even had de th'one all pushed one-sided.
>
> Go God hollered "Git back! Get back!" And they misunderstood Him and thought He said, "Git black," and they been black ever since. (32–33)

Hardly a curse, blackness is just a blunder, the result here not of a crime but of simple exuberance and misunderstanding. Yet the oddity of Gold's "lie" consists of her inability to conceptualize people before color. In addition, her account of how "de colored folks" jumped up and then misunderstood God, thereby getting "black" instead of "back," hints that blacks are kept back by their color.

In a 1937 version of a chapter later revised for publication in Hurston's autobiography, *Dust Tracks on a Road* (1942), the same fable surfaces, but this time told directly by the author. Hurston explains how God looked at various portions of the multitude in front of him, proclaiming some "red people" and others "yellow" and "white" and finally wondering aloud to Gabriel about "miss[ing] some hosts":

> "You go hunt 'em up and tell 'em I say they better come quick if they want any color. Fool with me and I won't give out no more." So Gabriel went round everywhere hunting till way after while he found the lost multitudes down by the Sea of Life asleep under a tree. (305–6)

From here the "Get back!" "Get black!" story resumes, but in what a different modality. Instead of "and they been black ever since," Hurston writes in her own voice: "So they got black and just kept the thing agoing" (306). For color, though still nothing but a mistake, is clearly desirable here and Hurston uses her parable to conclude "we are no race. We are just a collection of people who overslept our time and got caught in the draft" (306).

All narratives about how people "got" black or white or red or yellow defamiliarize color by providing an explanation for it. In contrast to the more strenuously original images of racial origins crafted by Spencer and Nugent, however, Hurston returned to hegemonic stories of ethnogenesis that had functioned so effectively as subordinating decrees of bondage that even her revisionary efforts to make them work for (rather than against) African Americans remained in part baffled. Sadly, what Alain Locke called "the timid conventionalism which racial disparagement has forced upon the Negro mind in America"—what I would term the

powerful conformity which America's racial disparagement forced upon all its citizens—did at times hamper the imaginations of even some of the most inventive,
irreverent of twentieth-century artists. One of the greatest songs Fats Waller made
famous, "Black and Blue," echoes "The First One" in its conflation of color with
punishment: "I'm white inside, But that don't help my case," the lyrics of Andy
Razaf state; "Cause I can't hide, What's in my face." As if composed for Hurston's
Ham, the song asks, "What did I do, to be so black and blue?" and then it attests
to Ham's belief that "My only sin is in my skin." Struggling to construct positive
     pretations of inherited narratives that present color negatively, Waller—like
    ʌurston—remained caught up in tensions that continue to typify the efforts of even
the most progressive thinkers about race.

Yet the aesthetic energies with which such artists as Anne Spencer, Richard
Bruce Nugent, and Zora Neale Hurston imbued the black race nevertheless contributed to the incursion of the African-American into Western literary traditions.
Locke's belief that the "artistic discovery of African art came at a time when there
was a marked decadence and sterility in certain forms of European plastic art expression, due to generations of the inbreeding of style and idiom" (258), explains
why and how African forms transformed the paintings of Matisse, Picasso, Derain,
and Utrillo, the sculpture of Epstein, Lipschitz, and Modigliani, the poetry of Guil-
laume Apollinaire and Blaise Cendrars (the artists cited in Locke's essay "The
Legacy of the Ancestral Arts"). One contemporary critic points to the paradox in
Locke's attempt to convince "the Negro to stop imitating reactionary Europeans
and to start imitating progressive ones" (Michaels, *Our America*, 86), though of
course Locke assumed black artists would derive from Africa an ancestral legacy
that might bring them in touch with their own origins. Unbeknownst to Locke,
however, many white poets writing at the same time he produced *The New Negro*
(1925) adopted African cadences and African-American idioms to revitalize
the "decadence and sterility" of European linguistic expression, indeed to cure
or at least invigorate the "white-man-who-has-problems-believing-in-his-own-
existence." With much less right to assert direct kinship with African culture than
Locke, the lost generation associated with high modernism managed to find itself
in what its members took to be ancient tribal rhythms and futuristic urban slang to
which these writers (acknowledged they) could lay no legitimate claim.

4

DE MODERN DO MR. BONES

(and All That Ventriloquist Jazz)

> Oh! tis consummation
> Devoutly to be wished,
> To end your heartache by a sleep;
> When likely to be dished,
> Shuffle off your mortal coil,
> Do just so,
> Wheel about and turn about
> And jump Jim Crow.
> —Anonymous Minstrel

> De fust great epitaph was written by Homer . . . He wrote de "Oddity." It is de story ob Ulysses. We know Ulysses' las' name—it was Grant. De "Oddity" is written in heroic cutlets wid miasmatic feet. Does you know what a miasmatic foot is? Well, dat is de meter. An' I don' mean de gas meter an I don' mean de water meter. It mean de heavenly meateor what comes shootin' from de stars.
> —Anonymous Minstrel

> —Mr Bones, you too advancer with your song,
> muching of which are wrong.
> —John Berryman

Why did Gertrude Stein take "the first definite step away from the nineteenth century and into the twentieth century in literature" by writing not only about but also as "Melanctha the negress" (Stein, 50)? What does it mean that the outrageous promoters of the Dada movement banged on drums while performing "Negergedichte" or "Negro poems" in the Cabaret Voltaire's 1916 avant-garde shows in Zurich? Is there a connection between Vachel Lindsay's frenzied recitation of "The Congo" at a banquet sponsored by Harriet Monroe's magazine *Poetry* and the patron Carl Van Vechten's decision to title his novel about Harlem after the speech of a Lennox Avenue character who declares, "I jes' nacherly think dis heah is Nigger Heaven" (15)? Or between T. S. Eliot's use of the nickname "Possum" (or Pound's of "Brer Rabbit") and Nancy Cunard's creation of footnotes for works she

134

composed in African-American slang? How much and what kind of meaning should we assign to William Carlos Williams' placing toward the conclusion of *Paterson* (1946–1958) this quotation from *Really the Blues* (1946), the memoir of a jazz musician named Mezz Mezzrow who was born Jewish but considered himself Negro: "You could dig the colored man's real message and get in there with him. . . . inspiration's mammy was with me" (221)?

Certainly many of the white proponents of modernism immersed themselves in black culture and in particular in various attempts at a racial ventriloquism they associated with linguistic experimentation. Nor is this surprising if we take to its logical conclusion a point that Ralph Ellison made about black dialect. Considering the efforts of Americans to distinguish the New World from the Old, Ellison noted the importance of "the vernacular which gave expression to that very newness of spirit and outlook of which the leaders of the [American] nation liked to boast" ("Going to the Territory," 142). During the era in which Pound's injunction to "Make It New" resounded, black language practices—as they had been encoded by earlier (often white-authored) texts—offered an irresistible strategy for revitalizing the stale conventionalities of traditional forms, giving resonance to James Baldwin's assertion that "he who would enter the twenty-first century must come by way of me" (Baker, *Modernism*, 61).

In his contribution to Nancy Cunard's *Negro* anthology (1934), the composer George Antheil historicized this phenomenon of the blackening of the arts in painting (Gauguin, Picasso) and music (Stravinsky, Dvořák):

> The great war had come and gone, we had been robbed and ransacked of everything; and we were on the march again. Therefore we welcomed this sunburnt and primitive feeling, we laid out blankets in the sun and it killed all of our civilized microbes. The Negro came naturally into this blazing light, and has remained there. The black man (the exact opposite color of ourselves) has appeared to us suddenly like a true phenomenon. Like a photograph of ourselves he is the sole negative from which a positive may be drawn. (351)

Even before World War I, of course, the Negro (usually imagined as male) had become in the white mind a symbol of natural spontaneity, healthy exuberance, physical rhythms, the genuine or authentic. "Our fascination with the native," the cultural studies critic Rey Chow explains, has often been "a desire to hold on to an unchanging certainty somewhere outside our own 'fake' experience" (53). Indeed, it was precisely the prejudicial logic of such a stereotype of the vital authenticity of the primitive that led black writers to eschew dialect during the period white poets embraced it.

Most of the African-American contemporaries of Lindsay and Van Vechten rejected black vernacular as politically and aesthetically retrograde because it reinforced an image of the ignorant, stumbling, bumbling fool whose ungrammatical malapropisms were spouted by the blackfaced minstrel. Lest natural spontaneity or healthy exuberance slide into the stupidity usually attributed to animals and children, it had to be renounced or denounced. In other words, to offset a damaging view of black intellectual inferiority, some African-American writers in the first quarter of the twentieth century exhibited a kind of hypercorrect conventionality. According to Henry Louis Gates, Jr., many of the Harlem Renaissance poets extensively borrowed the forms of white poetry while eschewing what was singular about the speech of blacks (*Figures*, 181).[1] With the work of Langston Hughes and Sterling Brown providing the obvious exception to the rule, it is paradoxical that just as black dialect disappeared from the verse produced by African Americans, it surfaced with surprising vitality in the compositions of their white contemporaries.[2]

This may be why the only scholarly attention the phenomenon of racial ventriloquism has received comes by way of disapproval. Michael North's useful *The Dialect of Modernism*—with its documentation of the black talk white modernists used in their revolt against authoritarianism—views such appropriations as a "slumming in slang" that perpetuates racial slurs as well as the privileged position of whites (82). Similarly, Aldon Lynn Nielsen's important *White American Poets and the Racial Discourse in the Twentieth Century* reads twentieth-century white poets' "objectification of the racial other" as "romantic racism" (11).[3] Along with Marianna Torgovnick's *Gone Primitive*, these books demonstrate that the minstrel tradition, the fiction of Harriet Beecher Stowe (*Uncle Tom's Cabin* (1852)), the folklore of Joel Chandler Harris (*Uncle Remus* (1881), *The Tar-Baby* (1904), and *Uncle Remus and Br'er Rabbit* (1906)), and the movies based on Edgar Rice Burroughs's series (*Tarzan of the Apes* (1912)) were phenomenally popular and influential, shaping modernist writers' representations of black speech and contributing to racist stereotypes that placed Africans as well as African Americans outside the bounds of culture by associating blackness with ineptitude, passivity, or savagery. As Torgovnick has pointed out, the primitive is defined as "different from (usually opposite to) the present" so as to fulfill the needs of the present: "Voiceless, it lets us speak for it. It is our ventriloquist's dummy—or so we like to think" (9).

Yet in the "black literature" composed by twentieth-century white authors, the white poet or novelist speaks through the African dummy's mouth in a black talk that often presents itself as back talk. That is, most writers exploiting black rhythms and vernacular felt themselves to be tapping a dissident lexicon of subversive power, one at odds with the hegemonic cadences of mainstream culture as well as their own normative conformity to it. To the African-American reader, such an undertaking may seem like just another form of stereotypical appropriation. About John Berryman's famous decision to play the roles of Tambo and Bones "in that needful black idiom / offending me," Michael Harper flatly decides, "your ear lied. / *That slave in you was white blood forced to derision*" (10; emphasis his). Notwithstanding his ethical condemnation ("your ear lied"), Harper's analysis provides a clue for understanding the psychological and historical designs of racial ventriloquism in the modern minstrelsy of Berryman's poetic precursors; it also illuminates the major role linguistic racechanges played in the lives and works of several highly influential white patrons of the Harlem Renaissance. Ralph Ellison's reactions to Berryman's use of dialect supply a comparable lead when the novelist explained that despite his "preference" for "idiomatic rendering" and despite his "suspicion that Berryman was casting me as a long-distant Mister Interlocutor—

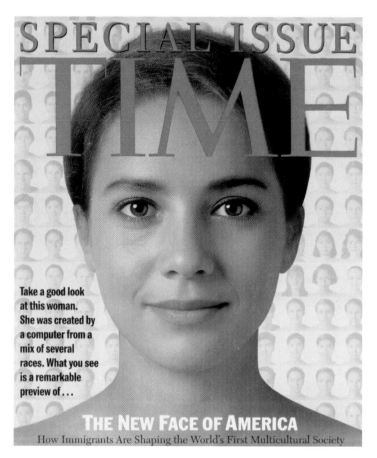

Eve, *Time* magazine cover girl. Special Issue, Fall 1993. Courtesy Time-Life.

Robert Colescott, *Eat Dem Taters* (1975). Acrylic on canvas, 59 x 79 in. Courtesy Phyllis Kind Gallery, New York and Chicago.

Robert Colescott, *George Washington Carver Crossing the Delaware: Page from an American History Textbook* (1975). Acrylic on canvas, 54 x 108 in. Courtesy Phyllis Kind Gallery, New York and Chicago.

Robert Colescott, *Shirley Temple Black and Bill Robinson White* (1980). Acrylic on canvas, 84 x 72 in. Courtesy Phyllis Kind Gallery, New York and Chicago.

Robert Colescott, *Les demoiselles d'Alabama: Vestidas* (1985). Acrylic on canvas, 96 x 92 in. Courtesy Phyllis Kind Gallery, New York and Chicago.

Robert Colescott, *Knowledge of the Past Is the Key to the Future (St. Sebastian)* (1986). Acrylic on canvas, 84 x 72 in. Courtesy Phyllis Kind Gallery, New York and Chicago.

or was it Mister Tambo?—" in the *Dream Songs*, Ellison himself "wasn't about to let the poetry of what [Berryman] was saying be interrupted by the dictates of my ear for Afro-American speech" (Mariani, *Dream Song*, 387). Though, like Harper, we might find fault with any appropriation by whites of black-inflected language and though, like Ellison, we might find such simulations inadequate as "idiomatic rendering[s]" of "Afro-American speech," we may have to admit that some of the most banal *and* some of the most brilliant experiments in twentieth-century poetry relied on cross-racial ventriloquism.

Perhaps because of its outrageous reliance on patently unrealistic or blatantly racist stereotypes, black English in twentieth-century literature contributes to the carnivalesque effect produced by pointedly self-parodic texts that seek to disrupt by mixing genres as well as lexical registers. As is the case in the fictional technique that the Russian theorist Bakhtin called "parodic stylization," the "intentions of the represent*ed* discourse are at odds with the intentions of the represent*ing* discourse" (364; emphasis mine). The printed white word contains and frames the represented speech of blacks, with the resulting collage contrasting belated written and originatory oral modalities often, as George Antheil had intuited, to dramatize the search of a society sickened by "civilized microbes" for a radiation-type therapy or cure derived from the blazing intensity of the African. In other words, black speech has a kind of fresh vitality that turns against the staid, stale, stupid decorums of the King's English. The very necessity of swerving toward subversive black talk, which holds out the possibility of reviving tediously traditional language forms, reveals the poverty and dessication of white culture. Whether conceived to be as ancient as African chants (what in this chapter I will call "Boomlay BOOM") or as new as African-American slang (what, following many, I term "Dis and Dat"), the vivacity or verve of African rhythms and African-American vernacular posed a threat to the established order for some as well as a promise for others. Indeed, in the pages to come we will note an ideological shift in emphasis over the course of the twentieth century: Black diction, which is repeatedly identified with a pre- or post-civilized energy, first tends to be exploited by practitioners who vilify it as anathema to Western civilization and only later in the century is it reimagined as redemptive.

But, regardless of their politics, all texts exploiting racial ventriloquism inevitably shuttle between defending against and welcoming energies of Otherness. The African-oral is written as if it hardly understands itself (and thus it must be desperately in need of the white writer who condescends to express it); however, the African-oral is supposed to capture primordial, essential meanings (and thus the mysterious potency of its energies captivate the white scribe).[4] What John Edgar Wideman identifies as the "high density of 'sound effects'" in folk narratives—performative strategies such as onomatopoetic words, syncopation, dialogue, phatic chants, word repetitions, rhetorical questions, parallel phrases, call and response patterns, notations indicating a percussive delivery, rhyme—finds its way into modern texts composed in imitation African rhythms (Boomlay BOOM) and African-American vernacular (Dis and Dat) that deride blacks but also backfire to mock white society as well as the white writer himself (74).

Though Wideman has argued that *"difference* in the dialect tradition clearly signaled *deficiency"* (60), improper grammar, eccentric orthography, slovenly pronunciation, comic malapropisms, and far-fetched words could also point to *difference* as *deviance* at a historical moment when alienated Euro-American writers
sought to escape the horror, the horror of Western civilization and what it had
wrought. Defying the efforts of scholars to distinguish the cadences and lexicons
rooted in the speech of real slaves from the bogus stage-Negro vernacular created
by whites, the literature of modernism problematizes such a clear-cut division.[5]
Similarly, the Africanist presence in experimental twentieth-century literature often stands not only for the new and the old but also for the genuine as well as the
ersatz. Although, as Chow puts it, "our fascination with the native" reflects "a desire to hold on to an unchanging certainty somewhere outside our own 'fake' experience," many twentieth-century white artists understood that such a figure for
the authentic was of their own making and thus simply another form of fakery.

In the passage from the *Negro* anthology quoted above, after all, Antheil stated
that blacks appeared *"like* a true phenomenon" (emphasis mine). Embedded, as it
usually is, within the hegemonic diction of the poet's culture, black talk signals the
wish to represent the authentic and the flagrant impossibility of doing so. Modernist experimentation in racial ventriloquism therefore needs to be distinguished
from, say, the black slave narratives produced by white abolitionists or other
crossover texts that attempted verisimilitude so as to pass their authors off as authentically colored.[6] Instead, what we confront in reading Lindsay's or Cunard's
or Mezzrow's renditions of African or African-American language are so obviously pidgin versions of the Other or are so pointedly marked as foreign (thus in
need of translation) that they force us to come to terms with the profound ide-
olectical differences which render all people incapable of communicating.[7] To the
extent that exaggerated stereotyping increasingly calls attention to white authors'
inability to represent the black Other, the works of later-twentieth-century writers
self-consciously meditate on their failure to represent the white self. For if the
writer cannot understand or render the Other, the work demonstrates that we cannot understand *any* other or, for that matter, each other. What Michael Harper diagnosed as *"white blood forced to derision"* constitutes the gothic self-mockery of
this heteroglossia, a poetics based on a curious impasse: the wish to engage the authenticity of the Other—to call it into being—and the fated sense that such an effort is doomed from the start.[8]

That so many racial ventriloquists—like Lindsay and Cunard, Mezzrow and
Berryman—would have viewed themselves as ardent advocates of racial equality
complicates our understanding of their motives. Perhaps in this regard bell hooks
furnishes the best framework for understanding how racial ventriloquism operates
as an attempted racechange:

> The desire to make contact with those bodies deemed Other, with no apparent will to
> dominate, assuages the guilt of the past, even takes the form of a defiant gesture where
> one denies accountability and historical connection. Most importantly, it establishes
> a contemporary narrative where *the suffering imposed by structures of domination on
> those designated Other is deflected* by an emphasis on seduction and longing where

the desire is not to make the Other over in one's image but *to become the Other*. (*Black Looks*, 25; emphasis mine)

Even as black rhythmic and lexical styles enabled many modernists to estrange language, they offered a (broken) promise that the white writer could become the Other and so often enmeshed practitioners in various fantasies of racechange. The race for modernity was African, according to a number of twentieth-century poets, patrons, and their more contemporary successors, many of whom sought to speak for and even as the blacks they (knew they only) pretended to be.

Modern Minstrelsy's Boomlay BOOM

For what reason is attention to the sufferings imposed by structures of domination deflected into a desire to become the Other or at least a desire to play at being the Other temporarily, as an inspiring experiment or exciting interlude? bell hooks supplies one answer: to assuage the guilt of the past or deny accountability for it. A related explanation is furnished by the anthropologist Renato Rosaldo:

> A person kills somebody, and then mourns the victim. In more attenuated form, someone deliberately alters a form of life, and then regrets that things have not remained as they were prior to the intervention. At one more remove, people destroy their environment, and then they worship nature. In any of its versions, imperialist nostalgia uses a pose of "innocent yearning" both to capture people's imaginations and to conceal its complicity with often brutal domination. (69–70)

After the slave system efficiently destroyed African culture and bodies, after the minstrel shows and blackface films effectively repeated an act of spirit-murder against African Americans, the basis for white guilt hardly needs to be explained. However, Rosaldo's concept of "imperialist nostalgia" illuminates the reasons why pseudo-African and African-American intonations functioned paradoxically as a form of complicity with brutal domination and as a compensatory lament deploring such domination. Since, as Adrienne Rich has remarked in a different context, "nostalgia is only amnesia turned around" ("Turning," 306), one face of imperialist nostalgia is what one might call imperialist amnesia.

Throughout the twentieth century, American, expatriate, and British poets used standard English inflected by rhythms marked as African in works overtly complicitous with brutal domination while others exploited African-American dialect to deplore such domination. Though they vary in their ideological designs and in their linguistic experimentation, early and later deployments of African rhythms, on the one hand, signal nostalgia for the oral, the originatory, the primordial, the real, the genuine; on the other hand, they denote white writers' consciousness that they are using not an undiluted but a minstrel-speak version of black talk that melds the genuine to the ersatz, generating a spurious speech to which the white imagination will perpetually be condemned. Among practitioners of what I am calling the Boomlay BOOM (ersatz African rhythms produced with standard English lexicons), Vachel Lindsay, Edith Sitwell, and T. S. Eliot illuminate the dynamics of imperialist nostalgia and amnesia even as they demonstrate the major role racial ventriloquism played in poetic experimentation. Despite their assaults on the culture and identity of black people, the reader's attention is deflected onto the taboo racechanges with which these racial ventriloquists flirt.

"Every kind of a war-drum ever heard. Then a Minstrel's Heaven, then a glorified Camp Meeting. Boomlay Boomlay Boomlay Boom!": This was how Vachel Lindsay described the "Congo piece" he began writing after visiting "vaudeville [and] . . . at last grasp[ing] what those painted folks are up to" (Ruggles, 210–11). Indeed, Lindsay believed that, given Americans' hatred of verse, the poet could aquire a sizable public only by cashing in on the popularity of, say, Bert Williams's ragtime hit "My Castle on the Nile"—"Inlaid diamonds on de flo', / A baboon butler at mah do'"—and thus producing the "Higher Vaudeville." "I am inventing a sort of ragtime manner that deceives [the audience] into thinking they are at a vaudeville show," Lindsay explained, although he admitted, "I have all my life abhorred" vaudeville (Yatron, 115; Ruggles, 211). Juba dancers at the Chicago World's Fair contributed to the rhythms of the poem, but so did his father's reading of *Uncle Remus*, Conrad's description of the "mighty big river . . . resembling an immense snake uncoiled" in *Heart of Darkness*, and Carlyle's query in *The French Revolution*:

> Does not the Black African take of Sticks and Old Clothes what will suffice and of these, cunningly combining them, fabricate for himself an Eidolon (Idol, or *Thing Seen*), and name it *Mumbo-Jumbo*? (6)

The patently grotesque logic of "The Congo"'s narrative depicts American blacks as genealogically linked to a sinister, heathen African race but able ultimately to be redeemed through Christianity. The first two sections—"Their Basic Savagery" and "Their Irrepressible High Spirits"—therefore move back and forth between twentieth-century American Negroes and primordial African savages. In Part I, "Fat Black bucks in a wine-barrel room" pay obeisance to the Congo God of destruction, Mumbo-Jumbo, as do "Tattooed cannibals [who] danced in files." A boisterous Negro subculture in America ("Barrel-house kings, with feet unstable, / Sagged and reeled and pounded on the table") remains tethered to an Africa figured as barbaric cannibalism ("the boom of the blood-lust song / And a thighbone beating on a tin-pan gong" (3)). Similarly, in Part II, "cake-walk royalty," juba dancers, a baboon butler, and a parrot band perform to the raucous delight of "witch men . . . with a sinister air" (5). The final solution appears in the last section, "The Hope of Their Religion," which moves to "the slums of the town" where a "good old negro" preaches to a congregation whose members repent "their stupor and savagery and sin and wrong" (6) so that "Mumbo-Jumbo will die in the jungle" and "Pioneer angels" can clear the way for a neat and clean "Congo paradise" (6). Ludicrous in the transparency of its racism, "The Congo" supplies its poet the role of missionary, shouldering the white man's burden to kill the African god who threatens to "hoo-doo" Western civilization.

The text of "The Congo"—with its stereotypically black rhythms glossed by directorial reading instructions in the prose marginalia—recalls Bakhtin's description of the clash between represent*ing* discourses that demolish represent*ed* languages in "parodic stylization" (364). From this perspective, the onomatopoetic and phatic words, syncopation, repetition, and percussive delivery of "The Congo" effectively ridicule and condemn the religious traditions and aesthetic styles identified as African and African-American. But the listeners who laughed at Lindsay's first performance were probably not tickled so much by its racism as by his flamboyantly weird delivery, just as those who made it his signature act were less enthralled by its message, more by the frenzied rolling of his eyes, the shooting of his hands, the rising of his voice to a whoop or a yelp and its falling to a whisper. Written accounts of Lindsay's impassioned performances as well as extant recordings make him sound like a versifying Al Jolson.[9] Curiously, too, the enormous popularity of the poem seemed to punish Lindsay for his cross-racial impersonation by forcing him repeatedly to stand in the place of the Other: Determined not to accede to the public's demands, he explained, "'I will *not* be a *slave* to my yesterdays'" (Ruggles, 412).

"People destroy their environment, and then they worship nature": If we apply the logic of Rosaldo's thinking about imperialist nostalgia to modernist heteroglossia, it becomes clear that Lindsay demonizes African Americans and then reveres their animated vitality (which he himself stages), for the effect of "The Congo" depends less on its genocidal plot and more on the verbal exuberance of its "high density of 'sound effects'" derived from African and African-American folk conventions. Pounding and singing, laughing and beating, preaching and prancing are the activities attributed within the poem to blacks but actually undertaken by the white performer. One passage, to be recited "with growing speed and sharply marked dance-rhythm," requires the white poet-performer to replicate the strutting of the black cake-walkers being described:

> And they pranced with their butterfly partners there,
> Coal-black maidens with pearls in their hair,
> Knee-skirts trimmed with the jassamine sweet,
> And bells on their ankles and little black feet. (5)

With their percussive four beats, these lines emphasize the pageantry, color, and vitality of a black culture that can never be fully captured through the pallor of print, but that the performer-poet seeks to replicate.

It does seem as if the topic of the poem gave Lindsay and his audience permission to engage with verbal intensity not just in "romantic racism" or "slumming in slang" but also in the mimetic rivalry of an incantatory chanting, singing, hymning, humming, slapping, drumming. All of "The Congo"'s lines aspire to the insistent, nonsensical condition of "Boomlay, boomlay, boomlay, BOOM." That is, the sense of the language is drained away by the repetition of sounds and words, by the alliteration, rhyme, and especially the preeminence of a rhythm so insistent it taps, claps, or drums through words. Phonetic similarity replaces semantic significance, as the ethnocentric effort to dethrone the African spiritual rituals of Mumbo Jumbo boomerangs to jettison the Western poet into his own mumbo jumbo of gibberish. Understandably, then, the strong beat and syncopation of Lindsay's "Higher Vaudeville" led Edgar Lee Masters to refer to "The Congo" as

"Beethoven jazz" (324).[10] Its prose gloss turns the text into a score, explaining to actor-chanters the speed, intonation, pitch, pausing, accents, emphasis, tone, emotion, and song tunes advisable for an effective performance. "With a touch of negro dialect and as rapidly as possible toward the end," one such stage direction reads (5).

Yet a "touch of negro dialect" that can be turned on, then turned off proves how consciously Lindsay wrote as a white for whites. That Lindsay understood himself to be involved in a less than authentic "Study of the Negro Race"—his subtitle to the poem and purported purpose in composing it—finds evidence throughout. First "Their" savagery, "Their" spirits, and "Their" religion: The pronoun of the section titles illustrates his acknowledged distance from the race he attempts to delineate. Second, the drunken barrel-house kings with their silk umbrellas and the cake-walking royalty would be instantly recognizable as types of the minstrel dandy. Third, Lindsay concedes that he and other whites have manipulated black representation: Ancient African voo-doo becomes "A roaring, epic, *rag-time tune*," a product of the contemporary Western imagination; the "negro fairyland" inhabited by the cake-walkers appears by "A *minstrel* river" (4). Finally, it is possible to read the end of the poem as an admission that white efforts to control black representation will be doomed to failure. Although the conclusion of "The Congo" emphatically states that the god of Africa is dead, a far-away vulture speaks the last lines of the poem: "Mumbo-Jumbo will hoo-doo you. / Mumbo . . . Jumbo . . . will . . . hoo-doo . . . you." To be recited in a "penetrating, terrified whisper," these broken phrases bespeak the author's admission that his curse poem will fail to extirpate the alien powers of Otherness that haunt his imagination and shape his artistry.

Lindsay is often ignored in histories of twentieth-century poetry because judged to be exceptionally reactionary in his racism. However, he was much more liberal than many of his poetic contemporaries and he first performed "The Congo" at a Lincoln Day banquet held in Springfield.[11] When Lindsay justified his pacifism during World War I, he said he would rather have died "of his own will mount[ing] a blazing pyre . . . by the side or in place of some black who had not trial by jury" than in the trenches (Ruggles, 250). "By the side or *in the place of some black*": Lindsay's self-sacrificial fantasy of racechange informed the poet's conviction that "the only way to end lynching would be to thrust yourself into the thick of such a mob and *make the men slay you instead of the Negro*. 'When they realized what they had done,'" Lindsay was supposed to have said, "'their hearts would be touched, their consciences shocked'" (Ruggles, 138; emphasis mine).[12] Even in the midst of describing the destructive ferocity of African savagry, Lindsay's "Congo" contains lines blaming black violence on white imperialism, including a grisly injunction that we "Listen to the yell of Leopold's ghost"; the Belgian King's exploitation of the Congo earns him "demons . . . / Cutting his hands off, down in Hell" (4). Although the booming drumbeats of "black bucks" and "barrel-house kings" lead Lindsay to explain, "THEN I had religion, THEN I had a vision. / I could not turn from their revel in derision" (3), he feels nothing but derision for the well-earned sufferings of King Leopold II punished in hell.

But if Lindsay cannot be discounted on account of virulent racism, neither can he be categorized as if outside the label "modernism," even though he is often presented as a formally conservative poet whose populist enthusiasm marked him as the very opposite of the experimental, elitist modernists. As prominent a poet as William Butler Yeats, commending "the half-sung, half-spoken delivery of such vaudeville acts as Tambo and Bones dialogues, which had an apparent spontaneity, and a quick-fire, incantatory rhythm," stated at the *Poetry* banquet recitation that "all that survived in America of the much-to-be-desired 'primitive singing of poetry' and the Greek lyric chant was American Vaudeville and Vachel Lindsay" (Massa, 231). Precisely "the half-sung, half-spoken delivery" of Tambo and Bones dialogues drew experimental writers rarely linked either to American vaudeville or Vachel Lindsay, at least in part because black talk enabled them to enact their estrangement from the pieties and proprieties of Western culture, to mark their awareness that such an alienation never guaranteed any bona fide alternative to Western culture, and to engage in unraveling meaning-making itself.[13]

What distinguishes the poetry of Boomlay BOOM in the twentieth century is its nonsensical hilarity, its anarchic incomprehensibility. When modernist writers heeded "The rattle of the bones, and chuckle spread from ear to ear," as T. S. Eliot did in *The Waste Land* (II.186), they used racial impersonation simultaneously to make the old new and the new old. And they did so by exploiting two of Lindsay's strategies: First, as Edith Sitwell's "Gold Coast Customs" (1928) illustrates, they produced incantatory mumbo jumbo by sustaining (what they thought to be) percussive African rhythms, emphasizing sound at the expense of sense; second, as T. S. Eliot's *Sweeney Agonistes* (1926–27) demonstrates, they set those rhythms within the framework of vaudeville and in so doing uncovered the links between the projects of modernism and minstrelsy, both of which exploited nonsense to ridicule the high seriousness of Western culture's monuments of unaging intellect.

Sitwell shared with Lindsay a fascination with Boomlay BOOM, though "Gold Coast Customs" seems even more saturated with revulsion at the knocking of savage bones on the portals of civilization than is "The Congo." When in the late forties Humphrey Searle, a practitioner of the twelve-tone scale and student of Webern, composed a musical setting to "Gold Coast Customs," he used a particularly full percussion section—two side drums, tenor drum, bass drum, tom-tom, triangle, cymbals, gong, and so on—to establish what one critic calls "the ground rhythm of the African tom-tom which gives the poem its rhythmical unity" (Singleton, 73). And Searle himself explained that "in the last movement at 'Bahunda, Banbangala, Barumbe, Bonge' (Section 24), whip, rattle, bass drum, two piccolos and a shouting chorus make an effect suggested by an African war-chant, whistled and shouted to the accompaniment of tom-toms and clapped hands" (Singleton, 74). He was drawing on a tradition of *musique nègre* that had shaped Stravinsky's *Le Sacre du printemps* (1913) and his *Ragtime* (1918), Milhaud's *La Creation du monde* (1924), and Poulenc's *Rapsodie nègre* (1917), in which a voice "singing only four pitches in a descending scalar pattern" recites such lines as "tota nou nou, nou nou ranga / lo lo lulu ma ta ma sou" (G. Watkins, 105).[14]

Echoes of the percussive, four-beat alliterative lines of "The Congo" toll in the opening of Sitwell's poem in which "Munza rattles his bones in the dusk, / Lurking in murk because he must" (7). Only the first explanatory note (on an Ashantee custom of killing slaves so as to use their blood in funeral services for the rich) and the closing footnote (documenting King Munza's reign in 1874 over the Monbuttoo) make any sense at all out of her mumbo jumbo. Instead of sense, sound links the three phantasmagoric settings of "Gold Coast Customs": the Ashantee tribal ceremonies, the decadent parties of one Lady Bamburgher, and a dock scene of sailors and prostitutes. Presented as if a poetic version of cinematic montage, all three share inexplicable but convulsive images of cannibalism, animality, corruption, and degeneration. As in the work of Lindsay, once again we have the narrative logic of a text that condemns black people for a fatal physicality at odds with morality or spirituality: According to Sitwell's notes, "The Negroes indulge [their] perfect contempt for humanity" in their "devouring of human flesh" (61).

A protest against the spiritual cannibalism of the postwar period, "Gold Coast Customs" condemns European civilization for its resemblance to Africa. Black mud, white bones and skulls, rotting flesh, devouring worms, monkey skins, rat-fat souls, and plague spots proliferate here, as there. But, as in "The Congo," the odd paradox emerges that the poet's voice finds its source of energy in (an albeit grotesquely stereotyped) Africa, "the threshold where history began" (16), an originatory place that keeps the poet enthralled by the "The cannibal drums [which] still roll in the mud / To the bones of the King's mother laved in blood." Sitwell herself seems to intuit the oddity of cross-racial identification early in the poem: The speaker refers mysteriously to "A bugbear bone that bellows white / As the ventriloquist sound of light" (8). Once again, an erstatz primitivism fuels modernist experimentation, for the poet repeatedly, passionately ventriloquizes "the bellowing bones" (28): "Rattle and beat what seemed a drum, / Rattle and beat it with a bone" (21). While most of the many photographed and painted portraits of Edith Sitwell emphasized her pallor and asceticism, a 1934 oil by Stella Bowen appears to invoke "Gold Coast Customs" by showing Sitwell's famously aristocratic hands grasping a black mask over her white face (Fig. 4.1).[15]

As if explaining the genealogy of "The Congo" and "Gold Coast Customs," T. S. Eliot once argued that "Poetry begins . . . with a savage beating a drum in a jungle" ("Beating of a Drum," 12).[16] But what Eliot's work lays bare is how self-consciously indebted the practitioners of the Boomlay BOOM tradition remained to flauntingly unreal representations of the primitive derived from minstrelsy, vaudeville, music halls, and Hollywood films.[17] Just as "The Congo" hinted at Lindsay's guilty awareness that he was engaged in an ersatz form of linguistic racechange, Eliot—who had prefaced "The Hollow Men" (1925) with Conrad's "*Mistah Kurtz—he dead*"—exploited "the hollow ring" of appropriated but admittedly spurious discourses.[18] This paradigmatic modernist, who accepted the nicknames Possum, Uncle Tom, and Tar Baby from Ezra Pound (himself nicknamed Br'er Rabbit)[19] and who for many years wrote pornographic verses about "King Bolo and His Great Black Queen," was drawn to black talk as a forbidden language that would enable him simultaneously to express and deride his most secret and fearful fantasies, or so a femicidal drama composed during the disintegration of his first marriage indicates.

Figure 4.1 Stella Bowen, *Hands of Edith Sitwell with Mask* (1934), oil. Courtesy of David Higham Associates.

After completing *The Waste Land*, Eliot used the minstrel endmen Tambo and Bones, music-hall dialogue and song, insistent rhythms, incantatory repetition of nonsense words, and descriptions of a cannibal island to frame an unfinished pastische that he considered "the most original of his compositions" (Ackroyd, 146). Published only in fragmentary form, *Sweeney Agonistes* appears at first quite different from "The Congo" or "Gold Coast Customs" in subject at least; however, it was supposed to be accompanied by light drum taps to accentuate the beats; one of its first readers, Arnold Bennett, called it a "jazz play" (Everett, 248); and Eliot himself later titled it "Fragment of a Comic Minstrelsy" (North, 87). As Barbara Everett has pointed out, the two verse dialogues that Eliot completed contrast the super-literacy of epigraphs from Aeschylus and St. John of the Cross with the subliteracy of American speech to establish what she calls "the medium of the comic demotic" (251).

Originally titled *Wanna Go Home, Baby?* and often read as a statement about modernist homelessness, the hallucinatory action of *Sweeney Agonistes* occurs in a rented flat occupied by Doris and Dusty. In Part I, "Fragment of a Prologue," these two smart tarts read their fortunes in cards, à la Madame Sosostris; they are then visited by a number of gentlemen callers who explain that they will not settle down because they find London "*a little too gay*" (19; emphasis mine).[20] The stress on misrule—geographic and sexual—surfaces again at the start of Part II, "Fragment of an Agon," in which Sweeney appears, threatening to carry Doris off to a cannibal isle: He wants to "gobble" her up and "convert" her "Into a stew. / A nice little, white little, missionary stew" (23). The cannibal island itself he imagines as the antithesis of London—no gramophones, no motor cars; when Sweeney emphasizes the nothingness to which he wishes to convey Doris, she replies, "I'd be bored." Doris's ennui presumably spells Western alienation from nature and from the ontological grounds of being, a tedium that may also mask her dread that she would really "be bored"—sexually or violently penetrated. "A woman runs a terrible risk," Doris admits, as Sweeney recounts tales of lurid sex crimes against female victims kept in baths of Lysol.

Minstrel and music hall numbers enabled Eliot to articulate and ridicule misogynist impulses he labeled barbaric or primitive at a time when he resented the demands made by his increasingly hysterical and unhappy wife.[21] The flagrant factitiousness of vaudeville, its zany unreality, allowed Eliot to intimate that modern man will never be able to capture the exhilarating primacy of the primitive. Although, as Sweeney explains, "Any man might do a girl in / Any man has to, needs to, wants to / Once in a lifetime, do a girl in" (28), this latter-day seedy thug will never manage to take Doris to the cannibal isle upon which such a consummation could be more than wished, for his island is comprised entirely out of the never-never land of vaudevillean stagecraft, or so the songs of "Snow and Swarts" indicate. As if to emphasize the showy theatricality of music hall scripts not to be taken too seriously, one such song—a version of "Under the Bamboo Tree," whose lyrics were composed in 1902 in a collaboration that included James Weldon Johnson—is performed by "Swarts as Tambo, Snow as Bones."

Even as the contrast of black (German *schwartz*) and white (snow or cocaine) reveals that their prototype is the harlequin (sporting his checkered costume, his black mask, and his phallic scepter), the two endmen make a mockery of realistic faith in any genuine state of nature

> *Where the Gauguin maids*
> *In the banyan shades*
> *Wear palmleaf drapery*
> *Under the bam*
> *Under the boo*
> *Under the bamboo tree.* (25–26)

The music hall status of Eliot's Tambo and Bones signals the impossibility of Sweeney enacting his femicidal fantasies. Minstrelsy stands, on the one hand, for the endurance of murderous instincts in the psyche of Western man and, on the other, the degeneration of such masculinism to a farcically improbable show-stopper possible only "Under the bam / Under the boo" where "Two live as one/ One live as two" (20).[22] (That the first black minstrel, Juba, advertised his "Imitation Dances" by explaining he would "give correct Imitation Dances of all the principal Ethiopian Dancers in the United States. After which he [would] give an imitation of himself" (Toll, 43) indicates how fully immersed minstrel mimicry was in artifice from its very inception.)

Inhabiting a fallen linguistic realm, Eliot's characters—haunted by guilt at their murderous desires and using a language contaminated by racial guilt—end up with the dissolution of all relationships and with the entropic deterioration of language into the nihilistic clowning of Vachel Lindsay's higher vaudeville: "Hoo / Hoo / Hoo / Knock Knock Knock" (31).[23] Just as the minstrels ridiculed high culture in their jumble of mistaken words and their mock pomposity, constructing burlesques that made a travesty of Western traditions, *Sweeney Agonistes* turned to minstrelsy as a remedy for but also a sign of the dessication of Western culture. Nihilistic hilarity at a hodge-podge of jostling registers—Biblical quotations and music hall patter, vaudeville slapstick and "coon" songs, jazz numbers and slang syncopations—emanates from otherwise quite different minstrel and modernist texts, in Eliot's case clearly motivated by the perplexity of a sense of masculine insufficiency that finds no outlet for rage against women. In more general terms, though, it is surprising how minstrel and modernist productions share a fascination with incongruity, given the obvious contrast between the popular stage and the abstruse experiments of the avant-garde.

The jumbled parodies that I used as the first two epigraphs of this chapter show how American popular culture in the nineteenth century used blackface performances to reinvent the Old World's culture in the irreverent New World's image. Just as Hamlet's suicidal soliloquy about what dreams may come after "we have shuffled off this mortal coil" degenerates into the choreographic imperative to "Shuffle off your mortal coil, / Do just so, / Wheel about and turn about / And jump Jim Crow," Eliot's *Waste Land* performs a "Shakespeherian Rag" (II.128); just as Homer's *Odyssey* devolves in minstrel-speak into the "oddity," while heroic couplets become "heroic cutlets" and poetic meter becomes the "gas meter" or the "heavenly meateor," *The Waste Land* transforms Marvell's "But at my back I always hear / Time's winged chariot hurrying near" into "But at my back in a cold blast I hear / The rattle of the bones, and chuckle spread from ear to ear" (III.185–86) while Eliot's next work substituted the thuggish Sweeney for Milton's heroic *Samson Agonistes*.

A comparable incongruity characterizes the beginning of *Sweeney Agonistes* (Aeschylus and St. John of the Cross) and its ending (the "Hoo / Hoo / Hoo" in "FULL CHORUS"). Through repetition and an insistence on sound over sense, the minstrel and the modernist drained high cultural texts of their seriousness, thereby making a travesty of the classical and biblical touchstones of Western civilization. According to Raymond Williams, the avant-garde often attempted "to dispense with language altogether, as too hopelessly compromised," or to substitute what Artaud called "'a different language of nature,'" which Williams equates with "vaudeville" (70).[24] In its anarchic glee at constructing a pastiche of incoherent bits and bites from high and low culture, the modernist's signifying shared common cause with the minstrel's flirtation with nonsense, his tendency to shore fragments against or amid the ruins.[25]

Given many modernists' alienation from conventional, linear, logical, causal structures of aesthetic forms and modes of intellection, it is hardly surprising that a number of Eliot's contemporaries were drawn to what has been called the "altiloquent speech" of stage blacks, a language full of sound and fury but signifying next to nothing. Gertrude Stein's booming repetition of the word "always" in "Melanchta"—"you so stupid *always* to me and *always* just bother with your *always* asking to me" (408, emphasis mine)—represents one deployment of the Boomlay BOOM that is linked to minstrelsy through the image of another (disturbingly stereotypical) refrain: "the wide, abandoned laughter that makes the warm broad glow of negro sunshine." If to one of Stein's critics the moralizings of her Negro hero sound like "the voice of the white bourgeoisie coming through a black mannikin," another hears in the "libidinous blues" of Melanctha herself "the stirrings of white desire passed through a fictive veil of blackness" (Nielsen, 28). In any case, that William Carlos Williams wrote the line "Drum, drum, drum, drum, drum" in "Ol' Bunk's Band" (1948, II.149) and that Gregory Corso composed the line "BING BANG BONG BOOM bee bear baboon" in "Bomb" (1958; 179) proves that the Boomlay BOOM tradition of Lindsay, Sitwell, Eliot, and Stein ended not with a whimper but with a BOOM and a baboon.[26]

Attraction to a sang-froid shaped by the drumming chants, incomprehensible incantations, and ersatz murmurs of countless stage endmen and screen cannibals catapulted writers from Lindsay to Corso into displaying the centrality of modernist minstrelsy in the evolution of twentieth-century poetry, clarifying the uses served by a nonwhite, Africanlike presence in the white imagination. Their racial ventriloquism might be considered a type of body language, stream-of-consciousness, free association, automatic writing, hermetic definition, or any other number of outré linguistic formulations. For the white imagination, a resonant imagery of artistry resides in the black man Hart Crane imagined wandering "Between his tambourine, stuck on the wall, / And, in Africa, a carcass quick with flies" ("Black Tambourine," 1926). As if negotiating between the minstrel tradition of the tambourine and the fly-infested African carcass, as if seeking—in the words of Hart Crane—"to dye" words "with a peculiarity of meaning" (*Letters*, 77), the proponents of Dada broadcast the bankruptcy of European aesthetic traditions with "Negro poems" or *Negergedichte*: "TRABADYA LA MODJERE MAGAMORE MAGAGERE TRABADJA BONO" was recited in the Cabaret Voltaire to the poundings of a big bass drum and punctuated with what one critic calls the "bones-in-the-nose" of a periodic "umbah-umbah" (Marcus, *Lipstick Traces*, 19).

The Patrons' Dis and Dat

During the twenties and thirties, the pseudo-Africanism of the Boomlay BOOMers was most strikingly embodied on the person of Nancy Cunard, a poet turned editor whose money and influence helped white as well as black artists. In many of the celebrated pictures taken of her, Cunard—sporting her personal trademark of African bracelets—looks like she is about to embark on a trip to Lindsay's Congo, Sitwell's Gold Coast, or Eliot's cannibal isle for a photo op to illustrate Rosaldo's concept of imperialist nostalgia. And Cunard also employed black talk, although her use of it exemplifies the second type of linguistic experimentation generated in the twentieth century by racial ventriloquism, namely the exploitation not of African rhythms but of African-American slang by patrons and poets alike. In the same years that two white vaudevillians, Freeman Gosden and Charles Correll, produced *Amos 'n' Andy* on the radio (that is, from 1925 until 1932), writers like Cunard, Carl Van Vechten, and e. e. cummings eschewed the Boomlay BOOM for Dis and Dat, repudiating ersatz African rhythms so as to focus on equally factitious African-American idioms.

If attraction is filtered through revulsion against the African in Lindsay's, Sitwell's, and Eliot's racial ventriloquism, at first glance Cunard's passionate commitment to reversing the defamation of non-European cultures seems to transform her imitation of African ways into a sincere, unmitigated form of flattery. Indeed, Cunard's image is informed by the same dedication to civil rights that shaped her heated attacks against racial prejudice in her scathing broadside "Black Man and White Ladyship" (1931), a defense of her partnership with the black musician Henry Crowder, and in her monumental *Negro* anthology, a massive collection of anthropological, ethnographic, historical, critical, poetic, personal, and pictorial documents on the achievements of Africans, West Indians, South Americans, and African Americans composed by some 150 contributors, two-thirds of them black. Although critics of the publishing venture tended to use racechange to slander the anthologist—"Auntie Nancy's Cabin—Down Among the Black Gentlemen of Harlem" ran the headline of a particularly egregious article in the *Empire News* (Chisholm, 278–79)—Cunard had "lived to see black become less black and white turn less white through shame," or so her friend Solita Solano claimed (Solano, 77). Constantin Brancusi's portrait of Nancy Cunard (1925–27), reflecting his preoccupation with ovoid, abstract forms over and against personal features, alludes to her fascination with and commitment to African and African-American artistry by invoking his earlier sculpture, *The White Negress* (1923); as one critic explains, "something of Nancy's gaity is captured in the crowning whorl, which appears to represent a more vivacious version of the topknot in *The White Negress*" (G. Watkins, 169).

The racechanging possibilities apparent in both of Brancusi's works had always haunted Cunard's imagination. As the six-year-old child of a British shipping magnate, she once recalled, she had dreamed about "Africans dancing and drumming around me, and I one of them, though still white, knowing, mysteriously enough, how to dance in their own manner" (Cunard, *Grand Man*, 140). Barbara Ker-

Seymer's shot of the adult Cunard—linking the fur collar with the tiger-striped background and juxtaposing the black turban and its dark netting with the pale face—mixes primitive and modern, savage and civilized to present the exotically erotic Cunard as a wild and gamey hybrid (Fig. 4.2). As if participating in the higher vaudeville of "The Congo," "Gold Coast Customs," or *Sweeney Agonistes*, Cunard in a Cecil Beaton photograph sports a plumed headdress and, again photographed by Beaton, she is positioned before black and white polka dots, exhibiting bangled arms and a glossy skullcap (evoking the brilliantined hair of Josephine Baker), signs of the carnivalesque (Figs. 4.3 and 4.4), for here totemic items marked as Other flaunt the campy self-costuming at play. The outré bangles, wig, and feathers emphasize precisely the ontological fullness of being that Cunard attributed to black people:

> it is the zest that the Negroes put in, and the enjoyment they get out of, things that causes one more envy in the ofay. Notice how many of the whites are unreal in America; they are *dim*. But the Negro is very real; he is *there*. (*Negro*, 69)

Yet despite her admiration for the vitality of African Americans (typically engendered male in her mind), Cunard's envious self-fashioning hints at the same ambivalent dynamic at work in the poems of, say, Lindsay, Eliot, and Sitwell. The very model of the modern woman, Cunard (in Beaton's pictures especially) reeks of a sophistication and privilege based on displaying the highly commodified, commercialized merchandise of difference. In her bad-girl self-displays, she might be imagined as miming sexual slavery within the *tableaux vivant* of a classy brothel or, in more contemporary terms, modeling the goods on sale in a *Banana Republic* brochure or selling the perfume *Safari* in Bloomingdale's. Similarly, her use of black slang (ofay is pig latin for foe and a term for whites) bespeaks her appropriation of a culture very much not her own.

The phrase "*Fay, Ofay, Fagingy Fagade*: a white person" appears in the glossary entitled "Some Negro Slang" and attached to one of Cunard's contributions to her *Negro* anthology (75). So do several other terms that could have easily been used against her. Was she a "*Jig-chaser*: white person who runs after Negroes" (76)? A prototype of "*Miss Ann, Mr Eddie, Mr Charley*: wealthy social white people" (76)? Cunard's list of defined expressions calls attention to the white patron's schizophrenic self-loathing, her fascination with—but also hesitancy about—speaking the language of the Other. The word "*Boody*" Cunard glosses as a "light-hearted term for what Mommer does her loving with" (75). "Mommer" here resonates with the desire to represent black experience and the difficulty of doing so, as does the tonal glitch of the coy "*Tail, a piece of*: see *Boody*" (77). In addition, Cunard's earnest insistence that many Negroes in New York use "finger-language" (78) and speak "Sanguadny," a "distinct language" invented by them in the theatrical world and incomprehensible to "evil *ofays*"—including herself—testifies to the weird distortions bred by her fervid fantasies about black linguistic power.

Perhaps most notably in the poem "Equatorial Way," Cunard used black slang, in this case too (as so often evident in her work) associated with a male persona. The dedication for her edition of Henry Crowder's musical scores, *Henry Music* (1930), "Equatorial Way" displays her anxieties about such linguistic appropria-

Figure 4.2   Barbara Ker-Seymer, Nancy Cunard with veil (1930). Photography Collection, Harry Ransom Humanities Research Center, The University of Texas at Austin; courtesy of Barbara A. Roett.

Figure 4.3   Cecil Beaton, Nancy Cunard in feathers. Kay Boyle Collection, Special Collections/Morris Library, Southern Illinois University at Carbondale.

Figure 4.4   Cecil Beaton, Nancy Cunard with bangles. Courtesy of Sotheby's Belgravia.

151

tion, again through definitions (here provided in numbered footnotes set in parentheses and sprinkled throughout the poem). Cunard's speaker sets out to leave "cotton lands, / Ole-stuff coons in Dixie bands," as he travels "To where the Congo waters roll":

> This aint no (4) white man's nigger
> *Nor was*—but I've grown bigger
> The further away from you
> Further, longer away from you
> My (5) cracker moon.

The notes define "white man's nigger" as "A cringing or dispirited negro playing up to, i.e. bullied by whites" and "cracker" as "southerners with violent prejudice apt to explode."

The jacket of the volume in which this poem appears displays precisely the odd mixture of "love and theft" that Eric Lott sees at work in nineteenth-century minstrelsy and that reverberates through Cunard's black talk (Fig. 4.5). On the one hand, with a photomontage designed by Man Ray, Cunard produced a book honoring her lover's musical creativity that features a handsome portrait of the man himself. On the other, his shoulders seem oddly burdened by what look to be more of the African bracelets that are piled at the bottom of the picture. If these are the bangles on her own arms (if she is standing hidden behind him), they seem ominously to weigh him down like a kind of head- or neckbrace reminiscent of punitive devices in slavery. Has Henry Crowder been shackled by Nancy Cunard's patronage, turned into a "white [woman's] nigger"? Were the other black artists she supported so tethered? In ancient Rome, *Webster's New World Dictionary* explains, a patron was "a person who had freed his slave but still retained a certain paternal control over him."

Precisely this sort of tension makes even Cunard's most radical contributions to the Harlem Renaissance appear at times sinister. In her *Negro* anthology, for example, she included W.E.B. Du Bois's essay on "Black America" (explaining that "So-called black America is of every conceivable hue and shade, and white America is by no means 'lily-white'" (152)), but prefaced the contribution with a parochial attack on Du Bois's "Reactionary Negro Organization," in which she invoked the standards of the Communist Party to judge the NAACP and find its leader wanting. Although numerous satiric portraits of Cunard may have been in part motivated by racist and sexist resentment at her revolutionary values and lifestyle, what still emerges from them is a portrait of a vamp who used her social status, her money, and her promiscuity to work her willful ways.[27] Comparable ironies might speak, too, through Janet Flanner's recollection of seeing Henry Crowder's bruised face and being told what happened: "Just braceletwork, Miss Janet," Crowder was supposed to have said with the linguistic shuffle (feigned or not) of the paid escort into which he had declined. Or in Harold Acton's equally damning recollection that Cunard would instruct Crowder to "Be more *African*," only to receive the musician's plaintive reply, "But I *ain't* African. I'm *American*" (Chisholm, 186). As Ann Douglas astutely puts it, in Crowder's memoir, *As Won-*

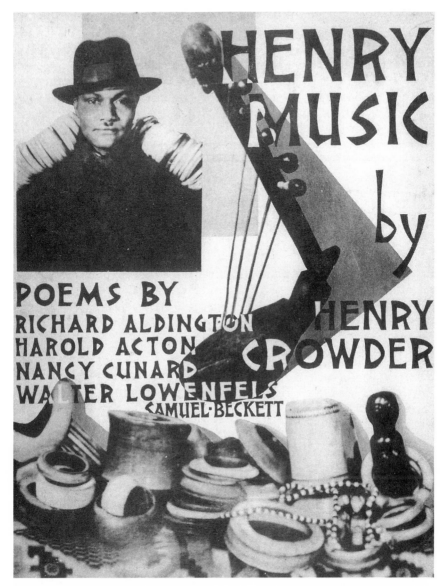

Figure 4.5   Cover designed by Man Ray of *Henry Music* (1930). Courtesy of Lilly Library, Indiana University.

derful as All That? (composed in 1935), "it is Nancy who plays the savage, Crowder the civilized role; she's the aggressor, he's the victim" (278).

Curiously, the other major patron of the Harlem Renaissance, Carl Van Vechten, also became notorious for a Dis and Dat ventriloquism that threatened to fetishize African-American difference. Although Cunard prided herself on a realism about race that she felt Van Vechten lacked, her attraction to "the zest" and "enjoyment" of being "very real" clearly propelled his "addiction" to African Americans (Kellner, *"Keep,"* 7).[28] Before and after the controversy set in motion by the publication of his portrait of Harlem, the bestselling novel *Nigger Heaven* (1926), Carl Van Vechten attained the same notorious identity in America that Cunard achieved in Europe, becoming a principal publicity icon of racechange during the Jazz Age (even as he publicized Harlem celebrities and visitors in his astonishingly numerous photographic portraits). A popular song of the time, "Go Harlem," advised listeners to "Go inspectin' like Van Vechten!" and he did attend Harlem's nightclubs, transvestite costume balls, and A'lelia Walker's 136th Street salon so frequently that (though he traveled by cab and at night) *Vanity Fair* claimed he was getting a heavy tan (Kellner, *Carl Van Vechten*, 198). Ignoring the fair complexion and blond hair of the Midwesterner, Miguel Covarrubias produced several caricatures which capture not so much Van Vechten in blackface as Van Vechten the African American.

Titled "A Prediction" (Fig. 4.6), one of Covarrubias's images prophesies that the color of the Harlemites with whom Van Vechten fraternized would somehow rub off on him. A different racechange narrative was told by Avery Hopwood, whose cautionary remarks to readers of *Nigger Heaven* sardonically hint that the

Figure 4.6 Miguel Covarrubias, *A Prediction*. Courtesy of Beinecke Library, Yale University.

whiteness of Van Vechten was a fiction: "I am explaining," Hopwood confided to Van Vechten, "that you really see little of Harlem, these days, but that you saw a great deal of it before you *passed*. They are all so surprised to hear about your Negro strain, but I tell them that your best friends *always knew*" (Kellner, *Carl Van Vechten*, 221). Similarly, in Rudolph Fisher's novel *The Walls of Jericho* (1928) a character patterned on Van Vechten declares, "'Downtown I'm only passing. These,' he waved grandiloquently [at blacks], 'are my people'" (117). Another cartoon by Covarrubias captures Van Vechten engaged in a strenuous version of the lindy hop, the black bottom, or the Charleston, again as a black man. Exactly this emphasis on Van Vechten's commonality with African Americans imbues Zora Neale Hurston's affectionate comment that "If Carl was a people instead of a person, I could then say, these are my people" (Kellner, *Carl Van Vechten*, 207).

The brouhaha over its title demonstrates, however, that the language of *Nigger Heaven* and in particular its white author's use of black vernacular shocked many readers. Van Vechten's father objected, as did W.E.B. Du Bois, to what the latter called "an astonishing and wearisome hodgepodge of laboriously stated facts, quotations and expressions" (Kellner, *Carl Van Vechten*, 209). Yet the novel influenced Claude McKay's landmark narrative, *Home to Harlem* (1928), regardless of his boast that "what I write is urged out of my blood. / There is no white man who could write my book" (*Selected Poems*, 50). And a number of powerful, independent black thinkers not only condoned but actually collaborated in Van Vechten's Dis and Dat. James Weldon Johnson, Walter White, and Rudolph Fisher read the galley proofs of *Nigger Heaven* for what they referred to as authenticity; Langston Hughes provided original lyrics to replace lines from the deleted song *Shake That Thing* (for which Van Vechten had forgotten to get copyright permission). Describing the process of revision before publication, Van Vechten's biographer calls "the working over of dialect . . . almost mathematical, as in the change from the conventional and inaccurate 'Dis am Nigger Heaven' to 'Dis heah is Nigger Heaven'" (220). Van Vechten, who used his connections in black cultural circles to engage in what Sollors calls "ethnic transvestism," produced a text that—like those purportedly real slave narratives authored by white abolitionists and unlike the more flagrantly ersatz productions of his contemporaries—raises crucial questions about who has what right to deploy racially inflected lexicons and experiences; however, even his collaborative work with African-American authorities displays subtle markings of its white author's unease at his linguistic appropriations.

"Ah calls et, specherly tonight, Ah calls et Nigger Heaven! I jes' nacherly think dis heah is Nigger Heaven" (15): A Lenox Avenue prostitute delivers this line early in the novel; yet—as if to underline the author's discomfort—a footnote later concedes that "While this informal epithet is freely used by Negroes among themselves, not only as a term of opprobrium, but also actually as a term of endearment, its employment by a white person is always fiercely resented" (26). Another sign of uneasiness may be the exploitation of what is called "eye dialect" in a contradictory manner: that is, "*Ah* calls et" but "*I* jes' nacherly think." A 1926 article in *The Crisis*, "The Negro in Art: How Shall He Be Portrayed?" by Van Vechten, further demonstrates his awareness of his precarious position as a linguistic trespasser whose borrowings might be viewed as poaching:

> Are Negro writers going to write about this exotic material while it is still fresh or will they continue to make a free gift of it to white authors who will exploit it until not a drop of vitality remains? (Kellner, "*Keep*," 65)

Clearly Van Vechten understood that his own aesthetic project would be judged a form of vampirism, draining the last drops of vitality out of fresh black material and eventually earning him the name "Von Vampton" in Ishmael Reed's satiric novel *Mumbo Jumbo* (1972).[29]

Whether or not their critics were justified in accusing them of vamping or vampirism, Cunard and Van Vechten combined outrage against racial injustice with a deep regard for African-American culture, a mixture of motives that distanced them from their (white) origins, providing them entrance into—but not citizenship in—another (black) country. Like Cunard, who denied personal accountability for a past injurious to black people while asking her white audience to shoulder such responsibility, Van Vechten used black talk to exhibit his commonality with the Other. Like Cunard's list, "Some Negro Slang," the vocabulary index at the end of *Nigger Heaven* signals identification (the white insider who understands the slang of blacks) and estrangement (the white newcomer or foreigner who admits his Ur-community of white readers will be mystified by such argot). In other words, the linguistic inventory as a genre registers the tension at work in twentieth-century racial ventriloquism. From *arnchy* (a person who puts on airs) and *August ham* (watermelon) to *struggle-buggy* (Ford) and *unsheik* (divorce), the slang of *Nigger Heaven* places on exhibit black linguistic strangeness, though Van Vechten's glossary flaunts more self-parodic playfulness than Cunard's, even sending the reader on a wild goose chase: "*boody*: see hootchie-pap" as well as "*hootchie-pap*: see boody" (285–86).

Taken together, Cunard and Van Vechten can stand for a generation of white artists crossing over into racially ghettoized material (often for libertarian as well as aesthetic reasons) and in the process deploying Dis and Dat: Waldo Frank in *Holiday* (1923), Eugene O'Neill in *All God's Chillun Got Wings* (1924), Sherwood Anderson in *Dark Laughter* (1925), DuBose Heyward in *Porgy* (1925), Marc Connelly in *The Green Pastures* (1930), and of course George Gershwin in *Porgy and Bess* (1935).[30] Notwithstanding their various levels of knowledge and sensitivity about black culture, all these white ventriloquists of dialect revert to the predicament of Cunard's line in "Equatorial Way": "This aint no white man's nigger." The very gestures they make toward ethnographic authenticity are set off by signs of their awareness that their counterfeits were plagiarized, sham, or simply simulated. With its grammatical and spelling mistakes—its double negatives, loss of final letters, appropriation of ghetto lingo, and give-and-take backchat—Cunard's Dis and Dat smacks of minstrelsy, as do any number of passages from *Nigger Heaven*.[31]

In the period when Freeman Gosden and Charles Correll made *Amos 'n' Andy* a smash hit with both white and black audiences, a number of white poets inadvertently displayed imperialist nostalgia and amnesia in their deployment of a racial ventriloquism that assumed with Cunard that whites are "unreal" or "*dim*" whereas blacks are "very real." Thus, William Carlos Williams's "Shoot It Jimmy!" (1923) sought to "Get the rhythm" of "Banjo jazz" (I.216). Wallace Stevens, who compared colonist to colonized in "Nudity at the Capital" and "Nudity in the Colonies" (1936), signed at least one personal letter with the name Sambo.[32] Two years after hearing Lindsay recite at the *Poetry* banquet, Carl Sandburg began a poem whose first lines are "I am the nigger. / Singer of songs . . . " ("Nigger," 23) and later he recorded the speech of a woman describing another "woman what / hustles / Never keeps nothin' / For all her hustlin'" ("Harrison Street Court," 64). Just as Amos 'n' Andy's "Recordin' to my figgers in de book" or "You gotta be repaired for that" perpetuated minstrel traditions, the Dis and Dat talk that surfaced in the work of white poets reveals (as strikingly as did the verse of Boomlay BOOM) minstrelsy's impact on modern literary diction. Possibly the most popular show ever broadcast on radio and still considered "the first great radio show," *Amos 'n' Andy*'s favorite sayings ("Ain't dat sumptin'" and "Holy mackerel") changed the nation's speech patterns, just as their malapropisms cracked up white as well as black audiences ("I denies the allegation," Kingfish pontificated to the judge, "and I resents the alligator").[33]

That a fine line divides comic hilarity from grotesque stereotyping becomes clear in the particularly gruesome evidence of minstrelsy's influence on e. e. cummings's surrealistic play *Him* (1927), specifically in the play-within-the-play composed by the blocked artist-hero (who is cummings's surrogate and named in the objective case, Him). One scene prefaces a black ensemble singing and dancing "Frankie and Johnie" with a dialogue between two "coalblack figures" engaged in the phatic patter of minstrelsy:

MALE(*Nervously*):   Who you nigga?
FEMALE (*Looking up, answers lazily*):   Ahs de ground.
MALE (*Apprehensively*):   Who de ground?
FEMALE (*Proudly*):   Ahs de ground.
MALE (*Fearfully*):   Wot, you de ground?
FEMALE (*Insolently*):   Yas ahs de ground, ahs de ripe rich deep sweet sleek an sleepy ground, de G-R-O-U-N-D GROUND. (49)

After a censor rises in the audience to stop their vulgarities, he is frightened out of the theater by Frankie showing him an amputated penis or, as this proleptic Lorena Bobbitt puts it, "The BEST PART OF THE MAN / WHO DONE ME WRONG" (56).[34] Although the above dialogue matches the racist stereotypes produced by minstrelsy's ridicule of the grammatical mistakes, confused pomposities, and malapropisms of Tambo and Bones, the avowedly liberal cummings turned to the demotic energy he sought to tap in black talk as an antidote to the hypocrisy and sterility of standard English, for—like Cunard—cummings believed about blacks, "Theys sO alive," a conviction meant to boomerang against the ontological inferiority or dimness of whites (*Complete Poems*, 622). As with the Boomlay BOOM works, Dis and Dat slang illustrates the ways in which twentieth-century racial ventriloquism recycled nineteenth-century minstrel traditions by playing them out in the campy, nihilistic cadences of "the rattle of the bones, and chuckle spread from ear to ear." Like the practitioners of Boomlay BOOM, the twentieth-century speakers of Dis and Dat denied black people verbal intentionality or integrity and then paradoxically lauded that lacking as a kind of anarchic playfulness. Therefore, like the minstrels, modernist ventriloquists repeatedly returned to touchstone texts about race and in doing so re-inscribed the association of African Americans with pre-linguistic being. Just as the minstrels obsessively recycled *Uncle Tom's Cabin*, for example, e. e. cummings produced a ballet entitled *Tom* (1931) that amounts to modernist minstrelsy.[35]

Cummings's exuberant African-American characters in *Tom* continued to be mysteriously inclined to the atavistism so evident among the inhabitants of Lindsay's "Congo" and Sitwell's "Gold Coast," or, for that matter, Heyward's Catfish Row, whose jubulent Dis and Dat community remains as "Exotic as the Congo, and still able to abandon themselves utterly to the wild joy of fantastic play" (115). Yet in his later work, cummings seems to be striving for a more sensitive approach to racial ventriloquism, one that would take hold in the literature produced after the Second World War. Consider the jazzy rhythms of a poem cummings published in 1940, verse inflected by the enormous impact of black music embodied in

> one slipslouch twi
> tterstamp
> coon wid a plon
> kykerplung
> guit
> ar

The guitar player, a jazz man—who "sho am / wick / id"—stands for a wickedness associated with the powerful forces of the Freudian id, with inebriation and "joy (eye kinely thank yoo)" (*Complete Poems*, 519). Like so many practitioners of Boomlay BOOM as well as Dis and Dat, cummings falls under the influence of jazz, drugs, and urbanity and thereby follows the advice he proffered in another poem where he urges his readers to "touch the black skin / of an angel named imagination" (639). In their admittedly racist deployments of minstrelsy, the ventriloquists of modernism nevertheless touched their muse and found the source of their inspiration to be black.

Self-Derisive Black Talk

The effect of the blues and of jazz on white ventriloquists from the forties on can be demonstrated most effectively through the achievement of Milton "Mezz" Mezzrow, a musician whose 1946 autobiography dramatizes the evolving relationship between racial ventriloquism and racechange. At the end of his memoir *Really the Blues* (whose very title highlights the problem of authenticity), Mezzrow provided a glossary like those of Cunard and Van Vechten, defining his own name, "The

Mezz," as *"the best brand of marihuana; anything unusually good"* (376), a term immortalized in the song "If You're a Viper": "Dreamed about a reefer five foot long, / The mighty mezz but not too strong" (215). Mezzrow, whose book includes a fairly long account of various "Jive" sessions with a "translation" provided in an appendix (354–60), had been born Jewish in Chicago and called a "nigger-lover" in the South.[36] After a prison stint in 1918, he quickly came to believe about the other inmates that he "not only loved those colored boys, but I was one of them— I felt closer to them than I felt to the whites" so

> I was going to spend all my time from then on sticking close to Negroes. They were my kind of people. And I was going to learn their music and play it for the rest of my days. *I was going to be a musician, a Negro musician*, hipping the world about the blues the way only Negroes can. (18; emphasis mine)

And at the triumphant moment he enters the "serene exaltation" of playing "real authentic jazz" with his clarinet, he does become Jimmy Noone, Johnny Dodds, Sidney Bechet, Tubby Hall, Baby Dodds, Zutty Singleton, King Oliver, Tommy Ladnier, "and yes, Louis too, the one and only Pops, the greatest of them all" (322–23).

Yet in his capacity as an autobiographer Mezzrow himself admits the difficulty of his linguistic position: Street "lingo has to be *heard*, not seen"; even if written down, it "would sound like plain gibberish"; for "how can any outsider latch on to the real flavor of a secret code in which *tick twenty* means ten o'clock and *line forty* means the price is twenty dollars; friends are addressed as *gate* or *slot*, verbal short-hand for *gatemouth* and *slotmouth*, which are inner-circle racial jokes to begin with" (220)? A sea change occurs between the transcription of jive—

SECOND CAT: Never no crummy, chummy. I'm gonna lay a drape under the trey of knockers for Tenth Street and I'll be on the scene wearin' the green (216)

—and its translation:

SECOND CAT: I never lie, friend. I'm going to bring a suit to the pawnshop to raise ten dollars, and I'll show up with some money. (355)

Like his heightened awareness of the difficulties of shuttling between two lan-guages, his sexual explicitness, his fascination with black music, and his absorp-tion with drugs, Mezzrow's comprehension of the overwhelming racism of white society signals not a break so much as a shift in emphasis in the deployment of racial ventriloquism after the Second World War. Mezzrow, who was drawn to the "feeling of brotherhood" in Harlem, believed that "the oppression that rules" the lives of African Americans "has caused a kind of fraternity to spring up"; being black means being "at the bottom of the pile, with all the weight of white society crushing you" (228). William Carlos Williams, who in *Paterson* wryly explained that everything he had written was for "the birds / or Mezz Mezzrow" (221), was also drawn to racial ventriloquism as a means to establish a fraternity with an op-pression that generated great music.[37]

After hearing Bunk Johnson's jazz band in 1945, Williams began work on "Boogie woogie writing" (84), a project related to his earlier view that African Americans were imbued with an authenticity bred of their existential nothingness; *In the American Grain* (1925) included, too, Williams's predictive declaration, "I wish I might write a book of [the black man's] improvisations in slang" (211) as well as his tribute to the African-American minstrel Bert Williams. Williams's attraction to black music and to the black Williams found an outlet in a collaborative work he set out to write in a jazzy, impromptu manner,[38] a novel entitled "Man Orchid" about a racechanging character who claims "I am black. Therefore I am white. Black, white. White black. Ampersand, quicksand: what's the difference?" (101). A study of the schizophrenia of American culture, the work suggests some sensitivity about racial identity, or so this meditation on its title indicates:

> Why the orchid?—to begin with. There's the old, tiresome and at bottom snobbish literary assumption that the Negro in America is an exotic bloom. Negro equals jungle. Despite the fact that he has been here longer than the second, third, even ninth generation Eurp [*sic*] European—Negro equals jungle. Then why doesn't the ofay bank president of German descent equal Black Forest? the Rutherford doctor of Welsh descent equal the cromlechs? or Welsh rarebit? (111)

Although many white writers of Williams's generation and of the next exploited black dialect after midcentury, they did so with an intensified apprehension about reductive stereotypes. As in the modernist period, during the second half of the twentieth century African rhythms and African-American vernacular assuage the burden of the past, denying accountability for guilt, but with more ideological footwork indicative of white sympathy for black oppression. "Look at me," postmodernist novelists and poets seem to say, "so deeply committed to alienation, so Other-identified as to be black." Curiously, though, their racial ventriloquism increasingly also exhibits an extraordinary self-consciousness about (their own collusion in) the racist roots of a discourse that maintains the subordination of people of color, a knowledge in part fashioned by the slang permeating the productions of the beat generation, whose artists made talking black/talking back *au courant* among dissidents. It was no accident that a so-called "holy barbarian" like Allen Ginsberg began his monumental beat poem *Howl* (1956) by describing his hysterical, naked, mad comrades "dragging themselves through the negro streets" or that he phrased his protest against "America" (1956) in terms of his identification with scapegoated African Americans: "America I am the Scottsboro boys" (1. 60).[39]

Yet the two mid-century writers who most brilliantly tackled the problematic ethics of racial ventriloquism—one in fiction, one in poetry—went far beyond the beats in the subtlety of their analyses. William Faulkner and John Berryman explore the comic demotic as a manifestation of the self-derision bred by white guilt about racial injustice. Ventriloquism's minstrel comedy becomes black humor in the works of both: Faulkner's tragic fiction satirizes humor at the expense of blacks as one more indication of a white stupidity and arrogance so profound as to call into question his own aesthetic project; Berryman's verse teeters always on the absurdly horrific, the grotesque, the painful exposure of the white speaker's linguistic bad faith. What fascinates both writers is their own entanglement in—attraction toward but also revulsion against—a racial ventriloquism they know to be damaging to African Americans and unscrupulous for Euro-Americans, though endlessly enticing. Both achieved the consummate feat of their artistry by representing their realization that their effort to find in an Africanist presence an escape from their own fake experiences would be a doomed undertaking.

The title story of Faulkner's *Go Down, Moses* (1940) shrewdly contrasts the languages of whites and blacks throughout, concentrating especially on the guilt-ridden, Harvard-educated lawyer Gavin Stevens's inability to comprehend the grief Mollie Worsham Beauchamp expresses over her dead grandson. Drawing upon the old spiritual that furnishes Faulkner's title, Mollie's incantatory lament with her brother—

> "Sold him in Egypt and now he dead."
> "Oh yes, Lord. Sold him in Egypt."
> "And now he dead."
> "Sold him to Pharaoh." (363)

—silences, flusters, and excludes the white lawyer, even as it expresses her understanding that this plea for a savior to "let my people go" comes too late for Butch, the lost grandchild, "now he dead." Baffled but sympathetic, Stevens sets out to enlist the charity of the white community to pay for Butch's funeral.

Beginning with an image of a black man incarcerated after killing a Chicago policeman and eventually executed, Faulkner's story ends with a telling moment that diagnoses racial ventriloquism as a reflex of white shame over the lasting, debilitating inheritance of slavery. That legacy means both the hardened grandson and the mourning grandmother are in danger of losing their voices. The brief sketch of Butch's few moments before execution portrays a fated gangster or gambler, complete with lacquered hair, fawn-colored flannel suit, and "a voice which was anything under the sun but a southern voice or even a negro voice" (351).[40] But the powerful "negro voice" of his grandmother is also threatened by the end of the narrative when the editor of the town newspaper explains to Stevens how Mollie had requested him to print the story of her grandson's death and funeral:

> "She said, 'Is you gonter put hit in de paper?"
> "What?"
> "That's what I said," the editor said. "And she said it again: 'Is you gonter put hit in de paper? I wants hit all in de paper. All of hit.'" (364–65)

Three aspects of this request strike the editor as ludicrous: that Mollie does not understand the details of her grandson's shameful end, that she cannot read, and that she speaks differently from him. By depicting a white man parodying the speech of a black woman—not in her own diction (as represented in the story) but in conventional black dialect—Faulkner examines racial impersonation as an act of violence comparable to that at work in the dynamics of blackface. "'Is you gonter put hit in de paper?'" becomes a kind of death sentence or spirit-murder. For the newspaper editor distances himself from the Other (she is so different from me) through incorporation (I can be her) that effectively destroys (she need not exist). If Mollie has been erased by the editor's impersonation of her, does she serve as an index of Faulkner's authorial arrogance as well? Are the African-American characters Faulkner created a reflex of his guilty awareness that he is not the Other and, indeed, that his linguistic transgressions have helped to Other black people?

Like the writing of the obituary which Mollie would not be able to read, the recording of the editor's mimicry of Mollie's speech effactually marks Faulkner's recognition of the iniquity of his own ventriloquism—because, of course, Mollie's speeches in the narrative (as "directly" presented earlier) have also been constructed by a white man, namely, Faulkner himself. As if producing evidence of his own continued entanglement in debilitating racial lies, Faulkner's tale sentimentalizes the charity of whites—the townspeople generously respect and fund Mollie's wish for a funeral in spite of their condescending incomprehension—and thereby deflects the reader's attention away from Mollie's tragedy. The reader ends up weeping over the pathos of the town's efforts at restitution rather than the black community's losses. In "Go Down, Moses," the author of numerous African-American characters presents the ethical complications behind minstrelsy's ongoing influence, casting suspicion on the art of racial ventriloquism that served as the basis of his own artistry and that soon brought so much flack to William Styron for *The Confessions of Nat Turner* (1967).

It seems paradoxical that the contributors to *William Styron's Nat Turner: Ten Black Writers Respond* (1968) agreed with Styron's own statement that "most Southern white people *cannot* know or touch black people," that the contemporary African American "may feel that it is too late to be known, and that the desire to know him reeks of outrageous condescension" (Styron, 135). Of course, the brouhaha at the publication of Styron's fictionalized account of a slave insurrectionist proved that the civil rights movement had intervened to usher in a period inhospitable to whites' use of black talk: During the early fifties, the NAACP managed to force CBS to suspend production of the hugely successful TV adaptation of *Amos 'n' Andy*.[41] Seeking to cancel both the TV and radio versions, NAACP critics believed the "show tends to strengthen the conclusion among uninformed and prejudiced people that Negroes are inferior, lazy, dumb, and dishonest" (M. Watkins, 521).

So we must understand the Tambo and Bones routines interspersed throughout the poems of Berryman's *The Dream Songs* (1964, 1968) as part of the stubborn depravity of its main character, Henry, and not just a manifestation of the liberal sympathy his author claimed when he described his identification with Jews and blacks who suffer the stigma of difference: "I feel extremely lucky to be white" (Linebarger, 85), Berryman explained, demonstrating his understanding of what today is called white privilege. A devotee of Bessie Smith, Victoria Spivey, and Teddy Grace, Berryman resembled cummings and Williams in his effort to utilize jazz and blues rhythms. Given his sensitivity to racism and his appreciation of black culture, Berryman surely understood the points Patricia J. Williams has recently made about "black speech" which is invariably marked "as low-status" when used by whites: that it is "very annoying to us black people," that it "makes most of you white people sound ridiculous," and that any attempt to "'sound like' should probably be avoided" (*Rooster's Egg*, 199–200).

Yet Berryman persisted in what he knew to be an especially degrading form of racial ventriloquism, a fact made evident by the major impact on him of Carl Wittke's book on minstrelsy, *Tambo and Bones*: "'GO IN, BRACK MAN, DE DAY'S YO' OWN,'" taken from *Tambo and Bones*, stands as the first epigraph of *77 Dream Songs*. The sentiment voiced here and throughout Berryman's *Dream Songs* often sounds liberal or even radical; however, the language adopted is that of a highly contaminated Dis and Dat.[42] Indeed, so adulterated is Berryman's black talk that it calls attention to the act of ventriloquism, foregrounding its status as a debased imitation and thereby its tendency to veer into a performance something like a drag show. Take, for example, the opening of this poem about the failure of integration after the historic 1954 Supreme Court decision:

> Afters eight years, be less dan eight percent,
> distinguish' friend, of coloured wif de whites
> in de School, in de Souf.
> —Is coloured gobs, is coloured officers,
> Mr Bones. Dat's nuffin? —Uncle Tom,
> sweep shut yo mouf,
>
> is million flocking from de proper job,
> de fairest houses & de churches eben.
> —You may be right, Friend Bones.
> Indeed you is. Dey flyin ober de world,
> de pilots, ober ofays. (60)

The first speaker, Henry, rarely talks in black talk, but here he uses it to protest against segregation in Southern schools. After being questioned by the second speaker about advances in the military, Henry calls his interlocutor an Uncle Tom and earns his agreement that job, housing, and even religious discrimination will result in some kind of race warfare. The poem ends with the two men sadly concurring, "mos peoples gonna *lose*."

Who are these two amicable antagonists doing this linguistic drag? In an introductory note Berryman describes Henry as "a white American in early middle age sometimes in blackface, who has suffered an irreversible loss and talks about himself sometimes in the first person, sometimes in the third, sometimes even in the second; he has a friend, never named, who addresses him as Mr Bones and variants thereof." Not to be confused with the poet, Henry House or Henry Cat or Huffy Henry finds a critic, a comforter, a companion in his counterpart, who frequently employs black talk, playing Tambo to Henry's Bones. Like earlier practitioners of Boomlay BOOM and Dis and Dat, Berryman remains fascinated by the ways in which racial ventriloquism unmakes meaning. The second poem, dedicated to Daddy Rice, who jumped Jim Crow in 1828, remains incomprehensible mumbo jumbo in its use of slang ("The jane is zoned!"), its opting for sound over sense ("Have ev'ybody head for Maine, / utility-man take a train?"), its ungrammatical syntax and nonreferential pronouns ("Arrive a time when all coons lose dere grip, / but is he come?"), and its puns ("Poll-cats" for people who vote or col-lectors of poll-tax or the cutters of poles/trees).[43] Toward the end of *The Dream Songs*, the poet admits, "These Songs are not meant to be understood, you under-stand. / They are only meant to terrify & comfort" (366).

Why would Berryman focus his verse on injustice—social, political, racial—in a language so polluted with the guilt of past oppressions? Or, as Aldon Lynn Nielsen phrases this question, "How seriously can readers take an argument for the recognition of the rights of Afro-Americans when that argument is couched in de-risive terms and made in the course of an oneiric 'coon show'?" (143). But per-haps readers are meant to take seriously not simply the civil rights contentions but their incongruent relation to the contemptuous framework in which they appear, a framework that mordantly measures the failure of even the most sympathetic Euro-Americans. At least in part, the self-consciously white Berryman represents his predominantly white audience's stereotypical image of blacks so to examine one of his major obsessions and the one upon which his greatness as a confessional poet rests, namely, the difficulty of altering what is known to be destructive, the compulsive nature of evil, the recalcitrance of subjectivity despite the enlighten-ment furnished by reason, the inflexibility of habits known to be deleterious. Dis and Dat's retrograde pleasures give Berryman a chance to display his addiction to a host of damaging activities he knows to be harmful not only to himself (drink-ing, whoring around, smoking, suicidal abjection) but also to the culture at large (consumerism, militarism, racism).

To begin with, though, *The Dream Songs* presents the relationship of Tambo and Bones as a consolation, for Tambo provides solace, ballast, companionship, and a sense of perspective for the usually anguished Henry. Whenever Henry gets over-ly melodramatic, morbid, or maudlin, Tambo grounds him in the easy intimacy of the practical and everyday. In some poems, then, Tambo plays shrink or father con-fessor to Mr. Bones as patient or sinner, though neither exhibits much hope for a cure:

> The glories of the world struck me, made me aria, once.
> —What happen then, Mr. Bones?
> if be you cares to say. (26)

Later in the sequence when Henry, going out the door with his "cigs," his "flask-ie," and his "crystal cock," asks a blessing, Tambo's realism brings him down to earth:

> —Mr. Bones,
> you makes too much
> démand. I might be 'fording you a hat:
> it gonna rain. (64)

Lusty Henry—as in "Love her he doesn't but the thought he puts / into that young woman / would launch a national product"—encounters Tambo's exasperated, avuncular deterrents: "—Mr. Bones, *please*" (69).[44] Vaudevillean give-and-take recaptures an easy, playful bonding between men, adding credence to Leslie

Fiedler's insight about Americans that they are "Born theoretically white," but "are permitted to pass . . . [their] adolescence as imaginary Negroes" (134). Its inane energies also serve as a kind of antidote to depressing seriousness as well as a reminder that the world is a stage and the show must go on. In the midst of what Henry calls the "lonely whines" he whips out in times of "fleeing double"—that is, seeing double and fleeing trouble and being so muddled as not to be able to say which—Tambo calls for a song and dance (114). At Henry's grief over a childhood loss, Tambo offers a handkerchief and advice: "now set / your left foot by my shoulder, all that jazz, / . . . hum a little, Mr. Bones" (76).

One of the rare poems in which Tambo predominates focuses on the central tragedy of Berryman's life, the suicide of his father during his youth, but does so by framing the memory with vaudevillean trappings that counteract bathos:

> —That's enough of that, Mr. Bones. *Some* lady you make.
> Honour the burnt cork, be a vaudeville man,
> I'll sing you now a song
> the like of which may bring your heart to break:
> he's gone! and we don't know where. (143)

The poem focuses on the child's sense of abandonment and guilt by shifting between Tambo's "you was just a little" and Henry's plaintive "He was going to swim out, with me forevers." Only through the distance created by this dual fictionalization of himself, only through the banter of these two blackfaced endmen going through the paces of their numbers, is the pain of recollection bearable for the poet. A corrective to melancholia, Tambo stands for endurance and survival not by ignoring pain or injustice but by joking about it. He is a self-defined "pro-man," strutting "out from the wings" even and especially when "it's curtain-call" time (220).

"Harms and the child I sing": Berryman's neologisms in what he calls his "minstrelsy" (231) allow him to bumble into insights, here the conflation between arms and harm, man and child (149). Similarly, Tambo's garbled, punning supposition that Henry's "got a lessen up your slave" (84) rings true for Berryman, too: minstrelsy's enslaved characters furnish him with lessons from a Blakean Bible of Hell to teach in a fallen language that lessens the humanity of blacks and whites alike. Throughout *The Dream Songs*, racial impersonation flaunts itself as an ersatz, campy form of drag. Though Tambo parenthetically remarks about their routines "Some time we'll do it again, / in whiteface" (220), blackface emphasizes the vulgarity, the speciousness, the pointlessness of Berryman's surrealistic actors and their routines. Mr. Bones is Berryman's fanciful penis, his prancing skeleton, engaged in an endlessly entertaining dance of love and death, providing cheap thrills not only for those readers Sylvia Plath called "the peanut-crunching crowd" but also to divert his own attention away from the end he always craved ("Lady Lazarus," 26).

"Negroes, ignite! you have nothing to use but your brains" (232). Each parodic substitution in this line echoes with the original to elaborate upon Berryman's comment on the legacy of racial ventriloquism he had inherited. Negroes, the workers of the white imagination, should give up on the Marxist hope of uniting and ignite instead, in fighting or rioting, in rage or in creative energy, or so Henry proclaims in a poem about his struggle to stay off the sauce, to wait upon the Lord, to free his life by controlling his fate. With nothing to lose and everything to gain, blacks should use what they have, for only their brains or what Blake called "mental strife" can break down the chains that bind them. Or perhaps blacks should lose their brains because their minds retard the liberating act of igniting. But of course such prosey translations fall into precisely the platitudes and pieties Berryman abhorred as a vacuous mode of liberal self-certification; "When the mind dies," he admonished sardonically, "it exudes rich critical prose" (170). And, in fact, Berryman remained unconvinced that brains (black or white) could break the chains of societal habits or personal additions.

Tambo's response to Henry's painful efforts to remain sober and receive religious certitude allows Berryman to racialize his thoughts about physical failing, spiritual falling. Calling for a drink—"one-two, the old thrones / topple, dead sober. The decanter, pal! / Pascal, we free & loose"—Henry haplessly fails, falling back into his old ways, reaching for a drink but also refusing Pascal's reasoning about the existence of God. Pascal probably drops into this poem about the dark night of the soul, placing "cagey bets" with the poet, because his belief in God was based on his view that there was nothing to lose and everything to gain from such a wager. Just as the poet stubbornly and irrationally refuses such a consolation of philosophy, "Negroes" (also with nothing to lose, everything to gain) will be no more successful in their quest for social freedom than he in his quest for the rectitude of sobriety and faith. Though the garbled language of Dis and Dat made it inevitable that Berryman would be misconstrued, his levity signifies his helpless acquiescence in a sordid discourse, a corrupt social order.

Embedding himself in a debased linguistic past so as to dramatize the hopelessness of the libertarian causes he championed, Berryman analyzed the self-derisive fatalism he felt about himself as a promoter of a grievous past. Tambo's retort to Mr. Bones—"you too advancer with your song, / muching of which are wrong" (99)—stands as a final epigraph for a self-reflexive tradition of racial ventriloquism that testifies to the acknowledged inability of white artists to represent the black Other and, by extension, the white self that longs to escape solipsism by knowing (or owning its own) Otherness. For Berryman, the failure to find a language to break out of his own and civilization's doomed patterns returns him repeatedly to the inauthenticity of whites talking black. What the modernists viewed as a dialect of energy and liberation had become a dead-end, a self-conscious register of corruption for the post-modernist. Berryman's achievement consists in laying bare the drollery and despair that infiltrate racial parodies in the lives of Euro-Americans who feel driven to speak what they suspect they cannot feel: the tantalizing interiority of the Other.

In contemporary times, admissions of white guilt about linguistic racechange often present white black talk either as an indefensible but enthralling trope of condescension or of exploitation. John Barth's The Floating Opera (1956, 1967) offers a good example of the former analysis in its conclusion which features the

"Ethiopian Tidewater Minstrels" show. Barth's suicide-obsessed hero, the aptly named Todd (*tod* is German for death), immediately understands the pathetic attraction of the "knights of the burnt cork" (238):

> Tambo and Bones vindicated our ordinariness; made us secure in the face of mere book learning; their every triumph over Mr. Interlocutor was a pat on our backs. Indeed, a double pat: for were not Tambo and Bones but irresponsible Negroes? (239)

Curiously, however, the climactic performance of *Adam's Original & Unparalleled Floating Opera* convinces the melancholy Todd not to commit suicide and does so in part by persuading him of the senselessness not only of living but of dying. Precisely the nihilistic hilarity, the threadbare facticity and absurdity of the actors' impersonations on the showboat provide an ironic but sustaining image of the games people play not only in art but in life.

Far more disturbing in its analysis of black talk as a sexual exploitation and perversion of whites is Bernard Malamud's *The Tenants* (1971), a meta-critical novel about two novelists, the Jewish one named Lesser but usually called "the writer," and the African American named sometimes Bill Spearmint, sometimes Willie Shakespear, but usually called "the black." The work of fiction Bill begins composing includes a chapter about his drunken mother and

> an ofay who liked to pretend to talk nigger talk. It made him feel good to do it though it was fake black talk. He did not come from the South, he came from Scranton, Pa. He came to my mama because she charged one dollar and it wasn't before long that he used to get it for free. (94–95)

As the narrative slips from third to first person and we enter Bill's autobiographical account of the humiliations of his mother and of himself as a child witness, the horror of the ofay's "nigger talk" feels like a kind of rape.

In Bill's text, the white man (known as Rubber Dick because of his "big prick") returns one night when the mother is gone. Offering money to the nine-year-old black boy—"Heah's a quotah mo. Now unzip mah pants and the money is yo's. Bof the dime and the quotah"—Rubber Dick makes a proposition terrifying to Willie, but somehow less horrifying than his fake black talk:

> "Don't take it out, please," I asked him.
> "Not till you show me kin you open yo mouf wide an covah yo teef wif yo lips like this."
> He showed me how to cover my teeth.
> "I will do it if you stop talking nigger talk to me."
> He said honey he would, and also I was a smart boy and he loved me very much. He was talking like a whitey again. (96)

For the black author of the scene, mourning the childhood degradations he had suffered, the bought boy manages to obtain—with his mouth made into a receptacle for the white man's speech. A gruesome deal is struck; ersatz black talk relinquished, white semen accepted. But the white creator of the black writer of the scene stands accused by it of verbal propositions condemning blacks to an enforced prostitution comparable to the sexual abuse of children, for Malamud knows himself to be Lesser, realizes that in writing about Bill he is writing about the sort of man who "do not wish his words to be in your book" (195), and understands too that minstrel nightmares—"What he done did see, / He gnawin this white bone, / What that you eatin, Mr. Bones?" (133)—continue to haunt not only his characters' imagination but also his own. As the plot of *The Tenants* progresses and the black and white central characters trade places in an antagonistic *folie à deux* that can lead only to their common annihilation, each "feels"—but cannot speak—"the anguish of the other" (211).

5

PSYCHOPATHOLOGIES OF BLACK ENVY

Queer Colors

That the PENIS of an African is larger than that of an European has, I believe, been shewn in every anatomical school in London. Preparations of them are preserved in most anatomical museums; and I have one in mine.
—Dr. Charles White

[T]he Negro is fixated at the genital; or at any rate he has been fixated there. Two realms: the intellectual and the sexual. An erection on Rodin's *Thinker* is a shocking thought. One cannot decently "have a hard on" everywhere. The Negro symbolizes the biological danger; the Jew, the intellectual danger.
—Frantz Fanon

"You know how I'd like to fuck her now? I just realized—if I could get into a *spade bag* . . . like if I could pretend to be a spade . . . yeah, that's it, *spade-rape bag*. You think she'd lie still for some *burnt cork*, B.?"
—Terry Southern

On its July 27, 1994, cover, a notorious issue of *Time* magazine—featuring a "photo-illustration" of O. J. Simpson's mug shot that darkened his skin, blurred his features, and thickened the stubble on his chin—transformed one of America's most beloved athletes into the country's most familiar bogeyman. Its designer, Matt Mahurin, used a computer to produce the illustration because he wanted "a more somber photo, for a compelling story—an American tragedy" (*Herald-Times*, June 22, 1994, p. A3). Like Dreiser's novel of that name, the American tragedy to which the cover legend referred is domestic violence, in the Simpson case the wife-battering that allegedly ended in the death of Nicole Brown Simpson. But perhaps another tragedy, one of racial violence against men, is enacted by the reproduction itself, specifically through its use of blackface to execute a character assassination. Blacken the man, *Time* magazine implies, and you simultaneously drain him of moral discernment while accentuating his physicality, thus intensifying his brawn even as you criminalize it.

Unlike the colonized subject analyzed in Fanon's psychological study of racism, a black man who adopts the culture of the civilizing nation and thus "becomes whiter as he renounces his blackness, his jungle" (18), O. J. Simpson seemed "to many whites" like "a fellow white man [who] grew darker as the proceedings went on" (*Time*, Oct. 16, 1995, p. 43). Mahurin's illustration, then, functioned something like the portrait of Dorian Gray, predicting the hero's fall from grace. As hypermasculinized as the blackface rapists Gus and Lynch in *The Birth of a Nation*, Simpson is nevertheless arrested like the ineffective, boyish Jolson in *The Jazz Singer*, for the mug shot frames the man, transforming him into a mugger whose macho days are numbered. As Fanon slyly hints in one of my epigraphs, the biological danger posed by the black man's "hard on" paradoxically exempts him from modeling the perfection epitomized by Rodin's *Thinker*. As the passage of dialogue from Terry Southern's novel *Blue Movie* (1970) intimates, then, white people could project masculinist proclivities and misogynist antipathies onto personified "*spade-rape bag[s]*."[1]

That the stereotype of the black rapist coexists with the equally resilient image of the black eunuch; that behind the "buck" of, for example, *The Birth of a Nation* lurks the "boy" of, for instance, *The Jazz Singer* means the image of the black man has displayed both an intensification and a diminishment of masculinity. Two powerfully disturbing portraits of black men created by white artists—one fictional, one photographic—furnish primal scenes of instruction in which the displaying of male genitalia reveals the anxieties that shape contradictory constructions of black masculinity and that explain the nature of explicitly sexual fantasies of racechange during the second half of the twentieth century. In particular, Saul Bellow's novel *Mr. Sammler's Planet* (1970) and Robert Mapplethorpe's photograph "Man in Polyester Suit" (1980) deploy shockingly explicit images that, on the one hand, correlate black male subjectivity with the body and specifically with the penis, an association that has obviously contributed to the idea of the hypermasculinized black stud; on the other hand, by virtue of exposing the black penis for/to the white gaze, both artists deflate it, thereby self-consciously participating in the manifold ways in which a racist culture wrests authority and symbolic power from African Americans.

Bellow and Mapplethorpe muster the gruesome logic that stimulates eroticized fantasies of racechange in the post-World War II period. Put in Lacanian terms, this reasoning supposes that the black man who *is* his penis neither has nor ever will have the phallus.[2] To be sure, as any orthodox Lacanian would immediately interject, all men have penises, but none possesses the phallus. Not a real organ but instead an attribute of power or meaning, the phallus remains a signifier beyond the reach of all human beings. Yet, as Jane Gallop has pointed out in her cleverly entitled "Phallus/Penis: Same Difference," ever since Freud termed the woman's version of the castration complex "penis envy," the phallus belonging to the ideal other has been confused with the penis of an embodied male subject (124).[3] That male subject whose penis often seemed to embody the phallus was of course implicitly white. What Bellow and Mapplethorpe lay bare in their quite different ways is how the black man provides what—taking a clue from Edward Carpenter—we might call an Intermediate Type, a fantastic image of a nonphallic penis or an anti-establishment masculinism, one that repels the novelist but attracts the photographer.[4]

Mr. Sammler's Planet, Bellow's study of an Eastern European Holocaust survivor in New York City, dramatizes its central character's alienation as he attempts to inhabit a world he can only partially affirm after having been literally buried alive by the Nazis during the Second World War. Early in the novel, Sammler intently observes a black pickpocket who eventually sees the aging immigrant watching him. Acknowledging his fascination in the crime but fleeing the scene, Sammler finds himself confronted by the criminal in the lobby of his apartment building. Although the African American "no more spoke than a puma would," he delivers a silent message or warning:

> The black man had opened his fly and taken out his penis. It was displayed to Sammler with great oval testicles, a large tan-and-purple uncircumcised thing—a tube, a snake; metallic hairs bristled at the thick base and the tip curled beyond the supporting, demonstrating hand, suggesting the fleshly mobility of an elephant's trunk, though the skin was somewhat iridescent rather than thick or rough. (49)

"It was displayed": The passive voice here hints that the black man himself does not or cannot control his bestial penis. Because "The thing was shown with mystifying certitude," even "lordliness," Sammler responds to the "shock" of this experience by wondering "what was the object of displaying the genitalia?" and by recalling a scene of phallic exhibitionism attributed to a President of the United States who demanded to know from representatives of the press "whether a man so well hung could not be trusted to lead his country" (66). What power of intimidation and violence links the black pickpocket and the white Commander-in-Chief, mesmerizing Sammler?

To some extent, Sammler's voyeurism accords romance to the "princeliness" of the black con man ostensibly motivated by "an idea of *noblesse*" (294), one indication that the survivor prefers the somewhat iridescent genitals of the pickpocket to the messiness of female sexuality: "Females were naturally more prone to grossness, had more smells, needed more washing, clipping, binding, pruning, grooming, perfuming, and training" (36). Still, metallic and tubelike, the uncircumcized black penis in its rank physicality faintly repels the fastidious immigrant so understandably terrified of weaponry but also of nature, of the earthly tomb into which the Nazis had once long ago thrown him as if dead. Given "the sex ideology" of the day, the black man's "huge piece of sex flesh, half-tumescent in its pride," may symbolize "superlegitimacy or sovereignty" to the bankrupt society at large. But to sardonic Sammler, who has mastered the lessons of the body in pain, it quickly descends to the level of ridiculous physical protuberances: snakes, elephants' trunks, and anteaters' snouts (55).

The scene of exposure in *Mr. Sammler's Planet* is not unrelated to an infamously sardonic query put by Bellow that implicitly sets the terms civilization and Africa in opposition: "Who is the Tolstoi of the Zulus?"[5] According to squeamish Sammler, "the sexual ways of the seraglio and of the Congo bush" would contaminate

Enlightenment ideals (of "Liberty, Fraternity, Equality"), substituting in their stead such presumably immoral, inane principles as "Adultery," "the rights of women," "the unity of the different races affirmed," and "the right to be uninhibited, spontaneous, urinating, defecating, belching, coupling in all positions . . . " (32–33). For the displaced European, as for his creator, "the peculiar aim of sexual niggerhood for everyone" (162) must be defeated because the "superlegitimacy" of the black man's organ merely reflects corrupt social values—the lying, cheating, bullying criminality that saturates American culture from the bottom to the top, from the petty thief on the street to the President in the White House. Yet the fact that the pickpocket is last seen in Bellow's book struggling for possession of a camera (which contains shots of his pickpocketing activity) and bloodied from a beating inflicted at Sammler's instigation hints at the black prince's vulnerability. He has to be rescued eventually by the conscience-stricken philosopher king, Sammler, or he would be pummeled to death.[6] Despite the "intense animal pressing-power, the terrific swelling of the neck and the tightness of the buttocks" of this walking muscular member of society, he is last seen prostrate on the pavement, his face crushed, his skin gashed, his cheeks bloodied, fully liable to painful intimations of his own mortality.

With its focus on a bared black penis jutting out of the trunk of an otherwise fully clothed man, Robert Mapplethorpe's "Man in Polyester Suit" (Fig. 5.1) almost seems to place the viewer in the position of Sammler surprised in his lobby even as it meditates on Bellow's concluding vision of the black man vanquished by his inability to wrest control over the shots a camera has taken of his crimes. For Mapplethorpe draws attention to the ways in which African-American men have been refused jurisdiction over the representation of their own sexuality. Decapitated, the model of Mapplethorpe's audacious photograph stands disclosed, though fully clothed, symbolized by his sex. Indeed, the shocking contrast between the costume of culture (at least mythologically created to cover the sexual parts) and the exhibited sexual organ highlights the exposed flesh. The thrill of an erotic photo of an exposed man posing for the male photographer in part derives from the camera's height and angle, which brings the Sammler-like voyeur to his knees, situating him quite definitively and respectfully at eye level with what's central here, the sex that is the point of the picture, the male/male desire that connects Mapplethorpe and his subject.

Yet, as if he were a suspect or a specimen, the model's face must be hidden from view. As in cartoons of dressed-up animals, moreover, his relaxed penis emerges out of the suit like the tail of a puma or the trunk of an elephant or the snout of an anteater, biological nature putting the lie to the costume of culture. And the title emphasizes the generic disposition of this "Man" not in *a* specific outfit but instead "in Polyester Suit," wording that puts on display an ethnographic oddity (like "Animal in Human Clothing"). The sex at the center of the picture simply is the man who merely wears the polyester suit. Paradoxically, the visual evidence of masculinity here—because it exists for the viewer's inspection—emasculates the passive object of the photographer's gaze. A portrait of the signified, not the signifier, a picture of a visible and physical object rather than a veiled symbol of law

Figure 5.1   Robert Mapplethorpe, *Man in Polyester Suit* (1980), unique gelatin silver print, 40 × 30 in. Collection of Baldwin Fong. Copyright © 1980, The Estate of Robert Mapplethorpe/courtesy of A+C Anthology.

or lack, the photograph disempowers. For the "dark-veined, heavy thing" that is the literal penis, as Nancy K. Miller points out, remains "prosaic," unmediated by highminded concepts of the symbolic order that cluster about the magisterial phallus (145). Even the most standardized clothes of Western culture cannot fashion Mapplethorpe's headless model into a properly authoritative man.

What is it about this particular picture—as well as the many other images in the

Black Book (1986) collection—that makes it seem even more dangerous than far more violent, contorted shots like, for instance, the photographer's self-portrait with a whip handle inserted into his anus? Does "Man in Polyester Suit," endorsing the view of the eighteenth-century Dr. Charles White that "the PENIS of an African is larger than that of an European," prove that Mapplethorpe took the picture because he simply wanted to "have one" in his own possession? Emasculating by hypermasculinizing its subject, the photograph could—by fixing him at the physical level of the penis—contribute to those dangerous mythologies of black male predation on white women that were often used to warn against miscegenation or to justify lynching at the turn of the century.[7]

By means of cropping and lighting, Kobena Mercer and Isaac Julien have argued, the camera's fetishistic attention to one body part "affirms and denies that most fixed of racial myths in the white man's mind: that all black men have got bigger willies than he has" (150).[8] Excessive sexuality or an inability to control sexual passion—often imagined in terms of the large penis—has always characterized the male Other, be he a Jew, a homosexual, or a black.[9] So the decapitated trunk of the subject seems to deprive the man in the suit of subjectivity. Mindless matter devoid of morals or manners, "the Negro is eclipsed"—to use Fanon's phrasing—for "He is turned into a penis. He *is* a penis" (120). No wonder that one critic has linked this photograph to Mapplethorpe's penchant for "domineering erotic routines," especially "coprophagy" (since its "compulsory diet of excrement" symbolically punished black lovers for "their crime in having caused him to desire them" (Conrad 90)).

Still, the model clearly has consented to this pose which just as obviously occurs within the careful lighting of a studio. As Richard Avedon understood about the photographic studio which isolates people from their environment, subjects there "become in a sense . . . symbolic of themselves" (Sontag, 187). In addition, symmetry in Mapplethorpe's design stresses the representative content and artifice of the shot. A studied piece of white shirt peeks out of the fly to frame the penis, much as the skin on the shaft sets off the hidden head, much as the delicately veined hands balance the delicately veined "third hand," displaying the sensitivity of flesh as opposed to the real insult here: the clueless polyester. With its subject's quarter-angled pose, arms slightly bent, the image does seem "a parody of men's fashion photography of the Sears catalog school" (Sante, 46). An enemy of the synthetic respectability postulated by the cheap fabric of the suit, the model— like the photographer—thumbs his metaphorical nose at the viewer, flaunting his flagrant defiance of the rules. Therefore the picture puns on the word "exposure" in sexuality and in photography. Who is the pervert here: the black man exposing himself or the white photographer making his exposures; the people who enjoy the picture or the critic who reproduces it in her book? In other words, is the prurience of the viewer addressed by Mapplethorpe and his model, as if they were saying to the likes of Saul Bellow and his Mr. Sammler, "This is how you whites really see all blacks"?[10] Does black skin mean whites see no face at all?

What nauseates Bellow and fascinates Mapplethorpe is an uncanny, different kind of masculinism, an excessively physical masculinity stripped of traditionally patriarchal privilege. Certainly the sexual fantasies of racechange composed by white men and women from midcentury on return over and over again to the black penis-not-a-phallus, ringing changes on a phenomenon I am calling "black envy" to invoke Freud's idea of "penis envy."[11] Since American culture denied most black men "the Name of the Father"—the genealogical, linguistic, economic authority traditionally signified by the phallus—the black man excommunicated from the symbolic suffered an iconographic devolution into the penis incarnate and then was pathologized by whites fearful or ashamed about their own representational violence. Because of such double binds, however, the black man who had historically been denied the patronymic and defined as three-fifths of a citizen could also offer an alternative, alluring model of the masculine, one lacking oppressive claims to a restrictive superiority.[12] When what Mira Schor considers the prevalent "pattern of diminishing or hiding the penis" was finally broken by twentieth-century painters, sculptors, and photographers, the represented biological appendage could unveil the phallus, undermining its power (6, 15). If, as Schor speculates, "black men may be allowed big penises because, in the myopia of a Eurocentric culture, they are *denied* the *phallus* of language and history" (12), they might become especially resonant images of an unmediated, illegal, anarchic eroticism.

Whereas Freud wrote about a penis envy that supposedly only affected women, I will focus here on the black envy expressed by white men and women of letters who have imagined blackness as a renegade, masculine Third Sex divested of patriarchal entitlement (a mode of thinking that fetishizes black men even as it effectively obliterates the existence of black women).[13] During the period following the Second World War, when conventional models of masculinity had proved themselves demonstrably destructive and outdated, the trope of the penis-not-a-phallus became especially glamorous as a way of flirting with titillating alternatives to normative heterosexuality. As in Bellow's *Mr. Sammler's Planet* and Mapplethorpe's "Man in Polyester Suit," the genital distinctiveness ascribed to the black man by the white homosexualizes their bond: Sammler's spying on the pickpocket bespeaks a voyeuristic pleasure the black character intuits; even though he conceals his subject's face, Mapplethorpe wants the "Man in Polyester Suit" out, at least as out as the photographer himself is. Precisely the intensification and diminishment of masculinity characteristic of the African American's image also frequently mark the male homosexual (typecast, say, as macho biker or effete fairy) and blackness does at times take on the color of deviance for white writers. As we shall see, the strange combination of hypersexuality and emasculation may even oddly lesbianize the black man. The penis-not-a-phallus makes the black male character neither traditionally male nor female, neither paternal nor maternal, and so he provides the white imagination with an escape route from the boredom of the family romance, the pieties and proprieties of customary roles.

The essays and novels discussed in these pages affiliate the mutability of racechange with the flexibility of transgressive and difficult to categorize erotic desires.[14] Pathologized, the imagined black stud—on whom are projected criminalized or perverted forms of masculinity—can become a model for whites (what they want to become) or an erotic object (what they wish to have) and so the texts in which he appears tend to collapse heterosexual and homosexual categories as they blur racial borders. Racial ambiguity, in other words, attends sexual ambivalence and vice-versa. To the greater or lesser degree that sexual and racial suppleness prompts anxiety, essayists and novelists exhibit more or less pronounced cases of what Eve Kosofsky Sedgwick calls "definitional panic" (167). "Color me queer," the racechangers in this chapter seem to say, or "queerness colors me," though their white creators vary in the extent to which apprehension leads them to annihilate the representative of deviance.

The second half of this chapter will describe how the magnetism of such a scenario shaped portraits of racechange as sexchange in fiction by Ernest Hemingway and Lois Gould, specifically the former's *Garden of Eden* (c. 1946–61) and the latter's *A Sea-Change* (1976) in which white female characters live out their wish to become black men. However, first we will see that the black penis-not-a-phallus also fascinated such writers as Norman Mailer, Jack Kerouac, and John Howard Griffin, who uncover a psychopathology of fear, admiration, and envy of—as well as identification with and attraction toward—the black stud during the fifties and sixties. Queer colors are the object of fascination, but the subjects enthralled are mostly straight writers who wish to take a holiday from the banality of heterosexual roles. Just a holiday though: The metaphorically perverse only looks like it will threaten the status quo, for it ends up strengthening the satisfying closure of a heterosexually defined happily-ever-after. Initially in these narratives, disgust with traditional gender roles turns white men and women toward a perversity that in turn attaches itself to the racechanged character; however, eventually the blackness of the Third Sex works to retain difference and thus ultimately to enable a heterosexuality otherwise imperiled.

Throughout both sections of this chapter, the mutability implicit in racechange scenarios inflects sexuality with an elusive pliancy; conversely, the blurring of normative categories of eroticism contributes to the permeable boundaries of racial borderlines. Flirting with the idea of breaking taboos against interracial love and same-sex desire, the authors and characters in thrall to black envy temporarily eschew the boring categories "black," "white," "straight," "gay" for scenarios propelled by more slippery, seductive terms. "What alternative to the phallus is there?" Jessica Benjamin has inquired in her study of domination and desire. The fantasy of the penis-not-a-phallus has clearly been debilitating to actual African-American people; yet it illuminates the titillating uses to which the Other has been put in narratives tapping black envy to imagine eros outside the standard Oedipal plot. Enthralled by a traditionally retrograde racial script, writers like Mailer, Hemingway, and Gould seem to ask, "What's love got to do with it?" when sadism, masochism, fetishism, sodomy, adultery, regression, and polygamy are just so much more fun.

The White Negro's Desire for the Black Man

In a meditation entitled "The Black Boy Looks at the White Boy," about his intermittent friendship with Norman Mailer, James Baldwin approached the odd double bind of black men imbued with hypothetical sexual powers even as they are drained of political or social potency:

> I think that I know something about the American masculinity which most men of my generation do not know because they have not been menaced by it in the way that I have been. It is still true, alas, that to be an American Negro male is also to be a kind of walking phallic symbol: which means that one pays, in one's own personality, for the sexual insecurity of others. The relationship, therefore, of a black boy to a white boy is a very complex thing. (217)

Menaced by "the" American masculinity, Baldwin feels himself sufficiently removed from it to analyze it; because of white men's "sexual insecurity," the African American remains always a "*walking* phallic *symbol*," a symbol for whites that never possesses the phallus in its own right.[15] Understandably, then, Baldwin condemns Mailer's impassioned essay "The White Negro" (1957) as an instance of an "antique vision" of blacks. Indeed, Baldwin bases his "resistance to the title" on his suspicion that "the sorely menaced sexuality of Negroes" is maligned by Mailer "in order to justify the white man's own sexual panic" (230).

The "sexual panic" so evident in Mailer's essay includes white men's fears about impotence, emasculation, sexual ineptitude, physical inferiority, and whiteness as well as "homosexual panic," the term Sedgwick uses to describe heterosexual men's fear of homosexuality.[16] For Mailer's attraction to the pathologized image of the black stud teeters between admiration of a role model and desire for an erotic partner. Just as important, Mailer's racechanging fantasy of a "White Negro," which enabled him to play out his rebellion against traditional definitions of masculinity as well as his attraction to illicit forms of eroticism, typifies a racial crossover that accelerated in the late forties and fifties to flower in the sixties. Describing this phenomenon, Malcolm X explained that "A few of the white men around Harlem, younger ones we called 'hippies,' acted more Negro than Negroes" (94). The Otherness of the "White Negro" enabled Mailer to lay the groundwork for the beats and beatniks, the hippies and yippies who so often took the black man as a model for their rebellion against the bourgeois respectability of the authoritarian white patriarch. Racechange for Mailer and his followers empowered them to experience, on the one hand, their revulsion against conventional sex roles and, on the other, their attraction to outlawed alternatives to them. Although Baldwin's indictment of "The White Negro"'s "offensive nonsense" captures the pathos of Mailer's effort to become "hip," Baldwin failed to see the ways in which the white writer's black envy accords with the black novelist's own sense of what it means to be "a Negro man" (232), let alone a white boy looking at a "walking phallic symbol."

Panic, specifically panic about outworn masculine roles, informs the very beginning of Mailer's essay with its horror at concentration camps, atom bombs, and a Western "civilization founded upon the Faustian urge to dominate nature" (583). For Mailer, what emerged out of the Second World War was an acknowledgment that "no matter how crippled and perverted an image of man was the society he had created, it was nonetheless his creation" (583). Composed at the end of the fifties, the essay—attributing the "conformity and depression" of the period to fear and a collective failure of nerve—begins with white self-loathing and a crisis in male identity. The existentialist hipster who emerges as a new hero out of this landscape offers the only hope of masculine survival:

> *if one is to be a man,* almost any kind of unconventional action often takes disproportionate courage. So it is no accident that *the source of Hip is the Negro* for he has been living on the margin between totalitarianism and democracy for two centuries. (585; emphasis mine)

As Baldwin intuited, Mailer identifies black culture with sex and primitivism: "Jazz is orgasm" (586), he insists; "Hip is the sophistication of the wise primitive in a giant jungle" (589), he intones. And the hipster-Negro is also criminalized into a "psychopath [who] murders—if he has the courage—out of the necessity to purge his violence" (593). Childlike in his nihilism, beyond good and evil, the hipster-Negro could as easily be a left-wing revolutionary as a fascist: "Hip . . . is the affirmation of the barbarian for it requires a primitive passion about human nature to believe that individual acts of violence are always to be preferred to the collective violence of the State" (601). How new is the hipster-Negro if in him is only reinscribed the stereotype of the oversexed, psychopathic, aggressive barbarian typified by a character like Gus in *Birth of a Nation*—even though these attributes are now valued positively rather than negatively?[17] To the extent that its author was "in the grip of a bad case of the I've-got-the-pseudo-anglo-saxon-technological-male menopausal-twentieth-century-civilized man's blues" (as Michele Wallace puts it (42)), the concept of the White Negro offensively stereotypes black culture.

It seems appropriate that a photographic negative appears on the cover of the book version of Mailer's essay (Fig. 5.2) since its central figure is, in the words of one critic, "an inverted image" of the Other whose devalorized attributes (primitivism, violence, insanity) were simply revalorized as emblems of alienation from dominant cultural norms (Mercer, "Skin Head," 21). Two precursors of Mailer—Hart Crane and e. e. cummings—flirted with exactly such a "strategic self-othering" through fantasies of the physically daunting black outsider (Mercer, "Skin Head," 21). Hart Crane's terrified dream of finding himself floating in a canoe or rowboat toward a waterfall concludes with his seeing a naked Negro on a nearby shore, a black man whose huge penis convinces Crane of his own insignificant genitals, "tiny as a baby's" (Unterecker, 501). Similarly, when e. e. cummings is imprisoned in *The Enormous Room* (1922), he encounters another inmate more confident than the poet could ever be, "a beautiful pillar of black strutting muscle" whose grin and musical laugh create an "effect on the spectators [which] was instantaneous; they roared and danced with joy" (197).

One narrative line interwoven in Crane's and cummings's accounts is unraveled by Sherwood Anderson's story "The Man Who Became a Woman" (1923) when a scared and lonesome young man is found by "two big buck niggers" who take him for the girl he fears himself to be (219).[18] Part castration anxiety, part projection, part desire, the image of the formidable Other reinforces Crane's and cummings's insecurity about their own deficiency, but it also speaks of a wish cummings silent-

the
white
negro

norman
mailer

75¢

Figure 5.2 Cover of *The White Negro*. Copyright © 1960 by City Lights Books, reprinted by permission.

ly puts to the grinning, strutting black muscle (so reminiscent of minstrelsy's version of the African American): If only in the privacy of his mind, cummings prays to Jean, "Take me up (carefully;as if I were a toy)and play carefully with me,once or twice,before I and you go suddenly all limp and foolish" (*sic*; 214). The homosexual subtext—hardly acknowledged yet so thinly veiled—means that the potent black Other offers the promise of a tender companion who is not female as well as respite from self-loathing for the white man who seeks to be like the Other, to be with the Other, to be loved by the Other, as indeed Norman Mailer does throughout "The White Negro." Several factors may get lost in too quick a condemnation of Mailer's polemic: first, his appreciation of subversive survival skills conditioned by the oppression of African Americans; second, the open secret of his desire for some kind of sexualized union with black men.

At the close of "The White Negro," Mailer describes "the most intense conditions of exploitation, cruelty, violence, frustration, and lust" that bred the Negro's "passionate instinct about the meaning of life" (604). The hipster needs to absorb "the existentialist synapses of the Negro" (587) because the African American always has understood the dangerous edge upon which he attempted to live his precarious life. Anti-social and rebellious in the theater of the present, the hipster can learn survival strategies by modeling himself upon "the Negro [who] knows more about the ugliness and danger of life than the White" (602). Like Lenny Bruce, the comedian Jonathan Miller called the "sick white negro," Mailer ridiculed liberal platitudes about American justice to dramatize the ongoing history of racial persecution. Like Bruce, too, Mailer admired the tenacity of black people faced with constant discrimination as well as what he lauded as their nihilistic disillusionment about American culture.

Despite his loathing of Mailer's essay, Baldwin comes very close to Mailer's view of the existentialist wisdom and grit conferred on African Americans by their marginalization in a culture out to destroy them. Baldwin believes that

> to become a Negro man, let alone a Negro artist, one had to make oneself up as one went along. This had to be done in the not-at-all-metaphorical teeth of the world's determination to destroy you. The world had prepared no place for you, and if the world had its way, no place would ever exist. (*Nobody*, 232)

Although he realizes that society has prepared no place for *anyone*, Baldwin knows about white delusions of grandeur and in particular about white men who (assuming "the world is theirs") "expect the world to help them in the achievement of their identity" (232). In other words, he shares with Mailer a belief that the exile and consequent self-fashioning of black men glamorize them with Byronic alienation, Joycean cunning, and the grace under pressure Hemingway named the model of courage.

What Mailer adds to this mix is a Lawrentian blood consciousness infused by his own cross-racial desire. According to Mailer, the "Negro, not being privileged to gratify his self-esteem," chose instead to derive from "perversion, promiscuity, pimping, drug addiction, rape . . . a morality of the bottom" (594). Connecting the "emergence of the Negro" with the eruption of a psychic rebellion "against the anti-sexual foundation of every organized power in America" (603), he fantasizes about congress between whites and Negroes:

> In such places as Greenwich Village, *a ménage-à-trois* was completed—the bohemian and the juvenile delinquent came face-to-face with the Negro, and the hipster was a fact in American life. If marijuana was *the wedding ring, the child* was the language of Hip. . . . And *in this wedding of the white and the black* it was the Negro who brought the cultural *dowry*. (586; emphasis mine)

Leslie Fiedler has described the longing that imbues *Huckleberry Finn*, the Leatherstocking novels, and *Moby Dick* as the wish that "Our dark-skinned beloved will take us in . . . when we have been cut off, or have cut ourselves off, from all others" (150). Isolated and alienated, Mailer's bohemian and juvenile delinquent also dream of their "acceptance at the breast [they have] most utterly offended" (Fiedler, "Come Back," 151). Fiedler's "notion of the Negro as the unblemished bride" (148) informs Mailer's longing for the "wedding" of white and black men, where the Negro furnishes the "dowry" and a new mulatto language emerges to express the rebellious thoughts of the outlawed hybrid.[19]

A figure of the Not-Yet-Born out of male bonding, the White Negro would speak this miscegenated tongue. A racechanging simulacrum emerging out of a drug dream of mutability, the hipster becomes the fantasy son of three coupling white and black men. With its Man Ray look of a negative, the photograph on the copy of the City Lights edition of Mailer's essay traces the ghostly presence of an embryonic creature in search of an allusive embodiment. Although, in fact, black power activism authorized many African Americans to reject whites, Mailer's essay heralds the civil rights movement as a honeymoon between Euro-American and African-American men.[20] "The White Negro" is the proleptic offspring of that interracial fraternity, a testament to the orgasmic Negro's transformation into the white author's adoring and adored spouse. Unacknowledged same-sex and interracial desire—both taboo—combine to produce the titillating frisson of Mailer's text.

Thus, the character of the White Negro illuminates Mailer's awareness of the slippages between heterosexuality and homoeroticism, heterosexuality's tendency (when calculated premeditation fails) to blur with/into homosexuality.[21] Despite their purported content, Hart Crane's dream of the Negro with huge genitals and e. e. cummings's account of the "pillar of black strutting muscle" locate themselves on precisely such a continuum. Ditto Sherwood Anderson's "The Man Who Became a Woman." In Mailer's pantheon, the White Negro stands between the boxer (Sonny Liston, Muhammad Ali) and "The Homosexual Villain," the gay man most straight men fear they may be. Like the boxer whose "body has become a live part of his brain" ("Ten Thousand," 110), the hipster-Negro will confront any crisis, determined to win contests of love or hate, because "the nihilism of Hip proposes as its final tendency that every social restraint and category be removed," returning "us to ourselves, at no matter what price in individual violence" ("White Negro," 601). In his "search after the good orgasm" (594), he resembles the sexually athletic protagonist of "The Time of Her Time" whose copulation with a woman starts as a boxing match: "I threw her a fuck the equivalent of a fifteen-round fight" (*Advertisements*, 501). Significantly, however, the thrusts of Mailer's hero in this story culminate in an act of sodomy that causes his partner to accuse him of unsuccessfully repressing his homosexuality: "Your whole life is a lie, and you do nothing but run away from the homosexual that is you" (603).[22]

As in the bed, so in the boxing ring "the accusation of homosexuality arouses a major passion in many men; they spend their lives resisting it with a biological force" (243). Mailer's retrospective *Advertisements for Myself* (1959) includes a brief newspaper column that explains how black envy enabled him to express (if only covertly) homosexual desire: his wish to be like the black man, his desire for the black man. Attributing the causes of racial injustice to white men's fears about "the sexual potency of the Negro," Mailer used the column as an opportunity to analyze sexual rivalry between black and white men:

> The comedy is that the white loathes the idea of the Negro attaining equality in the classroom because the white feels that the Negro already enjoys sensual superiority. So the white unconsciously feels that the balance has been kept, that the old arrangement was fair. The Negro had his sexual supremacy and the white had his white supremacy. (332)

That such an estimation teetered on an admission of white male desire for black men was immediately understood by William Faulkner, who was sent Mailer's words and responded that he had "heard this idea expressed several times . . .

though not before by a man." Faulkner's attributing such a sentiment to "ladies, northern or middle western ladies, usually around 40 or 45 years of age," did not amuse Mailer ("I did not laugh so very much when I read this," he deadpans à la Gertrude Stein), but caused him to write back that he, for one, "would not be surprised" if the "timid" Mr. Faulkner "has had his best and most intense conversations with sensitive middle-aged ladies" (333). Hilariously transparent in their gay-baiting, both writers flirt with the idea of articulating their attraction toward black sexual potency by projecting it onto those tired symbols of prudish sublimation—45-year-old ladies.

As if to confess and simultaneously contain consciousness of his own desire for what Fiedler calls "the Negro as the unblemished bride," throughout "The White Negro" Mailer links the hipster to the homosexual stigmatized in the fifties as arrested, sick, and impotent. Besides reiterating a tired and pointedly anti-homosexual ideology, Mailer's identification of queers with impotence, effeminacy, and illness as well as his valorization of aggression probably contributed to the reaction of a gay artist like Allen Ginsberg, who remembered thinking about "The White Negro" that the "notion of the hipster as being cool and psychopathic and cutting his way through society was a kind of macho folly that we giggled at" (Manso, 257).[23] Prescient in its vision of the civil rights movement or what Mailer calls "the rise of the Negro," his essay may exhibit "macho folly," but that folly often blends into a fantasy *folie à deux* or *trois* about white and black men engaged in activism visualized not as "desegregation but [as] miscegenation."

To the extent that the White Negro uses his thralldom to black envy as a way to prove "the oedipal world is not the whole world" (Benjamin, 94), he poses a threat to straight, staid gender definitions in the fifties. An amalgam of his differently colored male parents, the White Negro exhibits (traditionally) masculine autonomy, individuation, activity; however, raging against the phallic order of authority, rationality, and power in the world, he evinces traditionally feminine emotional empathy and a desire for intersubjective merging. Precisely for this reason and despite Mailer's overt homophobia, the highly charged deviancy of the White Negro resists the usual homo/heterosexual categories. So central in "The White Negro" and *Love and Death in the American Novel*, white men's dreams of a "wedding" with black men emerge with striking clarity in the works of many of Mailer's and Fiedler's contemporaries. Whether overtly homosexual or heterosexual, representations of black envy during the post–World War II era employ sexual categories that keep on breaking down or merging. To the extent that black envy stems from white (not black) men, it reflects white men's fantasies of a masculinity before or beyond the phallic stage, their wish to escape the burden of the phallus through a route that retains the pleasures of the penis.

The most striking use of racechange in a distinctly homosexual setting of black envy occurs in the photographs of Carl Van Vechten, who emphasizes the shared pain, pressure, and fetishization of ostracized white and black gay men.[24] Even in the nature of his bequests, Carl Van Vechten sought to advance racechange since he left his abundant photographs of black artists to mostly white Yale University, his archives on white artists to mostly black Fisk. Only recently, as Jonathan Weinberg's pioneering essay on Van Vechten's "Queer Collection" demonstrates, have scholars realized that this celebrated promoter of the Harlem Renaissance put together some twenty scrapbooks of pictures and newspaper clippings that constitute "homemade sex books, early and private forerunners of Madonna's best-seller" (28). Two portraits of Saint Sebastian—one with a white model, one with a black—justify Weinberg's view that "changing the race of [the] model raises disturbing associations. For us today, the tied arms and outdoor setting might evoke less the early-Christian martyr than a modern lynching" (36; Fig. 5.3).

That the patron of the Harlem Renaissance was drawn to Sebastian seems hardly surprising, since this third-century martyr served as the patron saint of a masochistically inflected homosexuality for many artists. The staging of his sanctification usually features a beautiful, naked youth whose flesh is riddled with arrows in a scene that extends suspense by protracting suffering; the mixture of pain due to phallic penetration and pleasure in transcendence made Sebastian a particularly resonant prototype of the ecstatic torment of a supreme erotic experience. With his eyes shut and his arms clutching the stake or tree against which he is impaled, the black model in Van Vechten's picture looks ravished in both senses of the word: raped and sent into ecstasies. Like Mapplethorpe's photographs in the *Black Book*, however, Van Vechten's racechanged "shot" of Sebastian hints that when a white boy looks at a black boy he may manage to dislodge the more traditional figure of the fetishized female nude only by glamorizing the (already potentially subordinated) black subject as a model of feminized masochism. As curvaceous as a woman, black St. Sebastian sports two arrows strategically placed on either side of his genitals, making a V, something like the iconic V for Venus or vagina. Though he is supposed to appear thrilled at being pierced by the skewed arrows, Van Vechten's target of opportunity—displayed like sexual meat—may seem uncomfortably scapegoated or skewered (something like shish kebab).

If Van Vechten performs a racechange on St. Sebastian to intensify the thrill at arresting time before saintly reward or sexual consumation, Francis Picabia's gouache *Oiseau et tortue* (Bird and turtle, 1949; Fig. 5.4) presents its strangely colored central figure to hint at an androgynous sexuality. The hermaphroditic and biracial center of attention here—neither black nor white, neither male nor female—engages in a kind of life or death struggle as if to establish new categories of being that would violently rescind the ordinary either/or binaries of gender, sexual orientation, and race. Using the trope of the spotted Negro, Picabia draws attention to achromatism, usually held to be hideous or a sign of illness but here a signature of the fluid boundaries between what are often taken to be distinct species or kinds of being.[25] The mottled skin denotes a hybridity comparable to the bisexuality of the body, intimating that racechange and sexchange together undo conventional modes of being and seeing. Once again, in other words, the strangely colored White Negro—like Edward Carpenter's Intermediate Type—annuls the polarity of standard gender categories.

In supposedly straight contexts, too, black becomes a color favored to figure deviant forms of eroticism that defy ordinary heterosexual plots. In fact, racial Otherness guards against sexual Otherness; for white men of letters, an enticing black

Figure 5.3 Carl Van Vechten, *Saint Sebastian*. Courtesy of Beinecke Library, Yale University. Courtesy of Joseph Solomon, Executor of the Estate of Carl Van Vechten.

masculinity can defend against women. The most aggressively heterosexual book to exhibit black envy is Jack Kerouac's *On the Road* (1957), especially in a passage later hailed by Eldridge Cleaver as symptomatic of white youth's "rejection of the conformity which America expected" (72). The third section begins with the narrator, Sal Paradise, strolling in the "violet dark," wishing he "could exchange worlds with the happy, true-hearted, ecstatic Negroes of America" (149):

At lilac evening I walked with every muscle aching amongst the lights of 27th and Welton in the Denver coloured section, *wishing I were a Negro*, feeling that the best the white world had offered was not enough ecstasy for me, not enough life, joy, kicks, darkness, music, not enough night. (148; emphasis mine)

As in *The Subterraneans* (1958), where he describes his "old dream of wanting to be vital, alive like a Negro or an Indian or a Denver Jap or a New York Puerto Rican" (70), Kerouac was disgusted by what he took to be white rationality and self-consciousness.

Drugs, jazz, and male bonding with the innocent but scapegoated victims of racism, all to be found on "the negro streets" Ginsberg walked when declaring "I am the Scottsboro boys" typify the wish for some sort of racechange in consciousness that animated the beat generation. *On the Road* describes what happens when Sal meets up with his white buddy Dean Moriarty, who immediately deserts

Figure 5.4 Francis Picabia, *Oiseau et tortue* (Bird and turtle, 1925–27), gouache on paper, 25¾ × 19¾ in. Courtesy of the Metropolitan Museum of Art, Alfred Stieglitz Collection, 1949.

his pregnant wife and baby, putting "bitterness, recriminations, advice, morality, sadness—everything . . . behind him" so as to embrace "the ragged and ecstatic joy of pure being" (161). In a sawdust saloon filled with "colored men in Saturday-night suits" (162), Dean almost seems to copulate with an orgasmic tenorman:

> Dean was directly in front of him with his face lowered to the bell of the horn, clapping his hands, pouring sweat on the man's keys, and the man noticed and laughed in his horn a long quivering crazy laugh, and . . . finally the tenorman decided to blow his top and crouched down and held a note in high C for a long time as everything else crashed along and the cries increased and I thought the cops would come swarming from the nearest precinct. Dean was in a trance. (163)

Notwithstanding Kerouac's intermittent put-downs of "queers," the same love that joins white hero and black musician also flourished between white buddies on the roads they took to flee from family responsibilities in general, wives and children in particular. Just as Sal, staring at Dean who gazes back at Sal, often feels something "click" between them, many photographs of their prototypes—Kerouac himself and Neal Cassady—present the duo with arms entangled, looking boyishly fraternal. As Paul Goodman knew, "Beat culture, unlike the American standard of living, is essentially for men" (185), a point presumably made too by the camaraderie fostered by jazz and drugs.

Curiously, even the enemies of "The Know-Nothing Bohemians" adopted the rhetoric of cross-racial longing. The phrase just quoted is the title of Norman Podhoretz's 1958 attack on Ginsberg and Kerouac (and specifically the latter's "idyllic picture of Negro life" so similar to Southern attempts "to convince the world that things were just as fine as fine could be for the slaves" (311)). Yet Podhoretz's essay "My Negro Problem—And Ours" (1963) contains the same stock of black envy spiced with a dash of homoeroticism evident in "The White Negro" and *On the Road*:

> just as in childhood *I envied Negroes* for what seemed to me *their superior masculinity*, so *I envy them* today for what seems to be their superior physical grace and beauty. I have come to value physical grace very highly and I am now capable of *aching with all my being when I watch a Negro couple* on the dance floor, or *a Negro playing* baseball or basketball. They are on the kind of terms with their own bodies that I should like to be on with mine, and for that precious quality they seem blessed to me. (99; emphasis mine)[26]

Podhoretz represents himself as a liberal in race matters, one who would even learn—if necessary—to let his sister or daughter marry "one" (101). But the ache he feels while watching Negro athletes may mean the hypothetical sister or daughter has been put in place as a kind of surrogate. In one of the stills Dick Gregory includes in his satiric book on American racism in the sixties, *What's Happening?* (1965), the black comic hints as much about the sexually hidden motives of even the most prejudiced of law enforcement officers (Fig. 5.5). "You can't marry my sister," the white sheriff explains to the black aristocrat, "but if you're as rich as you look, you can marry me."

From the fifties and sixties on, libertarians and bigots alike shared an obsessive

Figure 5.5 Dick Gregory, "You can't marry my sister, but if you're as rich as you look, you can marry me," from Dick Gregory, *What's Happening?* (Dutton 1965), photographs by Jerry Yulsman. Courtesy of Dick Gregory.

black envy. Indeed, the allegedly enlightened Podhoretz's aching admiration recalls the reactions of the racist Southerners who pass the blackened, hitch-hiking John Howard Griffin on the road during the daylight, but stop to pick him up after dark. This disturbing section of *Black Like Me* castigates the pornographic imagination of white men, their "morbid curiosity about the sexual life of the Negro" whom they see "as an inexhaustible sex-machine with oversized genitals and a vast store of experiences, immensely varied" (85). A kind of confessional, the dark car at night becomes a "ghoulish" place of white men's "pantings" as they take to "hounding" Griffin for his "sexual reminiscences" (85). Significantly, then, white men are shown propositioning a presumably black man to hear his accounts of sex. As if situating himself in the voyeuristic place of Bellow's Sammler or Mapplethorpe's camera, one especially prurient driver who "had never seen a Negro naked" asks Griffin to expose himself; after he is refused, the young man feels the need to explain, "I wasn't going to do anything to you. . . . I'm not a queer, or anything" (89).[27] If we return to the Terry Southern quotation at the start of this chapter, keeping in mind the absence of women from the scenes of Griffin's dialogues, it may seem that the speaker who wants to "pretend to be a spade" is less excited by the fantasy female figure to be raped than by the act of actually "get[ting] into a *spade bag*."

Cases of white men's black envy make strange bedfellows in popular American culture during the second half of the twentieth century. According to Greil Marcus, early rock 'n' roll "must have been a bit like a white foray into darktown, a combination of a blackface minstrel show and night riding—romantic as hell, a little dangerous, a little ridiculous" (*Mystery Train*, 176). Though Elvis Presley didn't need to exile himself from his own community as Mezz Mezzrow and Johnny Otis "and so many *real white Negroes*" did (182; emphasis mine), the King nevertheless remained indebted to the black music upon which he drew, as did Jimmie Rogers, Dock Boggs, and Bob Dylan. Assessing the ethics of that debt, Marcus asks, "What *does* Huck owe Jim, especially when Jim is really Huck in blackface and everyone smells loot?" (180). "Elvis was sexy," according to one popular music historian, "not clean-cut, wholesome, white-bread, Hollywood sexy but sexy in the aggressive earthy manner associated by whites with black males" (George, 62–63). The prominence of black cultural forms, which "served as a model for middle-class youths in the 1950s," may explain why "bad" teens ("hoods" as well as "beats") wore "black turtleneck shirts, black stockings, black sunglasses" (Breines, 19, 148).

Mick Jagger and Keith Richards—as if confirming Marcus's view of rock 'n' roll as white forays into darktown—initially bonded over their mutual obsession with Chuck Berry and Muddy Waters; however, during their first tour of the States a mistaken Murray the K warned them "there was not much hope for them in America because if Americans wanted the music of Chuck Berry and Muddy Waters they would listen to the original, and anyway white people most certainly did not want what was considered 'nigger music.' . . . And it would not be realistic to hope that black people would want to listen to young Englishmen playing the blues" (Schofield, 68). Another type of England's youth culture, "the mods" in mid-sixties London displayed "an emotional affinity with black people" that "was transposed into style," according to Dick Hebdige: The (blatantly stereotyped) model of "the Black Man" made possible the view that "work was insignificant, irrelevant; vanity and arrogance were permissible, even desirable qualities, and a more furtive and ambiguous sense of masculinity" could be achieved through "a sleight of hand, through 'soul'" (Hebdige 53–54).

Black envy—so prevalent in rock music's metaphorical blackface—shaped the civil rights movement as well. In a 1964 interview with Bradford Daniel for *The Progressive*, John Howard Griffin described the "intellectual fad" of white liberals as a kind of love affair with African Americans: "liberals . . . embrace all Negroes because they are Negroes"; they "tend to adopt the attitude: 'You bring the whiskey and I'll bring the Negro,' to a party or a meeting" (15).[28] Not only were various quests for countercultural authenticity imagined in terms of an archaic Africa, the pathologized hypervirility of the black man continued to propel the imaginations of political activists from widely divergent perspectives.[29] According to Michele Wallace, who believes that "the manhood America finally conceded to blacks was the manhood of a psychopath" (48), the "curiously psychopathic energy at work in the black man's pursuit of his manhood (Black Power)" derived from the influence of Norman Mailer's fantasies on militants like LeRoi Jones and Eldridge Cleaver (47, 39): "Yes, white men were perversely obsessed with the black man's genitals but the obsession turned out to be a communicable disease and in the sixties black men came down with high fevers" (73).

For Jones (later Amiri Baraka) and Cleaver, in turn, the supermasculinization of the black power movement could lead to the virulent homophobia of the former's comment that "Most American white men are trained to be fags" (*Home*, 216) or of the latter's judgment that "Homosexuality is a sickness, just as are baby-rape or wanting to become the head of General Motors" (110).[30] Cleaver's subsequent effort to market "real men's pants," featuring large and dangling cotton-stuffed codpieces, serves as a symbol of what the social critic Stanley Crouch calls "the priapic version of black 'manhood' that slithered from behind the black power movement's fly" (106–7). As if to confirm the idea that racism may be rooted not only in white men's jealous imagining of black macho but also in their racechanging impersonations of that macho, the writings of the ex-KKK leader and recurrent Republican candidate David Duke include *African Atto*, a street-fighting manual for urban blacks that he wrote under the pseudonym Mohammed X in order to collect the names of black militants.[31]

What Does the Lesbian White Negro Want?

Despite their manifold differences, the common project of Norman Mailer, Jack Kerouac, Norman Podhoretz, John Howard Griffin, and Eldridge Cleaver—their effort to locate through black men a dissident masculinity before or beyond the phallic—demonstrates its limits in their unconscious but not therefore less emphatic contempt for women. To become racially Other somehow licenses violence against women. Obviously, Mailer's flirtation with a "morality of the bottom" ratified "perversion, promiscuity, pimping, drug addition, rape" (603) in ways that could easily constitute a danger for the sex he considered secondary. In other words, the supposedly revolutionary renegade often shares with the authoritarian men against whom he rebels a scorn for women whose femininity is equated with castration. Although, as Jane Gallop has pointed out, "To distinguish penis from phallus would [appear to] be to locate some masculinity that does not necessarily obliterate the feminine" (125), women *are* eclipsed in such texts as "The White Negro" and *On the Road*. What happens when the psychopathology of black envy surfaces not in a white male but in a white female context? Here, too, we will see that queer colors—though attractive as one aspect of a seductive revolt against traditional and debilitating gender roles—nevertheless ultimately play themselves out in scenarios that continue to identify women with castration and that oddly end up buttressing heterosexual as well as racist structures.

Given the long history of the black stud/white female victim in propaganda and pornography, it is no wonder that white women have written quite openly about their fear of the "*spade-rape bag*." Indeed, a touchstone psychoanalytic essay about femininity begins with a meditation on the meaning of such dread. Joan Rivière's "Womanliness as a Masquerade" (1929)—which argues that "women who wish for masculinity may put on a mask of womanliness to avert anxiety and the retribution feared from men" (35)—includes a case study of an intellectually proficient woman who believes her ambitions supplant her father, who propitiates father-figures by flirting, and who associates such flirtation with a youthful fantasy:

> This phantasy . . . had been very common in her childhood and youth, which had been spent in the Southern States of America; if a negro came to attack her, she planned to defend herself by making him kiss her and make love to her (ultimately so that she could then deliver him over to justice). But there was a further determinant of the obsessive behaviour. In a dream . . . she was in terror alone in the house; then a negro came in and found her washing clothes, with her sleeves rolled up and arms exposed. She resisted him, with the secret intention of attracting him sexually, and he began to admire her arms and caress them and her breasts. (37)

Rivière goes on to explain what she takes to be the dream's meaning: The girl was alone in the house because she had killed her parents so she dreaded their retribution and she defended herself from charges of ambitiousness by playing a menial role, thereby disguising herself as "merely a castrated woman" (38). Convinced that her intellectual gifts have turned her into a man, she feigns femininity by means of flirtatious ogling.

Rivière remains perfectly satisfied with her conflating of the white parents so feared by the daughter with the phantom Negro breaking in: Both are frighteningly powerful and therefore must be assuaged with seductive coquetting.[32] But what if the girl's "*making* [the negro] kiss her and make love to her" or resisting "with the secret *intention of attracting* him sexually" (emphasis mine) can be read as a way of rebelling against the authority of the white parents, finishing them off? If the young woman's intellectual displays are experienced as an apprehensive "possession of the father's penis," perhaps she longs to entice the black man to take up her cause. Put another way, just as she wishes for an intellectual proficiency equal to—but not identical with—the father's, she dreams of aligning herself with a black masculinity equal to—but not identical with—the father's. Conceivably, then, she wishes to join with the black man, become part of the black man, become the black man, to exploit him as an instrument to complete the castration of the white father. Two novels by Ernest Hemingway and Lois Gould propose exactly such a dynamic. More surprising than representations of white women's anxieties about the black rapist are portraits hinting that—like white men—white women are also capable of flirting with the stereotype of the black renegade, identifying with it, and thus relishing the fantasy of getting into a "*spade-rape bag*."

In other words, white men were not alone in their desire to model themselves on the dark stud. Male- and female-authored heroines also enact their own misogyny through the figure of the black penis-not-a-phallus. This is a misogyny women experience because of their alienation from a demeaning, secondary, trivializing, weakening construction of femininity, a femininity that makes women feel vulnerable and frightened, dependent upon feigned flirations and in need of paternal protection.[33] Both Hemingway's *Garden of Eden* and Gould's *A Sea-Change* present portraits of female characters nauseated by such an enfeebling femininity and driven by anxieties about their subordination to revenge themselves against men. In revolt against the same gender polarity that disgusted the White Negro, Hemingway's and Gould's heroines appear to reject the rational reality principle of the father (or conventionally masculine) as well as the intimacy, emotionalism, and affectivity of the mother (or traditionally feminine). By means of a black envy that causes them to darken themselves, they stage racechange as a sexchange that turns them into White Negroes, queer hipsters or outlaws who compete with white men for white women. This is why in both these texts the lesbian looks so dark and so male. Paradoxically, then, we will see that even the most seemingly seditious racechange narratives ultimately work to support a compromised, endangered heterosexuality.

Turning dark in *The Garden of Eden* and *A Sea-Change* means turning queer; both Hemingway's and Gould's heroines uncover bizarre slippages between lesbianism, transsexuality, blackness, and heterosexual sadism. For Hemingway's Catherine Bourne and Gould's Jessie Waterman, to become black means gaining seditious, prohibited, masculine potency; however, it also means a fugitive status that continues to subject them to political as well as social marginality. Disrupting the patriarchal order, the rebellious lesbians in these two novels at least temporarily refute traditional sexual arrangements, but only by employing the profoundly retrograde racial configuration of the pathologized black stud.

Hemingway, who worked on the posthumously published *Garden of Eden* from 1946 until his death in 1961, used his title to point to the mythic design upon which he hung his narrative of "an intelligent woman uncontrollably envious of her husband's success as a writer" (to use the prefatory words of the editor who helped shape—by cutting—the only version that is now available in print).[34] Pen and penis envy motivate Catherine, David Bourne's bride of three weeks, who interrupts their idyllic swimming and fishing, their Edenic eating and sleeping and lovemaking during a honeymoon in Avignon to embark on "a wonderful dangerous surprise": "I'm going to be changed," she explains before going off to get her hair "cropped as short as a boy's" (12, 14–15). The boy's haircut leads directly to transgression—"Dave, you don't mind if we've gone to the devil, do you?"—and the fall is a sexual one. When Catherine takes on the character of "Peter," asking David to become "my girl Catherine," she effects her temptation through the act of sodomy:

> He lay there and felt something and then her hand holding him and searching lower and he helped with his hands and then lay back in the dark and did not think at all and only felt the weight and the strangeness inside and she said, "Now you can't tell who is who can you?" (17)

The "dark magic of the change" at first only occurs at night, but Catherine wants "to be darker" and that wish forecasts the impossibility of her containing the process that will inexorably lead, as in the original myth, to shame, recrimination, and expulsion. "I'll be your African girl," she vows, dedicating herself to getting "darker than an Indian" and "further away from other people" (30).[35] Yet the tanning process that blackens Catherine's skin demonstrates that the "African girl" she wants to be is "Peter" penetrating David. Nor is Hemingway's association of "dark" or "African" ways with sodomy eccentric. Throughout *Women in Love*

(1921) as well as his later essays, Hemingway's English counterpart describes sodomy as "the African process." According to D. H. Lawrence, "African degradation" occurs at "the darkest, deepest, strangest life-source . . . at the back and base of the loins."[36] As Diana Fuss has shown, Freud also established his theories about the origin of culture by equating "primitivity and homosexuality" as the "inversions" that had to be repressed or made taboo (*Identification Papers,* 36).

For Catherine, being black means attaining the pleasure of becoming physically active in the penetration of her lover without claiming the legitimacy or respectability of any socially sanctioned authority. Indeed, she seeks precisely the psychopathic violence and nihilistic courage of Mailer's alienated hipster. After another haircut followed by bouts of anxiety about sex- and racechanges that hook her like a compulsion or addiction, it becomes clear that Catherine's need to "be a boy" requires David's "change" into "my dearest only girl" (56), illustrating Hemingway's tendency to imagine homosexuality in heterosexual terms. Given her nickname, "Devil," Catherine would use her transgressive seductions to bear David Bourne away to a sexual wilderness where he will be reborn as a girl. When he submits to having his hair cut just like hers and then lightened to a color of no color, something like her pearls, he finds it futile to fly from the hell which is himself. For, unlike Samson, he has voluntarily and knowingly submitted to the rape of his locks.

After being turned into a twin image of Catherine and playing her role in bed, David looks in the mirror and admits responsibility for the change: "Don't ever say anyone tempted you or that anyone bitched you," he advises himself, because "You like it" (84–85). With their brown skin and their lightened hair, the pair looks not only like each other but also like Man Ray's photographic "solarizations" or the cover of Mailer's "The White Negro," as if their outré reversals mean to highlight their refusal to conform to conventional gender and race roles, their playing with a dangerous androgyny and hybridity. The punk contrast Catherine designs between the couple's tanned skin and the whitening of their hair emphasizes their self-made, artificial, singular being, her cosmetological effort to break not only sexual and racial taboos but also normative physiological types. As Toni Morrison explains in her reading of the novel, "Catherine is both black and white, both male and female" and thus destined for madness (*Playing,* 87–88). All too predictably, then, the next "dark change" the "African girl" instigates involves her taking a female lover.

When Catherine brings Marita into the relationship, David's passive, pensive query—"Whose girl is she?"—indicates that Catherine enjoys having Marita as an erotic partner, but Catherine also relishes playing the man by bringing a gift to her girl David ("I brought you a dark girl for a present," she tells him (103)); in addition, she savors being one of two lovers for her husband David ("be nice to your girls," she instructs him (103)). Just as her turning David into a kind of twin gives the marriage a tang of incest, the *ménage à trois* breaks several taboos, allowing Catherine to flirt with adultery, lesbianism, polygamy. In her compulsion to experience whatever sexual permutations and combinations she can imagine, this licentious "African girl" recalls Lawrence's meditation on a West African fetish, a female statue that represents

> mindless, progressive knowledge through the senses, knowledge arrested and ending in the senses, mystic knowledge in disintegration and dissolution, knowledge such as the beetles have, which live purely within the world of corruption and cold dissolution. (*Women in Love*, 330)

For a while, David allows the two girls "to take turns" with him as he is drained of agency by Catherine's demonic invention of competing life stories that redirect his aesthetic energies onto herself. What can save our hero from what Lawrence calls "knowledge in dissolution, the African knowledge," not to mention "knowledge such as the beetles have"? Although living with two wives would be allowed "in Africa if I was registered Mohammedan" (144), David increasingly sees Catherine as neurotically flaunting her economic support of him and complaining either that she is not allowed to read the stories she has financed or labeling them "bestial" and "horrible" (157). But as he resumes work on his writing David luckily finds a way back to a reborn masculininity, conveniently allowing "Hemingway to play out the familiar male fantasy of converting a lesbian to another way of sexuality" (Comley and Scholes, 97). To add piquancy to David's victory, he does so by winning Marita away from Catherine, reestablishing as normative his heterosexuality as well as his imaginative autonomy, and banishing Catherine to the hinterlands where any Eve turned Lilith belongs.

No wonder that Marita happily recovers from (sick) homosexuality to attain (sound) heterosexuality. To begin with, she herself views lesbianism as "only something girls do because they have nothing better" (120). So as to confirm a Victorian diagnosis of homosexuality as masturbatory self-abuse, Catherine's sexual experimentation, affecting her like a drug, leaves her feeling empty, dead, hollow, exhausted. Headed for a breakdown, Hemingway's heroine inhabits a wired, weird world in which colors are too bright, time seems speeded up, and bouts of hectic alcoholism follow enervating periods of lassitude. Her nemesis is soon nicknamed "Heiress" and "Haya" ("the one who blushes, the modest one" (142)) by a David who sees where his future lies, for Marita serves as an antidotal, sacerdotal Mary to Catherine's transgressive Eve-turned-Lilith, making his fall a fortunate one indeed. Significantly, David rescues himself from mindless African dissolution by writing African tales reminiscent of Hemingway's own hunting tales and those of his major precursor, Rudyard Kipling. Indeed, the last quarter of the published version of *The Garden of Eden* progresses by splicing the main plot of the novel— Catherine's breakdowns, her increasing hostility toward David's writing and his affair with Marita, her climactic burning of the only copy of his writing, and her abject note on leaving the newly constituted couple—with David's interpolated narrative about his father on an elephant hunt. Why does Hemingway shuttle the reader between a feminized Europe in an erotic present and a masculine Africa in an adventurous past?

The autobiographical story upon which David works so assiduously concerns a

young boy's trip with his father and his father's native guide, Juma, to track an ancient elephant that the soon repentant David and his dog, Kibo, had glimpsed one
mystic night in the moonlight: "The bull wasn't doing anyone any harm and now
we've tracked him to where he came to see his dead friend and now we're going
to kill him. It's my fault. I betrayed him" (181). The adult David completes "a very
young boy's story" by noting about his central character, "The elephant was his
hero now as his father had been for a long time" (201). Why does the murder of
the elephant in the interpolated tale lead directly to Catherine's burning of David's
manuscripts in the main narrative and her expulsion from his future?[37] Does
David's participation in the crime of (writing about) murdering the elephant somehow lead to punishment exacted by Catherine, an act which in turn requires her
own annihilation?

Catherine hints at a wildness she shares with the ancient, huge mammal in an
excised portion of the manuscript: "you are lucky to have a wife that is a wild animal instead of a domestic animal," she informs David (Ms. 1/1/23–24). Like the
elephant, hunted for his ivory tusks, "the darkest white girl in the world," who
sports hair so blond it looks "just like ivory" (169) and who ascribes her ability to
get dark to her "lion color" (30), seems doomed. After David the writer records the
murder of the elephant, Catherine returns to act "for" the repressed, destroying
David's tale. She merits her own destruction because she represents the male author's dependency upon dangerously unmanning sources of inspiration. Just as the
young boy David loved but learned to accept his complicity in the betrayal of the
elephant, the grown-up David loves but learns he must vanquish his "African girl."
Presenting a portrait of the artist as colonizer, Hemingway admits with some guilt
his reliance on an Otherness with which he cannot abide: African wilderness/sex-
ual wildness furnish the aphrodisiac to fuel the writing that sentences them to ex-
termination.

Yet, unlike David, who cannot be persuaded by Catherine to write about her escapades, Hemingway *does* focus much of his novel on Catherine. In so doing and
also by making David's African tale so nostalgic, Hemingway gains several degrees of distance from his hero. Closer to the self-consciously ersatz "African girl,"
Hemingway marks his awareness of a primitivism constructed by the Western
imagination and therefore already compromised by producing David's tale as a
parodically formulaic initiation story. Like Catherine, Hemingway mourned a father dead by suicide, experienced cross-dressing that turned him into an androgynous twin (of his sister), and believed that good writers should destroy much of
their writing. Indeed, just as Catherine recalls Catherine Earnshaw of *Wuthering
Heights* in her passionate belief that she is David, David is Catherine and so is
Hemingway himself, who uses Catherine's female gender to camouflage the ways
she encodes his own fascination with sexual transgression. The African queen of
The Garden of Eden is queer, Hemingway's drag persona. (Paradoxically, such a
lesbian self-image can be understood as oddly bracing Hemingway's view of his
heterosexuality as if he were exclaiming "even if I were a woman, I'd still desire
women—not men, never men.")

Dramatizing Hemingway's contradictory version of himself as imperialist and as lesbian, *The Garden of Eden* remains surprisingly fair-minded in its analysis of the sexual antagonism of its protagonists. Catherine at her most seductively sinister lavishes attention on David—"Let me feel your hair girl . . . . you have lovely lips. Shut your eyes girl"—so as to teach him "it isn't so easy to be a girl if you're really one. If you really feel things" (86). To some extent, then, both the race- and the sexchange are contextualized by her wish to write or paint and her knowledge that she cannot execute her aesthetic ambitions, except on herself. Being typed as a girl means being "a god damned bore" as well as "Scenes, hysteria, false accusations, temperament" (70), so her crafty plots reflect her nervous, nihilistic efforts to circumvent the creative nullity she experiences as a woman.[38]

Black envy in *The Garden of Eden* is pen and penis (not phallus) envy; Catherine's wish to become the darkest white girl merges with her desire to become her husband's twin, depraved seducer, or Devil (not her husband's husband, father, or God). Yet because body parts other than the penis—hands, hair, skin—as well as symbolic accoutrements—a car, a female lover, money—allow her to appropriate masculine powers, it may be possible to appraise Catherine's response to the narcissistic wound of femininity as a quest not for a penis and not for a phallus (which Lacan associates with law, authority, legitimacy) but for an illicit substitute that disguises that wound while still leaving a trace of its threat.[39] This formulation would identify blackness as a fetish—a sexually overvalued part of the body or inanimate object—just as it is in the photographs of Man Ray and the photomontages of Hannah Höch. Not a phallic symbol, a fetish is a substitute for the missing penis, which is exciting precisely because it is "seen as authentically different from the missing penis" (Bersani and Dutoit, 68). Blackness as a fetish gives Catherine something comparable to, evocative of, but different from male genitalia.

In any case, however, Hemingway ultimately punishes Catherine's Satanic ambition, for he retains the conventional notion that the white man with a penis should have the phallus or the fetish, the signifying power and authority. Even at her darkest Catherine remains merely a male manqué, an imitation boy (Peter) who will never grow into a man. Women's anxiety about powerlessness takes a quite different turn in Lois Gould's more surrealistic *A Sea-Change* whose heroine also dreams of aligning herself with a black masculinity equal to—but not identical with—the father's. Like Rivière's patient and Hemingway's Catherine, Gould's central character wishes to become the black man to complete the castration of the white father. But the female novelist grants this wish, depicting her white heroine undergoing a fully actualized sex- and racechange. Whether or not Gould read Hemingway's short story "The Sea Change" (1938)—an encapsulated version of *The Garden of Eden* about a tanned, short-haired young woman's decision to leave her male partner for another woman as well as his helpless chagrin at this turn of events—Gould's *Sea-Change* deflates Hemingway's fantasy of converting the sick lesbian into a healthy heterosexual, meditating instead on the threat to masculine perogative racially transgressive sexchanges inaugurate.[40]

Gould's Jessie Waterman is imbued with fury generated by envy of men and feminine self-loathing. In a dreamlike flashback of a scene that may or may not have actually occurred but that recurs throughout the narrative, Jessie remembers being subjected to the terrifying breaking and entering of a *b*lack *g*unman she calls B.G. What horrifies her about the episode is her terror when B.G. caressed her breasts with his gun as well as her physical responsiveness when she followed his orders and embraced it with her mouth, felt it entering her smoothly, "sliding it, so easily, as if into a lubricated holster" (83), calling it by her husband's name, Roy (from *roi*, French for king). The twofold effect of the nightmarish experience involves a confusion of cocked gun and gunning cock, of rapist and husband, of sex and death: "Roy had come Ah, Jessie, Ahh, red-and-black, her blood and B.G.'s cock/gun Roy had come exploding finally Ah Jessie Ahh" (122). The conflation of masculinity with femicidal sadism, femininity with masochistic victimization inevitably results in a revulsion against heterosexuality. Because the phallus/penis/gun—"Loaded aiming at you"—slips into the place of the camera which previously ruled Jessie's modeling career, she becomes increasingly alienated by the condescending, philandering husband—"a relic from the golden age of misogyny" (30)—who had kept her in this job and who (in some of the surrealistic retellings of the primal scene) colludes with B.G. in the rape.

But if the initial reaction to the haunting assault is revulsion, the more lasting is a mounting desire for retaliation which triggers a grotesque rebirth, a schizophrenic twinning along the lines of the brutal Mr. Hyde's emergence out of the benevolent Dr. Jekyll. (That one film version of Stevenson's Gothic tale performs a racechange on Mr. Hyde helps to explain the novella's influence on *A Sea-Change*, as do more contemporary interpretations of its doubling as an encoded approach to homosexual liasons.[41]) Described as "nursing her secret, which grew inside her like a tumor or a monstrous child" (24), Jessie (bearing her embryonic alter-ego) moves to remote Andrea Island with her daughter, Robin, and her stepdaughter Diane. Although the old vulnerable Jessie-identity seems "rooted, attached like a vestigial organ" (25), the new hardened B.G.-identity responds to the freedom of her commuting husband's removal by annihilating the "Soft, pliant core that would yield, would give way" (104). Besides the body-building exercising in which she devotedly engages, the hurricane Minerva fosters the evolution of Jessie into B.G. Named after the goddess of war, the storm turns Jessie into the veteran B.G. on an island named for andro or male.[42] Indeed, its fury obviously functions as the objective correlative of Jessie *Waterman*'s wish for a "real female weapon," like "quakes, volcanoes, whirlpools, cyclones. Even ocean currents. Powerful sucking devices in a female form" (47).

What actually transforms Jessie racially and sexually is a repetition of the act of rape—a reenactment with Jessie in control, first positioning herself again in the position of the raped victim and then in the place of the raping victimizer. At the beginning of this process, she engages the attentions of her friend Kate by trying out various sadistic erotic advances. As her attraction to Roy indicates, Kate stands for an earlier, more submissive version of Jessie. But by kissing Jessie's breasts, the enthralled Kate can still call the "skeleton" feminine Jessie out of the "closet" that the black gunman B.G. fears he has become (111). To prove B.G. more than just a closet, Jessie first notes that Kate seems attracted by the temporarily waylaid coastguardsman Leo Bailey (and even more fascinated when she discovers he had participated once in a gang bang). Then Jessie sets up a *ménage à trois*. Getting Kate so drunk that she passes out, Jessie impersonates her friend, urging Bailey to engage in "hate-fucking" her "Hard, and cold, and very fast" until Jessie "tore open beneath him, until he broke her like a cheap toy" (120–1). Because this murderous act kills off the feminine Jessie, the person who emerges "would never again perceive the touch of her body, of her breasts, as an assault. . . . Here I am, B.G." (121).

Breaking into Kate's room, like entering Kate's body, gives B.G. his identity: "Slip in through the narrow opening of the sliding glass door. He would like the feel of that, the tightness squeezing him" (129). Out of the closet, Gould's violent White Negro is beyond the pale, something like Hyde in his demonic dedication to aggression. Using his gun on Kate as it had been used on Jessie, B.G. then holds it up to Leo Bailey's face: "Clean it for me, Surfman. Leo Bailey did that too" (134). Thus Jessie as the black gunman gets Leo Bailey to become complicitious in precisely the mysterious way Roy had been earlier and in the process blackmails the coastguardsman to secrecy. Displaying a satanic aggression that silences white men and women, B.G. talks black: "Aint no *but*, man" (134), he tells Leo; "I don't study about love, baby. I just know what I got to have to make it" (144), he whispers to Kate. An incarnation of precisely the sexual symbolism Baldwin decried, B.G. embodies the ferocity of Jessie Waterman's hatred of her earlier femininity, her leaping into "a *spade-bag*" not substantially different from the one that so attracted Terry Southern's hero.

With daughter and stepdaughter in tow, relocating to the even more remote Reef Island under cover of the supposed demise of Mrs. Jessie Waterman, the black gunman who names himself *Kil*roy reconstitutes his family, which goes unrecognized by the searching Roy. Whereas Hemingway's Catherine remains at best an imitation boy, Gould's B.G. becomes a stud powerful enough to compete successfully with the white patriarch. An anti-king in his liminal realm, the black, male Jessie inhabits a borderline place in culture, an outlaw who survives by virtue of his commitment to a control he can exert over a succession of women who fill in for the absent Kate. At the close of the novel, B.G. is joined by Kate, who embraces thralldom as her fate. In this triumphant sado-masochistic consummation, Gould bleakly suggests that the sea-change of sex- and racechange constitutes no change in gender arrangements at all. Thus *A Sea-Change* concurs with Jane Gallop's quip, "Penis, phallus—same difference." Black man, white man—same difference too. What does it mean that Jessie's anxieties about masculinity and revulsion against normative heterosexuality have issued in racechanging scenarios that ultimately restore the most sadomasochistic form of heterosexual coupling as well as the founding couple of racist propaganda: the black male rapist, white female victim?

The title of Gould's novel refers the reader to its epigraph about the physiological sexchanges of coral-reef fish in warm coastal areas; however, like Hemingway's "The Sea Change" it also invokes Shakespeare's *Tempest* (1623), a play about a number of transformations on a magical island and in particular a song of

Ariel's that T. S. Eliot had placed at the center of *The Waste Land* (1922) and Sylvia Plath had located at the center of her book of verse *Ariel* (1965):

> Full fathom five thy father lies,
>   Of his bones are coral made;
> Those are pearls that were his eyes;
>   Nothing of him that doth fade,
> But doth suffer a sea-change
> Into something rich and strange.
> Sea-nymphs hourly ring his knell . . . (I.ii.397–404)

Gould, who clearly shared Eliot's and Plath's fascination with transformation, re-mained particularly absorbed by the issue of domination. The novelist uses the pa-triarchal Roy and the renegade B.G. to call attention to Prospero's rule in Shake-speare's play, to Caliban's servitude to Prospero, and to the relationship between that subordination and rape fantasies. After the magus robbed Caliban of his in-heritance (the island which belonged to Caliban's mother, Sycorax), the native at-tempted to use sexual assault to take revenge against his colonizer, or so Prospero claims. His accusation—"thou didst seek to violate / The honour of my child"—meets with Caliban's implicit admission of guilt: "O ho, O ho! would't had been done! / Thou didst prevent me—I had peopled else / This isle with Calibans" (I.ii.346–51).[43]

Like Shakespeare, Gould may be found guilty of further cementing the chains that link ethnic difference with animality and a fearsome sexual aggression. Like Caliban, an inferior being "on whose nature / Nurture can never stick" (IV.i.188–9), B.G. remains stubbornly unregenerate, cursing the tyranny that brutalizes him, seeking a cruel revenge against the white patriarch by seizing the women men like Roy control. Unlike Shakespeare, though, Gould presents the native/rapist as a *white* fantasy. To this extent, her meditation on racechange in *A Sea-Change* un-covers the secret longing that imbues even the most racist imaginings of the black Other. Robert Browning used the figure of "Caliban upon Setebos" (1864) to make a similar point. His Caliban, musing upon the God who made him, illuminates the dynamics of creation that impelled Shakespeare to create Caliban but that also mo-tivates whites to construct blackness in the shape of, say, B.G.:

> He would not make what he mislikes or slights,
> An eyesore to Him, or not worth His pains:
> But did, in envy, listlessness, or sport,
> Make what Himself would fain, in a manner, be—
> Weaker in most points, stronger in a few,
> Worthy, and yet mere playthings all the while,
> Things He admires and mocks too—that is it. (ll. 59–65)

If B.G. embodies what Lois Gould and her heroine would fain be, he establish-es not only the strength of their revulsion against feminization but also the allure of the black rogue who can compete through sheer willfulness and badness with the patriarchal power of the white father. Yet since B.G. takes the place of Roy in the ownership of Kate, he proves that, even when the white father is buried five fathoms deep down in death, he subsists through psychic metamorphoses that continue to haunt the minds not only of men but also of women. Since nothing of the patriarch fades—he suffers a sea-change only when played in blackface by a white woman—B.G./Jessie and Kate as a couple hardly adumbrate a brave new world. On the one hand, the central female characters of Hemingway and Gould may simply be understood as a sign of these authors' homophobic, racist identification of white lesbians and black men with sick sadism. On the other, to the extent that both Catherine and Jessie are motivated to forge their plots about lesbianism and blackness because of their revulsion against the passivity and vulnerability they associate with white femininity, they may illuminate one racialized psychological strain that turns erotic love toward domination.[44]

Racechange fantasies, which put both Catherine and Jessie in touch with taboo, masculine impulses, allow Hemingway and Gould to elaborate upon the logic of Fanon, who views "the Negro" as "the predestined depository" of the white girl's aggression, arguing that "the fantasy of rape by a Negro is a variation of this emotion: 'I wish the Negro would rip me open as I would have ripped a woman open'" (179). Unfortunately, however, Fanon simply counters the debilitating myth of the black rapist with the equally disturbing myth of the white woman's desire to be raped (Fuss, *Identification Papers*, 156). Both Hemingway and Gould ground the desire to be a rapist and the desire to be raped in their female characters' hatred of white femininity. In *The Garden of Eden* and *A Sea-Change*, the logic goes something like this: White women's abhorrence of feminization leads to a projection of that hatred onto the penis-not-a-phallus and a fantasy of becoming the dark Third or Intermediate Sex. What this analysis adds to Fanon's is the idea that the Negro is the depository of the white girl's conflicted aggression against her own femininity.

Like Freud, Hemingway and Gould connect lesbianism with the wish for a penis or a penis substitute. But Freud's propensity to see "the lesbian as masculine solves the problem of lesbian sexuality by rendering it as essentially heterosexual" (Roof, *A Lure of Knowledge*, 211), whereas black envy—the wish for a black penis—creates a mixed figure in *The Garden of Eden* and *A Sea-Change*, for the lesbian is a woman who thinks she has an erotic power capable of successfully competing with—but not the same as—white men's. Still, to the extent that race triggers sexchanges and so functions to maintain difference (to allay anxieties about representing lesbian sameness), both Hemingway and Gould reiterate Freud's tendency to collapse lesbian sexuality into the heterosexual paradigm. Indeed, racechange as sexchange transforms lesbianism into heterosexuality: Instead of two women coupling, the portrait of lesbianism provided by Hemingway consists of dark "Peter" (Catherine) with "his girl" (David), just as Gould presents "B.G." (Jessie) with "his" girl (Kate). As Judith Roof has demonstrated using many other narratives, "the metaphorically perverse both threatens to short-circuit and leads toward a satisfying, very heterosexual closure" (*Come as You Are*, xxxiv).

Next to both novels' association of primitivism and deviancy, moreover, lurks the iconography of slavery—locks and chains, whips, head constraints and hoods, leather straps. In addition, the fact that slaves were forced to submit to sexual acts has imaginatively fused the sadomasochistic to racial impersonation, regardless of which role is adopted (since, as Gould points out, the parts of dominator and dominated can be switched). White female characters like Jessie and Kate, enthralled by the idea of a dominator, exhibit the masochism dramatized in a series of disturbing photographs of Nancy Cunard taken by Barbara Ker-Seymer, a German photographer, and recently brought to the attention of scholars by Jane Marcus.[45] Both the "solarizations" and the traditional shots display a starved creature Marcus terms "a white slave" whose neck is encircled by beaded necklaces that appear to strangle, bind, or leash her (Figs. 5.6 and 5.7). According to Marcus's analysis, this "reenactment of black slave bondage in the self-staging of [a] white body" should be read "as a site for political protest against racism" and not "as a perverse pornography": Cunard "really meant the performance of bondage to signify her political bonding with black culture" (42). Maybe.

However, if we interpret this racechanging figure more skeptically as Jessie Waterman at the start of her dreadful intimacy with B.G. or as Kate at the end of her equally appalling mating with Jessie-turned-B.G., then the mimicry of slavery Cunard performs stages the female White Negro's desirous encounter with the "spade-rape bag." Cunard's eroticizing of a master/slave psychology could be said to perpetuate racial and sexual scripts of thralldom that bequeath only the most degrading form of power to men, that of sexual domination; only the most demeaning form of submission to women, that of anorexic self-abasement. Although Gould's characters see the black man as a sadist while Cunard views the female slave as a masochist, both glamorize the sadomasochistic deviance of color.

Like the photos of Cunard, then, the conclusion of Gould's *A Sea-Change* implies that, as Sylvia Plath put it, "Every woman adores a Fascist, / The boot in the face, the brute / Brute heart of a brute like you" ("Daddy," l.48–50). Inveighing against "the black man who / Bit [her] pretty red heart in two," Plath is motivated by grief and rage to perform a racechange on the father to whom she remains enthralled even as she determines to plant "a stake in [his] fat black heart" (l.53–55, 76). Once again in the history of racechanging iconography, as it did in *The Jazz Singer*, Jewishness emerges to play an unforeseeable (if erratic) part, for Plath pits the black, male Nazi against the white, female Jew. Whereas Norman Mailer's and Saul Bellow's quite different engagements with the Negro construct the American Jew's masculinity, Jewishness is marked feminine in Plath's work. But all three writers continue to equate blackness with what Fanon called "the biological danger" of the penis, Jewishness with "the intellectual danger" of subjectivity itself.

Because "Peter" or "B.G." or the "black man who / Bit my pretty red heart in two" does not exist, white people will supply, invent, or become him. Addressing white fearful projections about the penis-not-a-phallus, Adrian Piper's cross-dressing performance in the early seventies, *Mythic Being*, included notes explaining how her Afro, bell bottoms, and dark glasses made her

> swagger, stride, lope, lower my eyebrows, raise my shoulders, sit with my legs wide apart on the subway, so as to accommodate my protruding genitalia. (Golden, 26)

Figure 5.6 *Barbara Ker-Seymer, Nancy Cunard solarization.* Photography Collection, Harry Ransom Humanities Research Center, The University of Texas at Austin; courtesy of Barbara A. Roett.

Figure 5.7 (*Below*) Barbara Ker-Seymer, Nancy Cunard in neck gear. Photography Collection, Harry Ransom Humanities Research Center, The University of Texas at Austin; courtesy of Barbara A. Roett.

And the portrait of herself she created from *Mythic Being* contains the words "I embody everything you most hate and fear." Similarly, Piper's later installation *Four Intruders Plus Alarm Systems* (1980) projected slide and sound images of black men as interlopers, images predetermined by the same white fears and fantasies Toni Morrison addresses in her fiction (Golden, 26). Most pointedly, Morrison's *Sula* (1973) includes a speech by a male character who seems to be meditating on the consequences of the black "*spade-rape bag*" for black men:

> White men love you. They spend so much time worrying about your penis they forget their own. The only thing they want to do is cut off a nigger's privates. And if that ain't love and respect I don't know what is. And white women? They chase you all to every corner of the earth, feel for you under every bed. I knew a white woman wouldn't leave the house after 6 o'clock for fear one of you would snatch her. Now ain't that love? They think rape soon's they see you, and if they don't get the rape they looking for, they scream it anyway just so the search won't be in vain. (103)

Besides illuminating the reasons why O. J. Simpson's picture underwent a darkening and why, even more recently, Susan Smith depicted the "murderer" of the children she herself actually killed as a black man, the logic of such bitter testimony explains the sophisticated imagery of Bellow's *Mr. Sammler's Planet* and Mapplethorpe's "Man in Polyester Suit." As these and most of the other texts explored in this chapter prove, white fixation on the black penis has contributed not only to the blackmailing of the black man (the criminalizing of his sexuality) but also to the eclipse of the black woman, supplanting her from creative and critical view. Yet we will see in the next chapter that when she does come into focus, the African-American woman's image is less framed by an obsession with the magnetism of any one of her body parts, more focused on the question of who lays claim to the productions of her womb.

WHAT WILL THE MIXED CHILD DELIVER?

Conceiving Color Without Race

[T]he basic error of white comments about their own oppression is the assumption that they *know* the nature of their enslavement. This cannot be so, because if they really knew, they would liberate themselves by joining the revolution of the black community. They would destroy themselves and be born again as beautiful black people.

—James Cone

I almost felt the baby grow inside me, and I suddenly felt completely Black. . . . in that moment, walking down the street full of people who were miraculously unaware of the change in me, resting my hand lightly on my belly, I was as Black as anyone.

—Jane Lazarre

In my body were many bloods, some dark blood, all blended in the fire of six or more generations. I was, then, either a new type of man or the very oldest. . . . If I achieved greatness of human stature, then just to the degree that I did I would justify *all* the blood in me. If I proved worthless, then I would betray all.

—Jean Toomer

Shirley Temple Black and Bill Robinson White, a 1980 acrylic, is one of Robert Colescott's more sardonic experiments in racechange (see color insert). Picking berries on a garden path, a darkened Shirley and a lightened Bill pause to glance at each other, perhaps the moment before they will break out in a tap dance routine. As in so many of his other paintings, this picture converts characters traditionally portrayed as white into blacks, switching the races so as to ridicule, first, our assumptions about white hegemony in cultural scripts and, second, the caricaturing that infects almost all depictions of African Americans in mass-produced as well as elite art. Here the coincidence of Shirley Temple's married surname serves as Colescott's sly pretext for her racial metamorphosis. In a discussion of this painting recorded on the video *Robert Colescott: The One Two Punch* (1993), the artist explains that he was wondering what kind of society ours might have been if Shirley Temple had been black: What if America's sweetheart during the thirties were a little dark child?

Had we grown up with stories treasuring the sweetness of black children, Colescott's painting intimates, many of the other scripts that govern public and private life might have been less dangerous to the welfare of African Americans. Instead, of course, we expect to see the pampered white child at the center of a narrative in which she is waited on by the devoted black domestic. Shirley Temple frolicking with Bojangles typifies the coupling of white child/black adult-servant which is rendered so frequently that it has moved to the very center of American cultural history. From youthful Huck accompanied by Nigger Jim to adolescent Scarlett O'Hara costumed by her Mammy, the white youth attended by the black adult spells out a number of disturbing ideological lessons. Not only are blacks somehow childlike in their fawning dependency, but authority accrues to whiteness, which even at its most vulnerable and ignorant masters blackness. Were the tables turned, it would be whites who might have to struggle with anxieties about their insufficiency and debasement into a grateful servitude.

In part, Shirley Temple's whiteness can be attributed to the exclusion of blacks from the Blakean or Wordsworthian figure of the child as embodied wisdom, spontaneity, and joy, as if a people condemned to perpetual childishness must be robbed of childhood itself. Thus in *The Bluest Eye*, when Toni Morrison's outcast Pecola seeks the milk of human kindness reserved for a cherished offspring, she tries to lighten herself by drinking from a Shirley Temple cup. Loathing Shirley Temple, Pecola's healthier, less socialized friend, Claudia, believes instead that Bojangles is her friend, uncle, daddy, and that he "ought to have been soft-shoeing it and chuckling with" her (19). From the baby in the barn depicted in Renaissance paintings to *Alice in Wonderland* and the Bobbsey twins, from Valentine cupids and cherubs to the Snow Whites, Pinocchios, and Little Bo Peeps of fairy tales and nursery rhymes, the normative child of Western culture appears white (at least until quite recently).[1] If only inadvertently, the white child who figures as the protagonist in stories with a multiracial cast of characters attests to the centrality of the white race. Black mother surrogates could serve as wet nurses and mammies, black domestics could become "uncles" or "aunts"; however, they were supposed to lavish their attention on the well-being of the white heir apparent. Equally to the point, the beneficent surrogate parenting performed by the desexualized black caretaker drained away the threat of interracial sexuality (which might contaminate the "purity" of white lineage).

It is striking in this regard that, even though the racechanged Shirley Temple seems to grant Morrison's Claudia her wish of soft-shoeing it and chuckling with her very own Bojangles, Colescott's metamorphosed characters continue to suffer the consequences of racist imagery: Shirley Temple does not appear simply darkened, Bojangles simply lightened in skin tone.[2] Instead, racial transformation eroticizes the couple, draining away their innocence and infusing them with a vaguely perverse ribaldry. Why does the prancing Robinson White seem to be leering at the equally coquettish and rather hefty Temple Black? Does their berry picking hint at the saying "the darker the berry the sweeter the juice"? As one of the curators of Colescott's shows has remarked, "the older black man" had been so "effectively emasculated" by the Uncle Tom role as "to pose no sexual threat to American white females," but his racechange into a white fieldhand grants the Robinson figure potential virility (Sims, 5). At the same time, though, *is* Robinson simply whitened in Colescott's painting or does his lightening immediately jettison him into a minstrel role? In overalls—with the familiar gaping mouth, bowed legs, and glowing eyes—Colescott's Bill occupies a liminal position on the color line; whether a white man impersonating a black or a light-skinned black man, he ogles the dark child who grins back at him and together they illustrate an imagistic amplitude or physicalization that robs African-American girl children of their childhood. When the adorable Shirley Temple turns black, she devolves into soon-to-be gobbled up sexual food for a lecherous uncle-daddy. The one-two punch Colescott's work administers by switching the expected color of the child pertains to the shocking stories it uncovers about race and sex, a maneuver that male and female, black and white writers exploit in a curious narrative translation of Colescott's trope, namely the appearance of a child whose skin color appears unexpected or unprecedented, at odds with that of its parents.

Like Colescott, fiction writers from Kate Chopin and Jean Toomer to Gloria Naylor brood over the significance of the racechanged child in terms of sexuality, lineage, and cultural empowerment. What does it mean if the newborn baby looks visibly different from its parents, looks like it comes from another race? Would a white Mr. and Mrs. Temple feel about a mysteriously swarthy daughter that she decreased their value or even comprised an embarrassment that should be destroyed or disowned? What if the child attests to the amalgamation of races that had been declared not simply unwelcome but downright illegal? Until 1967 many states decreed interracial marriage a criminal act and its mixed-race offspring illegitimate.[3] In addition, the "one drop rule" meant that after the 1920 census all mulatto children were defined as black and thus disappeared as an identifiable group. Buttressing the "one drop rule" as well as many states' laws against miscegenation, turn-of-the-century eugenicists argued that "the result of the mixture of two races, in the long run, gives us a race reverting to the more ancient, generalized, and lower type. . . . The cross between a white man and a negro is a negro" (Doyle, 16). Thus, the mixed child produced by interracial relationships became conceptually inconceivable. As Colescott also hints, Shirley Temple has to be either white or black. In an autobiographical book published in 1994, Maureen Reddy, the white wife of a black man who writes about their children, points out that even today school applications, federal government documents, medical records, census reports, and job applications do not recognize "biracial" as a category (75).

Yet precisely a fascination with such a transgressive term shapes the way in which racechange played itself out in plots about the mixed child that surfaced repeatedly in twentieth-century fiction. This outlawed creature, according to Jane Lazarre, "has stalked the white nightmare for all of American history, born at times of transcending love, at others of twisted desire, a creature who threatens the boundaries we have drawn around ourselves—the hybrid" (*The Mother Knot*, 45).

Although Jean Toomer's denial of his African-American identity, his claim that "many bloods" ran in his veins, has been viewed as aberrant or retrograde,[4] the birth story of new breeds composed of mixed races appears with startling frequency possibly because it enabled both mainstream and African-American artists to meditate on the idea of color without race. Was that idea a nightmare or a dream come true?

In the interest of righting past wrongful thinking about miscegenation, one might hope that the dark infant demonized by white parents early in this period would reappear trailing clouds of glory later in the twentieth century, that the light-skinned child born to black parents would be dislodged from the center of their desires at the end of the century. And something like this paradigm shift does occur. Whereas early artists worry over the traditional problem of who will deliver the dark child, later ones consider the more fantastic, even apocalyptic forms of deliverance the dark child might hold out to or for society. Indeed, we shall see that the image of a white woman mothering, nursing, or tending the African-American baby eventually surfaced in imaginative literature as a sign of white efforts to offset a history of conflictual racial Othering. Nor is it surprising that the image of the unexpectedly colored infant has recently been so positively revalued because few people today are racially "pure," in any sense of that word. Not simply admonitions against choosing one identification over and against another, not merely vindications of the "mulatto" or "half-breed" previously shamed as a racial traitor, fictional meditations on the mixed child exploit racechange to elaborate upon Jean Toomer's awareness of how "many bloods" run through the veins of most people. At their most optimistic, some of these narratives—attempting to envision a post-racist time—celebrate the permeable boundaries between mother and hybrid child as a panracial antidote to racism, an intersubjective solution to the violence of a racist past.

Less predictable, though, are those black and white authors of the racechanged offspring who remain bleak about the redemptive possibilities of its subversive plot. For the multiracial child may inherit as its birthright only the lies, secrets, and silences that threaten not merely its well-being but its life and society's future. "To the Child, she held herself, her life, accountable" ("One Child," 362): The language in which Alice Walker praises the poet Muriel Rukeyser can be applied to the ethic adopted by most of the authors in this tradition, a maternal ethic which explains why so many of them are women. In contrast to most of the other race mutations studied in this book, the peculiar force of the child of a startling color depends upon a phenomenon neither chosen nor willed. The offspring's out-of-place, uncanny complexion means that racechange—not merely an impersonation, not volitional—ceases to be playful, speculative, or temporary and instead simply poses a challenge to a society organized in such a way as to deny the ambiguously raced child the familial space that accords personal and public identity. Since, as Fanon puts it, "the family is a miniature of the nation" (142), writers from Kate Chopin to Gloria Naylor resemble Rukeyser and Walker in finding in their elegiac writing about the racechanged child an alternative to the less constructive forms of rage that they feel at national injustices. Their accountability to the hybrid offspring (innocent but judged guilty) shapes their scathing portraits of family values based on racial taxonomies proved irrational, even vicious.

"Writing saved me," Walker explains, "from the sin and *inconvenience* of violence" ("One Child," 369). In the most embittered scripts, the racechanged baby taps the anger of African-American writers and the guilt of their white contemporaries, all of whom understand that, as Walker again puts it, "black children are to have less in their world so that . . . white children will have more" (374). Such anger and guilt are only enhanced by the secret the biracial infant holds, namely the lie commingled bloodlines put to historical accounts of a segregated culture. At their most optimistic, however, narratives about the racechanged baby hold out the promise of a redemptive transracial consciousness that does not merely mimic existing racial categories but transgressively traverses them. Taken together, then, stories about the mixed child hauntingly posit a variation on Jean Genet's assertion that "In white America the Blacks are the characters in which history is written. They are the ink that gives the white page its meaning" (*Prisoner of Love*, 213).[5] African Americans, according to the authors in this tradition, are the characters in which the genealogies of America were written in ink that most public or national histories attempted to blot out but that can be traced to discern different tellings of our common heritage.

The Color of Desire

Kate Chopin's 1892 story "Désirée's Baby" will serve as a touchstone for narrative use of the mixed-race child in this chapter because Chopin uses fairy-tale motifs and a set of ironic reversals to compose what amounts to multiple parables about interracial genealogy. This often anthologized tale turns on a shock administered to mother, father, and relatives when the most desirable of desired babies, born of a woman herself allegorically linked to desire, undergoes a racechange that transforms the infant from a valued beloved into an unwanted outcast. Each of the reversals that conclude Chopin's brilliant story (so similar to those devised by Maupassant and O'Henry) epitomizes alternative approaches to the narrative of the racechanged child. Yet in both ironic twists, the baby of desire and, indeed, desire itself remain doomed to extinction because they contradict warped definitions of the permissible in a segregated society. The clash between desire and the permissible plays itself out in the ironic contradictions between reproduction and the family. Family values which are firmly grounded in dualistic racial categories endanger life, liberty, and the pursuit of happiness, according to Chopin's tale, since a familial investment in racial dualism effectively murders desire (which knows no racial restrictions) as well as life itself.

The story begins with one Madame Valmondé who, going to visit Désirée and her baby, reflects back many years to Désirée herself as a toddler mysteriously found sleeping under a stone pillar. Madame Valmondé and her husband, accepting the foundling as a providential response to their childlessness, watched the girl grow "to be beautiful and gentle, affectionate and sincere."[6] With perfect fairy-tale logic, we are immediately told that eighteen years later, when Désirée stood before that very same stone pillar, she was immediately sighted by the aristocratic Armand Aubigny. Just returned from his early life and education in France, the young man deems Désirée the object of his desire. Despite her obscure origins and his own proud heritage, Armand determines on the marriage. Once this flashback account of past events ends, the visit of Madame Valmonde occurs and we are shown her consternation at looking at the infant: "This is not the baby! . . . . the child has grown, has changed," she exclaims.

Although at this point Désirée herself sees no transformation and remains delighted by her husband's pleasure at the appearance of a male offspring, soon she notices "an awful change in her husband's manner" as well as "an air of mystery among the blacks" toward whom his severity has increased. The inevitable scene of instruction occurs when the young mother watches her three-month-old baby being fanned by one of the children of a slave named La Blanche, a "little quadroon" boy. After Désirée "looked from her child to the boy who stood beside him, and back again; over and over," her "blood turned like ice in her veins, and a clammy moisture gathered upon her face." Asking her husband, "What does it mean?" Désirée is told "the child is not white; it means that you are not white." When she interjects that her hand is whiter than Armand's, he sneers, "As white as La Blanche's." The shocked wife's letter to her stepmother explaining, "I am not white. . . . I shall die" results in Madame Valmonde's loving offer of shelter; however, Désirée—feeling her husband's words stabbing her soul, wearing only a thin white garment—departs with her child, disappearing "among the reeds and willows that grew thick along the banks of the deep, sluggish bayou; and she did not come back again."

As Du Bois explained in "The Souls of White Folks" (the racechanged version of his more famous *Souls of Black Folk*), a "religion of whiteness" preaches that "whiteness is the ownership of the earth, forever and ever, Amen!" (339) so the now black Désirée must be expunged. The first, Ophelia-type ending of the story establishes the tale as a statement about the fatality of black maternity for mother and child. Désirée, engaged in an act of infanticide, commits suicide because her child's color reflects back, as in a glass darkly, to teach her that her light epidermis conceals her "real" racial identity and because she understands that (in a slave economy) her infant follows the condition of the mother into the dispossession spelled by namelessness. Thus, Chopin foregrounds patrilineage to examine the exclusion of blacks from kinship, property, and identity. That Désirée was "nameless" when she arrived at the stone pillar, that Armand possesses "one of the oldest and proudest" of names in Louisiana, and that at first Armand delights in "a boy, to bear his name": All these demonstrate the legitimacy of the white man, as does Désirée's demotion to La Blanche, whose light skin (because on a "black"-defined person) exemplifies not purity so much as legal blankness.[7]

Since there is no space appointed for the mixed offspring or for the baby's double, Désirée herself, they leave the world of culture to merge into the anonymity of nature. Although a son, her nameless child is as cut off as she from any kinship system and thus he is disinherited and fatally ungendered.[8] Always a baby, he will never grow to become a boy or a man. A statement about slavery as the death not only of Désirée and her baby but of desire itself, Chopin's narrative attributes the destruction of desire to the racially marked limits of the idea of the family. The black baby proves that Armand defines the family not in terms of the reproduction of children or even inheritors but in terms of the production of whiteness; biological offspring designated as not white must be excluded from membership.[9] The racially mixed infant who is labeled black signifies the white father's sexual rights over black women and his economic control over mother and child as well as his repudiation of paternity; the racechanged baby embodies the African-American mother's physiological tie to the child as well as her inability to protect it.

But of course the tale Chopin picks up after the blank space on the page and the passage of several weeks revises the first ending of Désirée's expulsion as an outcast black by performing yet another racechange. Burning a cradle, a priceless layette, silk and velvet gowns, bonnets and gloves in a kind of funeral pyre, Armand fanatically sets out to purify the presumably polluted space of the plantation. As if his wife were a witch or sorceress, he annihilates the costume of culture that disguised Désirée's alien identity, itself a threat to the purity of his lineage. In an all-consuming rage, Armand also sets fire to the letters Désirée had sent him. Then he sees the remnant of an old letter from the same drawer, a letter from his mother to his father: "'I thank the good God for having so arranged our lives that our dear Armand will never know that his mother, who adores him, belongs to the race that is cursed with the brand of slavery.'" Reading becomes his undoing because Chopin seeks to link the act of reading writing with larger issues about the interpretation of physical features.

When earlier Armand had read the baby's dark complexion as a sign of Désirée's race, he assumed the baby's materiality was maternal while its symbolic place in society was paternal. Then, banishing Désirée and her baby, he acted on what Patricia Yaeger calls "the temporal distance between insemination and parturition," which is an equally immense conceptual distance, as suggested by the adage "Mama's baby, Papa's maybe" (285). In other words, Armand saw visible links between Désirée and the baby, not between the infant and himself. If, as James Joyce put it, "paternity is a legal fiction," it could be abrogated; the child was effectively divorced by Armand when he cast Désirée out. Ironically, though, Armand discovers that he has fashioned a destiny for Désirée more justly suited to himself. Even more ironic, he suffers the fate of becoming Désirée's baby (just as his wife had in the earlier ending) at the moment he understands himself to be guilty of the "brand" he attaches to his offspring. Not the child, but he is born of a white man and a black woman. As readers, now, we reinterpret his earlier life in France as a sign of (what else?) the illicit sexuality of his parents. Visual as well as familial markers function so ambiguously that a pale wife has been defined as black while a dark husband has been taken to be white. The end of the tale effectively divides physiology from race, complexion from origin, making the visual unreliable. Indeed, though many readers assume that Armand's black matrilineage somehow turns Désirée white, the race of Chopin's heroine remains stubbornly indeterminate. Notwithstanding the predilection of most interpreters of the narrative, there is no logical reason to assume that since Armand is black, Désirée must be white.[10]

Because of that indeterminacy, "Désirée's Baby" manages to encapsulate a cluster of twentieth-century scripts about the dark child whose skin color does not match that of his parents: (1) narratives about white fathers and black mothers; (2) narratives about racially indeterminate women (who ought not become mothers); (3) narratives about black fathers and white mothers. As in the various conclusions of "Désirée's Baby," until very recently most artists depict the mixed offspring expelled from the human community or sentenced to undeserved suffering and almost certain death. As in its first ending, moreover, the majority of stories about biological hybridity have tended to center on the baby born of a white father and a black mother (to which this chapter will next turn). For Armand's original supposition has remained the normative one; the belief that the dark baby must be conceived within the black maternal body was a logic determined by the economy of slavery in which white masters established sexual rights over black female slaves. As if taking revenge for the innocent but helpless infant, Chopin's plot punishes Armand for his murderous arrogance and the punishment fits the crime. But vengeance may be carried out by hybrid characters themselves when the baby grows up to wage war against the white father who gives even as he denies love to the mother, life to the child.

Oedipal Rage Against the White Father

Although Ann Douglas has argued that "Freud's theories of what he called 'the family romance,' the tortured triangle of mother, father, and child that produces the Oedipus complex, had little to do with the African-American experience" (95), stories about the biracial child born of a white father and a black mother repeatedly return to Oedipal struggles.[11] Both white and black writers understand that the annihilation of desire dictated by the family's romance with white lineage necessarily breeds retaliatory fantasies in the dispossessed offspring; however, the plots they fashion respond differently to the dissonant appearance of the child born into a family in which it does not fit. Whereas such white writers as Mark Twain and William Faulkner reject or put off the promise of the biracial offspring who poses a threat to the white family, the African-American authors Marita Bonner and Langston Hughes indict a racist system which damages or imperils the future such children promise to bring into being.

Twain's *Pudd'nhead Wilson* provides a paradigm of the Oedipal rage for revenge instilled in the biracial son of a black single mother. The pale complexion of Twain's central character here, the light-skinned Tom who was born to the slave Roxy and switched with her master's heir in infancy, gives his mother the opportunity to save him from slavery. Pampered as his wealthy uncle's inheritor, Tom exhibits all the character flaws instilled by faulty upbringing, although Twain's ambiguous story also hints that the immorality of this cowardly liar and sneak should be attributed to a "native viciousness" (20) related to his genetic background. Whether because of nurture or nature, at a climactic point in the novel Tom blackens his face with burnt cork, arms himself with an Indian knife, creeps downstairs into his surrogate father's study to steal his money, and reacts quickly to hear-

ing the old man's cries of help: "Without hesitation he drove the knife home—and was free" (94), a phrase that expresses his Oedipal revenge against the man who stands in the place of his father, the authority whom he seeks to supplant. That even the best of white fathers jeopardizes mother and child by means of his power of excommunicating them from (the security of) the family is what fosters interracial hatred and intergenerational rivalry.[12]

Far more equivocal about what the ex-slave Harriet Jacobs called the "tangled skeins" of "the genealogies of slavery" (121), William Faulkner examines the psychology of Twain's position when he considers the reasons why the white family represses the mixed child who threatens if not the father directly then the old patrilineal ways. The story "Delta Autumn" in *Go Down Moses* (1942) evocatively presents a woman who appears to be white, who turns black before the eyes of the aging Isaac (Ike) McCaslin, and who holds in her arms a biracial baby (whose father is McCaslin's white relative Roth Edmonds). Though she sounds like "a Northerner" (343), the mysterious mother mentions an aunt taking in washing, thereby providing a clue that leads Ike to look at "the pale lips, the skin pallid and dead-looking yet not ill, the dark and tragic and foreknowing eyes" and proclaim her "a nigger"; in the same passage, he also thinks about inter-racial unions, *"Maybe in a thousand or two thousand years in America, . . . but not now!"* (344).

The blanket-swaddled bundle must be trundled off, along with the woman who is paid to leave and told to marry a black man. That Ike has divested himself of his inheritance in order to expiate the sins of his grandfather—who begot a child upon his own slave daughter—makes this act exceptionally ironic. Horrified by a social order in which white privilege shapes ownership of property, family, and law, the compensation Ike McCaslin offers mother and child nevertheless remains only money, exactly the reparation his grandfather proffered to his biracial offspring as a way of paying them off for disowning them: Cash *"was cheaper than saying My son to a nigger . . . "* ("The Bear," 258). Although Faulkner's central character has renounced his white inheritance as contaminated, Ike McCaslin's withdrawal from the nameless young woman—herself a living embodiment of his grandfather's miscegenation—dramatizes his continued entrapment in a shameful past that has not paid adequate restitution. Thus, the mother of "Delta Autumn" carries not only the baby but the moral weight of the tale.[13] Not accepting the infant that would bring the bifurcated lines of the family together means that Faulkner's representative patriarch is doomed to remain entrapped in an exhausted, guilty past.

If in different ways Twain and Faulkner make the family the victim of the out-of-place child, African-American authors sympathize with the rage of the child against a familial system that dispossesses, or so the rivalrous feelings expressed in a poem entitled "Mulatto" (1925) by Claude McKay suggest:

> Because I am the white man's son—his own,
> Bearing his bastard birth-mark on my face,
> I will dispute his title to his throne,
> Forever fight him for my rightful place.

As in Twain's novel, at the end of McKay's poem the speaker is spurred on by hate to determine on the murder of his father:

> When falls the hour I shall not hesitate
> Into my father's heart to plunge the knife
> To gain the utmost freedom that is life. (*Passion*, 126)

Two contemporaries of McKay's, Marita Bonner and Langston Hughes, published racialized revisions of the Oedipal story that examine the patricidal anger of a mulatto child. In particular, Bonner's "One Boy's Story" (1927) almost reads like an allegory about the self-destructiveness this author presents as paradigmatic in all biracial boys' psychosexual development.

The eleven-year-old child who is the central character of Bonner's resonant narrative, Donald Gage, lives with his seamstress mother, dimly aware of their liminal status as people of color in the white town. Although he knows one of her customers, a childless Mrs. Swyburne, observes him sadly, wishing she could have a son just like him, the well-behaved Donald refrains from explaining she cannot, "Cause I'm colored and you aren't" (80). Visits from Mr. Swyburne perplex him, but the books he brings intrigue the boy who becomes especially absorbed by tales about "Orestes who went home from the Trojan War and found his mother had married his father's brother so he killed them" and "about Oedipus—a Greek too— who put out his eyes to hurt himself because he killed his father and married his mother by mistake" (81–82). In response to the child's fascination with epic heroes, Mr. Swyburne proudly exclaims "he has the blood" and the reader understands—even though Donald does not yet—that the white man is his biological father and that his mother is trying to extricate herself from the ongoing relationship she has maintained with him.

When Mrs. Gage's vain attempts to break away from the white father of her son issue in a fight with Swyburne that is witnessed by Donald, he takes out his slingshot and aims a stone that kills the man. Less like David stalking Goliath, more like Oedipus who unwittingly murdered his father at the crossroads and equally unknowingly embraced his mother, Donald finds the touch of his mother fatal. Her hold impales him on her breast pin, which first scratches his mouth and then sticks into his tongue. The resulting infection means that to save his life he will have to lose his tongue and the ability to speak. About the "black stump" in his mouth, "shaped like a forked whip," Donald sometimes pretends, "I am Orestes with the Furies' whips in my mouth for killing a man. . . . I am Oedipus and . . . I cut it out for killing my own father" (91). But what Bonner best captures in this grotesque tale is the unmanning of Donald. A sign of castration, the cut-off tongue links Donald not only to the maimed yet heroic Oedipus and Orestes but also to the silenced, raped Philomel (whose tongue is cut so she cannot accuse her powerful rapist, a king).

Just as Désirée's baby never grows up, "One Boy's Story" tells the narrator's story of remaining a lost boy.[14] From its very first sentence—"I'm glad they got me shut up in here"—to its conclusion, Donald is trapped and silenced by a father who lays claim to his mother but relinquishes any familial tie. The Oedipal crisis

cannot be resolved because the biological father refuses to perform the societal function of the father—refuses, that is, to provide the name, property, status, home, protection, or education that would enable the son to secede him. The story of the son who cannot become a man ends not only with patricidal fury but with a fatal identification with the African-American mother who—despite her loving kindness—inflicts a wounding dispossession. At the end, the hybridity of Bonner's central character breeds self-consuming rage as well as painfully enforced silence: "I am bearing my Furies and my clipped tongue like a Swyburne and a Gage—'cause I am both of them" (91).

Langston Hughes's historical play *Mulatto: A Tragedy of the Deep South* (1931)—like the story "Father and Son" (1933) based on it—turns on exactly the psychosexual dynamic described by Twain, McKay, and Bonner, a variation on the theme of the mulatto tragically doomed to illegitimacy and schizophrenia. As such critics as Judith Berzon, Werner Sollors, and Heather Hathaway have pointed out, Greek themes of incest and obscure familial origins accrue in American literature to melodramas of the "tragic mulatto" in a racially divided society. Hughes' Bert, the mixed son of Colonel Norwood with "proud thin features like his father's," finds himself treated as his father's slave (2). His mother, the black housekeeper on the plantation and mistress of Colonel Norwood, becomes convinced their son is mad when he grandly struts about asking, "Isn't this my old man's house? Ain't I his son and heir?" (15). Although he repeatedly exclaims, "I'm not a nigger, Colonel Tom. I'm your son," the master of the plantation insists, "Nigger women don't know the fathers. You're a bastard" (23). Earlier in their lives, too, the conflict of father and son occurred over naming. Bert received his first physical punishment when the Colonel "beat him for callin' him 'papa'" (14). Their struggle escalates until the son murders his father and then commits suicide to escape a lynching mob.

According to his mother, Cora, Bert represents countless others: "White mens, and colored womens, and little bastard chilluns—that's de old way of de South—... mixtries, mixtries" (30–31); mixes of blood, mixed-up ancestries, mysterious (family) trees. The son in Hughes's play dies on his mother's bed, arrested in the maternal realm, no less fatally divided from the symbolic order of (white) masculine legitimacy than Bonner's Donald. Named after the mythic Greek maiden abducted and raped by the god of the underworld, Cora is right that Bert stands for other doomed characters, even in Hughes's own *oeuvre*. The tormented figure of Hughes's poem "Mulatto" (1927), for example, speaks lines that echo those of Bert—*"I am your son, white man!"*—while the father sounds like Colonel Norwood: *"You are my son! / Like hell!"* (100). Similarly, the speaker of the poem "Cross" (1925), who is "neither white nor black," looks upon his old man's death "in a fine big house" and his mother's "in a shack," wondering not only where he will die but how he can live in the doublecross of his biracial inheritance (58–59).

To "mixtries," the white father must seem a little more than kin, but less than kind. Whether murdered, maddened, ungendered, or simply expelled from the human community, the biracial offspring in narratives about the white father/black mother remains disinherited, hidden from public history, a shameful burden or secret.[15] In a novel entitled *Kindred* (1979) that looks back on American slavery, Octavia E. Butler weighs the origins of the biracial child in illegitimacy and rape against what Jacobs called the "tangled skeins" of slavery's ongoing genealogies. A curious blend of historical slave narrative and science-fiction time travel, the work features a contemporary black woman named Dana who shuttles between southern California in the 1970s and an antebellum plantation in Maryland. In particular, she is snatched back to the past so as to rescue her white progenitor, slave owner Rufus Weylin, who must live and mate with his slave Alice Greenwood until their child Hagar is born. That it is Hagar who will give birth to a lineage (eventuating ultimately in the birth of Dana) evokes the biblical slave-girl Hagar as a prototypical black single mother: Used by Abraham as a surrogate when his wife Sarah is sterile, Hagar is expelled with her illegitimate son Ishmael.[16] As a genealogical statement, *Kindred* portrays the one bit of hope it proffers when—after the death by hanging of Alice—her children begin to call Rufus "Daddy" (253), a sign of his new willingness to acknowledge familial ties that in turn allows Dana to win for them certificates of freedom. Despite the family's romance with whiteness, American history is written in the ink of mated (not married) black and white characters.[17]

Racial Ambiguity and (Childless) Prostitution

If we turn away from Armand's conventional idea of the narrative and toward the second conclusion of "Désirée's Baby," Chopin's far less traditional ending remains more openly ambiguous than her first, for though we presumably know that Armand is the black father of the mixed child, we remain unsure about Désirée's racial background. In this regard, the story resists racial categories altogether. The "dark" baby and father have undergone a racechange from white to black; however, the orphan Désirée remains a figure as nebulous and elusive as desire itself. We had thought her black when she departed for the sluggish bayou; we may have labeled her white when the dark color of her baby was assumed to be the result of Armand's black mother; ultimately, however, we cannot ascertain her own lineage and the baby's dark color may be derived from both parents' mysteriously distant or unknown African lineage.

Perhaps, like the author of a recent autobiography entitled *Notes of a White Black Woman*, Désirée would describe herself as "living on the margins of race" because she believes herself to be "a black American with white skin"; or perhaps Désirée would describe herself as "living on the margins of race" because she assumes herself to be outcast as a white woman who has entered into a sexual relationship with "a black American with white skin" (Scales-Trent, 7). In either case, her indeterminate status means that a definitively color-coded culture must deny her maternal status since her offspring threatens to contaminate the racial purity of white lineage. The racially mutable figure of Désirée, destined at the end to a kind of perpetual oscillation or an unending series of racechanges, establishes a curious link between the white woman defined as illegitimate in her sexuality and the African-American woman, the fallen and the black female, because to bear an unexpectedly colored baby is to register oneself as fallen or sexual—an available black woman, a degenerate white woman—and thus (paradoxically) unfit for motherhood. When doubled with black women—as two potential aspects of one self or as mistress and maid—white women's eroticism, lawlessness, and primitivism are multiplied. For the cultural assumption remained, as one widely read nineteenth-century natural historian put it, that "Negresses carry voluptuousness to a degree of lascivity unknown in [the European] climate."[18]

In its protest against the damning of biracial affiliations and its radical refusal to spell out the secret of Désirée's genealogy, Chopin's tale resembles Charles Chesnutt's "White Weeds" (1974), a story unpublished in his lifetime which also insists on the unstable racial identity of its heroine. Indeed, a female character of obscure origins who is about to be married to an established Professor Carson of Danforth University functions in Chesnutt's narrative as if she were the nemesis Chopin's Désirée might have desired for Armand. The story evolves as a series of mysterious vignettes revolving around Professor Carson's alarm concerning an anonymous letter slandering his wife-to-be followed by his depression after the wedding and subsequent death. Why is Professor Carson's funeral surrealistically staged by his widow as a lavish wedding ceremony, complete with love songs and a casket made to resemble a couch, the "Wedding March" from *Lohengrin*, and Mrs. Carson clad in bridal array?

Only later does the reader discover that the tormented groom had told his bride about the letter's "monstrous calumny," although no one "looking at [her] fair face . . . [could] believe that one drop of Negro blood coursed through [her] veins" (401). Like Armand, in other words, the Professor feared that his fair wife was African American. Again like Armand, Professor Carson insisted that "men and women are either white or black. Those who are not all white are all black," but his bride refuses to give him any assurance that she does not derive from black lineage. Instead, with Jamesian ambiguity she insisted, "I shall certainly not deny it" (402). As if acting out a rebelliousness one might wish for Chopin's heroine, Mrs. Carson persists in precisely the unknowability of racial identity that the orphaned Désirée actually embodies. At least one reason why Professor Carson's bride refuses to reveal the secret of her racial ancestry has to do with the sexual impact of racechange on a woman: It would eroticize or even prostitute her.

Professor Carson's abhorrence—"Nothing could ever make me feel that the touch of a Negress was not pollution"—comes from his mother's suffering when her husband, a planter with numerous slaves, took "some poor unfortunate of color" as his mistress (402). A promise at the maternal deathbed that he would never commit "this sin" causes the fastidious Professor to seek the assurance of his wife about her whiteness. Her refusal to do so apparently leads not only to their alienation in marriage but also to his morbidity and death. In both the funeral-qua-wedding and the title, whiteness—emblematizing an obsessive, self-destructive anxiety about blood stains and strains—takes on the color of grief. Like Miss Havisham in Dickens's *Great Expectations* (1861), Mrs. Carson marks the wedding day as the inauguration of a life-in-death, the commencement of a broken heart. Wearing white weeds, the widow also connects the death of her marriage with the consummation of her desire. Since Mrs. Carson's marriage had been a living death, her husband's death means life to her. The source of the narrative's power derives from its heroine's refusal to accept race as a definition of identity—even if, *especially if*, that identity is maternal and thus capable of producing what Professor Carson calls "children . . . show[ing] traces of their descent from an inferior and degraded race" (402).[19]

The fact that ontological insecurity destroys Professor Carson, who finds himself maddened by his inability to tell if the woman in his bed is a respectable wife or an illicit whore, suggests the fragility of men's control over their future racial lineage. Given the uncertainty of his bride's background, he only knows that she must never become the mother of his children. To admit to being an African American would put the mother and her children beyond the pale. Thus, Mrs. Carson's stubborn silence constitutes a refusal to move along the trajectory of Désirée from sanctification to demonization, from the representative of home to the emblem of homelessness. Yet black or white, Chopin's heroine—as the mother of a dark child—is doomed, exactly as her predecessor La Blanche had been. If black, she devolves into sexual chattel; if white, she must be stigmatized for having been possessed by a black man. Since Désirée remarks that her husband can hear their baby crying "as far away as La Blanche's cabin," perhaps Armand has retained La Blanche as his whore after his wedding, a fate he may have set aside for Désirée, too, once he suspected her of African ancestry.[20]

Exactly this path paved by racechange—from propriety to prostitution—constitutes the progress of the biracial child Amantha Starr of Robert Penn Warren's historical novel *Band of Angels* (1955). The only daughter of a nameless, dead woman and a devoted white planter who neglected to manumit her, Amantha plummets from Edenic freedom to hellish bondage at her father's death when she is enslaved to be sold to pay his debts. At several points in the narrative, Warren's light-skinned heroine experiences a jolting, jarring form of racechange. Like the "ex-coloured man" who narrates James Weldon Johnson's passing narrative and who feels himself "growing black and thick-featured and crimp-haired" when he reveals his African-American roots (204), at certain moments Amantha looks at herself, seeing

> the stain of the black blood swelling through my veins—yes, I actually saw some such picture in my head, a flood darkening through all the arteries and veins of my body— no, a stain spreading in a glass of clear water. (228)

At a later point in the book, however, when the young woman attempts to identify herself with black characters, she feels as if

> a strong galvanic current had been passed through my being to jerk me out of my torpor, to jerk me scrambling up, not in fear, in some deeper necessity, uttering the unplanned words, the words that burst out of me.
> The words were: "I'm not nigger, I'm not nigger—I'm white." (332)

Perpetually oscillating in her racial identity, Amanda knows as completely as did Désirée and Mrs. Carson that to be "nigger" for a woman means being sold as

Figure 6.1   Édouard Manet, *Olympia* (1863). Courtesy Musée d'Orsay, Paris.

sexual merchandise,[21] a form of exploitation which was buttressed by nineteenth-century iconography in art and in medicine. As Sander Gilman has demonstrated, aesthetic and anatomical imagery linked "two seemingly unrelated female images—the icon of the Hottentot female and the icon of the prostitute" (206). Perhaps for this reason, racechange when it occurs in the white female of the species tends to physicalize, much as it did in Colescott's portrait of "Shirley Temple Black." The same dynamic is at work in the racechanges performed on two touchstone paintings, both of which established links between the black female body and white prostitution: Édouard Manet's *Olympia* (1863) and Pablo Picasso's *Les demoiselles d'Avignon* (1907). Although Gilman quite reasonably uses Manet's famous portrait of *Olympia* (Fig. 6.1) to establish the connection between women, sex for sale, and nonwhites, the racechanging parodies of this picture produced by Picasso and Larry Rivers make the point even more explicit.

The black cat coupled with the black maid on the extreme right of Manet's original painting stand for the "pussy" which the thin model coyly hides beneath her hand but which the hefty servant offers the viewer in the shape of a bouquet symbolizing the female genitals and echoed by the exotic flower worn in her mistress's hair. A revision of and homage to Titian's *Venus of Urbino* (1538), Manet's canvas plays various tones of white (the naked skin of the courtesan, rumpled sheets and pillows, silk robe and slippers) against many dark tones (the brown skin of the Negress, dark green curtains, black alley cat). Carrying the gift from a past or future gentleman caller, the maid eyes the mistress as if replicating the gaze to which the mistress brazenly attends, the voyeuristic stare of the spectator who is placed in the position of next client or departing caller. (No wonder that in *Fremde Schön-heit* (discussed in the opening chapter) Hannah Höch bestows such huge though sunken eyes upon her reinvention of Manet's model.) Theodore Reff has demonstrated that *Olympia*, which "seems in fact to mark the real beginning of modern art" (59), brings together a heady Baudelairean brew of "la Venus noire," "fleurs du mal," and a witchy feline fetish, a blend of animal magnetism and moral indifference, ostentatious luxury and commodified primitivism dependent on the doubling of the white courtesan and her black attendant (91–94).

As Marianna Torgovnick points out, both Picasso's *Parody of Manet's "Olympia"* (Fig. 6.2) and Rivers's *I Like Olympia in Black Face* (Fig. 6.3) equate blackness with prostitution and a more explicit physicality (102). In Picasso's canvas, the dark female figure's pronounced thighs and belly as well as her exposed pubic hair emphasize her fleshliness (in contrast to the thinner white model at the center of Manet's painting and the emaciated customers in Picasso's). By producing a picture of himself pointing at the reclining Negress, Picasso stresses his self-consciousness about his own absorption with the African as the subject of modern art. In Rivers's parody, reciprocity in black and white means that when black turns white, white turns black. Not merely a portrait of a single prostitute, the scene has become a whorehouse or harem, complete with titillating interracial lesbian overtones.[22] Playing with the same sort of oscillating racechanges that doom Chopin's and Chesnutt's heroines, Picasso and Rivers produce canvases that oddly medicalize their subjects, hinting at hospital beds, patients anatomically displayed as curiosities, and attendant visitor-voyeurs. Female sexuality, whether black or white, appears vaguely aberrant or even potentially contaminating. If, as Lorraine O'Grady has remarked, the female body, like a coin, has an obverse and a reverse side—"White is what woman is; not-white . . . is what she had better not be"—then the impossibility of separating the two dooms both to pollution (14); it dooms both to childlessness as well, since the pariah's "sterility" stands iconographically in opposition to the sacred mother's "fertility."

Many critics have observed that Picasso's *Les demoiselles d'Avignon* (originally called "The Brothel of Avignon" and partially inspired by *Olympia*) fits Iberian, African, or Oceanic masks onto the inhabitants of a Parisian bordello to conflate the Otherness of primitivism with the Otherness of female sexuality (Fig. 6.4). Like *Parody of Manet's "Olympia"* and *I Like Olympia in Black Face*, Picasso's modernist breakthrough—undertaken soon after his trip to the ethnographic collections at the Trocadero—can be linked to syphilophobia since original drafts of the picture include a dessicated male figure as well as a doctor.[23] As the Africanization of the faces deepens toward the right side of the canvas in the head of the standing *demoiselle* (whose features most resemble the masks of tribal peoples), what William Rubin calls "the unprecedented *brut* or raw coloring and the slashing painterly attack" become more evident, emphasizing the physicality of the oil medium itself (*Les demoiselles*, 105). By destylizing or fleshing out black female figures, Robert Colescott's *Les demoiselles d'Alabama: Vestidas, 1985* (see color insert) ridicules not only Picasso's sexual anxieties but also modernist commodi-

Figure 6.2 Pablo Picasso, *Parody of Manet's "Olympia"* (1907). Copyright ©
1989, ARS N.Y./SPADEM.

Figure 6.3 Larry Rivers, *I Like Olympia in Black Face* (1970), mixed media construction, 71⅝ × 76⅜ × 39⅜″. Copyright © 1996 by Larry Rivers/Licensed by VAGA, New
York. Collection, Musée National d'art Moderne, Centre Georges Pompidou, Paris; courtesy ARS N.Y.

Figure 6.4   Pablo Picasso, *Les demoiselles d'Avignon*, Paris (June–July 1907), oil on canvas, 8′ × 7′8″. Copyright © 1996 The Museum of Modern Art, New York, acquired through the Lillie P. Bliss Bequest.

fications of women and of Africans. According to Lowery S. Sims, "Colescott de-abstracts the Picasso composition . . . , which was abstracted under the influence of African art, and he restores these female apparitions to their original European painterly manifestations" (8). Since Picasso used African art to make European conventions abstract, Colescott moves Picasso's Africanism back toward European images. From Colescott's point of view, "the irony is partly that what most people (including me) know about African conventions comes from Cubist art"; he goes on to ask, "Could a knowledge of European art be so derived as well?" (Sims, 8).

Colescott's question can be answered in the affirmative after we note that removing the masks from the prostitutes in the whorehouse involves depicting their various colors, costumes, and body shapes in such a manner as to make the whore strutting her stuff for the male customer evoke the slave on an auction block. In the fleshly passivity of their line-up, there is something slavish about the prostitute, something prostituted about the slave. Whereas Picasso used geometric planes and abstraction to emphasize the stylized constructedness of even the naked body and thus degendered his subjects, Colescott employs a combination of realistic and comic book techniques to stress the materiality of his decidedly female models. His picture thereby insists that the object of the Western gaze has always been female and that the reified, fetishized female model remains a crucial convention in European art. Colescott centrally locates a wedge of red—a berry? a watermelon?—that mimics the shape of minstrelsy's smiling lips as well as the lipstick-red lips of the whores, thus linking both with the lower (vaginal) lips preferred to anyone in the market for forbidden fruit.

That the trollop on the left looks a bit like Picasso only underlines Colescott's critique of the uses to which the Spanish modernist put African and female images.[24] Taken together with *Olympia* and her racechanged avatars, *Les demoiselles d'Alabama*'s subjects continue to make the mixed child inconceivable since the prostitute in art and in literature may bring pleasure or pain, orgasm or syphilis, but she rarely bears children into the world. Only childlessness insures that a racially indeterminate lineage will not pollute pure origins, as Chesnutt's Professor Carson understood. In the case of *Olympia* and her progenitors, pets, not babies, appear on her bedsheets, embodiments of her willingness to submit herself not only to a devolution into physicality but also to ownership. Zora Neale Hurston's phrase "The 'Pet' Negro System" (1943) adds resonance to Dorothy Sayers's definition of the feminine as "the human-not-quite-human," and together they hint at the reciprocity between the white prostitute and the dark Other singled out for affection by its owner. J.-J. Grandville's parodic version of *Olympia*, entitled *I Was Lazy* (1842), graphically identifies the model reclining on her couch with her pet; the face of the human figure is quite definitively that of a cat (Reff, 72).

The white woman who has trafficked in darkness is not simply prostituted and animalized but also twinned with black women so as to suggest a range of perversities from bestiality to lesbianism. As with the black stud stereotype, the hypersexuality of the Africanist female could take bizarre shapes, as it does perhaps most notoriously in the "Hot Voodoo" nightclub number of Josef von Sternberg's movie *Blonde Venus* (1929) after Marlene Dietrich strips off a gorilla suit and sports a blond Afro while gyrating to jungle drum beats in front of a chorus line of African-American women decked in black Afros. When Dietrich removes her gorilla suit to show the cabaret audience her white hands and face, she herself becomes an amalgam of Fay Wray and King Kong (Figs. 6.5 and 6.6). Both beauty and beast, Dietrich half in, half out of her ape costume recalls the transformation of She-Who-Must-Be-Obeyed at the end of Rider Haggard's late Victorian bestseller *She* (1887). His exquisite heroine, Ayesha, devolves into a wrinkled, brown female animal, "no larger than a big ape" (308). Like Haggard's She, Dietrich—encircled by gyrating black women toting spears (threatening castration) and

Figure 6.5   Marlene Dietrich as King Kong in *Blonde Venus* (1929). Courtesy of Museum of Modern Art Film Stills Archive.

Figure 6.6   Marlene Dietrich as Fay Wray in *Blonde Venus* (1929). Courtesy of Museum of Modern Art Film Stills Archive.

shields painted with vagina dentata (more castration)—no longer knows right from wrong because those insidious "voodoo" drums have caused her conscience to "take a vacation." To the extent that the weary irony and the German-inflected English of her performance-within-the performance emphasize the star's jaded distance from Africa, it is hardly surprising that Dietrich reminds one of her most perceptive critics of the role model for Haggard's She-Who-Must-Be-Obeyed, namely "what the Mona Lisa had been for Walter Pater—a tantalizing, enigmatic woman framed by a decadent gloom, whose face hinted at delicious perversities" (Naremore, 143).

Not only does the "Hot Voodoo" number insinuate that the races are two species—the white one human, the black not—but what Freud called "the dark continent" of female sexuality surfaces in these frames to mark the heroine's role as *femme fatale* as well as her abdication of her maternal respectability.[25] Like Manet's *Olympia*, the nightclub scene brings together a Baudelairean brew of animal magnetism, "la Venus noire," and commodified primitivism through the doubling of the white courtesan and her Africanist attendants. As Dietrich is surrounded by a chorus line of partially naked showgirl-natives, the woman famous for emanating an eroticism that floated free of gender appears to pose the threat and the promise of color released from race in a degenerate (but titillating) deviancy. Reduced to a widow or a whore, robbed of maternity, or simply animalized, the white woman coupled with blackness typifies what Calvin C. Hernton calls the "slut concept," the idea that "any white woman with a Negro [is considered] fair game" (53).[26] Even in the thinking of a critic as savvy as Hernton, the view prevails that "it is the racial meaning of Negro sexuality, in all of its pornography, that the white woman *expects* and *demands* when she becomes intimate with a Negro" (50), whether or not "a Negro" is the male of the species, as Hernton assumes. When the character he calls "the White-Negro woman" undergoes a racechange, she "has that 'gyrating gait,' that bouncing of the shoulders as she talks, that slur in the voice, that earthy twirl in her pelvis when she dances . . ." (51).[27]

The Pre-Oedipal Union of White Mother, Dark Baby

To turn to a final interpretation of the conclusion of Chopin's tale, what if Désirée's baby is born of a black father and a white mother? Such a denouement is, of course, the most shocking of all, from a historical perspective, because the idea of a black father/white mother was made unspeakable during slavery and Reconstruction. In *Incidents in the Life of a Slave Girl*, Harriet Jacobs explains that, although the infant of a black mother immediately became the property of the white father, the baby born of a white mistress who selected a slave on the plantation to be the father of her child would be smothered at birth or banished from sight (81). No wonder that even the most racist eugenicist admonitions—"The cross between a white man and a negro is a negro"—take for granted the white father, black mother. Not only the privations suffered by the central character of the first published novel by an African American but also the obscurity of the book itself—it disappeared into oblivion for more than a century—may be related to Harriet Wilson's depiction in *Our Nig* (1859) of an interracial marriage between a white wife and a black husband. Both the presences and the absences in twentieth-century literature imply that the mandates of a history of slavery and lynching still operate. Significantly, however, transgressive narratives about the white mother/black offspring eventually issue in a libertarian script, one that imbues the multiracial child with an almost magical transracial aura.

An especially evocative, lyrical story about dark children born to a white mother, which appears near the beginning of Jean Toomer's classic *Cane* (1923), captures the calamitous as well as the potentially redemptive aspects of the white mother/black child dyad. An opening and closing paragraph—

> Becky was the white woman who had two Negro sons. She's dead; they've gone away. The pines whisper to Jesus. The Bible flaps its leaves with an aimless rustle on her mound. (7)

—brackets the tale, functioning like a refrain or an epigraph, so as to establish the sketch as an elegy of a pariah. White and black communities alike ostracize Becky after the first "Negro son" was engendered by what the whites in the town call a "Damn buck nigger" and what the blacks call a "Low-down nigger with no self-respect." Gossip from both sides conspires to destroy Becky's sanity, though she does not reveal the father's identity (and thereby saves him from the lynching other sections of *Cane* describe). Against the crime of miscegenation and racial disloyalty, blacks and whites "joined hands to cast her out" onto a "narrow strip of land between the railroad and the road," a location fitting her liminal status in the town.

But like other scapegoats, Becky takes on magical significance to those who have exiled her. Although "No one ever saw her," train passengers throw papers on the "Ground islandized between the road and railroad track," something like the prayers strewn on religious shrines, while townsfolk secretly bring her sweet potatoes and corn, something like offerings or propitiations. When her five-year-old boy appears carrying a dark baby, everyone knows but no one says anything about the second child, for people had told themselves "that Becky now was dead" (8). The pronoun "we" surfaces in this section of the narrative to make it clear that the community remains monolithic in its scorn of the "Sullen and cunning" boys who, in turn, curse white and black people alike. Since the young men don't know or care if they are "White or colored" and since neither racial group will take them in, Becky's sons "answered black and white folks by shooting up two men and leaving town." The departure of the renegades leads to the repeated refrain "O pines, whisper to Jesus" as the narrator explains the community's dread that Becky's ghost haunts the cabin.

One Sunday, on a trip home from a neighboring church, an unnamed but now individualized narrator sees his horses frightened as they come onto Becky's cabin. Terrified himself, he witnesses the ground trembling as a ghost train rumbles by and the chimney falls down with a hollow thud. A glance at the door tells him and his companion, Barlo, that Becky would have been buried by the bricks, if she were in there: "I thought I heard a groan. Barlo, mumbling something, threw his Bible on the pile" (9). As a number of readers have explained, Becky becomes invisible because her racial transgression has broken the ban against cross-racial mothering; however, she also becomes a haunting, even shamanistic presence, indeed the spirit of the place that both black and white people placate, feed, worship (Baker, *Singers of Daybreak*, 59; Doyle, 84). Like Désirée, Becky remains an outcast whose dark children blackened her character. But Toomer's prose poem insists it is the very unthinkability of Becky's life story that obsesses the racially segregated community.[28]

Refusing to accept the idea of black babies born of white maternal bodies, both blacks and whites isolate, punish, and then bow down to the woman who incarnates their secret desires. Like the return of the repressed, Becky's spectral life-in-death on the edge of town transmutes her into an uncanny haunting presence. Just as Becky moves from scapegoat to saint, the figure of the white mother of the dark child evolves from pariah to madonna over the course of the twentieth century. The identity of her child, too, undergoes a transformation, as the move from the term "mulatto" (meaning a sterile mule) to the terms "mixed," "hybrid," "biracial," and "multi-ethnic" demonstrates. Through the story of a woman made into a taboo—consecrated but forbidden, polluted but sacred—Toomer provides a framework for understanding the relative silence of imaginative writers on the narrative of the white mother of the mixed child, a silence maintained until very recently. Even when that silence was broken, the narrative seems at first to have generated grotesquely incommensurate, Gothic consequences.

Countee Cullen's lament in his poem "Near White" (1925)—that those "Ambiguous of race . . . stand/ By one disowned, scorned of another"—underscores the fates of fictional and nonfictional products of the white mother, black father (*Color*, 11). At the turn of the century, according to Ida B. Wells, apocryphal stories about the members of integrated clubs giving birth to black babies were used to warn white women against including African Americans in their ranks. That monitory tales cautioning against the dangers of miscegenation endured long into the century Bessie Head's *A Question of Power* (1973) proves.[29] For the African writer's autobiographical novel presents a protagonist told about her biracial origins by a school principal who seems to see them as legal proof of the girl's culpability:

> "We have a full docket on you. You must be very careful. Your mother was insane. If you're not careful you'll get insane just like your mother. Your mother was a white woman. They had to lock her up, as she was having a child by the stable boy, who was a native." (16)

The quintessential victim of racism, Head's heroine is viewed as a half-breed or untouchable. A character in Zora Neale Hurston's novel *Jonah's Gourd Vine* (1934) illuminates the same dynamic at work in American society when he explains, "dese half-white niggers [are thought to have] got de worst part uh bofe de white and de black folks" (9), a claim sustained in contemporary times by one Gregory Howard Williams—the "whitest colored boy" most people had seen—who attributed the prejudice he experienced while growing up in the Midwest during the 1950s to whites' revulsion against the "'bestial mongrel mulatto'" (93).[30]

Notwithstanding the persistence of pessimistic accounts of the biracial off-spring, in recent times several contemporary literary women brood on the story of the biracial child born of the white mother so as to induce a kind of redemptive racechange in the psychology of nonblack readers. If "among politically committed and enlightened whites," as Adrian Piper has contended, "the inability to acknowledge their probable African ancestry is the last outpost of racism" (234), then white parenting of black children may constitute one vanguard in a movement of changing racial consciousness. According to Piper, "for whites to acknowledge their blackness is . . . much the same as for men to acknowledge their femininity and for Christians to acknowledge their Judaic heritage. It is to reinternalize the external scapegoat through attention to which they have sought to escape their own sense of inferiority" (235). How better reinternalize the external scapegoat than by bearing the black baby within the white body? How better acknowledge blackness than by giving birth to, nursing, or nurturing the black child?

Such contemporary women of letters as Marilyn Hacker, Jane Lazarre, Sherley Anne Williams, and Grace Paley engage nonblack readers in imagining their African ancestry by celebrating consciousness of color without race, transcendent epiphanies achieved through the image of the dark child fostered by the white parent. In the place of the warring father and Oedipal son, they excavate the pacific pre-Oedipal bonding of mother and baby to delineate the possibilities not only of fluid ego boundaries between self and Other but also blurred racial boundaries between white mother and biracial infant. Implicitly agreeing with James Baldwin's belief that one cannot "cease playing a role simply because one has begun to understand it" (*Price of the Ticket*, 291), these contemporary poets and fiction writers envision the interdependence as well as the merging of races through the complicated two-in-oneness of the mother/child dyad, a couple which leads them to meditations similar to Baldwin's reflection that "each of us, helplessly and forever, contains the other—male in female, female in male, white in black, and black in white" (*Price of the Ticket*, 690).

Marilyn Hacker and Jane Lazarre, writing respectively in autobiographical verse and prose forms, depict the pregnancy of the white mother, the birth of the dark child as an awakening into a consciousness different from the normative one of racial conflict or competition. Bearing the multiracial child delivers the mother into a new conception of not simply admitting or acknowledging but embracing and loving difference. Representative of much of her work on this subject, Hacker's sonnet about the birth of her biracial daughter deserves to be quoted in full:

> "I'm pregnant," I wrote to her in delight
> from London, thirty, married, in print. A fools-
> cap sheet scrawled slantwise with one minuscule
> sentence came back. "I hope your child is white."
> I couldn't tear the pieces small enough.
> I hoped she'd be black as the ace of spades,

> though hybrid beige heredity had made
> that as unlikely as the spun-gold stuff
> sprouted after her neonatal fur.
> I grudgingly acknowledged her "good hair,"
> which wasn't, very, from my point of view.
> "No tar brush left," her father's mother said.
> "She's Jewish and she's white," from her cranked bed
> mine smugly snapped.
> She's Black. She is a Jew.

Rebellious toward her aged, ill mother, Hacker identifies her delight in the mysterious child she is carrying with her pleasure in her own authority and authorship. "Thirty, married, in print," she writes a letter about her pregnancy and imagines a baby "black as the ace of spades." Her mother's conventionally prejudiced response arrives in a "minuscule sentence" "scrawled" on "A foolscap sheet" only to be torn into small pieces. Although the mother-to-be worries about "hybrid beige heredity" on the father's side, her mother-in-law appears to be pleased that there is "no tar brush left." Firmly rejecting the terms of her mother and her mother-in-law, Hacker's poem turns into a love sonnet in its last line of welcome where the child's transracial identity cannot be summed up in one sentence but needs two separate but equal declarations on the page, both combined in the unprecedented mix of the child.[31] The "unlikely . . . neonatal fur" sprouting on Hacker's baby signals its unpredictable difference from what had come before and presages the older child's color of "gold on lion-gold" in a later poem where the mother-poet directly claims that "mixed races swell the lexicon," generating new words and new perceptions like that of the "Bedouin for *sand*, or Eskimo / for *snow*" (45).

Just as giving birth to the biracial child alienates Hacker from the conventional racial consciousness of her cranky mother and mother-in-law, the white writer Jane Lazarre in *The Mother Knot* feels herself undergoing a racechange when she realizes she is pregnant with her black husband's child: "Resting my hand lightly on my belly, I was as Black as anyone" (18). But it is not until the birth of her baby that her identification with the infant effectively alienates her from white people, specifically when she witnesses incomprehensible white fear of blackness. At the hospital where her first son is born, she watches the nurses holding her boy and notes "the same fear lurking around the edges of their faces as I had seen in other white faces, in town, in stories, in our housing complex, when they spoke of Bobby Seale," a civil rights activist just as unintimidating as her infant son because incarcerated at the time (45). In her confessional novel *Worlds Beyond My Control* (1991), Lazarre's shameful awareness of white people's unfounded fear of African Americans jettisons her fictional surrogate into a series of racechanges in consciousness.

Because the heroine's son Daniel understands that white people do not perceive him or his father as persons but instead witness only color, Julia begins to feel "her skin is scorched by their blackness, like a branding iron would scorch her skin. Her skin seems to go up in smoke from a body that is hot, wounded" (95). Although her other son, Anthony, composes a poem about "*Warring races divided / yet in-*

side of me / the two races beautifully united," Julia wonders if her husband ever regrets that he married someone white, only to be charmed by his mock shock: "—Oh my God . . . You're white?" (100–101). Terrified throughout her writing about letting her children go out into a world especially inhospitable to black young men, Julia nevertheless learns from them to imagine clay roads inside her body turning into rich layers of mud and being transformed until she is "as black and blue" as her husband and children: "I am black inside where loss, language, and courage will root for as long as I live" (176). As if writing from the position of one of Lazarre's sons and imbued with precisely the sense of biracial subjectivity that fascinates her, James McBride—one of twelve siblings brought up by a black father and a Jewish mother who defined herself as not "white" but simply "light-skinned"—explains in his memoir, *The Color of Water* (1996), that as a child he "would have preferred that Mommy were black"; however, as as adult "I feel privileged to have come from two worlds. My view of the world is not merely that of a black man but that of a black man with something of a Jewish soul" (15, 79).

In an analysis of precisely the taboo Hacker, Lazarre, and Ruth McBride Jordan have broken, Patricia J. Williams asks a series of resonant questions about white mothering of black children:

> Is there not something unseemly, in our society, about the spectacle of a white woman mothering a black child? A white woman giving totally to a black child; a black child totally and demandingly dependent for everything, sustenance itself, from a white woman. The image of a white woman suckling a black child; the image of a black child sucking for its life from the bosom of a white woman. The utter interdependence of such an image; the merging it implies; the giving up of boundary; the encompassing of other within self; the unbounded generosity and interconnectedness of such an image. (*Alchemy*, 226–27)

Elsewhere, envisioning a way to "integrate this world from the inside out," Williams argues that "We must shake up biological normativity" and goes so far as to "suggest guerrilla insemination to challenge the notion of choice" (the privileging of white characteristics); "it will be disembodied black seed that will swell white bellies; the symbolically sacred vessel of the white womb will bring the complication home to the guarded intimacy of white families, and into the madonna worship of the larger culture" (*Alchemy*, 188). (Such seemingly outré ideas take on plangency in the context of cases like that of Wilma and Willem Stuart, the Dutch couple whose experience with in-vitro fertilization produced one light- and one dark-skinned baby because a technician unwittingly reused a pipette that still contained sperm from a previous insemination.[32])

Probably the most ironic approach to the taboo described by Williams surfaces in a brilliant short story by Muriel Spark about the racial limits of Western culture's madonna worship as well as its mythology about the maternal instinct. "The Black Madonna" (1960) focuses on a couple of progressive Catholics—Raymond and Lou Parker—whose liberalism is unmasked by the horror they experience at their bringing a black baby into the world. Even at the beginning, Spark's tale juxtaposes the patronizing Parkers' befriending of two Jamaicans with certain strains in the relationship. After a visit to Lou's impoverished sister, for example, black Henry Pierce has the temerity to compare her psychology to "the slum mentality . . . back home," but Lou resents the comparison; "what a cheek *him* talking like a snob. At least Elizabeth's white" (13). Or, again, when the other Jamaican, Oxford St. John, looks at the glass in her kitchen and refers to himself as black, "Lou thought . . . it was not the thing to say" (13). Yet the Raymonds continue to pray for the welfare of the two immigrants, and after those prayers are met by the aesthetically distinctive icon in their parish church, Lou and Raymond "decided to put in for a baby to the Black Madonna" (16). Of course their prayers are answered in a manner they could hardly expect.

Appearing "terribly red" at first (20), the newborn is perfect, yet the couple is shocked to discover "the baby will certainly be brown, if not indeed black" (21). Lou refuses to feed the infant, an enraged Raymond wonders if it was Oxford who is to blame, Lou's sister informs them of color on her father's side, but nothing placates the horrified pair. "If it was anyone else's child I would think it was all right," Raymond explains; "It's just the thought of it being mine, and people thinking it isn't" (26). Lou agrees, declaring to a neighbor, "Imagine it for yourself, waking up to find you've had a black baby that everyone thinks has a nigger for its father" (26). When they put the baby up for adoption, the priest says it is the "*right*" thing to do, though it would have been a "*good*" thing to have kept it. The difference between "right" and "good" is the contrast between the facade of liberalism Lou and Raymond practice and the love they cannot find within themselves. The black Madonna seems to work the will of "a coloured God [who] is not asleep," playing exactly the trick on the priggish couple that they deserve. When "the symbolically sacred vessel of the white womb" swells with "black seed," it brings home the complications of unacknowledged racism, as Williams predicted it would. Spark's madonna is black because in this satirist's view racism has incapacitated whites, proven them incapable of loving—or mothering—the Other.

Like Patricia J. Williams, though more cynically, Muriel Spark broods on the possibility of the interdependence of mother and child, the permeable boundaries between mother and infant, posing an antidote to racism in a fostering of the Other within the self. Similarly, in *Dessa Rose* (1986), Sherley Anne Williams's imaginative account of a nineteenth-century slave rebellion, the "unseemly" scene of a white woman suckling a black child first horrifies the baby's slave mother but eventually foreshadows reciprocity between blacks and whites. Here, a runaway who has just given birth, the eponymous Dessa, awakes in shock to witness a white woman nursing the black newborn. Miss Rufel, a mother and a plantation mistress presiding over a refuge for runaways, had responded to the tiny, bloodied baby with painful intensity and "only when his cries were stilled and she looked down upon the sleek black head, the nut-brown face flattened against the pearly paleness of her breast, had she become conscious of what she was doing" (105). Embarrassed, she feels "somehow vindicated" by the confusion of the African Americans in her household, though mortified, too, "at becoming wet nurse for a darky" (106). What wins out is the pleasure the white mistress takes at "the contrast between [the infant's] mulberry-colored mouth and the pink areola surrounding her nipple, between his caramel-colored fist and the rosy cream of her breast" (106).

At first Dessa's vision of Rufel nursing her baby goes "against everything she had been taught to think about white women but to inspect that fact too closely was almost to deny her own existence" (123). However, Rufel clearly acts this way in gratitude and reciprocity for the acts of kindness of her Mammy. Indeed, because of the goodness of this shadowy figure as well as the white woman's growing awareness that she knew nothing at all about Mammy as a person in her own right, rueful Rufel expects "all darkies to be like Mammy. *Like family*" (135; emphasis mine). Eventually, just as the mistress begins to admit her ignorance about Mammy, to concede that kinship had been forced on Mammy, even the resentful and understandably wary Dessa learns that Rufel "wasn't that foolish. But where white peoples look at black and see something ugly, something hateful, she saw color" (184). Finally, together with other runaways, Rufel and Dessa enter into a con game on slaveholders, with Rufel playing the role of "Mistress" and Dessa playing the role of "Mammy." The fictiveness of their impersonations has been underscored not only by a series of complex disagreements and dialogues they have sustained about Mammies and mothers but also by the fact that Rufel has actually functioned as Mammy for Dessa's baby.[33]

Besides shaking up what Patricia J. Williams calls "biological normativity," the racechanged baby nursed by its loving mother or mother surrogate holds out the promise of difference not simply recognized but relished. Writing about what the mother-infant couple teaches, the psychologist Jessica Benjamin points out that "In getting pleasure *with* the other and taking pleasure *in* the other, we engage in mutual recognition" (126). The "intersubjective mode where two subjects meet"—mother and child, man and woman, black and white—negotiates between separateness and relatedness, bounded and unbounded possibilities, holding out some future solution to past conflictual sexual or racial Othering. For this reason, the nurtured biracial child can become a utopian icon of transracial consciousness. One of the happiest subjects interviewed in Lise Funderburg's *Black, White, Other: Biracial Americans Talk about Race and Identity* (1994) explained that she feels "ahead of everybody else . . . because I'm already mixed. I have this hidden theory that eventually everybody in the world is going to be mixed with something or another, so I got a jump on it" (298).[34]

Grace Paley would agree with the biracial son in Lazarre's *Worlds Beyond My Control* about the mixed child representing "*Warring races divided / yet inside of me / the two races beautifully united*" and with Lise Funderburg's optimistic subject. Indeed, in two quite different stories, Paley uses the hybridity of the mixed race child to capture the possibility of a redemptive future truce in race warfare. As narrated by its central character, an aged Jewish pharmacist, "Zagrowsky Tells" (1985) examines a miraculous transformation from racial hate to racial love. Accompanied by his black five-year-old grandson Emanuel, Zagrowsky tells his story to Faith, a woman who once many years earlier had picketed his store because he refused to serve African Americans or kept them waiting or served them rudely. Although he admits that he had wanted "to discourage" black people from moving into the neighborhood, although he used to respond to interracial couples with "Ugh—disgusting! It shouldn't be allowed!" (158, 165), he clearly has learned to love "raising a little boy brown like a coffee bean" (159). Convinced that his wife's nervousness has given his daughter Cissy her mental illness—he believes that "genes . . . [are] where the whole story is written down" (154)—Zagrowsky is shocked when she finds herself pregnant in the mental institution to which she has been confined and impregnated by "a black man with a green thumb"—the gardener (169). At first, the old man thinks to himself, "I can't stand it. I refuse. Out of my Cissy, who looked like a piece of gold, would come a black child" (168), but soon the child becomes his "little best friend" (169), convincing Zagrowsky that "long ago we were mostly dark" and "there are plenty black Jews" (171).

Just as Jean Toomer looked upon *Cane* as "a spiritual fusion analogous to the fact of racial intermingling" (Hutchinson, "Jean Toomer," 231), the biracial offspring in Paley's work holds out the promise of a mystical merging. The hybrid child becomes a messianic wonder worker in the gospel according to Zagrowsky but also in the good news of "At That Time, or The History of a Joke" (1981). In the earlier story, Faith finds newborn faith in a child named Emanuel (Hebrew for messiah) born to a mother who used to sing Handel's *Messiah*, especially two songs: "One is about the Gentiles will see the light and the other is, Look! a virgin will conceive a son" (162). Zagrowsky, who himself believes that the boy is "a golden present" from "Egypt," is told by Faith that Emanuel is born from Ishmael who is born from Abraham's union with Hagar (the slave of his barren wife, Sarah). As in Octavia Butler's *Kindred*, the biblical story of Hagar identifies African-American women with an enforced surrogacy that could be defined as rape, single parenthood, exile, and radical encounters with divinity. In any case, the dark child earlier despised and rejected becomes an uncanny savior.

Composed in a more tongue-in-cheek style, the postmodernist fable "At That Time, or The History of a Joke" takes up the idea of the dark child as a messiah in a technologically advanced time when "most people were willing to donate organs" and one woman received a uterine transplant only immediately to discover that her womb held "a darling rolled-up foetus": "It was unfurled in due time and lo! it was black as the night which rests our day-worn eyes." Again the child is a herald of redemption, as the aptly named scientist Dr. Heiliger calls out "see how the myth of man advances on the back of technological achievement and behold without conceiving a virgin has borne a son." All the people celebrate except for certain Jews weeping "It is not He!" As always, the Jews are right. After the authorities take away their TVs and shortwaves, the doctor admits, "Yes, it is a girl. A virgin born of a virgin." Paley's parodic parable concludes with the joy of the world, for "By that time, sexism and racism had no public life, though they were still sometimes practiced by adults at home."

On the one hand, as if elaborating upon Charlotte Perkins Gilman's view that male-authored religions were death-centered while female-created spiritualities would be birth-centered, Paley envisions the holy black girl's umbilicus becoming a spiritual symbol to put next to that of the cross; on the other, she imagines the stiff-necked Jews still discontented, exclaiming "we need another Virgin Birth like our blessed dead want cupping by ancient holistic practitioners." That with varying degrees of joy, anxiety, and hilarity Hacker, Lazarre, and Paley mythologize dark babies in explicitly Jewish contexts reflects the many artistic links between blacks and Jews, associations embodied at the start of the century in the cross-racial artistry of performers like Irving Berlin, Sophie Tucker, Eddie Cantor, and Al Jolson; at midcentury, connections manifest in Norman Mailer's "White Negro," and at its close in Anna Deavere Smith's *Fires in the Mirror* (1993), a dramatic performance in which the talented actress impersonates Lubavitchers and blacks at war in the Crown Heights section of Brooklyn. As Deavere Smith's play proves, it would, of course, be foolish to ignore divisions between and within African-American and Jewish communities during the past several decades, including charges of paternalism leveled against Jewish supporters of civil rights, accusations of anti-Semitism aimed at black leaders, and outrage about racialized class boundaries that have kept a greater percentage of African Americans than Jews in poverty. Indeed, Jewish–black racechanges often address precisely these tensions. In addition, however, the mythologizing of the Jewish, black child suggests that the discourse of Judaism—by traversing ethnic, religious, regional, and racial categories—might set the stage for less agonistic approaches to difference.[35] (It seems significant, in this regard, that Fanon modeled his ideas about racism on Sartre's study *Anti-Semite and Jew*.[36])

For such women of letters as Muriel Spark and Sherley Anne Williams, as for Hacker, Lazarre, and Paley, the hybridity of the child signals an apocalyptic racial consciousness, a distinct rupture from the past into an unprecedented, strange, post-racist future. According to Lise Funderburg, biracial people "necessarily have to break new ground in their own relationships" since they can never replicate their family of origin, "that intersection of two separate groups" (197). Empowering whites to experience the individuality of the Other on a visceral level, the mixed children of contemporary fiction usher into being a rejuvenated world order not further away than the middle of the next century when white Americans will constitute a minority of the national population.

Black Parents and the Racechanged Offspring

In 1972, when the National Association of Black Social Workers passed a resolution against the adoption of black children by white parents, it issued what F. James Davis has called "a ringing endorsement of the one-drop rule" (129). Arguing that black children need role models to gain confidence in their identities, the social workers considered the racial match between parent and child "essential to maintaining pride in the black ethnic identity" (168). By 1995, interracial adoptions were officially or unofficially barred in 43 states (*Newsweek*, Feb. 13, 1995).[37] From the perspective of the National Association of Black Social Workers, do fantasies of the unpredictably colored baby simply illuminate one more nefarious attempt at white appropriation of black bodies or one more representation of white authority over black? Have the most scrupulously imaginative efforts at restitution for the long history of suffering inflicted by whites on blacks only transmuted the childishness and primitivism which were attributed to African Americans so as to justify whites playing a role *in loco parentis*?

By trying to fashion scripts in which African Americans affect the lives of whites personally, in which family responsibilities are restructured along interracial lines, in which racial competition is replaced by interracial nurturance that benefits both parent and child, authors of the narrative of the white-mothered black offspring seek to escape the dynamics of Othering that permeate racism. Supplanting Shirley Temple, the mixed child appears as a Blakean "Infant Joy" or a Wordsworthian "best Philosopher" or "Nature's Priest." Yet of course such black and white thinkers as Patricia J. Williams and Grace Paley understand that the terms with which they describe the organic revolution they seek remain inevitably contaminated by the culture they inhabit. *Charitas* could devolve into charity; parenting into patronizing.[38] Too often, Patricia J. Williams explains, "gray babies" under a "waved banner of aggressive miscegenation" become "the optimist's antidote to everything" (*Rooster's Egg*, 189–90). Despite loving intentions, then, creators of a story about whites bearing, birthing, or nursing black offspring could be accused of slipping back into the habit of whites defining themselves vis-à-vis subordinated black bodies.

Recently, as if defending against imperializing encounters, a number of writers have revised the narrative of the racechanged child by imagining its appearance within the black family. Whereas historically literature records white families depreciating the gift of black life, at times (albeit infrequently) it has included imaginative accounts of blacks devaluing the gift of white life.[39] When the white child is imagined inexplicably materializing in the black family, it can create exactly the response of shock, alarm, even horror generated by the dark offspring in characters like Chopin's Armand and Hughes's Colonel Norwood, for the light-skinned child may be rejected as a denial or abandonment of (black) origins. Though it is hardly surprising that celebrating blackness can entail demonizing whiteness, even the lightest baby in the black family remains inescapably, categorically African American (because of the ongoing influence of the "one-drop rule"). This asymmetry means that white racism never translates simply into black racism; even black parents bent on killing their light offspring cannot simply be accused of hostility against whites, for they collude in a culture hostile primarily to African Americans.

The striking contrast between Zora Neale Hurston's play *Color Struck* (1926) and Alyce Miller's short story "Color Struck" (1994) exemplifies a shift in narrative treatment of the light-skinned child born to the black mother. At the beginning of the drama produced during the Harlem Renaissance, Hurston's insecure heroine, Emma, remains firmly convinced that her dark skin color makes her unlovable. For this reason, she has rejected a black lover (jealously believing John desirous of lighter women) and has given birth out of wedlock to a child whose complexion suggests that the father is white. Years later, after John has returned to express his devotion again, Emma remains so blinded by overvaluations of whiteness (so "color-struck") that she lets her sick daughter die, rather than leave her alone with him in order to go for a doctor; the ailing child is condemned to death because the mother believes her suitor would molest the bedridden girl. Apparently, a light epidermis—even on a feverish little girl—casts an inexorably alluring spell. Exemplifying the sort of psychotic racial self-hatred Hurston would go on to examine in the character of Mrs. Turner in *Their Eyes Were Watching God*, the color-struck mother effectively murders the light child she has brought into the world.

Just as disturbed by the eruption of whiteness in the family as Emma is enthralled by it, the parents in Alyce Miller's story "Color Struck" are shocked by the appearance of their third child. For the mother Caldonia, a caesarian birth has contributed to her sense that the white "child had not really come out of her own body" (108) but was instead some kind of ghastly "mix-up" (128) or "blunder, a genetic contretemps" (110). Although Caldonia had read an article entitled "White Couple Gives Birth to Black Baby," she cannot simply reverse its message to comprehend her own situation because "a black woman's baby, no matter how light, would always be black" (110). According to the estranged mother, the child, who seems "cold and foreign" (110), a "tiny wriggling shrimplike creature," must be tended in the dark like "a household plant" (120) or a shameful secret. Haunted by her fear that she will never be able to love the child, Caldonia cannot find a name for the infant even weeks after the birth. If Hurston's mother adores whiteness (though she kills it), Miller's finds it vaguely repulsive (though she nurtures it).

When her brother's date arrives at Thanksgiving and turns out to have the coloring of the baby, Caldonia's extended family coos over the "same pretty complexion" they share (125), but Caldonia remains upset and calls the baby "albino" not simply to signify its sensitivity to light but to indicate her refusal to conform to their "color-struck" values (122–23). Arranging "the baby's pink mouth at her brown breast" (147), she sees that the white girlfriend will never respond to the advances of her dark brother, and she does not "know which was worse, going through life toward blindness or going through life white. In a way, it was kind of the same thing" (128). Caldonia's wish to name the baby Ebony is greeted by her husband with incredulity; however, the final sentence of the story—"she wasn't blaming anyone but herself for the pinch in her heart that prevented her from running right upstairs and calling the child by her rightful name" (129)—suggests, on the one hand, that the baby must be named Ebony so as to be loved within the black family and, on the other, that nobody knows the child's name.

Throughout the narrative of the racechanged child, of course, a fascination with the new child signals an interest in imagining the parent-self reborn with an altered demeanor. In other words, the child can be read as an avatar embodying one of the parent's potential futures. For Alyce Miller's central character, the slippage between whiteness and a disabling albinism means such a rebirth constitutes a genetic mistake.[40] The white-self emerges again as a fallen one in two dystopic reveries on what racial rebirth might mean for the African-American poet. June Jordan's "What Would I Do White" (1967) and Lucille Clifton's "my dream about being white" (1987) use racechange fantasies to identify whiteness with a kind of ghostly invisibility or insubstantial nonbeing. Jordan answers the question of her title with a poem that can be summed up in the word "nothing." If she were "full / of not exactly beans," she would forget her furs, ignore the doorman, and "inspire big returns to equity / the equity of capital I am / accustomed to accept." The final couplet—"I would do nothing. / That would be enough."—hints that the white woman on view as a decorous object, unproductive except as a kind of investment or commodity, is herself nobody. Similarly, in Clifton's dream of being white, negativity abounds. With "no lips" and "no behind," the poet reborn white finds herself "wearing / white history / but there's no future / in those clothes" so she strips and wakes up dancing. Like Soyinka, Jordan and Clifton hint at a black fullness of being, white nothingness that could propel precisely the anxieties among Euro-Americans that in turn lead to obsessive racial mimicries and masquerades.

Inevitable as retaliatory devaluations of whiteness (like those of Jordan and Clifton) may be, their insufficiency as a response against racism is examined by Gloria Naylor, whose ambitious novel *Linden Hills* (1985) provides a sort of coda to this chapter through its meditation on the vertiginous destructiveness of racial impersonation for the African-American community. Here the legitimate but shockingly light-skinned baby born into a black family is as despised as the dark child in slave times. Though endowed with the "same squat bowlegs, the same protruding eyes and puffed lips" as his father, the son's white complexion makes him appear to his father like "a ghostly presence that mocked everything his fathers had built" (18). As in Alyce Miller's tale, then, the child goes unnamed, but in this case for the first five years of life. Clearly Naylor, like Miller, is interested in the idea of black replications of white racism. Ultimately, however, both writers insist that even the lightest or the most assimilated African Americans remain categorized as implacably, essentially black. Ironically, only when black people try (unsuccessfully) to model themselves on whites in *Linden Hills* do they learn to loath difference; only when black people imitate whites do they commit the crime of murdering Otherness. Naylor's highly paradoxical novel thus turns on mimicry and mirroring, racial impersonation as a dead end.

A revision of Dante's *Inferno*, *Linden Hills* describes a wealthy black suburb whose citizens pay for their success with various forms of torment, from suicide and infidelity to loveless marriages and a sense of lifelessness. When blacks model their communities on the competitive, entrepreneurial system of whites, the resulting racechange kills or perverts. The select families chosen to receive mortgages are given "a thousand years and a day to sit right there and forget what it means to be black" (16), somewhat like Nathan Hare's *Black Anglo-Saxons* (1965), those "social schizophrenics" who—because they are black on the outside, white on the inside—are dubbed "Oreos." Although advertised as a "beautiful, black wad of spit right in the white eye of America," Linden Hills "wasn't black; it was successful" (9, 17). Following up on this grotesque logic, one of its fanatically conformist citizens, hungry for professional advancement in the white business world, makes "his blackness . . . disappear" by avoiding sex and controlling his diet so as to regulate his bowel movements (102–4). Similarly, a top executive at IBM kills herself after selling her soul to the corporation, while a lawyer suffers a life-in-death marriage when he relinquishes his male lover to defuse homophobic rumors that threaten his career.

At the bottom of this sordid, sad world, in the very pitch of power, is Satanic Luther Nedeed's house, surrounded by a frozen lake and given the number 999 because in this neighborhood up is down (the wealthier houses are lower down the hill) and 666 is the sign of the beast.[41] Unlike his ancestors who wed light-skinned brides, each of whom produced one very dark and froglike son, a duplicate of the father, Luther Nedeed married a dark "shadow" of a woman, Willa Prescott Nedeed, who has given birth to a white child resembling her grandmother. Because Luther considers the boy a bastard or because his wife has failed in her appointed task to recreate him, Nedeed incarcerates his wife and son in the basement, a kind of underworld beneath the hell of his house. Willa survives in part by interpreting the documents left behind by wives of earlier Nedeeds—diaries, photographs, cookbooks—whose stories reveal the effacement through which they submitted to their husbands' denial of their value as anything except what Margaret Homans calls "disposable machines for replicating men" (369).

The death of the six-year-old boy, a dead end for the Nedeed line, awakens the complicitous Willa, who finally realizes that she has herself walked down the steps into the basement and so she can walk back up. Carrying her ghostly white son, Willa revolts against the slavery inflicted on herself and on all the other wives of Nedeed men. In a brilliant revision of Charlotte Brontë's *Jane Eyre*, where maddened Bertha Mason Rochester escapes her confinement in the attic of the ancestral mansion of Thornfield Hall and climbs to the roof to set it afire, Willa ascends from the basement to struggle with her husband and in the process sets the house afire. Her dead white child serves as an emblem of the deathliness of the psychological racechanges that created Linden Hills in the first place. In other words, the son dies because he was always destined to be merely a simulacrum or copy of whiteness, a symbol of the fatality and futility of the black middle class's effort to prove itself "just like" whites. Significantly, Willa's boy is murdered by the black man who wants to "forget what it means to be black": A white impersonator, Luther Nedeed becomes the apotheosis of evil when he acts like Chopin's Armand and Hughes's Colonel Norwood, refusing to father the son he masters. That he destroys himself and his lineage in the process proves that black racism remains a contradiction-in-terms for Naylor; it injures only black people and thus perpetuates the hurts inflicted by white racism.[42]

Eventually, the ghost story Naylor tells eulogizes all the rejected children haunting the conscience of the nation. As Lillian Smith once put it, "Little ghosts playing and laughing and weeping on the edge of the southern memory can be a haunting thing" (120). Whether unexpectedly dark or light, then, racechanged children in fiction act as ghostly instructors on the subject of the family's romance with whiteness. In his meditation on "Family Romances" (1909), Freud claimed that most children remain persuaded for a good portion of their early lives that their mundane biological parents could not possibly be their real parents, for a magisterial sense of privilege and power endows young children with the fantasy that they must derive from royal lineage. Children convinced that they have an Emperor and Empress for father and mother demote their actual parents into mere caretakers, substituting in their stead exalted parents of "better birth," altogether "grander people" (76–77). If we read this psychological trope not only in the Oedipal context provided by Freud but also in the framework of most psychologists' belief that babies and young children do not register any awareness of a racial identity, narratives of the racechanged child suggest that all colored but unraced babies are mismatched with parents pledging allegiance to a single racial identity. The shock administered by stories of racechanged children has everything to do with startling representations of the monochromatic adult self at odds with its own uncannily colorful embodiments.

Perhaps no African-American visual artist has presented a better portrait of the comforting familiarity of stultifying, monochromatic racial identities than Horace Pippin in his painting *Mr. Prejudice* (1943), a picture portraying a world split in two (Fig. 6.7). This ironic treatment of what one critic calls "the threat to wartime unity posed by the persistence of racial segregation in the United States" places the central image of the Allied effort in the Second World War, the V-for-Victory, so as to divide blacks from whites (Wilson, 61). Black soldiers and sailors, black artisans and workers occupy the left side of the canvas with the towering figure of the Statue of Liberty as their avatar. White soldiers and craftsman, workers and farmers occupy the right side of the picture with the towering figure of a Ku Klux Klansman as their avatar. Although mirroring goes on (between Islamic fundamentalist and Klansman, for instance), interchanges and racechanges remain impossible between black and white citizens or cultures. To insure widened divisions, white Mr. Prejudice drives a wedge into the very crux of the V, threatening to transform wartime unity into postwar divisiveness. Neither the prewar idea of the melting pot of assimilation nor the postwar ideal of the salad bar of cultural pluralism seems feasible in a framework that so severs America. That bigotry is personified as a "Mr." and that all the figures except the stone statue are male highlight the iconography of the V which traditionally stands not only for wartime victory but also for the vagina, the virgin, Venus herself, the female generative principle. Read this way, Pippin's canvas imagines a wounding penetration, an injurious rape presaging the destruction of the womb, the place of reproduction. As writers from Chopin to Toomer, from Spark to Naylor understood, perhaps only the annihilation of life and love itself will insure a lasting divorce between black and white.

Although the history of racechange in the twentieth century attests to repeated attempts to imagine racial mutations that confirm, attack, confound, or move beyond the conventional meanings of black and white in America, racial polarity has a kind of obdurate recalcitrance, a stubborn and stupid obstinacy that withstands such imaginings. Perhaps such permutations remain thin and partial because they so often assume the priority or superiority of white over and against black or because of the flimsiness of aesthetic phenomena vis-à-vis the material recalcitrance of race relations in the United States. With none of the redeeming value it displays in, say, Picabia's portrait of the androgynous White Negro, racechange crucifies in Robert Colescott's most tragic approach to the subject. His biracial figure returns to the "mixtries" of Langston Hughes through the saint sanctified by Carl Van Vechten to merge the homosexual as a blameless victim of heterosexual society with the hybrid as a casualty of racist society. Executed in what one critic calls

Figure 6.7 Horace Pippin, *Mr. Prejudice* (1943), oil on canvas, 18 × 14 in. Gift of Dr. and Mrs. Matthew T. Moore; courtesy of the Philadelphia Museum of Art.

a "luridly Neo-Expressionist style," Colescott's painting "Knowledge of the Past Is the Key to the Future (St. Sebastian)" (1986; see color insert) explicitly applies the St. Sebastian figure and the White Negro to the trope of the tragic mulatto or self-divided hermaphrodite (Johnson, 149). The central figure, whose left half is a black man and whose right half is a white woman, appears bound and pierced, in part because of a schizophrenic splitting of the biracial, bisexed body.

Above the central figure, two heads—tethered together—signify the attachments between black women and white men in America, bonds that bind. Whether a portrait of the historical reality of interracial coupling (a coercive white master exercising his right to rape the black female slave) or a picture of the main subject's familial genealogy (a voluntarily entered-upon union), the "not" of miscegenation turns the marriage "knot" into a lynching rope or a murderous noose. Such a genealogy, social or personal, casts the Saint as an outlaw, strung up as a sacrifice, subjected to the torment of becoming an enigmatic contradiction-in-terms, a Du Boisian icon of warring "double consciousness." Fixed in a living hell of gender and racial tensions, Colescott's racechanged offspring will join his only companions, the skulls on the bottom left of the canvas that foretell the inexorable fate of all those who abrogate conventional categories defining difference. Within the barren valley of the shadow of death that is Western civilization, the solid, sullied flesh of whites and blacks alike brings only pain, the sole release its melting away to reveal macabre skeletons with their rictus of a grin. Saint Sebastian is only the latest in a long line of martyrs. Outlawed, criminalized, and then worshipped, the saint punished for sexual, racial transgressions suffers the martyrdom of an ambiguous racial and sexual identity that defies normative classifications. Strapped to his stake, Colescott's protagonist experiences the color line Du Bois considered the central problem of the twentieth century as only a lash.

7

THE EDIBLE COMPLEX

A Postscript

I conceive there is more barbarism in eating a man alive than in eating him dead. . . .
> —Montaigne

The Negro is America's metaphor.
> —Richard Wright

Of every hue and caste am I. . . . I resist any thing better than my own diversity.
> —Walt Whitman

In the relation of the self (the same) to the Other, the Other is distant, he is the stranger; but if I reverse this relation, the Other relates to me as if I were the Other and thus causes me to take leave of my identity. . . . When thus I am wrested from myself, there remains a passivity bereft of self (sheer alterity, the other without unity).
> —Maurice Blanchot

Born white and Jewish, the chameleon-hero of Woody Allen's *Zelig* (1983) subsequently becomes not only black and Native American but also Irish, Italian, Mexican, and Chinese; judged a "triple threat" by the Ku Klux Klan, he embodies the "hybridity, impurity, intermingling, the transformation that comes of new and unexpected combinations of human beings" to which an intrepid Salman Rushdie dedicated his *Satanic Verses* (1988).[1] When Steve Martin starts a comic film by recalling "I was born a poor black child," when Karl Lagerfeld photographs the model Naomi Campbell as a black Scarlett for a fashion collection presented with a *Gone with the Wind* twist, even flippant contemporary approaches to racechange appear to tap its subversive potential, disrupting the racist complacency many earlier deployments bolstered. The performance artist Adrian Piper, who meditates in her essays on whether the idea of race might soon become obsolete, put together the exhibit and the volume *Colored People* (in 1987 and 1991 respectively) by coloring and categorizing sixteen people's photographs according to such moods as "scarlet with embarrassment" or "tickled pink." Also fascinated with the anarchic promise of double-crossing the color line, Iké Udé used computer graphics to produce in his *Celluloid Frames* exhibit (of 1995) racechanged versions of one of Marilyn Monroe's most famous images and one of Mapplethorpe's most infamous in order to criticize the tendency of consumer culture to portray "difference as 'damned otherness.'" Like a surprising number of writers and film-makers working at the close of this century, Piper and Udé concretize the denaturalizing of race implicit in the idea of racechanges as well as the diverse roles they have played over time in manifold settings and media.

Denaturalizing: To translate Simone de Beauvoir's famous remark about femininity from a context of gender to a framework of race, racechange demonstrates that one is not born but becomes a white; one is not born but becomes a black. Diversity: Cross-racial imitations have appeared in startlingly different contexts throughout the pages of this book. Although racial masquerades seem murderous in their intent as they enact replacement (of the self for the Other), they appear loving as they emphasize resemblance (of the self with the Other). Conscious or unconscious, voluntary or involuntary, racial impersonations can be set within homosexual, heterosexual, bisexual, and ambiguously sexual scenarios. Not always the sites of erotic investment, they may constitute a political venture. We have seen, too, that cross-racial fantasies appear in nonironic, mimetic frameworks or they parade a parodic excess that turns them into self-mocking performances. Some racial masquerades act to police boundaries; however, others abrogate definitional limits. In various contexts and media, racial representations teeter between identification (the wish to be the Other), desire (the wish to have the Other), and disavowal (the wish to disengage from the Other).

Yet, oddly and disturbingly, cross-racial impersonations have often sustained racist conceptualizations. Why did the denaturalizing potential and diversity of racechange so rarely find egalitarian expression?[2] In earlier chapters, I have primarily emphasized the motives for racechange; however, what exactly are its effects? If I ask and answer a question usually put to doctoral students defending their completed dissertations in the humanities—how did the material surprise you in the course of your writing?—I have to admit to finding myself somewhat alarmed that racechange (as employed by artists from D. W. Griffith to Zora Neale Hurston, from Mark Twain to Fannie Hurst and William Faulkner, from Vachel Lindsay and T. S. Eliot to Lois Gould) remained circumscribed so often within narratives that either endorse or acquiesce in racist totalizing as well as the social injustices such totalizing validates. I want to speculate in this postscript on why racechange has served racist ends in this country's cultural past before I conclude by claiming that its structure nevertheless continues to hold out the promise of bridging the gap between black and white. What I will end up suggesting, then, is that racechange has historically buttressed the very totalizing that its dynamic calls into question. Thus the liberating potential of racechanging iconography is only now being tapped in various performances, meditations, films, and art works that use cross-racial imagery to enact or envision post-racist ways of being and perceiving.

Racist Totalizing

One of the more bizarre moments in Edgar Allan Poe's *The Narrative of Arthur Gordon Pym* (1837) occurs in an episode that forecloses any possibility of cross-racial interaction when a captive cannibal opens his lips to disclose black teeth. To the white hero who finds himself floating in a canoe in the Antarctic Ocean at the end of Poe's unfinished narrative, the dark-skinned savage appears so violently terrified by whiteness that he goes into convulsions, first, at the sign of a linen handkerchief and, then, as a fine white powder resembling ashes begins to fall from an apocalyptic sky. After being questioned about the motives of his countrymen in destroying Pym's companions, Nu-Nu's dread incapacitates him from affording a rational reply:

> He still obstinately lay in the bottom of the boat; and, upon our reiterating the questions as to the motive made use only of idiotic gesticulations, such as raising with his forefinger the upper lip, and displaying the teeth which lay beneath it. These were black. We had never before seen the teeth of an inhabitant of Tsalal. (194)

Not just skin deep, racial difference permeates and saturates all aspects of being, dividing Europeans from Africans anatomically, genetically, skeletally, absolutely.[3] The mark of racist totalizing inflicted by a fictional trope like black teeth on a character such as Nu-Nu depends on a simple mental trajectory. By the word "totalizing," I mean that trajectory to encompass two assumptions: that all blacks are alike and also that all blacks are completely and immutably different, utterly distinct from whites. (I use blacks in the place of those racially totalized since whites in America remain in the default position of a humanity presumed to be raceless.) The idea of race as absolute or monolithic—the notion that racial dissimilarity permeates every cell, each gene, all internal and external organs of the body, even its skeletal frame—surfaced repeatedly in Western history. For example, Poe's account summarizes a commonplace mindset described by Frantz Fanon with characteristic surrealism:

> And there one lies body to body with one's blackness or one's whiteness, in full narcissistic cry, each sealed into his own peculiarity. . . . (45)

As in the paintings of Horace Pippin and Robert Colescott that were reproduced in the last chapter, race operates decisively and divisively the way species does, to sunder the human race.

On Nu-Nu's home island of Tsalal, we are told, nothing white or light-colored was to be found. Similarly, Nu-Nu's black teeth accentuate difference, in this telling case the deviancy of his mouth which in turn draws attention back to his idiotic (yet somehow obstinate) silence as well as the obscene tastes of his blood-thirsty, barbaric people.[4] Yet of course Nu-Nu's cannibalism camouflages the engorging dynamics of a white creativity that incorporates Africanist presences to reproduce them for its own purposes. Like Lynch, the black politician in *The Birth of a Nation* who wants to lynch white people exactly as much as his creator sought to expunge blacks, the supposed orality of Poe's savage captive screens the exorbitant appetites of a white author whose racial representations are themselves a form of cannibalism; with a nod toward Sigmund Freud and bell hooks, we might term this dynamic "the edible complex."[5] The first epigraph of this postscript— Montaigne's critique of imperialists horrified by cannibalism yet themselves guilty of torturing natives "under the pretense of piety and religion"—remains pertinent vis-à-vis the dynamics of representation.

A quick glance confirms the fact that such different and differently situated thinkers as Herman Melville, Robert Lowell, and Thomas Jefferson meditated on a totalizing that permeated American thought and that in turn explains why racechange has historically served racist ends. At the very center of Herman Melville's fascinating "Benito Cereno" (1856), the tale of a slave mutiny, the brilliant rebel leader Babo strikes terror into the heart of his white captain not only by murdering the Spaniard's cocaptain and displaying the dead man's bones on the bow (substituted for the ship's figurehead), but also by exulting in the whiteness of the skeleton (which Babo uses to prove his triumph over this particular white man and white privilege in general): "The Negro Babo" asks Benito Cereno repeatedly about his cocaptain's remains "whether, from its whiteness, he should not think it a white's" (111). Just as Babo almost gets away with his conspiracy by playing on racist propositions (through his black black impersonation of a fawningly solicitous slave), his exultant display of the white bones uncovers the racist totalizing of his would-be enslavers. In contrast to the black skull and crossbones raised by the insurrectionary Africans in Robert Lowell's 1965 dramatic adaptation of Melville's tale stands the chalk-white skeleton dressed up in Benito Cereno's clothes and hailed by the slaves on board the ship:

> He is a white because his bones are white!
> He is a white because his bones are white! (208)

Although Lowell's Babu harbors some hope that Thomas Jefferson, the "King" of the American "Republic, would like to free his slaves," the rebel leader is immediately disabused of that illusion: "Jefferson [is] a gentleman and an American," which means "He's not lifting a finger to free his slaves" (195). And even a glimpse at the relatively liberal meditations of Thomas Jefferson in *Notes on the State of Virginia* (1787) provides evidence that he had internalized not simply the most transparently utilitarian platitudes about slaves—that they "require less sleep" or feel "griefs [that] are transient"—but also a racist totalizing based upon immutable physical distinctions purportedly permeating all aspects of being:

Whether the black of the negro resides in the reticular membrane between the skin and scarf-skin, or in the scarf-skin itself; whether it proceeds from the colour of the blood, the colour of the bile, or from that of some other secretion, the difference is fixed in nature, and is as real as if its seat and cause were better known to us. And is this difference of no importance? Is it not the foundation of a greater or less share of beauty in the two races? (138)

According to Jefferson, beauty cannot reside in "that eternal monotony . . . , that immoveable veil of black which covers all the emotions of the other race" (138).[6] To be sure, Jefferson sounds relatively moderate when he admits that "The opinion, that [blacks] are inferior in the faculties of reason and imagination, must be hazarded with great diffidence" (143). Still, he strikes a far more ominous tone when he melds race with species, judging the preference of slaves for whites to be as uniform "as is the preference of the Oran-ootan for the black women over those of his own species" (138).

As with fictional characters so with real people—at least with respect to the wound of such totalizing. Although Fanon tries on a "tight smile" when a little girl points at him—exclaiming to her mother "Look, a Negro!"—the psychiatrist admits that he "made myself an object" and that this process felt like "an amputation, an excision, a hemorrhage that spattered my whole body with black blood" (112). Like Nu-Nu's black teeth, Fanon's black blood signifies his complete Otherness; however, he stages that estrangement in the context of his internalization of a totalizing "racial epidermal schema" projected on him by whites, one requiring very thick skin indeed from the point of view of the person seeking (without much hope) to extricate himself from a position of alterity. How should we position cross-racial passing and posing in terms of racist totalizing?

Especially before civil rights legislation, affirmative action programs, and the emergence of a substantial black middle class, the white imagination tended to conform to the pattern of an edible complex that depends upon totalizing, picturing blacks as so saturated by Otherness that their disruptive, demonized energies had to be contained since they threaten the status quo. Several decades ago, Zora Neale Hurston compared her own situation to that of whites; regardless of her entanglement in prejudicial modes of conceptualizing race, her conclusion that whites remained victims of the fears they projected onto blacks still rings true today:

> The position of my white neighbor is much more difficult [than mine]. No brown specter pulls up a chair beside me when I sit down to eat. No dark ghost thrusts its leg against mine in bed. (153)

Brown specters and dark ghosts haunting the house of the white imagination attest to many artists' sometimes conscious, sometimes unconscious efforts to buttress privileges made fragile by the inevitable awareness produced in a democratic society that such entitlements are indefensible. Often in the American past, racechanges—undertaken by white artists for a variety of motives—testify to the construction of an Otherness compulsively annihilated.

Despite the anarchic potential of racechange, then, the aggregate of epidermal fungibility, or what I am tempted to call "epidermatics," almost always seems historically to have resulted in the subordination, muting, or obliteration of the Other. Whether driven by identification or disidentification, racechanges spotlight the crucial question posed by Diana Fuss in her recent book *Identification Papers*: "How can the other be brought into the domain of the knowable without annihilating the other *as other*—as precisely that which cannot be known?" (4). Like the politics that Fuss sees at work in Fanon's analysis of the violence of identification, cross-racial impersonations have illuminated "the material practices of exclusion, alienation, appropriation, and domination that transform other subjects into subjected others" (14). The paradox of this study is that they did so despite the wildly divergent, conscious aims of performers.

Here, then, are the equations that constitute the edible complex shaping seemingly antithetical attempts at cross-racial impersonation. They must be read with some attention to numbering, for the first Proposition 1 begins with resemblance while the second Proposition 1 antithetically starts with disavowal. Indeed, the first Proposition 1 looks like the most libertarian form of racechanging mutability whereas the second Proposition 1 looks like the most racist form of totalizing. Yet, if scanned as two sequences, they shockingly end up in the same irrationally monistic place:

1. I am like the Other.
2. I display my similarity to the Other.
3. I am the same as the Other.
4. I admit the Other within me.
5. I contain the Otherness of the Other within me.
—6. I represent the Other.
5. I contain the Otherness of the Other outside me.
4. I expel the Other outside me.
3. I am the opposite of the Other.
2. I display the Otherness of the Other.
1. I am nothing like the Other.

Starting from startlingly opposed attitudes toward Otherness, the subject nevertheless subjects the Other to ownership or control. If "I" represent the "Other," the "Other" is "my" construction. (The prohibition against graven images of divinity in the Hebrew Bible or the fear among some peoples that a photograph constitutes a form of soul-snatching might help contextualize the idea that representation poses the threat of violation.)

Whether one begins with internalization or externalization of the Other, identification or disavowal of identification, professed amity or enmity, the logic of the self that occupies the position of the universally representative, representing subject ends us possessing or dispossessing, engulfing or expelling Otherness. A catch-22 or double bind, the syntax of self and Other inevitably leads to the disappearance of the Other's Otherness.[7] Regardless of the route by which it is attained, the central Proposition 6 inexorably transmutes the Other into a surd or a voiceless sound. Thus, the history of representations of racechange provides a cautionary tale about the expropriating mechanics of mimesis in general. More specifically, the cross-racial masquerades presented in this book often tally the same irrational numbers, though they are motivated by widely divergent desires and dreams. Like those vegematics advertised on late-night television, epidermatics grind out with mindless rapidity identical, predictable patterns and shapes (bringing to mind the old adage, "no matter how you slice it . . . ").

Although white representations of blackness have moved in the course of the twentieth century from the mean mockery of blackface through the adulatory mimicry of imperialist nostalgia, from the confused erotics of black envy to the loving emphasis on interracial mutuality and mutability at work in narratives of the mixed child and in visual graphics of morphed hybrid beings, even the best-intentioned and most aesthetically exuberant imitations veer into incorporations that threaten to obliterate the Otherness of the Other: not just *The Birth of a Nation* but also *Swing Time*, not just Vachel Lindsay's "The Congo" but also John Berryman's *The Dream Songs*, not just Saul Bellow's *Mr. Sammler's Planet* but also Norman Mailer's "The White Negro," not just Al Jolson's but also Virginia Woolf's and John Howard Griffin's use of blackface, not just Mark Twain's *Pudd'nhead Wilson* but also Kate Chopin's "Désirée's Baby." (In an elegaic manner comparable to that adopted by Chopin, the racechanging works of such black artists as Anne Spencer, Charles Chesnutt, George Schuyler, Marita Bonner, Jean Toomer, and Gloria Naylor make this same point.) In other words, the purported politics of racechangers can vary dramatically, but the ethical problem that structures their performance tends to remain constant.

Keeping this in mind, what does it mean to return to the idea articulated in my introduction that America's first national theater, first motion pictures, first radio shows, and first new journalism as well as Europe's first experimental literature, painting, and photography were all marked by forms of cross-racial impersonation? Has a significant aspect of the evolution of modern Euro-American culture been achieved through the edible complex and the muting or what bell hooks calls "the eating" of the Other? Just as *The Birth of the Nation* and the birth of the nation's film industry depended upon staging the death of African Americans, could one contend that the genesis of twentieth-century radio, new journalism, experimental poetry, modernist painting, and avant-garde photography hinged at least in part on representations that possessed or dispossessed, engulfed or expelled the black Other? Edward Said's argument about European modernism—that its most prominent characteristics derive from collisions between Western society and native cultures constituted by the colonized—can be extended to twentieth-century American aesthetic productions which repeatedly framed themselves in terms of multiple collusions in the persistent disparity in power between the white and the black (188–91).

Though I have not told the whole story of black passing and white posing, though I have refrained from a teleological plot with a comic or tragic resolution, I have found myself returning again and again to a question this study cannot answer, the ethical inquiry at the center of cross-racial interaction: How can white people understand or sympathize with African-Americans without distorting or usurping their perspective? In the conclusion to her book about theorizing race and gender, Robyn Wiegman raises the same problem about "the transformatory hope of identifying with the pain and suffering of others [which] seems ever more bound to an imperialistic cast," and she goes on to ask, "is this the only fate for identification?" (200) Perhaps most of the racechanges recounted in these pages answer this question positively because they operate so intransigently within the categories of a sovereign, autonomous selfhood defined through whiteness and an Other colored black. As Fuss puts it,

> To invoke "the Other" as an ontological or existentialist category paradoxically risks
> eliding the very range and play of cultural differences that the designation is intend-
> ed to represent. Reliance upon the Other as a categorical imperative often works to
> flatten rather than to accentuate difference. (*Identification Papers*, 144)

The query "How can white people understand or sympathize with African-
Americans without distorting or usurping their perspective?" too glibly assumes
that there is such a perspective. Indeed, how can one posit a genuine, uncontami-
nated white cultural identity or a unique black racial autonomy, given the cross-
racial entanglements and influences mapped throughout these pages? What the
history of racechange teaches is that race and color are not immutable categories
but classifications with permeable boundaries. Or, to put it another way, that neither black nor white fill-in-the-blank—artistic productions, experiences, groups of
people—can be understood as unitary, entire, monolithic, coherent. Although the
epidermatics of cross-racial performances would flatten all cross-racial experiments to the level of the same evil white conspiracy, a recognition of their complex inflections and rhetorics makes for a more intricate comprehension of how
those experiments arbitrate or violate racial perimeters.

Transraciality

Only by understanding the complex heterogeneity hidden beneath the terms "I"
and "Other" can we avoid facile assumptions about a single, homogenized subjectivity or Otherness. When the manifold sorts of differences—beyond those
of complexion—multiply, perhaps the monolithic dualism that set the stage for
twentieth-century racechanges can break down. Yet—and this is a big "yet"—
"color has long been a powerful tool for assimilative erasure of class, religion, history, most ethnicity, gender and sexual orientation," or so Patricia J. Williams has
observed (*Rooster's Egg*, 188–89). Besides leveling many other differences, pigmentation has monotonously played into Western culture's favorite mind-body dualism. For too long the human face has been white, the object-face black—as, for
example, in Man Ray's photographs. (A glance back at some of Hannah Höch's
photomontages confirms her effort to undermine this equation.) As a number of
racechanging productions analyzed in this book intimate, the African American
has been more deeply inflected by an homogenized Otherness than other admittedly othered groups; the category "black" takes on what Patricia J. Williams calls
"irreducibility" in the racist imagination (192).

In *The Jazz Singer* or Claude McKay's "Near White," we have seen, blacks
function as precisely the limits by which other others (Jews and Chinese) could be
accepted into American society as white. Antithetically, blackness—when plastered on other others—serves to extend their marginalization: On the Renaissance
stage, according to James Shapiro, Jews were demonized as blackamoors; in contemporary times, according to Bharati Mukherjee, Indians in Toronto are asked,
"Why don't you go back to Africa?" (38). Yet if we break down the terms "black"
and "white," will the proliferation of more differences evade the fate of simply re-
fining the taxonomy by which we other others? Will dividing "white" into, say,

working-class, second-generation, lapsed Catholic, Irish-American afford more than just more claustrophobic pigeonholes? Or can an ineffable attentiveness to precisely those differences resistant to our analogizings save us from the erasures of Othering, as Wiegman has speculated (179–202)?

Whether "the Other" becomes an individuated "you" or multiply defined "others," a shift in syntax combined with attentiveness to differences resistant to our analogizings might help make the relationship between "black" and "white" bi-directional. As the world population becomes darker and the Euro-American becomes simply another other, such two-way traffic encourages self and other to change places, so "the Other relates to me as if I were the Other" (Blanchot, 18). What can be said on behalf of the performances studied in this book is that they provide an explanation for, even a prognostication of, that future evolution. For regardless of its historic contamination in racist totalizing, the structure of cross-racial impersonation poses a dialectic between self and Other that posits a third term, pointing toward "transraciality," a word Michael Awkward uses "to describe the adoption of physical traits of difference for the purpose of impersonating a racial other" (19). To distinguish the concept from the various modes of cross-racial passing and posing we have reviewed thus far, I would stress the ways in which transracial performers seek neither to become the Other (blending into or integrating within the Other's community like a passer) nor to flaunt their alienation from the Other (ridiculing the Other's mores like a poser). The word "cross-racial" means crossing over racial demarcations; however, the word "transracial" should imply dwelling within racial borderlands.

Securely positioned in the place of neither the self nor the Other, the racechanger demonstrates through the motility of performance how impossible it is to ascribe fixed meanings to racial or, for that matter, gendered differences (19–20). To the "either/or, both/and" with which I began this book, the transraciality of the racechanger posits a "neither/nor"—not in the conflicted, sad cadences of the "tragic mulatto" whose neither white nor black spells disastrous exile but in the flagrantly foreign heterogeneity implied by Rimbaud's "*Je est un autre*" ("I is an other") with its call for the acknowledgment not simply of accepting the Other but, as Julia Kristeva puts it, "of *being in his [or her] place*, and this means to imagine and make oneself other for oneself" (*Strangers* 13). In the thirties, the surrealist artist Claude Cahun explained her racechanging, sexchanging self-portraits by describing her principal pleasure as dreaming about alterity: "To imagine that I am another" (Phillips, 39). A whimsical approach to the vertiginous instability of "transraciality" might be furnished by the panethnic chameleon of Woody Allen's *Zelig* who, in the words of Ella Shohat and Robert Stam, "renders syncretism visible by offering us a figure who is at once Woody Allen, and therefore White and Jewish, *and* Black, Indian, Chinese, and Irish" (238). Or, for that matter, Mel Brooks's *Blazing Saddles* (1972) where whites sing "Ole Man River" and blacks sing "I Get No Kick from Champagne." Another and the one Awkward uses is provided by Michael Jackson.

Because the transraciality of a figure like Michael Jackson—"the radical revision of one's natural markings and the adoption of aspects of the human surface (especially skin, hair, and facial features) generally associated with the racial other"—insists on the mysteriousness of the racial other's cultural life, it distinguishes itself from passing: In Awkward's view, then, it may constitute "a distinct cultural and scopic possibility in our time" (181).[8] To the extent that cross-racial performers neither abandon origins nor pass into the other group's world, they create a new (volatile and not necessarily unified) racial category. In terms of its most liberating potential and despite its history, then, trans-racial transgressions can crack open any monolithic notion one might have about the coherent racial self. Two recent avant-garde films explore the scopic possibilities transraciality holds out by making white viewers self-conscious about the uses to which they put racial categories.

So blatantly post-modern is the performance artist Sandra Bernhard in her approach to the recalcitrant mysteriousness of the Other's cultural life that she sardonically turns her gaze onto herself as a prototypical white subject enraptured by black envy; she thereby seeks to dramatize the extent to which whiteness depends upon appropriative and patently synthetic presentations of blackness. From its beginning, Bernhard's movie *Without You I'm Nothing* (1990) melds racechange with sexchange when the camera pans away from a white man in eighteenth-century costume playing Bach on a spinet to a contemporary black woman picking up the same piece. Repeatedly filmed in a cabaret and introduced to bored black patrons by an MC who keeps misnaming her "Sarah Bernhardt," Bernhard—through heavily ironized performances, some in blackface—never captures anyone's attention, despite what Stanley Kauffmann calls her "guilt-cum-envy toward blacks" (26).

What the self-satirizing routines enact is Bernhard's understanding that her wish to gain the adulation of blacks is as morally reprehensible as her adulterated versions of their artistry. Invariably a bit off, the shuck and sham of Bernhard's ersatz racial concoctions remind us that it is only us whites playing black people for our own narcissistic purposes (though Bernhard teerers on the edge of an imitative fallacy that rebounds against her own egomania).[9] The film's title captures some of the paradoxes at work in white psychology, a line of thinking (within the mind of the white entertainer brooding on her black precursors and audience) which might be captured this way:

> Because "*Without you* I'm nothing," I desire you more than anything; however, because "*I am nothing* without you," I resent the way you make me feel dependent on you for my very existence. In fact, my loathing of myself for my dependency on you is only matched by my hatred of you. And so let me remind you, for once and all, that "*Without me* you're nothing." I am at the center here so count yourself lucky that I make and re-make you up, rescuing you from the nothingness to which you must remain ontologically wedded. Only when we both agree that "*You're nothing* without me" will it become apparent that "*I'm something* with or without you (aren't I?)."

Another recent movie, entitled *Suture* (1993), dramatizes the instability of transraciality—and by extension of such transgressively malleable figures as Jean

Toomer and Mezz Mezzrow—through the odd juxtaposition between the color blindness of its characters and an inevitable awareness of racial markers on the part of the viewing audience. A decent but impoverished African-American man named Clay suffers amnesia after his nefarious but wealthy white brother Vincent unsuccessfully attempts to stage his own death by murdering Clay. Placed inside Vincent's locale by deluded doctors and friends, the confused Clay inhabits his brother's identity, living his white brother's life without any of Vincent's acquaintances ever in any way noticing the racechange the scoundrel has undergone. In other words, we-the-viewers repeatedly see the African-American Clay being mistaken for his white brother Vincent.

After an enamored white woman praises the Greco-Roman beauty of Clay's nose and the slimness of his lips, the black man who has stepped into the white man's shoes decides to become Vincent, even though an avuncular psychiatrist warns that such an abrogation of Clay's originatory identity will lead to catastrophic consequences. When Vincent returns to reclaim his privileged life, Clay murders him and becomes him (even though Clay's memory has returned and he knows now who he "really" is). By the film's conclusion, Clay's happily-ever-after proves the shrink wrong, just as all of the characters' obliviousness about color hints that we viewers are stuck in old-fashioned notions about the significance of the visibility or the stability of racial identity, categories which in fact have no substantive reality within the world of the film. The black Clay therefore need not "pass" as the white Vincent since the African-American assumes and plays his brother's roles without in any way altering his dark complexion or African-American features.

Different though they are in terms of aesthetic ambitiousness and mass marketing, Hollywood films have recently exploited various types of transracial narratives to complicate normative notions about the color line. In *Silver Streak* (1976), *The Jerk* (1979), and *Heart Condition* (1990), for example, transraciality triggers the reversals in perspective that racechanges often deploy. *Silver Streak*'s Richard Pryor mentions Al Jolson when he instructs Gene Wilder on how to disguise himself as a black man to evade police looking for a white suspect, so it is hardly surprising that, shoe polish and shades and radio notwithstanding, Wilder remains unable to display the rhythmic acumen necessary to pass (Fig. 7.1). This same lacking is what tells Navin R. Johnson (aka Steve Martin) that he is not the natural-born child of his black parents (Fig. 7.2). *The Jerk*, which opens with Martin explaining "I was born a poor black child," includes a flashback to the "jump down, turn around, pick a bail of cotton" jamboree of Navin's childhood when his mother's confession about his adoption makes him burst out crying in horrified disbelief: "You mean, I'm going *to stay* this color?" *Heart Condition* remains just as sardonic about white deficiency when chubby, sweaty Bob Hoskins receives the heart of healthy, handsome, but murdered Denzel Washington. After Hoskins's racist buddies joke about the sort of organ transplant he really wants by displaying a huge black dildo on his hospital bedside tray, Hoskins-with-a-black-heart regains his lost soul by saving the child Denzel Washington fathered with the vulnerable white woman Hoskins had himself failed to foster at an earlier time of his life.

Figure 7.1   Gene Wilder and Richard Pryor in *Silver Streak* (1976). Courtesy of Photofest.

Figure 7.2   Steve Martin in *The Jerk* (1979). Courtesy of Museum of Modern Art Film Stills Archive.

The importance of transraciality in popular media may be bound up with what the novelist Trey Ellis views as a new phenomena extending the Black Arts movement into the eighties and nineties, namely the emergence of what he calls the "cultural mulatto," a figure "educated by a multi-racial mix of cultures [who] can also navigate easily in the white world" and who "no longer need[s] to deny or suppress any part of our complicated and sometimes contradictory cultural baggage to please either white people or black" (235). Ellis, pointing to the class basis of this new "post-bourgeois" movement, locates its origins in the production of a critical mass of black college graduates who are the children of college graduates (237). From the films of Spike Lee and the rap of Fishbone to the novels of Terry McMillan, samples of what Ellis jokingly calls the NBA (the New Black Aesthetic) empower a skeptical take on earlier black nationalist movements, flouting any "positivist black party line": Playwright George C. Wolfe's parodies of *A Raisin in the Sun* (1961) and *For Colored Girls* (1975) in his brilliantly satiric *The Colored Museum* (1987), for instance, refuse to whitewash the intricate experiences of African Americans whether or not white and/or black audiences (for whatever reason) wish to be given sanitized positive role models (236). When the extraordinary tap-dancer Savion Glover choreographed "The Uncle Huck-a-Buck Song" for his Broadway hit *Bring in 'Da Noise, Bring in 'Da Funk* (1996), he depicted what he judged to be Bill Robinson's limited repertoire as a reflex of his white audiences' demands on a black performer. Sardonically living out the dream of the little black girls in *The Bluest Eye*, Glover himself—mincing behind a life-size, floppy Shirley Temple doll strapped to his hands and feet—dances with a Bojangles who can be only as versatile as his racist viewers will allow.

As if exemplifying Ellis's vision of the cultural mulatto's multicultural mixing of traditions, Adrian Piper and Iké Udé focus on the portrait as a genre that can unravel racialized presuppositions about identity. Piper's *Colored People* consists of photographic self-portraits that sixteen subjects ("equal numbers of people of color and euroethnics, women and men") took in eight different shots of themselves, "each expressing facially the corresponding colloquial metaphor of color as mood." Presumably Piper herself colored them in as "Tickled Pink" or "Scarlet with Embarrassment," "Purple with Anger" or simply "Blue," "Green with Envy" or "Jaundiced Yellow," "White with Fear" or "Black Depression." The childlike strokes of crayon lines criss-crossing faces—often not staying within the heads' boundaries, at times looking weblike, at times like a cloud or a vise—connect people together on the basis of fleeting feelings fixed and framed.

The colored people in Iké Udé's *Celluoid Frames* are featured in movie posters created for nonexistent films through computer graphics. One such ad, "Norma Jean," features a familiarly posed but racechanged Marilyn Monroe fighting to keep her billowing dress from exposing her panties; though African American, "Norma Jean" remains quite definitively the movie star Marilyn Monroe (Fig. 7.3), an off-hand homage to Andy Warhol's marketing of multicolored Marilyns. The title of this ersatz poster for a "virtual" movie emphasizes the woman with bronze skin and dark hair who pre-existed the marketed Monroe. As Udé himself puts it, "the dark-haired beauty Norma Jean passed when she became the Snow-White

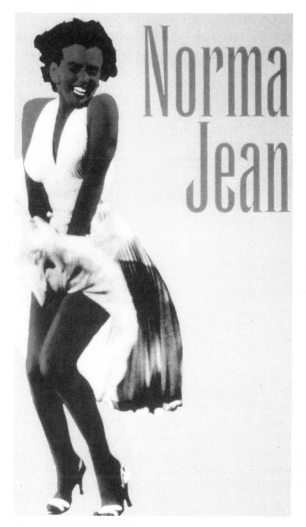

Figure 7.3 Iké Udé, *Norma Jean* (1995), from the *Celluloid Frames* series, cibachrome print, 34″ × 48″, computer manipulated photography. Courtesy of Wessel O'Connor Gallery.

Monroe, much as Madonna did too and via the same bottle of peroxide."[10] That the executive producer is listed in the print below as "Material Girl" or that the production design is said to be by "Peroxide Magic" makes clear and abundant sense.

But what does Udé mean by listing the director of photography as "Leni Riefenstahl" or the editor as "Himmler" or the director as "The Fuhrer"? Seeking to eliminate their "darker roots," both Monroe and Madonna opted for a form of blond ambition that bought into a Nordic notion of beauty, for "the bestselling blond em-

braces notions of the Aryan whiter-than-white." An article in Udé's aply named
magazine *aRUDE* explains about the marketing of Monroe as blond Venus, "Hollywood played Bosnia and she was ethnically cleansed" (33). Just as dedicated
as Iké Udé to exhibiting what Kobena Mercer terms "the unfinished business
of the post-Civil Rights era" and specifically to confronting the issue of ethnic
cleansing, Daniel Tisdale's 1988 series of images *Post-Plantation Pop* contrasts
"before" and "after" shots of several icons of ethnicity (like Harriet Tubman and
Paul Robeson) so that the retouched, glamorized, often Westernized photocopy
"documents the inexorable power of mass culture to drain off the aura of ethnic
iconicity—and hence to 'deracialize' identity—all the better to colonize and cannibalize difference, and thus homogenize and hegemonize it under the supremacy
of sameness" (Mercer, *Welcome to the Jungle*, 161).

Udé's most parodic approach to "ethnic iconicity," his "Man in Polyester Suit,"
exhibits a circumcised and racechanged version of Mapplethorpe's "Man in Polyester Suit" as a movie poster that attributes production design to "Newth Geng-
rich," editing to "Clarence Thomas," and directing of photography to "Jessey
Elms," presumably to connect repressive right-wing censorship or self-righteous
respectability with shockingly sexualized productions (Fig. 7.4). Mapplethorpe's
black-and-white "artistic" photograph has been reproduced and colorized on a
computer screen and therefore could presumably be mass marketed and plastered
on the walls of subway and bus stations or urban construction sites all over the
first, second, and third worlds. The contrast Udé highlights between the dark suit
and the pinkish penis and hands brings out Mapplethorpe's allusion to Sloan Wilson's sociological novel *Man in the Gray Flannel Suit* (1955); popularized in the
Gregory Peck film version, this critique of the corporate organization man's affluence, conformity, and cowardice in the fifties has been extended by Mapplethorpe's and his successor Udé's audacious retort to bourgeois puritanism. That
the timidity of the Man in the Gray Flannel Suit is not unrelated to the vulgar brava-
do and abusiveness of the male character in Mary McCarthy's short story "Man in
the Brooks Brother Shirt" (1941) suggests that repression must be gauged in terms
of economic privilege and that it can breed sexual exploitation. Because Udé has
circumcised the photographer's subject, he hints at a class (as well as a complexion) change. Is it more upsetting for white viewers to see a white, possibly Jewish, probably middle-class (or even (pardon the expression) pointedly professional) penis than one that always already embodied nothing but the brutishness of the
black man?[11]

Just as Udé features various racechanged and sexchanged portraits of himself
on the covers of parodic versions of *GQ* ("Conservative Skirts for the Working
Man") and *Town & Country* ("The Noble Savage Is Dead") to stress not only the
self's "constant want of re-invention" but also the need to affirm a "reverence for
difference that will redeem and liberate us" (35), the art critic Thomas McEvilley
has argued, "One is bound to betray one's own specific ethnic inheritance in the
attempt to open oneself to the reality of others." He therefore goes on to advocate
developing "the ability to switch value frameworks and cognitive frameworks at
will"; "the search for the Other then is a search for the newness of one's changing

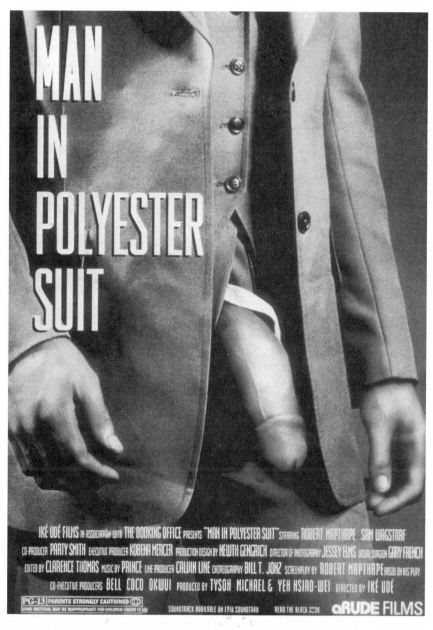

Figure 7.4 Iké Udé, *Man in Polyester Suit* (1995), from the *Celluloid Frames* series, cibachrome print, 34″ × 48″, computer manipulated photography. Courtesy of Wessel O'Connor Gallery.

self" (99–100, 104) or one's own transraciality. If we return to the issues raised by the propositions governing epidermatics, or epidermal fungibility, from the perspective of the transraciality at work in Udé's computer graphics and McEvilley's speculations, the central statement of the edible complex would itself undergo a transformation, for the self that represents the Other does not merely supplant others but also presents Otherness again. In other words, although the "re" in representation signifies *dis*placement of the Other, it also signifies a *re*placement staged by the self put in the position of reenacting Otherness again and with a difference. Who knows, racechange may go on to become a crucial aesthetic means of comprehending racial distinction without entrenching or denying it, as it does in the transracial skits of the white performance artist Eleanor Antin (whose personae include the Black King, the Black Ballerina, and the Black Nurse) and of the comics Eddie Murphy, Lily Tomlin, Billy Crystal, and Whoopi Goldberg. Just as their stand-up routines contrast inner being and outer appearance to disrupt racial totalizing, the avant-garde plays of Caryl Churchill, Adrienne Kennedy, and Suzan-Lori Parks reverse the mechanics of Othering in the way Blanchot describes in my final epigraph.

"Few people speak a language about race that is not their own," the performance artist Anna Deavere Smith cautions in her introduction to *Twilight: Los Angeles, 1992*, adding, "If more of us could actually speak from another point of view, like speaking another language, we could accelerate the flow of ideas." Documentary theater involves Deavere Smith in listening to and then repeating the stories of a host of very different people responding to a crisis like the L.A. riots. According to her, working aesthetically and psychologically both within and beyond the "boundaries of ethnicity" might "develop multifaceted identities" as well as "a more complex language": "Our race dialogue desperately needs this more complex language" (xxv). The consciousness she seeks involves neither the flattening-out of differences into samenesses nor their exaggeration into ghettoized partitions but awareness of the sometimes harmonious, sometimes cacophonous connections between related (not equated) narratives.[12]

"One aspect of symbolic inversion may be to break people out of their culturally defined, even biologically ascribed, roles," Victor Turner has commented. Just as psychologists employ sociodrama as a therapeutic technique that assigns to patients the roles of those with whom they are in conflict, ritual or dramatic symbolic inversion may topple age or sex or status barriers "to teach the meaning of the generic humanity; so that each person becomes the joker in the pack, the card who can be all cards, the method actor" (287–88). In addition, racechange uncovers the illusion of racial autonomy or purity, the inexorable reality of racial interdependency. Flying in the face of all insistences on racial totalizing or ethnic purity, transracial mutations put the lie to ideas of cultural homogeneity or authenticity, suggesting instead that mixing, merging, borrowing, and adapting remain inevitable and creative in the realm of the aesthetic. Pastiche and collage and parody, so characteristic of racechange representations, criss-cross the ethnic divides constructed by historians, abrogating all efforts at compartmentalizing discrete ethnic or racial productions. Cross-cultural, dialogic artistic productions address the analogies, competitions, frictions, juxtapositions, and distinctions between traditions that are thereby rendered strangely unfamiliar and new.

The influence of black culture on white (and vice versa) has such dizzying interactional effects that an artist like Colescott can play with the idea of an African-American painter translating hegemonic images of whites into portraits of blacks who in turn were created by whites. Questions of ethics—such as, should an ethnically specific tradition or genre be appropriated by outsiders?—operate on the illusion that cross-racial interactions can be regulated. Whether or not they *should* be, American history suggests that they *cannot* be.[13] What Barbara E. Johnson has called "*cultural* apartheid" remains impossible "once cultures enter dialogue, or conflict": "Cultures are not containable within boundaries" ("Response," 42). If, as the folklorist Roger Abrahams posits about the Civil War period, "the motives of the Southern white dancers who engaged in the black jig at the end of their formal dances are not that removed from those of the white bluesman, rapper, or break dancer," then the dynamic driving contemporary American culture may consist of an endless oscillation between white "aficionados of stylistically alternative performances" who adopt a distinctly Afro-American style and the invention of new, singular styles within black communities (157). From this perspective, many American aesthetic enterprises participate in what Sollors calls "ethnic transvestism," especially those produced by artists who endorse Walt Whitman's vision of himself (and by extension his view of humanity) as colored by "every hue and cast" and resisting "any thing better than my own diversity."[14]

It seems significant, finally, that several racechanging episodes help the theorist Patricia J. Williams whittle away at the "irreducibility of the category of 'black'" (*Rooster's Egg*, 192) that elsewhere in her critical writing understandably distresses her. In one such scenario, she finds herself in a hip-hop dance class populated entirely by Japanese so adept that she knows immediately that she is "in deep hip-hop trouble" (193). Williams undergoes three racechanges. When she enters the studio, she becomes "conspicuously black" and is taken for "The Real Thing"; however, after her ineptitude demonstrates that she is as far removed from hip-hop "as any American white person," she finds herself undergoing a whitening until she returns to the street where "I was completely black again" (194). Since the Japanese dancers (whose martial arts influenced hip-hop) were more enmeshed in this black cultural form, it was theirs, but she "couldn't help feeling that it was more 'mine' than 'theirs,' even though I had no claim" (194). Surprised—somewhat like Hurston in "How It Feels to Be Colored Me"—"to feel both so black *and* so *white*," Williams sees the event as an ambiguous "example of cultural hybridity that reasserts a co-optive status quo, or one that exceeds the limits of the body to imagine the harmonious potential of borrowed community" (192–93).

Williams's second reverie about racechange returns to the issue of black and Jewish relations that have so frequently shaped the history of cross-racial imaginative influence. She recalls seeing the vividly colorful paintings of an Auschwitz survivor, exquisitely lush in their brightness, but "in every last one of them there was a space of completely bare canvas, an empty patch in the shape of a human being." To the painter's wife, the bare patch presents the tragedy of unfinished work; to Williams, it means "the erasure of humanity that the Holocaust exacted" (*Rooster's Egg*, 209). The law scholar later has a dream that depends on the arrival of an intervening letter: A sister sends Williams "a microfiche copy of a property listing from the National Archives, documenting the existence of our enslaved great-great-grandmother." In her subsequent dream of the survivor's paintings,

> all those vivid landscapes with the bare body-shapes, and suddenly my great-great-grandmother appeared in the middle of each and every one of them. Suddenly she filled in all the empty spaces, and I looked into her face with the supernatural stillness of deep recollection. From that moment, I knew exactly who she was—every pore, every hair, every angle of her face. I would know her everywhere. (209)

Cultural property and cultural identity remain paradoxically both fixed and fused through Williams's powerful meditations on the vertiginous surprises of an appreciation of cultures not one's own that strains against simple appropriative gestures to aim instead at a kind of palimpsestic homage. The surd at the center of the survivor's paintings, the empty patch in the shape of a human being, remains a bare spot on his canvas but also becomes the only space poignant enough to hold Williams's own hurtful past. Beyond a politics of coexistence and what she calls "the handwringing about subject position" (118), Williams's negotiations hint at a visionary diversity that intensifies the reality of each unique inheritance.

Neither an erasure of the survivor's anti-figure by Williams's enslaved ancestress nor a conflation of the two, the dream refuses to reduce the Jewish experience of the Holocaust to the African-American experience of slavery or vice versa. Incommensurate, each heritage retains its own image, its own integrity. Yet the dream keeps the two figures and experiences in some sort of conversation—something like the momentary illumination that Fanon sees as the only solution to the separatism he imagines as two bodies, black and white, lying side by side:

> And there one lies body to body with one's blackness or one's whiteness, in full narcissistic cry, each sealed into his own peculiarity—with, it is true, now and then a flash or so, but these are threatened at their source. (45)

Uncannily, in a flash of insight threatened at its source Williams recognizes her relative—"I knew exactly who she was. . . . I would know her everywhere"—when the great-great-grandmother appears set in the foreign space of another's most poignant context of loss. Should the Auschwitz survivor be able to see his anti-figure filled in by Williams's apparition, would he, too, "know her" or own her as a redemptive reincarnation of what he had feared destroyed? Even if he viewed Williams's use of his space as appropriative, might he understand how appropriate it would seem from her point of view as a marker of "borrowed community"? Given this logic, would he have asked the question voiced by Bernard Malamud's Job-like Manischevitz: "So if God sends to me an angel, why a black?" (47).

Not in any way definitive, Bernard Malamud's vision of racechange in his story "Angel Levine" (1958) will nevertheless furnish the penultimate image of racial mutation in this extended study of the troubling friction between the aesthetics and

ethics of the skin trade that helped to shape American culture in the twentieth century. Although in *The Tenants* Malamud finds no solution to inter-racial animosi-
ty, in this tale he gains sufficient distance from it to gauge the possibilities of
achieving dialogues of understanding in a syncretistic society. After suffering as
many reverses as he can possibly stand—a fire in his shop, a son dead in war, a
runaway daughter, a wife wasting before his eyes—Manischevitz is visited by one
Alexander Levine, a "bona fide angel of God, within prescribed limitations" (46).
A disbeliever initially, Malamud's Jewish sufferer goes to Harlem in search of the
black angel only when further misery breaks down his skepticism. First he sees
"four Negroes wearing skullcaps" and reading "the Holy Word"—"On de face of
de water moved de speerit"—and then he finds an inebriated, carousing Levine—
spruced up in "shiny new checkered suit, pearl-gray derby, cigar, and big, two-tone
button shoes"—to whom Manischevitz must summon all his conviction to attest
"I think you are an angel from God" (52–53, 54–55). The parodic black talk of the
worshippers at the Harlem Ark, like the Harlequin pimp suit in the all too familiar
honky-tonk, reflects only the most obvious forms of stereotyping in this story. Yet
the proliferating ironies of the tale's final line—Manischevitz's marveling to his
now cured wife, "Believe me, there are Jews everywhere" (56)—disrupt all racial
complacencies. For probably one of the least remarkable aspects of the remarkable character of Angel Levine is his Jewishness.

Why is Malamud's Job not astonished that he joins the ranks of the biblical im-
mortals—Abraham and Lot—when his grief produces a sign from God? Why is
he not amazed that such a phenomenon as Jewish angels still exist, no less that
they visit the earth? Shouldn't he be surprised that simply and only his own act of
believing in the divine presence can empower Levine's agency? Why does this
contemporary Jew never express any shock about the uncanniness of natural su-
pernaturalism when Angel Levine manages not only to heal his wife but also to as-
cend to heaven on what look like "a pair of magnificent black wings" (56)? Instead, the miracle that blacks are not goyim takes precedence in Manischevitz's
mind, much to the amusement of his creator.[15] Parochial though he may be, Manischevitz has derived a lesson from his racechanged angel that demonstrates what
extraordinary magic it would take to transform individual cultural consciousness
into a multicultural conscience adequate to American society: Whether or not
Malamud and his readers agree, Manischevitz operates under the assumption that
crucial meanings reside not simply in the cultural or ethnic or religious heritage
he claims as his past but also in their continual entanglement in issues of self-
definition.[16]

Yet of course Malamud would no more ascribe to the idea that cultural identity
can ever fully stand for subjectivity or personhood than would Patricia J. Williams.
Like Henry Louis Gates, Malamud and Williams would probably "rebel at the notion that I can't be part of other groups, that I can't construct identities through
elective affinity, that race must be the most important thing about me" (Gates, *Colored People*, xv). Shedding the excessive physicality and sexuality usually attributed to blackness, Malamud's Angel Levine refutes Western notions of whiteness
as purity, absence, the universality accorded discorporated being. An intoxicated

Manischevitz has been guarded and guided by an immortal spirit in the shape of a human body, an uncanny better and othered self. If not he then his creator understands that racial dialogues and interactions begin to evolve when the bloated term "white" no longer is allowed to stand for spirituality or identity.[17] To repeat a point I made earlier, only by understanding the complex heterogeneity hidden beneath the term "self" or "one" or "I" can we avoid facile assumptions about a single, homogenized Otherness.

Is Manischevitz himself white, when his spiritual doppleganger is black? Since there are African-American Jews, can't there be—aren't there also—Canadian Islamics, Italian Buddhists, Ethiopian and Korean Catholics? And how are they related to Islamic Canadians, Buddhist Italians, and Catholic Ethiopians or Koreans? Of course blacks and Jews remain different (since Malamud does not deny blackness by putting it into an Old Testament costume), but neither absolutely nor diametrically so. And if blacks are Jews then Jews can be blacks, and after such knowledge, who can keep the categories sequestered? Manischevitz's black angel underscores the mystic manner in which we understand our relatedness to each other or the ways in which interiority never collapses simply into socially ascribed, racial or ethnic or gender or class positions.

This, it seems to me, is the point of John Edgar Wideman's albino character Brother Tate in *Sent for You Yesterday* (1983), a novel about a man described as "lighter than anybody else" who nevertheless "wasn't white," but whose "color changed." Whereas albinism for Ralph Ellison's *Invisible Man* (1952) eventually means being turned "transparent" by a "cruel, invisible ray" (434), for Wideman's narrator it signifies the fear that seeks out color as a category so as to camouflage the real terror about the common vulnerability all fleshly things remain heir to:

> I was a little afraid of him, afraid I'd see through him, under his skin, because there was no color to stop my eyes, no color which said there's a black man or a white man in front of you. I was afraid I'd see through that transparent envelope of skin to the bones and blood and guts of whatever he was. (15)[18]

The pervasive color-coding of human beings does assuage—but cannot defend against—generalized discomfort about the susceptible, live organism pulsing behind the fragile "envelope of skin." Albinism makes Brother Tate into something like an empty patch in the shape of a human body, one so alarming to a community organized along separatist lines that his light-colored, six-year-old son is burned to death as a human sacrifice.

"Depending on the time of day, on how much light was in a room, on how you were feeling when you ran into Brother Tate, his color changed" (15). In this regard, Wideman's seemingly eccentric character typifies the syncretic or hybrid self—the physical and aesthetic mutability of the racechanger whose performances undermine the notion that any racial type can posit a unified or fixed or epistemologically privileged term. The passage I have used as a second epigraph to this coda—Richard Wright's famous claim that "the Negro is America's metaphor"—sounds strikingly similar to Fanon's assertion that "The Negro is comparison" (211). Metaphor: the substitution of the one for the other, from the

Greek *metaphora*, meaning transport. Ideas about who constitutes "the one," what functions as "the other," and how such a substitution signifies transmute mysteriously under the pressure of those changing faces of every hue and caste that use their "elective affinities" to put the lie to "cultural apartheid." What will happen to our society when we understand Americans as not necessarily white or black people in thrall to the transporting figures of the edible complex?

NOTES

Epigraph Page: Du Bois, *Souls of Black Folk*, vii; Genet, *Blacks*, 3; Baldwin, *Notes of a Native Son*, 150; Morrison, *Playing in the Dark*, 38; Fuss, *Identification Papers*, 164.

Chapter 1. Adventures in the Skin Trade

Epigraphs: Washington, 100; Fanon, 110.

1. I am not making an argument about racial equality in ancient Tarquinia, although Frank M. Snowden, Jr., views the image of blacks in the ancient world as "highly favorable," claiming that "white-black relationships differ[ed] markedly from those that have developed in more color-conscious societies" (vii).

2. On the history of race defined as a binary, see Jordan, *White over Black*, and Jan-Mohamed, "The Economy of Manichean Allegory."

3. See Donna Haraway's meditation on "category confusion" and the way in which it has affected racial taxonomies in American history.

4. A recent article on "Mixed Blood" in the popular magazine *Psychology Today*, for example, explains that "our categories for the racial classification of people arbitrarily include certain dimensions (light versus dark skin) and exclude others (rounded versus elongated bodies). There is no biological basis for classifying race according to skin color instead of body form—or according to any other variable, for that matter. . . . race is a myth" (Jefferson M. Fish, Nov./Dec. 1995: 57).

5. Two portraits of André Breton that Man Ray shot in the thirties testify to his continued interest in racechange and sexchange: Breton as his own negative image and Breton as a cross between a nun and an aviator. Man Ray also produced a number of pictures of white faces peering through black netting or abstract white forms striated with black shadows. See Man Ray, *Man Ray: Photographs*, 65, 114, 161.

6. To be sure, minstrelsy and its offshoot, blackface in the movies, have received quite a bit of attention, mostly from American historians; however, literary critics have tended to confine their investigations into cross-racial masquerade to African-American passing characters.

7. According to James Weldon Johnson in *The Autobiography of an Ex-Coloured Man*, "it cannot be so embarrassing for a coloured man to be taken for white as for a white man to be taken for coloured; and I have heard of several cases of the latter kind" (172–73).

8. Victor Burgin explains that when the color white as "the sum totality of light" is contrasted with black as "the total absence of light," "elementary optical physics is recruited to the psychotic metaphysics of racism in which white is 'all' to black's 'nothing'" (70).

9. F. James Davis argues that, though the Plessy case is no longer law, "the nation's legal definition of who is black remains unchanged" since that time: *Who Is Black?*, 9.

10. I have profited from Walter Benn Michaels's analysis of the transformation of race into an identity and a culture at the beginning of the twentieth century in *Our America*, 122.

11. I am indebted to Christine Froula's speculations on this image.

12. In "Has Science Conquered the Color Line," White quotes this passage (written three years earlier) but now explains that "science is near making such a dream a reality" through monobenzyl ether of hydroquinone, which dermatologists have used to clear up discolorations of the skin.

13. Joyce Carol Oates exploits this same sort of technique throughout her play "Negative" (1991) in which "racial stereotypes are reversed, as in a photograph negative" (60).

14. See Lauren Berlant, "National Brands/National Body," in *Comparative American Identities*, 110–40.

15. Curiously, Hughes's satire turns into a series of sexual jokes when Mammy's male companion asks Audette for "some of that fine white bread" and then settles for pancakes with "jelly" on his.

16. Mary Ann Doane discusses this paradoxical scene in which Sarah Jane "assumes the expectations about blackness which are imposed upon her. She becomes the representation of blackness which is implicitly contrasted with her passing" (237). More specifically, a white actress playing a mulatto passer speaks the black talk she identifies with precisely the African-American culture this character seeks to disavow.

17. Hemenway points out that "The idea was not to fool black folks—who must have been amused by the strange sight—but to present a uniform color to white passersby" (211).

18. Recent evidence of ongoing concern about the iconography of Christainity appears in James McBride's *The Color of Water* (1996) where a Jewish mother tells her black son that God's spirit "doesn't have a color . . . God is the color of water" and where later another son protests against pictures of a white Jesus: "If they put Jesus in this picture here, and He ain't white, and He ain't black, they should make him gray. Jesus should be gray" (39, 41).

19. According to the late Senegalese writer Cheikh Anta Diop, European culture derives from Egypt and Egypt is African. Euclid and Cleopatra were black; the pyramid, hieroglyphics, the cult of the sun king were all the achievements of black Africa. Such theorists clearly were reacting against the view of, say, Arnold Toynbee in *A Study of History* who claimed that the only one of the races which did not make a creative contribution to civilization was the black race.

20. Perhaps because the black singers are so passionately reminiscent of their operatic prototypes in the film version of *Carmen Jones*, their diction—when it falls into stereotypical "dis and dat"—seems not simply ludicrous but demeaning.

21. See Walter Benn Michaels's discussion of Piper's essay in which he asks about her definition of being black as being identified by a white racist society as black: "On what grounds, then, can someone who is *not* identified by that society as black be said to be black?" (*Our America*, 133).

22. Omi and Winant argue that the concept of race cannot be reduced to an essence but that it also cannot be imagined as a mere illusion. In other words, even if there is nothing

fixed or objective or biological about race, it still plays a crucial role in structuring the social world.

23. According to Russell E. Coon, Chicago's Field Museum reopened its permanent Egyptian collections in 1988, including an interactive display labeled "See Yourself as an Ancient Egyptian." "Peering into a semi-reflective glass case, viewers confronted their own countenances, Egyptianized by the superimposition of a curly black wig and 'Egyptian' make-up" (11).

24. While *Rebirth of a Nation, Computer-Style* appears to revel in the "morphies" created out of a "straight 50–50 combination of the physical characteristics of their progenitors," it is interesting that the editors explain, "One of our tentative unions produced a distinctly feminine face—sitting atop a muscular neck and hairy chest." Clearly disturbed by the hermaphroditism of this image, they conclude, "Back to the mouse on that one."

25. Gail Ching-Liang Low describes the phenomenon of cultural cross-dressing from Sir Richard Burton to the Lawrence of Arabia legend in these terms which are borrowed from Robert Stoller's treatment of transvestism (where the cross-dresser relishes his awareness of his hidden maleness and thus plays at being a woman with the phallus) (96–97).

26. It is interesting that *Orlando* (1928), Woolf's novel about sexchange, depicts its hero becoming a heroine when she has joined with the gipsies, thus undergoing a racechange as well.

27. The artist Adrian Piper presented herself in whiteface and with a penciled mustache as "white man" in *Some Reflective Surfaces*, first performed in 1975. See Adrian Piper on "Passing for White, Passing for Black" (241) as well as Amelia Jones.

28. According to *Rolling Stone* magazine (March 10, 1994), John Mellencamp's video "When Jesus Left Birmingham" is the first from which MTV has censored faces. Mellencamp was asked to put computer-scrambled squares over parts of the video where guitarist David Grissom appears in blackface and backing vocalist Roberta Freeman appears in whiteface (18).

29. Ashley Tidey, in her dissertation-in-progress, puts it this way: "The white, in Fanon's view, does not have to 'be' anything for the black. The white man, is, in fact, unable to see the black man. This observation, however, does not discredit the fact that the white's identity is affected by that which he cannot identify/see. . . . [T]he white *does* define himself in relation to the black—*even though* he does not or cannot or refuses to 'see' the black. We must recognize, in other words, what the white does not: that is, that he (the white) not only projects his own anxieties, fears, and doubts onto the black but also that he introjects, figuratively speaking, the racial other" (Chapter 2, 51).

30. As Anne McClintock explains, "different forms of mimicry such as passing and cross-dressing deploy ambiguity in different ways," and she goes on to caution that "critical distinctions are lost if these historically variant cultural practices are collapsed under the ahistorical sign of the same" (65).

31. Until the historical and critical work of such thinkers as Robert Toll, Eric Lott, Michael Rogin, and Toni Morrison, white impersonations of blackness have gone largely ignored by American cultural historians because of morally important taboos that censure such spectacles and that also (though less reasonably) discourage analysis of them.

32. See Guillaumin, 37–67. She demonstrates "how belief in the physical existence of race is really an archetypal attitude of pseudo-materialism" (37). In addition, Anthony Appiah in "The Uncompleted Argument: Du Bois and the Illusion of Race" explains that race is a fiction with no empirical or scientific basis.

33. Eve Sedgwick's analysis of the arbitrariness of gender binaries in *Legacies* makes a similar point.

34. See Paul Gilroy's somewhat sardonic discussion of theorists who tout "the effluent from a constituted subjectivity that emerges contingently from the endless play of racial signification" (36).

35. For a discussion of the social construction of race that explains how obdurate that construction remains in contemporary America, see Guillaumin, "The Idea of Race," and Wiegman, Chapter 1. In *Essentially Speaking*, Diana Fuss includes a chapter that describes what is at stake in the argument over de-essentializing race for such critics as Henry Louis Gates, Jr., Houston Baker, and Barbara Christian (73–96). Fuss's last chapter of *Identification Papers* furnishes an excellent meditation on the implications of Fanon's racial analyses for the critic also interested in gender.

36. According to Omi and Winant, too, one should "avoid both the utopian framework which sees race as an illusion we can somehow 'get beyond,' and also the essentialist formation which sees race as something objective and fixed, a biological datum" (55). They argue that race must be understood as a "complex of social meanings constantly being transformed by political struggle" (55).

37. Although I do not want to fall into the fallacy of "chromatism," the term Gayatri Spivak uses to describe the problem of reducing race to the question of visible difference in skin color (235), twentieth-century narratives about skin color uncover the evolution of the meaning of the term "race."

38. See Susan Willis, who defines blackface "as a metaphor for the commodity" (189), and Homi Bhabha, who views "the racial stereotype of colonial discourse in terms of fetishism" (74).

39. In other words, this study accords with Eric Sundquist's belief that, although the black and white traditions in literature have been and can continue to be seen as separate, ultimately "they form a single tradition" (22). So-called "American culture" has become so embedded within and saturated by conventions generated by its black citizens that one may foresee a future in which it will be indistinguishable from "African-American culture." To be sure, black culture may always derive ways of differentiating itself from the white mainstream. And, of course, there are ways that mainstream culture continues to define itself in exclusionary terms and along racial lines.

40. What was recently described "as the worst hoax in the history of Australian publishing" illuminates the ongoing centrality of this issue. Susan Demidenko admitted that "her book *The Hand That Signed the Paper*, an account of the role of Ukrainians in atrocities against Jews during the Holocaust, was not based on her own family's history, as she had long insisted in defending the book's veracity." Not Ukrainian at all, Helen Darville (the pseudonomous Dimidenko) was the child of well-educated British immigrants to Australia. (*New York Times*, Sept. 26, 1995).

41. Consider the lesbian critic who is not Jewish writing about Gertrude Stein or the black critic who is not Islamic writing about Malcolm X. To match the "subject position" of the critic with that of the artist would inevitably involve the infinite regress that a Derridean would identify with an "abyssal question." Obviously, too, authors of narrative cannot posssibly limit themselves to the creation of characters only reflective of their ethnic, class, or social background, even if they tried to. In other words, as I argue in the last chapter, crossover work remains inevitable.

42. I am revising Andrew Sarris's famous observation that "the dramatic conflict in a Welles film often arises from the dialectical collision between morality and megalomania," mindful that Wells demonstrated a fascination with racial imaginings in his efforts to produce a version of Joseph Conrad's *Heart of Darkness*, in his production of a "Voodoo" *Mac-*

beth (discussed in Chapter 3), and in his blackface portrayal of *Othello*. For background on these matters, see Guerric DeBona.

Chapter 2. Spirit-Murder at the Movies

Epigraphs: Fanon, 231; Žižek, 23.

1. An exception to the notion that minstrelsy remained a nineteenth-century form is Mark A. Reid's argument that the most pervasive subtypes of African-American comedy in film retain various hybrid forms of minstrelsy: *Redefining Black Film*, 19–43. As recently as April 13–15, 1995, *The Minstrel Show*, a production of the Dance Center of Columbia College, Donald Byrd, and the Group, ran at the Shubert Theatre in Chicago.

2. See the discussion in Cripps, 25 and 14, and in M. Watkins, 185–86. The ways in which *Uncle Tom's Cabin* evolved through various silent and then sound movies has begun to be studied by Michele Wallace, who points out that the first movie in which Uncle Tom was played by a black actor also revises Stowe's plot in a scene where a black man responds directly against slavery by shooting and killing a white.

3. Woolf's comments about the phantom of the Angel in the House appear in "Professions for Women." I am suggesting that the blackface actor in films functions like a ghost in the movie house.

4. In Dixon's novel, Gus actually rapes the girl, and the act is described in bestial imagery evocative of *Dracula*: "A single tiger-spring, and the black claws of the beast sank into the soft white throat and she was still" (304).

5. According to Michael Rogin, the original version of the movie probably followed *The Clansman* and portrayed Gus raping Flora before she leaps to her death. Also, he explains that audiences in Los Angeles and the South saw footage of Gus's castration, now lost or unavailable but recorded by Seymour Stern: "'The Sword Became a Flashing Vision,'" 277–78.

6. Robert Lang argues that the villainy of Lynch "originates in the fact that he is neither white nor black—that is, he is worse than black." In other words, Lang sees the mulatto as the "living embodiment of a disturbance in the melodramatic field, in which one is *either* white *or* black" (20).

7. See Walter Benn Michaels, who argues in "The Souls of White Folk" that "The invisible Empire of the Knights of the Ku Klux Klan arises in rebellion against the 'visible' empire of the North and its black soldiers like the rapist 'Gus' who, as his full name—Augustus Caesar—makes clear, is to be regarded as an imperial storm trooper. In *The Clansman*, then, white Americans are understood not as imperialists but as the victims of imperialism" (187).

8. Lillian Gish explained that she was chosen over another actress because she was "very blonde and fragile-looking. The contrast with the dark man evidently pleased Mr. Griffith, for he said in front of everyone, 'Maybe she would be more effective than the mature figure I had in mind.'" Quoted by Rogin, "The Sword Became a Flashing Vision," 267.

9. Richard Schickel "does not believe" that Lynch wishes "to carry [Elsie] off and work his will upon her at leisure." Indeed, he attributes Lynch's motivation to shame and fear of being ridiculed for his proposal, imagining that his "true intention may be to kill her rather than allow her to expose his terrible secret, which is not that he lusts after her but that he truly loves her" (234).

10. Mimi White points out that one supposed "historical facsimile" of the state house of representatives in 1871 is based on a photograph of that House in 1870: "A gap between the source and the filmic representation is . . . immediately evident in the title-card itself, which situates events in 1871 and the source in 1870, prior to the depicted scene." See her *"The Birth of a Nation*: History as Pretext" in Lang, 218.

11, According to Dixon's preface to *The Clansman*, Thaddeus Stevens attempted "to Africanize ten great States of the American Union" after Lincoln's assassination.

12. It seems significant in this regard that although white minstrel performers like the celebrated Francis Leon produced seductive images of black women, no comparably attractive representation of black men appeared in nineteenth-century and turn-of-the-century minstrelsy. A Wood's Theatre playbill illustrates how black women—though often libeled and stereotyped—could appear attractive while black men always look grotesque; see Toll, 77.

13. The contrast between the earliest masquerades in black on British and American stages speaks to the divergence between blackface in *The Birth of a Nation* and in *The Jazz Singer*. The first black impersonators on the English-speaking stage played a satanic, black Aaron, the Moor in Shakespeare's *Titus Andronicus,* who would soon be outstripped in popularity by the less evil but equally destructive Othello; however, one of the first native American roles written for blackface on the American stage was the part of a fool named Sambo who would soon be eclipsed in popularity by dramatic renditions of Harriet Beecher Stowe's less silly but equally naive Uncle Tom. See the discussion of all these characters in Leonard, passim. On the use of blackface in early English literature (Renaissance emblem books and on the Jacobean stage), see Boose, 49–50, and Beemer, passim.

14. The commonality of the two movies is forecast by curious historical connections between Griffith and Jolson. After the appearance of *The Birth of a Nation* and before the filming of *The Jazz Singer*, Griffith planned to make a movie tentatively entitled either *Black and White* or *Mammy's Boy*, a crime story starring Al Jolson as an innocent detective using the appearance of a "guilty black face" to exonerate a falsely accused man (Geduld, 167). Another of Griffith's projects—*The Romance of a Jewess* (1908)—focused on the intermarriage of Jew and gentile at the center of *The Jazz Singer*. This odd coupling of Griffith and Jolson recurred when Jolson first approached Griffith with the idea of dramatizing Samson Raphaelson's story "The Day of Atonement" (Carringer, 12).

15. Theodore Tilton's famous remark that the black race is equal in moral faculties to the white woman and thus superior to white men—"The negro race is the feminine race of the world"—appears in *The Negro* (1863) and is often cited (for example in bell hooks, "Feminism Inside," 131).

16. Eric Lott has pointed out to me that this scene resembles a rape, "with Pop pulling off his belt and charging after Jakie into the bedroom, out of which the crying boy will shortly emerge" (private correspondence).

17. A telltale mistake in the written treatment of Jack's blackface suggests his feminization: Jack "goes up and takes [his mother's] hands in his. He starts to kiss her, then, remembers her [*sic*] make-up" (Carrianger, 120). Also, the word "queer"—used by Mary and the backer to stop Jack from giving into his family—seems to warn against an unmanly passivity.

18. I am indebted to Melissa Valiska Gregory for pointing out the resonance of this passage with respect to the Jolson poster and for discovering the next very striking image.

19. A good description of the standard late-nineteenth-century minstrel show appears in Huggins, 249–50. After a rousing opening number, blackfaced performers sat in a row in

the careless costume of Jim Crow (the rough barbarian) and the ruffled super-stylishness of Jim Dandy (the urban effete). The center man, called the interlocutor and sometimes remaining in whiteface, engaged the end men, Mr. Bones and Mr. Tambo, in comic routines: jokes, political speeches, sermons. The "olio" followed with songs and dances. A grand finale usually closed the show.

20. No wonder, then, that the name Sambo has been traced back to the sixteenth-century word "zambo," a type of monkey whose antics were considered natural, and that one of the first musical works in America, *The Disappointment* (1767), featured a comic black character called "Raccoon" (Boskin, 38 and 70).

21. Darkened skin itself might signify disappearance by evoking body parts charred by fire or gone dead from gangrene, as they do to the boy child of William Faulkner's *As I Lay Dying* (1930): Observing one brother's burnt back and another's gangrened leg, Vardaman thinks they "looked like a nigger's" (224).

22. Alexander Saxton quotes Harry McCarthy, *Deeds of Darkness* (1876), *Dick's Ethiopian Scenes* (1879), and Bert Richards's *Colored Senators, an Ethiopian Burlesque* (23).

23. A similar song performed by Moore & Burgess Minstrels in England describes a mouth, "a caution to see, / A better provision store never could be," which the singer has not found a way to kiss because "I'm afraid to go near her, I'm sure to be drowned" (Pickering, 197).

24. Claire Kahane argues that the young boy Nelson and his grandfather Mr. Head in O'Connor's story identify with the plaster figure of the Negro and thereby achieve "an acceptance of helplessness and mutual dependency": "O'Connor implies that they themselves are 'artificial niggers,' powerless and afraid before the contingencies of a threatening world" (183).

25. Alexander Saxton explains that the banjo song published in New York in 1863 is sung by a character who would like to respond to "Abram Linkum" by buying "up all de niggers—de niggers—de colored African-American citizens" in order to sell them; he then finds it "Geographically and emotionally" quite close to the maiming and lynching of blacks on the sidewalks of New York during the draft riots of the same year.

26. See O'Connor, "Judgement Day," 539.

27. In "'Democracy and Burnt Cork,'" Michael Rogin points out that by the mid-1930s, the genre had turned to backstage musicals about putting on a show or retrospective biographies of the central figures in the history of American popular music (4).

28. As Eric Lott has commented to me, however, the background legs are unable to keep up with Astaire and they end up giving in and going away. If the legs represent Robinson's, perhaps he is shown throwing in the towel, unable to compete with the brilliant Astaire (private correspondence).

Still, the background and foreground oscillate so as to produce doubling between the two dancers. To the extent that Fred Astaire's dance number pays homage to Bojangles, it differs from other productions that simply appropriated black arts. See Carol J. Clover on the film *Singin' in the Rain* (1952) with its "moralizing surface story . . . a guilty disavowal of the practices that went into its own making" (725). Clover argues that the film apparently looks at the immorality of appropriating another person's voice but really it rips off (without crediting) the dancing bodies of black men. Whereas "there was a perverse honesty to traditional blackface" which "does point to where credit might be due" (740), *Singin' in the Rain* "doesn't-but-does know" that the musical art upon which it depends is African-American in origin (742).

On Rice's "shadow dance," see M. Watkins, 84.

Chapter 3. Making White, Becoming Black

Epigraphs: Bible; Browne, 281.

1. See Sacks and Sacks.

2. See, for example, Houston Baker's rejection of Constance Rourke's assessment of the authenticity of minstrel traditions in *Modernism and the Harlem Renaissance*, 17.

3. I am indebted to Sandra M. Gilbert's ideas about "female female impersonation" here; see our *Letters from the Front*, chapter 2.

4. Werner Sollors, quoting Andrew Greeley's use of the term "ethnogenesis," explains that the word "nicely combines an organic sense (people, birth) with a faint biblical echo (Genesis) and helps to sacralize beginnings" (*Beyond Ethnicity*, 57). For a discussion of early American as well as Greek, Native American, and Islamic black-white founding myths, see the chapter on "Origins" in Sollors's forthcoming book *Neither Black nor White and Yet Both: Thematic Explorations of Interracial Literature*.

5. See Bailey. Insistent about grounding a positive black self-image on recalcitrant biblical texts, the scholar Cain Hope Felder argues about the famous Jeremiah passage that "To Jeremiah and to his listeners, it is unthinkable that the Cushites would want to change the way they look"; indeed, "the use of [Ham's descendants] in this passage suggests that Israel should use the Cushites as 'yardsticks' for assessing themselves." For Cain, the Ethiopians or Cushites and the leopard "have learned the advantages of being who they are, rulers of territories who are respected by and awesome to their neighbors," and because they have "no incentive for change," they are used to explain the situation of the people of Judah who "liv[ing] the life of sinning have learned the advantages of being sinners" (177).

Cain's exegetical acrobatics cannot hide the fact that Jeremiah's famous rhetorical questions are structured so as to equate the Ethiopian's color and the leopard's spots with sin: just as the Cushite cannot change his skin or the leopard his spots, the evil-doer cannot become virtuous.

6. Patricia J. Williams quotes a twenty-year-old study about "The Economics of the Baby Shortage" that created a controversy when its authors, Judge Richard Posner and his associate Elizabeth Landes, argued, "Were baby prices quoted as prices of soybean future are quoted, a racial ranking of these prices would be evident, with white baby prices higher than nonwhite baby prices" (*Rooster's Egg*, 217).

7. Even though Hurston's accomplishments won prizes during her lifetime and her novel *Their Eyes Were Watching God* has attained centrality in the college curriculum, her early work—like the poems of Spencer and the graphics of Nugent—has gone virtually unnoticed. Neither Spencer nor Bruce published a collection of their works in their lifetimes, compositions which remain obscure (especially in the latter's case) because still scattered in journals, and neither one has yet received the scholarship which might illuminate the shape of their careers. Spencer, who lived reclusively with her mother and husband in Lynchburg, Virginia, was mentored by James Weldon Johnson; Richard Bruce, the pseudonym for Bruce Nugent, moved from Washington, D.C., to New York City, pursuing a more flamboyantly public life during which he was befriended by Georgia Douglas Johnson, Langston Hughes, Wallace Thurman, and Aaron Douglas.

8. Maureen Honey explains that Spencer composed the poem after reading about a pregnant woman who was tortured by a lynch mob while trying to protect her husband who had killed a racist employer (9–10).

9. The word "fagot" most obviously stands for the wood that fuels the mob's violent burning of the black body; however, it also resonates with the British meaning of fag—a

boy who acts as a servant for another boy in a higher class—and the slang term for homosexual. Sugar cane takes on the ominous resonance of caning in this context.

10. As many critics have suggested, of course, it is possible to read the "ex-coloured" man's revulsion against the black victim as an index of his identification with whites and of the irony his author directs against him.

11. Ashley Tidey refashions Du Bois's term to comprehend a comparable (though different) form of what she calls "white double consciousness."

12. Anne Douglas includes a description of the ways in which *Shuffle Along* represented a return to minstrelsy in *Mongrel Manhattan*, 378.

13. According to Watkins, Pigmeat Markham was one of the last comics to work in blackface in the 1950s, and audiences were astonished to find (when he relinquished the burnt cork) that "he was actually darker than the makeup he had used" (p. 133).

14. But Mills also played the groom for the bridal production number "Mandy, Make Up Your Mind" and insisted on her rights to artistic independence, explaining, "I'm the despair of stage managers who want a player to act in a groove. No grooves for me. The stage isn't large enough for me at times" (Woll, 102, 106).

15. James De Jongh mentions two novels, *Strange Brother* (1931) by Blair Niles and *The Young and the Evil* (1933) by Charles Henri Ford and Parker Tyler that include descriptions of Harlem's gay scene (34).

16. Most biblical commentators examine a series of enigmas in this text. If Ham was guilty of disrespect toward his father, why is Canaan cursed? Why is Ham mentioned as the youngest son in one verse and listed as the second of three in another? Did Noah have three or four sons? Why does Noah counter his curse of Canaan with a blessing that Japheth "dwell in the tents of Shem"? By glossing over such confusions or dissolving them, Hurston's tale represses the ideological pressures that probably shaped the evolution of the text. As Cain Hope Felder has speculated, "Many of the difficulties within this passage find a solution once we allow the possibility that the original version of Genesis 9:18–27 referred only to Ham and his error and that a later version of the story, motivated by political developments in ancient Palestine, attempted to justify the subjugation of Canaanites by Shem's descendants (Israel) and those of Japheth (Philistines)" (131).

17. Therefore, as Umberto Cassuto has argued, "The Canaanites were to suffer the curse and the bondage not because of the sins of Ham, but because they themselves acted like Ham, because of their own transgressions, which resembled those attributed to Ham in this allegory" (155).

18. For an illuminating commentary on these passages and the uses to which they have been put, see Rice, 5–27. In "The Curse of Ham: A Case of Rabbinic Racism?," David M. Goldenberg argues that "the source of anti-Black prejudice in western civilization" has been "found in rabbinic literature" and he goes on to exonerate the Rabbinic writing from this charge. Not race but skin color was the subject of folktales that simply express a "somatic norm preference" for lighter complexions. In addition, faulty translations as well as enigmatic texts have contributed to the unfair charge of Jewish racism. See the collection on blacks and Jews edited by Jack Salzman and Cornel West (Oxford University Press, forthcoming).

19. Copher cites the sources of Graves and Patai as Sanhedrin 108B and *Tanhumaa Noah* 13, 15.

20. By the end of the thirteenth century in England, an otherwise quite liberal attack on the slavery of men of free ancestry in the *Mirror of Justices* contained a defense of the subjugation of serfs because "this serfage . . . comes from the curse which Noah pronounced

against Canaan, the son of his son Ham. . . . And thus are men serfs by divine law and this is accepted by human law and confirmed by canon law" (D. B. Davis, 97).

Winthrop D. Jordan's point, though in need of qualification, remains an important one: "It is suggestive that the first [widespread] Christian utilizations" of Talmudic and Midrashic sources came during a period of "overseas exploration" (18). On sixteenth- and seventeenth-century writers' approach to the origins of blackness vis-à-vis climatological and biblical explanations, see Boose, 42–44.

21. On the conflation of Cain and Ham, see J. Friedman, 99–105. He sees the basis of the metaphoric identification of Ham and Cain in the Middle Ages as a result of certain parallels in their stories: Each was a bad brother and son, lived before the earth was populated, and produced a cursed line. "The descendants of Cain and Ham seem, indeed, to have become ubiquitous by the thirteenth century, and almost any person or people viewed with distaste or hostility by a Christian writer was likely to receive honorary membership in their family, as genealogy was used to justify an unfriendly or suspicious attitude toward the peoples who dwelt on the fringes of the medieval Latin world" (103).

For another biblical identification of darkening with the sorrow of a curse, see Job 28–31:

> I go about blackened, but not by the sun;
>   I stand up in the assembly, and cry for help.
> I am a brother of jackals,
>   and a companion of ostriches.
> My skin turns black and falls from me,
>   And my bones burn with heat.
> My lyre is turned to mourning,
>   and my pipe to the voice of those who weep.

22. See "Selections from the Book of Moses," in which the following passage appears:

> 23   The land of Egypt being first discovered by a woman, who was the daughter of Ham, and the daughter of Egyptus, which in the Chaldean signifies Egypt, which signifies that which is forbidden;
> 24   When this woman discovered the land it was under water, who afterward settled her sons in it; and thus, from Ham, sprang that race which preserved the curse in the land. (Abraham 1:23–24) in J. Smith, 31.

23. On the one hand, in his 1791 sermon on "The Injustice and Impolicy of the Slave Trade" Jonathan Edwards, Jr., argued that the curse of Canaan "had no reference to the inhabitants of Guinea, or of Africa in general"; on the other, in his 1724 book on the *Present State of Virginia* the Reverend Hugh Jones viewed Africans as "descendants from some of the sons of *Canaan*," a race "in an especially Manner hateful to God" (J. Washington, 316, 395).

24. Disturbing as Josiah Priest's account of Genesis may seem, it looks benign in contrast to that of Dr. Samuel A. Cartwright, whose "Unity of the Human Race Disproved by the Hebrew Bible" appeared in the August 1860 issue of *De Bow's Review*. In Cartwright's surreal analysis, Ham was not the natural father but instead the "head man, manager, or overseer" of Canaan, who (like the serpent in the Garden) was not a member of the white (superior) race derived from Adam but instead a representative of a pre-Adamic breed ("the *naphesh chaiyal*" of Genesis 1:24 in which the Lord brings forth "living creatures" along with "cattle and creeping things and the beast of the earth" (129)). In the Garden, "Adam selected his slaves from that portion of the *naphesh chaiyah*, or inferior races, who had the hardest masters in the world—the serpents" (133). After Cain killed Abel, he corrupted the

Adamic race through miscegenation with this inferior race: "That they were black is inferred from the mark they put upon Cain" (134). In any case, God cursed Canaan (and not Ham) because Canaan was part of the "snake-worshipping race," a race that exhibits "no resentments for being flogged"; one "that liberty makes . . . miserable instead of happy"; one that resembles the snake crawling in the dust because it is a tribe of "*knee-benders*, literally and metaphorically, knee-benders in mind and body" (135).

25. In *The Fire Next Time*, Baldwin criticized not only Christianity for its racism but also Islam, and in particular its myth of origin that describes prehistory as all-black and depicts whites as the product of an experiment Allah allowed the Devil to perform (81).

26. At least one early commentator on slavery had used the Bible in a comparable way. The jurist Sir Edward Coke believed "That Bondage or Servitude was first inflicted for dishonouring of Parents: For Cham the Father of Canaan . . . seeing the Nakedness of his Father Noah, and shewing it in Derision to his Brethren, was therefore punished in his Son Canaan with Bondage." At the time of the flood, "all Things were common to all," but afterward battles arose and "then it was ordained by Constitutions of Nations . . . that he that was taken in Battle should remain Bond to his taker forever, and he to do with him, all that should come of him, his Will and Pleasure, as with his Beast, or any other Cattle, to give, or to sell, or to kill" (W. Jordan, 55–56).

27. Similarly, just as Oedipus unwittingly slept with his mother, Ham was accused of all kinds of sexual perversions, including incest with his parents. According to one seventeenth-century exegete, Ham's sin of looking on his father's nakedness should be interpreted as having "incestuous relations with one's mother; so Canaan was the child of Noah's wife and Ham" (Allen, 78). According to Robert Graves and Raphael Patai, moreover, the myth of Noah's three brothers "is related to the Greek myth of how five brothers . . . conspired against their father Uranus," who is castrated by one of them (122).

28. Also important, the absence of a covenant brings up the apocalyptic possibility of another flood. Since the first flood is described in horrific terms that recall the Second Passage—Noah drinks so as to forget the deathly waters "And bodies floating face up!" (83)—perhaps the crimes of slavery will bring about another catastrophe.

29. It is hardly surprising that Hurston got caught up in the contradictions of the biblical myth of origin. More recently, in *The African Origin of Civilization* (trans. 1974), Cheikh Anta Diop argues,

> If we assembled end to end all the Biblical quotations in Western works referring to the curse on Ham's progeny, they would without exaggeration be numerous enough to fill a library. In contrast, rare are the quotations pointing out the fact that the Egyptians belong among Ham's descendants. (246)

For Diop, "the ethnic designation of Ham and his progeny is implied in the etymology of the word used in Genesis" and proves that "a Negro Egypt" gave birth to Western civilization (45). According to Diop, Ham is "blackened" by subsequent commentators as "the ancestor of the Negroes," but then he is "whitened whenever one seeks the origin of civilization" (9).

Chapter 4. De Modern Do Mr. Bones (and All That Ventriloquist Jazz)

Epigraphs: quoted in Brown, 382; quoted in Haywood, 80; and Berryman, 99. Here and at the end of this chapter, I use the poem number (not the page number) that appears at the top of each of the verses in *The Dream Songs*, the one-volume edition of *77 Dream Songs* and *His Toy, His Dream, His Rest*.

1. Gates goes on to say, "Far too often, their models were not of the first order; these black mockingbirds did not supersede the creations of their borrowed forms." Similarly, to the editor of one anthology of black women's poetry from this era, the work seems "senti-mental and stilted" in form (Honey, 32). So that they would represent the race in a politi-cally correct manner, black writers were often encouraged by their mentors to conform to established aesthetic standards or congratulated for doing so. Countee Cullen's 1927 *Car-oling Dusk* anthology touted Jessie Fauset's debts to the Sorbonne and Lewis Alexander's reliance on haiku forms as well as Anne Spencer's use of imagism. Benjamin Brawley's re-view of "The Negro Literary Renaissance" rejected vers libre, jazz, blues, or vernacular in-fluences.

More recently, in the Program Notes of Shange's *Sassafrass, Cypress and Indigo* (1976), the author explains "i cant count the number of times i have vicerally wanted to attack de-form n maim the language that i waz taught to hate myself in/the language that perpetuates the notions that cause pain to every black child as he/she learns to speak of the world & the 'self'": quoted in Baker, *Workings of the Spirit*, 170–71.

2. Of course, the same argument cannot be made about prose fiction, given Zora Neale Hurston's extensive use of dialect in her stories and novels.

3. Although anyone interested in the subject of racial ventriloquism remains indebted to North, Nielsen, and Torgovnick, I am suggesting that they do not fully appreciate the ex-tent to which white practitioners of black talk are themselves highly critical of their own language performances. An exception to those who disapprove of cross-racial linguistic ex-perimentation is Sylvia Wallace Holton, *Down Home and Uptown*, which furnishes many and interesting readings of black speech in the writings of American whites.

4. My language here draws upon a related meditation on dual linguistic registers in the essay "Quotations of Voices" in Certeau, esp. 159–63.

5. The point Shelley Fisher Fishkin makes about American literature can thus be ex-tended to modernist literature in general: "The laws against miscegenation have been struck from the books. But unwritten laws prevent critics from acknowledging how fully black and white voices and traditions have mingled to create what we know as 'American' culture." See Fishkin, 142. Her comment also points to the unwritten history of how white writers read and were affected by black authors as well as unwritten theories about the dynamics of cross-racial influence.

6. In "'Authenticity,' or the Lesson of *Little Tree*," Gates describes the 1836 slave nar-rative of Archy Moore which was written by the white historian Richard Hildreth; *Autobi-ography of a Female Slave* (1857), a novel composed by the white woman Mattie Griffith; and the purportedly true narrative composed by the ersatz slave James Williams.

7. This discussion is based on an analysis of miscommunication within marriages (Mairs, 114). Mairs goes on to say about miscommunication in relationships that, although we tend to say, "I know exactly what you mean," most of us should admit, "I, for one, don't know exactly what I mean, much less what you mean."

8. As Michel de Certeau put it in a different context, "The written discourse which cites the speech of the other is not, cannot be, the discourse of the other" (78).

9. Lindsay recorded his poems in January 1931 under the auspices of Columbia Uni-versity (Ruggles, 408).

10. Ann Massa quotes the poet explaining that he "always hated Jazz" and so he dis-avowed this approach to his poetry (235). As with the Higher Vaudeville analogy, Lindsay suffered attraction and repulsion to the experimental techniques he shared with popular American artists, black and white.

11. In 1909 Lindsay composed a story entitled "The Golden Face People" (printed in

The Crisis) about a future America conquered by the Chinese in which he examined the dynamics of racial subordination and clearly did so because he sympathized with the plights of minorities in America.

12. Lindsay's conflicted attitude toward his performances illuminates the complexities of his cross-racial identification. Although he was "used up in shouting" what people always wanted to hear, although after each performance he suffered bouts of vertigo and depression, the dramatizations acted on him "like alcohol" (Ruggles, 305, 307). That Lindsay is quoted as describing the appeal of his tours "as a splendid and unending drunkenness" (Cusic, 22) and that he eventually committed suicide by drinking Lysol dramatize the toll of what Michael Harper diagnosed as *white blood forced to derision*."

13. To some extent, of course, such a linguistic crossover reflects many early twentieth-century attempts at verbal strangeness—multiple classical allusions, say, or the effort to make language aspire to the conditions of music or painting—and to some extent, too, racial ventriloquism manifests a fascination with border crossings that led exiled and expatriated writers to "unhouse" language, to use George Steiner's term. Closest in kind might be the influence of Asian traditions on, say, Ezra Pound and Amy Lowell. Yet unlike linguistic Otherness in the fashion of the far East, which tends toward understated elegance, simplicity of diction, sparsity of verbal brushstrokes, linguistic Otherness in the fashion of the black emphasizes ridiculously ornate and baroque structures of address or hilariously nonsensical ones.

14. Glenn Watkins describes Louis Bruenberg's musical rendition of Lindsay's *The Daniel Jazz* as a "fusion of Viennese chromaticism with ragtime and the blues" (180).

15. Significantly, too, the frontispiece design for Sitwell's *Façade*, a 1919 gouache by Gino Severini, featured the figures of two harlequins. See Salter, 54.

16. See Yeomans, 267–75, for an account of Eliot's use of black-defined rhythms: 267–75. James Clifford links literary modernism to the beginning of modern anthropology in *Predicament of Culture*.

17. Eliot recurrently turned to dialect (white working-class or black), as in "He Do the Police in Different Voices" (the epigraph of Part I of the drafted *Waste Land*) and in the quotation that opens "The Hollow Men": "Mistuh Kurtz—he dead." More to the point, the original version of *The Waste Land* began with vaudevillean tunes—"Meet me in the shadow of the watermelon Vine / Eva Iva Uva Emmaline" (*Facsimile*, 5)—and the completed text included references not only to the "rattle of the bones" but also to the popular tune about Mrs. Porter's daughter (who washed her "feet in soda water" (III.200)).

18. The phrase comes from Michelle Shocked, whose notes to *Arkansas Traveler* (1992) claim that "a blackface tradition is alive and well hidden behind a modern mask. I believe that 'blackening up' should be done correctly; as an exploration for the source of that hollow ring we mistakenly believe was immaculately conceived in Las Vegas, and in a context of true respect for the cultures we ape."

19. Both Nielsen and North devote pages to Pound's use of black vernacular in the *Pisan Cantos*: *Reading Race*, 66–72 and *The Dialect of Modernism*, 91–99.

20. As early as 1700, the word "gay" means addicted to social dissipations, though it does not take on the notion of homosexuality until the mid-twentieth century.

21. His notes about the play describe the murder and reappearance of one Mrs. Porter, while the first London stage production presented Sweeney pursuing the screaming Doris with a razor, to the horror of Vivienne Eliot (Gordon, 57–58). I am indebted to Sandra Gilbert for her work done on this play in *No Man's Land* but also for the scholarship she produced with Elliot Gilbert on Eliot's relationship to his first wife. Robert Crawford explains that Doctor F. L. Sweany was featured in an ad that fascinated the young Eliot in which men

"lacking in energy, strength and vigor" are offered a remedy for their sense that they are "wasting away" (28).

22. Repeatedly encouraging Doris to "Let Mr. Sweeney continue his story" about doing a girl in, Swarts and Snow bring intimations of death to Doris when she sees them as "spades"—the suit of the coffin.

23. Crawford cites a letter to Michael Roberts, July 19, 1935 (in the Berg), in which Eliot explains that Lindsay's work might pave the way for better things (161).

24. As Donald J. Gray has shown, it was probably the antic dispensing with normative sense in minstrel songs that attracted the consummate nonsense poet Lewis Carroll to minstrelsy; his early version of "The Mock Turtle's Song"—"Salmon come up! Salmon go down! / Salmon come twist your tail around!"—echoes the popular (ribald) "Sally, Come Up":

> Sally come up! Sally go down!
> Sally come twist your heel around!
> De old man he's gone down to town—
> Oh Sally come down de middle.

25. I have used the word "signifying" here to indicate an odd resemblance between the parodic gleefulness of overtly racist minstrel numbers and the impact of the signifying structures Henry Louis Gates, Jr., finds in the African-American tradition (*Figures*, 242). Within the Dis-and-Dat songs popular in the nineteenth century, many focused on high cultural figures:

> To Boston Part I den sail roun,
> Dey said de Dickens was in town;
> I ax dem who de Dickens was
> Dey sed 'twas massa Pickwick Box.
> Ring de Hoop! an blow de horn!
> Massa Dickens eat de corn.

This particular song is quoted in Wasserstrom, 343.

26. The efforts of the Boomlay BOOMers cannot be conflated but nevertheless dovetail with what D. H. Lawrence sought in the Etruscan tongue, namely words resonant with "some of Africa's imperturbable sang-froid" ("Cypresses," 296), for they display precisely Lawrence's alienation against the hollowness of traditional European vocabularies.

27. Cunard's very real contributions to Africans and African Americans may have been obscured by the notoriety she achieved when her highly publicized bad girl escapades broke all the gender rules of the day. She was supposed to have inspired a number of fictional *femmes fatales*, from Lady Brett Ashley in Hemingway's *The Sun Also Rises* (1926) and Lucy Tantamount in Aldous Huxley's *Point Counter Point* (1928) to the "lecherous octopus" qua "erotic boa constrictor" Constance in Richard Aldington's short story "Now Lies She There" in *Soft Answers* (1932).

28. Cunard's essay "Harlem Reviewed" (1934) fulminates against "Van Vechten and Co. [who] have made a revolting and cheap lithograph, so that Harlem, to a large idle-minded public, has come to mean nothing more whatsoever than a round of hooch-filled nightclubs after a round of 'snow' (cocaine) filled boudoirs" (*Negro*, 67–75).

29. As if to ward off such criticism, Van Vechten included an analysis of his novel's title by its gloomily Byronic hero—one Byron Kasson—who exclaims about "Nigger Heaven" that "We sit in our places in the gallery of this New York theatre and watch the white world sitting down below in the good seats in the orchestra. Occasionally they turn their

faces up towards us, their hard, cruel faces, to laugh or sneer, but they never beckon" (149). Surely Langston Hughes was right; Van Vechten understood "that old segregated heaven . . . Ain't no heaven at all" (Kellner, *"Keep A-Inchin'*," 9–10). In addition, as college-educated Byron's speeches prove, Van Vechten allows class and social contexts to define which black characters do and do not speak Dis and Dat.

Van Vechten's crucial role in the Harlem Renaissance may have been downplayed "by design," as Bruce Kellner indicates, because of the wish of scholars to promote an image of independent black consciousness. During his lifetime, many black intellectuals and artists praised Van Vechten's contributions to the civil rights cause and to the black arts in America. See Kellner, *"Keep A-Inchin'*," 11–12.

30. How many of the racial ventriloquists in this generation shared the embarrassment experienced by Connelly, one wonders, when words written as a lamentation—a forlorn God says, "I ain't comin' down to help you. I'm jest in de dozens and wanta feel a little better, dat's all"—received "audible reactions" from his cast of black actors: Although Connelly believed "in the dozens" meant "greatly depressed, one actor discreetly informed him that in Harlem 'you say it when someone is sleeping with his aunt'" (Connelly, 175). More ominous is the story told about the black actor playing the central character of O'Neill's *The Emperor Jones* (1920), specifically his effort to substitute the words "black baby" for the term "nigger"; the playwright (noted for his liberalism) threatened him: "If I ever catch you rewriting my lines again, you black bastard, I'm going to beat you up" (Bogard, 134).

31. Consider, for example, a conversation at the beginning of *Nigger Heaven* between two friends who play the numbers:

> What nummer?
> Seven-Nine-Eight.
> Whah you find et?
> Off'n a gal's fron' do'.
> Commin' ut?
> Goin' in. Ah went out duh back winder. Her daddy done come home widout writin'.
> Hush mah mouf!
> Ah doan mean mebbe. (4)

Dialect markers standardized in the nineteenth-century are quite apparent here: changes in *th* ("the" becomes "duh" and "mouth" becomes "mouf"), loss of final letters ("front" becomes "fron'"), nasalization ("going" becomes "goin'"), eye dialect ("maybe" become "mebbe"), loss of words ("Whah you find et?"), reduction of consonant clusters ("don't" becomes "doan"), an alternative verb system (where "came" would be expected "done come home" appears), and phonological substitutions ("et" for "it"). Given the context of cuckoldry and gambling, the vaudevillean give-and-take backchat links black street talk with laziness, ignorance, boastful strutting, much as it had been in the nineteenth-century minstrel show and the turn-of-the-century music hall.

32. See the letter dated December 3, 1908 in H. Stevens, 199. See also "Exposition of the Contents of a Cab," in which "Victoria Clementina, negress," brings to Stevens's mind "savage blooms; // Thridding the squawkiest jungle" (*Opus Posthumous*, 41).

33. See M. Watkins, 276 and 278, as well as Gates, *Colored People*, 23.

34. A second scene, drawing upon homophobic as well as racist burlesque conventions, features a "Roman" drama about two centurions shooting craps and joined first by an Ethiopian and then by "two Fairies in scarlet togas": "If daze anything worse than Christians," exclaims the slave, "it certainly am peddyrasts" (66). The exceptional homophobia

at work here comes into focus in the context of cummings's later explanation that the scene was about Bert Savoy, a comedian who appeared in Broadway musicals, and cummings's own conviction about the link between homosexuality and fascism; "in my experience, enthusiastic advocates of any form of totalitarianism are inclined to be nothing-if-not-queer, mentally if not otherwise" (Norman, 221).

35. See *Uncle Tom's Cabin* (1852), by George L. Aiken and George C. Howard, one of the first musical adaptations of the novel. It is interesting to compare minstrels' punning on the novel's cast and its settings so as to drain Stowe's jeremiad of polemical substance—

> We wur cakes.
> What kind ob cakes wur we?
> Jist black cakes.
> What kind ob cakes is Little Eva?
> Angel Cake!
> An Massa St. Clair
> An eclair (Toll, 94)—

—with e. e. cummings's script which seeks to revive the libertarian plea of Stowe's bestseller; however, in the process he sustained minstrel stereotypes of the physicality and atavism of black people. On *Uncle Tom's Cabin* as staged by minstrels, see also M. Watkins, 95.

36. Mezzrow explains about Ted Lewis, Sophie Tucker, Eddie Cantor, and Al Jolson that they "were heebs, and the boys had the feeling that we should all stick together and not knock the big names of 'our' race. I didn't go for that jive at all; being a Jew didn't mean a thing to me." His "real brothers" were "the colored musicians," and "not a lot of beat-up old hamfats who sang and played a commercial excuse for the real thing. I never could dig the phony idea of a race—if we were a 'race'—sticking together all the way, even when it meant turning your back on what was good or bad" (49).

37. Nielsen and North discuss Williams's contribution to the *Negro* anthology, "The Colored Girls of Passenack—Old and New," in the context of Williams's various recollections in prose and verse of voyeuristic scenes in which he spies at black servants as well as Williams's fascination with the black minstrel Bert Williams (Nielsen, 72–84, and North, 150–161).

38. See the account of this project by Mariani in "Williams' Black Novel," which explains that the prototype of Man Orchid was one Bucklin Moon whom Williams believed to be a light-skinned black but who was, in fact, Dutch.

39. *Holy Barbarians* was the title of a book about the beats composed by Lawrence Lipton. The beats' attitudes toward the black man as a kind of prototypical renegade are discussed in Chapter 5.

40. The loss of his "negro voice" may have begun with the loss of his home on the Edmonds's place, as Mollie explains: Butch was exiled from home for petty thievery. But it was surely accelerated afterward when a policeman in Jefferson felled him in the act of breaking and entering a store, causing him to curse "through his broken mouth, his teeth fixed into something like furious laughter through the blood" (354). From the beginning to the end of his brief life, Mollie's grandson has been constructed into a Butch: a butcher of other men, a man who will be butchered, but also a hyper-masculinized stud.

41. See Brasch for a discussion of the "more Standard than Black English" used on the TV show (224). Although *Amos 'n' Andy* was not renewed after its 1952–53 run, CBS syndicated the films to local television stations so the episodes continued to be aired. See Ely, 238–39.

42. On the issue of Berryman's ignorance of actual black experience, see Canarroe, who argues nevertheless that "Berryman's feelings of kinship actually are sincere, touchingly so, expressing the self-mockery of a victim, and that if his diction is at times exploitative his motives were nevertheless sound" (104).

43. A heroic effort to understand this poem is made by Kathe Davis, 30–45.

44. According to one reader, Berryman—"by giving his Conscience a black voice"— embodied through "a white face in blackvoice" the "sustained reproof that white America faces from its dialectic companion, blackness" (Vendler, 57).

Chapter 5. Psychopathologies of Black Envy

Epigraphs: quoted in Hoch, 52; Fanon, 165; Southern, 198.

1. When in *The Tenants* Bernard Malamud named his reclusive white writer Lesser and his bellicose black novelist took the pseudonym Will Spear, the narrative turned the depiction of their relationship into an analysis of dualism in which the (white) mind finds itself divided from and diminished by the fearful potency of the (black) body. In Fanon's terms, the Jewish intellectual menace confronts the Negro biological threat. Yet that Will Spear's most horrific memory involves being forced to perform fellatio and that Lesser robs Will of his girlfriend clearly undercuts the identification of the black man with the phallic spear.

2. See Gwen Bergner's excellent discussion of Fanon which examines the ways in which colonialism allocates social power according to skin color instead of penis possession: "To say that the phallus corresponds to whiteness is not to unhinge the phallus from the penis but to complicate the association. Racial and gender privilege are so intertwined that Fanon evokes castration to describe racial disempowerment" (79).

3. As Diana Fuss explains in *Essentially Speaking*, the Lacanian phallus remains "metonymically close to the penis and derives much of its signifying importance from this by no means arbitrary relation. It is precisely because a woman does not have a penis that her relation to the phallus, the signifying order, the order of language and the law, is so complicated and fraught with difficulties" (8).

4. Carpenter's phrase is meant to describe those beings "occupying an intermediate position between the two sexes" (185), people whose homosexuality makes them deviate from normative definitions of either the feminine or the masculine. It is interesting in this regard that Jean-Joseph Goux has recently argued that Greek philosophy did not equate the phallus with the penis but instead aligned it with the *logos*. In my formulation, then, the hyperbolic penis of the black man, his inflated virility, paradoxically ties him to the body, separating him from the phallus or *logos* (discussed in Silverman, 30–31).

5. See Atlas, 111. Significant in this regard is the response of Brent Staples to the novel: "Bellow wanted the dick remembered. He returned to it again and again as a symbol of spiritual decay. . . . I expected more of a man who could see to the soul. I expected a portrait of myself, not as the beast I'd been made out to be, but as who I was at heart" (220).

6. I am disagreeing with an interesting reading proposed by Stanley Crouch, who argues that Mr. Sammler is turned into a man by the red blood of the pickpocket wounded in the street, for he understands that "The thief is no longer a dandified puma or an animal, but a human being vulnerable to the hysteria at the nub of injustice" (108).

7. As Allen Ellenzweig has pointed out, "to view with irony Mapplethorpe's attitudes toward his black males may be a luxury only the gay white viewer can afford" (138).

8. See also Mercer, "Skin Head Sex Thing," 1–23. At the Playwrights Horizons on Theater Row in New York in December 1995, four new one-act plays entitled *Black Ink*

included Ed DuRante's "Man in Polyester Suit," a play about two friends, one black and one white, who attempt to come out and to out each other.

9. See the chapter on "Race and Sexuality: The Role of the Outsider," in Mosse, 133–52.

10. That the photo exposes whites (rather than blacks) is partially related to the fact that Milton Moore, Mapplethorpe's model and lover, is as uncircumcised as the pickpocket in Bellow's novel, which means that the shaft of the penis covers the head; still undisclosed, his penis could be said to be only peeking out of the foreskin.

Recently, in "Looking for Trouble," Kobena Mercer reversed his original belief that the photograph stereotyped black men (352, 354).

11. From Vachel Lindsay's "fat black bucks" to Cunard's "nigger . . . grown bigger," the black of modernism was masculine but hopelessly emasculated vis-à-vis white power, as was evident in Chapter 4.

12. In her consideration of the history of African-American culture in the context of Lacanian issues, "Mama's Baby, Papa's Maybe," Hortense Spillers explains that "'Family' as we practice and understand in 'in the West'—the vertical transfer of a bloodline, of a patronymic, . . . from *fathers* to *sons* and in the supposedly free exchange of affectional ties between a male and a female of *his* choice—becomes the mythically revered privilege of a free and freed community." Thus, "legal enslavement removed the African-American male not so much from sight as from *mimetic* view as a partner in the prevailing social fiction of the Father's name, the Father's law" (74 and 80).

13. In the chapter on the "male male impersonator" in *Letters from the Front*, Sandra Gilbert and I discuss "male penis envy," a phrase we derive from Joseph Heller and Woody Allen.

14. Although, as Eve Kosofsky Sedgwick has argued, "the gender of object choice . . . has remained as *the* dimension denoted by the now ubiquitous category of 'sexual orientation'" (8), racechange scripts clustering around black male sexuality call into question traditional binary definitions of hetero- versus homosexualities (much as Sedgwick herself does when in *Epistemology of the Closet* she poses some pungent, funny alternative ways of categorizing human sexuality).

15. Thus, Morris Dickstein encapsulates Baldwin's thematic project in the sentence, "How unbearably poignant . . . that he, the black man, so cruelly undermined, should ironically remain the mythical phallus, the object of the deepest sexual fantasies and expectations of white people" (169). Dickstein also makes the point that Baldwin served as a precursor for Mailer: *Advertisements for Myself* appeared four years after *Notes of a Native Son*, and Mailer's *Armies of the Night* "was quite deliberately Mailer's *Fire Next Time*" (162).

16. See Sedgwick's discussion of this term as "a name for 'a structural residue of terrorist potential, of *blackmailability*, of Western maleness through the leverage of homophobia'" in *Epistemology*, pp. 19–22.

17. An isolated rebel without a cause, the hipster-Negro-dummy through whom speaks the ventriloquist Norman Mailer makes the white writer sound kind of foolish when he boasts, "I am just one cat in a world of cool cats" (589). The "primitive vocabularies" (599) he self-consciously exhibits—with "words like go, and make it, and with it, and swing" (596)—appear dated, forced, adding verisimilitude to Baldwin's anecdote about some "Negro musicians" complaining that "the only trouble with that cat [Mailer] is that he's white" (231). In addition, Mailer's vignette about an illiterate "Negro friend" sustaining a discussion with an intellectual white girl "by swinging with the nuances of her voice" (586–87) is patronizing at best. Finally, the novelist resembles a puerile Raskolnikov when he justi-

fies the "courage" of murdering a "weak fifty-year-old man" as an attempt to violate private property and introduce "a dangerous element into one's life" (593).

18. Earlier in Anderson's tale, the narrator sees his face in a looking-glass over a bar and sees "a girl's face, and a lonesome and scared girl too" (207); although he explains he is "not any fairy" (209), the boy cannot find a voice to protest against the black men who think his body "pretty white and slender . . . like a young girl's body" and later speculates about his silence, "It may be that I was too ashamed of having turned into a girl and being afraid of a man to make any sound" (223).

19. A useful discussion of Fielder's anxious turn from "the homosexual" to "the homoerotic" in his formulation of interracial fraternity in American fiction appears in Wiegman, 149–78.

See, too, Joseph A. Boone's critique of orientalist homoerotics and in particular his analysis of the sexual contacts between white gay men and brown boys in the Near East. As with the white male/African-American male dynamic, here too the gay man's "object of desire remains simultaneously same and other, a source of troubling and unresolved identification and difference" (91). On Mailer's later reaction against what he himself called "his love affair with the Black soul, a sentimental orgy at its worst," see Wallace, 49.

20. In this respect, Mailer anticipates a comparable phenomenon Wiegman has mapped in popular movies and TV shows, namely the ways in which "the image of interracial fraternity [came] to signify the post-civil rights era" (149–50).

21. Analyzing slippages between homosexuality and homosocial relationships between women, Rich's "lesbian continuum" refers only to the ways in which women slide from sisterly and maternal forms of loving into same-sex sexual relationships. Since a girl's first love object is usually the mother, Rich argues, the basis for her loving is a same-sex relationship. Most theorists agree that homosexuality remains more firmly bracketed away from heterosexuality in the psychology of men. I refrain from using Eve Kosofsky Sedgwick's word "homosocial" to describe nongenital bonding between men because the slide from social to sexual language makes it impossible to distinguish homosocial from homosexual attachments in many of the texts imbued by black envy. Perhaps in the post-World War II period, blackness calls into being a taboo against miscegenation that makes possible the blurring of the hetero-/homosexual dichotomy Sedgwick sees as so crucial in Western culture.

22. The best discussion of this story and its connection not only to Mailer's boxing fantasies but also to *An American Dream* is Messenger, "Norman Mailer." Although here Mailer sounds curiously sophisticated in his recognition that no safe space of straight confidence exists, in "The Homosexual Villain" he testifies with a kind of stilted silliness to his amazing realization that "*My God, homosexuals are people too*" (225). Bad faith reeks from the prefatory remarks about Mailer's reaction on being asked to write the piece—"*I didn't know the first thing about homosexuality*"—and from the liberal breast-beating within it: "I did not *know* any homosexuals because obviously I did not want to" (223). Indeed, evaluating this essay, Mailer himself later viewed it as "the worst article I have ever written, conventional, empty, pious, the quintessence of the Square" (221).

23. In this regard, it would be interesting to study the difference between brown and black. Tapping the homosexual tradition established from Sir Richard Burton to Laurence of Arabia to Virginia Woolf (whose Orlando undergoes a racechange before the sexchange that turns him into her), the gay beats often played out their homosexuality in Morocco, Tangiers, Algiers, Mexico.

24. The blackening of the homosexual functioned historically as a kind of character assasination. During his tour in America, for example, racialized caricatures of Oscar Wilde

appeared in a number of newspapers and popular books, as if to indicate that the average American citizen conflated decadent homosexual and tawdry black tastes which were thought to mirror each other in their flamboyant, bizarre vulgarity. According to Wilde's biographers, students at the University of Rochester and Yale University hired black men, dressed them in formal attire with kid gloves, and paid them to parade in the lecture halls visited by the English speaker (Ellman, 184).

25. See the discussion of blots, spots, and skin in Stafford, 294–320. Michelle Cliff describes "The Girl from Martinique": "A piece of cloth wrapped her breasts and wound itself behind her . . . . she was *parti-colored* . . . . Patches of black bumped against ivory." A "checkerboard of a woman," she appears in a freak show (76). One of the earliest discussions of achromatism appears in Jefferson's *Notes on a State of Virginia*, 70–71.

26. Whether or not Podhoretz "had a clear crush" on Mailer, as Jules Feiffer once claimed (Manso, 269), his legitimizing of "The White Negro" with the *Partisan Review* crowd may have been related to his sharing with Mailer an appreciation of the beauty of black masculinity.

27. Lott notes that Norman Mailer's codification of "the renegade ethic of male sexuality conceived out of and projected onto black men" resurfaces in "the homosocial nature of the dialogues" of *Black Like Me*: "In these conversations," Lott explains, "white men's interest in black male sexuality is mediated by but also identifies them with the white women black men are supposed to crave" ("White Like Me," 487). Yet the racial voyeurism at work here slips easily out of the slick category of homosociality into homosexuality, since women may not even be mentioned.

28. Similarly, as Andrew Ross has observed, such countercultural spokesmen as the Yuppie leader Jerry Rubin and the electronic technology promoter Marshall McLuhan paid "Rousseauistic tributes" to a primitivism figured as African (123).

29. In Melvin Van Peebles's movie *Watermelon Man,* the white racist who wakes up to discover that he has turned black shadowboxes in the mirror with the fighter he fancies he has become and then quickly looks down into his pants (though he knows "that's an old wives' tale"). The same sort of scene occurs in the movie *Soul Man,* where a girl peeks down the pants of her blacked-up lover to see the difference race makes.

30. See Henry Louis Gates, Jr., on the homophobia of black nationalism in "Black Man's Burden," 78–79.

31. On Duke, see *Newsweek*, Nov. 18, 1991, pp. 24–28. Despite the pacifist leanings of its founder, Robert Bly, the Wild Man movement of the nineties encouraged men to come into contact with the savage self within by playing bongo drums and visiting sweat houses in the wilderness.

32. Jean Walton remarks on the fact that, for Rivière, "Only the imagined attacker's gender is significant, not his race" ("Re-Placing Race," 782) and further argues that "Rivière's indifference to the racialized components of her patient's fantasies is reproduced with a striking monotony by her feminist successors" (800). The white woman's fantasy of a Negro intruder propels the sex games of Joanna Burden in *Light in August* where Joe Christmas is supposed to act as if he is breaking into her house through a window until he finds her hiding in a closet or an empty room or beneath certain shrubs; "She would be wild then, in the close, breathing halfdark without walls, with her wild hair, each strand of which would seem to come alive like octopus tentacles, and her wild hands and her breathing: 'Negro! Negro! Negro!'" (285).

33. I have discussed this concept more fully in "Feminist Misogyny." In relation to women's attraction to the beats during the fifties, see Breines, esp. 127–66.

34. The 1500-page manuscript can be read in the Hemingway Collection at the Kennedy Library in Boston, Massachusetts. For a discussion of it, see Spilka as well as Comley and Scholes. Despite the ways in which the paperback version "went too far in concealing the darkness of this text" (Comley and Scholes, 103), I have confined my comments mostly to the edited version because it has necessarily become the classroom text of this work.

35. As Comley and Scholes explain, the manuscript includes more references to Catherine's Africanism. She tells Marita that first she was "a Kanaka. Now I'm working to be Somali" (98). Similarly, although David advises Marita, "Don't try and make yourself like a Wakamba or M'Bulu girl," he quickly agrees that "We'll go to Africa tonight" (99).

36. See Cornelia Nixon's discussion of sodomy, 44–49, 153–54, 223–28. Also Ford, 189–205.

37. Morrison explores the counterpoint between the two narratives at the end of *The Garden of Eden* by explaining, "Africa, imagined as innocent and under white control, is the inner story; Africanism, imagined as evil, chaotic, impenetrable, is the outer story" (*Playing in the Dark*, 89).

38. A likeness of Zelda Fitzgerald, who explained the tanning craze in *Save Me the Waltz* (1932) by declaring that "beautiful brown people . . . seem so free of secrets" (85), Catherine in this respect dramatizes the tragic incompatibility between white femininity and creative freedom.

39. Countering notions of the lesbian phallus, de Lauretis proposes a model of perverse desire based on fetishism. The lesbian subject, neither refusing nor accepting castration, disavows it, adopting masculinity as a fetish because "masculinity alone carries a strong connotation of sexual desire for the female body" (204, 243). See also Grosz, 39–54, and Adams, 261. Of course, all these speculations diverge from Freud's view that the fetishist is male. Naomi Schor explains that fetishism may function as a strategy for women: "By appropriating the fetishist's oscillation between denial and recognition of castration, women can effectively counter any move to reduce their bisexuality to a single one of its poles" (98).

40. In *The Garden of Eden* manuscript, Catherine thinks about her sexual changes as sea changes: "we must have the sun to make this sea change. The sea change was made in the night and it grows in the night and the darkness that she wants and needs now grows in the sun" (quoted in Comley and Scholes, 93).

41. *Dr. Jekyll and Mr. Hyde*, directed by Rouben Mamoulian with Fredric March, Miriam Hopkins, and Rose Hobart (1932) presents a character whose otherness teeters between black and Asian characteristics. For a homosexual interpretation of *Dr. Jekyll and Mr. Hyde*, see Showalter, *Sexual Anarchy*, 105–26.

42. See Rubenstein, "Intersexions," and Showalter, "Rethinking the Seventies," 249: "B.G. is both [Jessie's] demon lover and her own repressed violent potentiality."

43. On the uses to which Octave Mannoni and other theorists of colonization have put *The Tempest*, see Loomba, 149.

44. In her analysis of the tendency of erotic love to become domination, Jessica Benjamin links that drift to masculine psychosexual development:

> The need to sever the identification with the mother in order to be confirmed both as a separate person and as a male person—and for the boy these are hard to distinguish—often prevents the boy from recognizing his mother. She is not seen as an independent person (another subject), but as something other. . . . (76)

Using the novels of Hemingway and Gould, we could rewrite this script to explain lesbian sadism:

The need to sever the identification with [the feminine] in order to be confirmed . . .
as a separate person [which means being] a male person . . . often prevents [the young
woman] from recognizing [her] mother [or any woman]. She is not seen as an independent person (another subject), but as something other.

45. Although I am disagreeing with Jane Marcus's reading of these photographs, I am
indebted to her scholarship in "Bonding and Bondage."

Chapter 6. What Will the Mixed Child Deliver?

Epigraphs: Cone, 186; Lazarre, *Mother Knot*, 17–18; Toomer quoted in D. Turner, xiii.

1. An exception to this rule is Topsy in *Uncle Tom's Cabin*, but it is worth observing
that she was not born but "jes grew"; in other words, unsure of her own origins, she appears
to be a fact or force of nature rather than an individuated child.

In *Vicious Modernism*, James De Jongh discusses a poem by Barbara Bellow Watson entitled "Echoes in a Burnt Building" that reimagines Alice reborn as black in a burned-out
Wonderland (181).

2. Susan Willis makes a somewhat different point about Morrison's Claudia and
racechange when she argues that Christie, the Barbie doll's black equivalent, "is not wholly unlike the inception of a black Shirley Temple doll." According to Willis, however, such
black "replicants" are "devoid of cultural integrity" (183–84).

3. In *Loving v. Virginia*, the United States Supreme Court struck down laws against interracial marriage which existed in sixteen states at that time. As Naomi Zack explains in
Race and Mixed Race, "At one time or another before 1957, thirty-eight states had laws
against marriage between blacks and whites" (77). For historical background on attitudes
toward miscegenation and mulattoes, see Williamson, *New People*. That miscegenation has
been taboo throughout this country's past links American racism to South African apartheid,
a system which reclassified the white partner of a black person as "colored."

4. George Hutchinson points out that Henry Louis Gates, Jr., associates Toomer's insistence on his status as a mulatto with sexual lack when he claims, "Toomer's was a gesture of racial castration, which, if not silencing his voice literally, then at least transformed
his deep black bass into a false soprano" (228).

5. This statement about Genet's feeling that the disappearance of blacks would make
the United States "nothing" to him, appears late in the book which opens with the comment
"When I said the Blacks were the characters on the white page of America, that was too
easy an image: the truth really lies where I can never quite know it, in a love between two
Americans of different colour" (*Prisoner of Love*, 3).

6. Because this story is so very short and so very often anthologized, I've refrained from
including page numbers parenthetically in the text.

7. For a fuller account of this dynamics, see Peel, 223–37.

8. Hortense Spillers's important essay, "Mama's Baby, Papa's Maybe" informs this discussion, in particular her idea that slavery inflicted a process of ungendering.

9. See Zack, 34, for a discussion of the American white family as a "private institution
for breeding white people." According to the "one drop rule," to be white is to have no black
relatives at all; to be black is to have only one distant black ancestor. As Langston Hughes's
character Simple deadpans, "That drop is really powerful" (*Simple Takes A Wife*, 85).

10. To be sure, the model for Chopin's tale was Loca Sampite, the white wife of one Al-

bert Sampite (with whom Chopin had an affair) and a woman who—whem deserted by her husband—simply went back to her mother with her children (Toth, 215).

11. See especially Sollors, "'Never Was Born,'" and Hathaway. Hathaway argues, "The desire to kill the father for sleeping with the mother is intensified by the rejection of the 'black' son by the 'white' father because of racial 'impurities.' The violation of identity caused by miscegenation exacerbates oedipal motivations" (154).

12. In Harriet Jacobs's slave narrative, the autobiographical heroine Linda uses blackface to disguise herself to reach a safe hiding place in her grandmother's garret. Her determination to win freedom for herself and her children does not really require that she don a sailor's outfit and blacken her face with charcoal, as she walks through the streets of the town where "The father of my children came so near that I brushed against his arm; but he had no idea who I was" (172). Whereas Jacobs's protagonist uses blackface to reach a safe hiding place in a scene where burnt cork signals the deflation of black interiority to a racial brand or the devolution of personhood to property in a slave economy, Tom's blackened face seems to signify a murderous depravity innate in the mixed child.

13. That the mother's tale is framed by the shooting of a doe—by hunters instructed by McCaslin to understand that one should not hunt does "because if we did kill does in a few years there wouldn't even be any bucks left to kill" (331)—means that Faulkner views the expulsion of mother and child as a tragic loss for white as well as black generations, which in any case cannot really be distinguished in the mixed generations to come. Ike McCaslin's discovery of Roth Edmonds' miscegenation with a "doe . . . that walks on two legs" (321) teaches the old man that his own ancestry will endure only into a diminished future in the blood lines of kindred repudiated as family.

14. When a black man shows up in town and then at his mother's house, Donald—who has seen "no colored men"—responds to his predictable questions by explaining he wants to grow up to become "A colored man" (83–84). But the African-American man reacts to the linking of Mrs. Gage's name with Swyburne's by cursing "Nigger women" and the outraged boy hits him. Finally, the story suggests that the biracial son understands the black man's hostility when he says "Nigger women" (85), for the black man has been displaced and replaced by the shadowy white father and Donald will therefore never grow up to become a "colored man."

15. An evocative refrain from Toomer's *Cane* makes a similar point:

> rock a-by baby . . .
> Black mother sways, holding a white child on her bosom.
> when the bough bends . . .
> Her breath hums through the pine cones. (84)

The black mother disempowered, helpless against the catastrophe awaiting her offspring, or the black mother surrogate retaliating, surviving the catastrophe awaiting the infant she has wet-nursed or adopted: In either case the child comes down, cradle and all.

In Nadine Gordimer's short story "The Moment before the Gun Went Off" (1991), the narrative of the biracial offspring of white father and black mother remains a not-growing-up tale, a plot of childhood's end, of infant mortality. Gordimer's black mother stands silently with her eyes downcast at the grave of her son because, as her secret sexual union with a white man is meant to indicate, she cannot do anything but comply with her own hidden exploitation under South Africa's system of apartheid. See also the discussion of Hurston's play *Color Struck* (1926) at the end of this chapter.

16. Though expelled by Abraham, Hagar is promised by God that her son Ishmael will

also found a great nation. See Delores S. Williams's extended discussion of the Hagar story in *Sisters in the Wilderness*, 15–33.

17. Finally, after witnessing Hagar's freedom and thus the survival of her matrilineage, Dana exacts revenge by acting as a female Oedipus, murdering her white progenitor and struggling back through the thick wall of the past into his future, at the cost of her left arm (cut off at precisely the spot the master's fingers had grasped). Joining the slave narrative with H. G. Wells's plot of time travel, Butler manages to foreshorten "the distance between now and then," as Robert Crossley put it in his Introduction to *Kindred*, (Butler, xxiii).

18. The rest of the quote attributes the voluptuousness of black women to "their sexual organs [which] are much more developed than those of whites." J. J. Virety, *Histoire naturelle du genre human*, 3 vols. (Paris, 1824), II: 150, is quoted by Reff, 92. Reff explores the role of "the Negress" in paintings where she clearly signifies exoticism and eroticism.

19. As in Chesnutt's "Her Virginia Mammy" (1899), where a black mother withholds her identity from her daughter and even impersonates the girl's mammy, female silence underscores the tension between interracial desire and the family as a producer of whiteness. Similarly, in George Washington Cable's novella "Madame Delphine" (1881), a quadroon mistress swears that her daughter is not her child (again, so the girl can make a respectable match).

20. See Anna Shannon Elfenbein's discussion of "Désirée's Baby" (127–31).

21. After one trader insinuates, "A pretty girl like you are, maybe some young buck down in Louisianna'll buy you—one of those French fellers down there—and you know what he'll do?—do you know now? . . . He'll —————— you" (65), Amantha—though she had never heard the "vile word" spoken before—hears it ring "like a bell with all the clarity of knowledge, or rather, with the clarity of nightmare knowledge" (*Band of Angels*, 65). It seems worth mentioning that, even if only through the title, this text again alludes to *Hamlet*.

22. One of the paintings thought to lead to *Les demoiselles d'Avignon* is entitled *The Harem*, a 1906 oil in which Picasso shows "four nude Fernandes" who are bathing in a room (Rubin and Seckel, 35).

23. See the discussions of North, 67–70, and Torgovnick, 102. Also see Foster for a discussion of William Rubin's show "Primitivism" at the Museum of Modern Art, an attempt to qualify the "debased art-historical notion of causal influence" that replaced it with the vague notion of "affinity" (182–83). Foster points out that Picasso understood the African fetishes were used as weapons and perhaps himself appropriated them so as to use Otherness to ward away others (women, death, the primitive itself). Rubins discusses Picasso's anxieties about syphilis and the evolution of the figures of the sailor and the student (see esp. 55–60).

24. See Langston Hughes's meditation on Picasso's cubism and sexual diseases in "Cubes" (*Collected Poems*, 175–76).

25. When the stuttering black waiter explains to a customer that he wouldn't "be here" if the gorilla were real, *Blonde Venus* seems to hint that the fetishization of the stage Africanist presence keeps actual African Americans in their subservient place.

In her excellent discussion of this film, Mary Ann Doane reads the movie in the context of Freud's phrase—"dark continent"—which appears in "The Question of Lay Analysis" and is used to describe the psychology of girls who "'feel deeply their lack of a sexual organ that is equal in value to the male one'" (210). Also useful is Tania Modleski's analysis, 127–29.

26. Foregrounding the logic that informs all these works, Alice Walker's *Meridian* (1976) meditates on the ways in which the white woman in a black context becomes prostituted. A chapter entitled "Of Bitches and Wives" presents a black man living with a white

woman he would never marry and explaining, "It's just a matter of pussy. That's all. Just a matter of my *personal* taste in pussy," though he views his personal taste as an aspect of racial politics because "This is war, man, *war!* And all's fair that fucks with the suckers' minds!" (136). Here the sexualized white woman has undergone a kind of species change in the battle between black and white men.

Elsewhere in *Meridian*, another white female character attached to a black man, Lynne Rabinowitz, realizes that she can be raped because black men assume she is "fucking every nigger in sight" (163). That the six-year-old child of Lynne Rabinowitz and her black husband Truman Held suffers a horrible death clearly dramatizes the fatality of their inter-racial partnership. Although Lynne had been drawn to the black community because "to her black people had a unique beauty, a kind of last-gasp loveliness, which, in other races, had already become extinct" (157), she is abandoned by her white parents (who count her dead because of her inter-racial marriage) and by her black husband (whose best friend rapes her).

27. The instability of female racial identity functions as a kind of Rorschach test in Toni Morrison's short story "Recitatif" (1982), an experimental tale that provides highly ambiguous social details upon which readers must build racial categories. For though we are told that one of Morrison's central characters comes "from a whole other race" and that together the two girls look like "salt and pepper" (445–46), Morrison removes or confuses racial codes. In a fascinating introspection on her critical response to the story, Elizabeth Abel has explained that she took "the amplitude of the sexualized body" of one character as evidence of black skin; her racial iconography, it turned out, hinged "on the construction of embodiedness" (473–74). But, as we have seen and as Abel herself knows, fleshliness or physicalization—the amplitude or embodiedness of the prominently sexualized female body—has historically been raced black.

28. Therman B. O'Daniel points out that Becky breaks the taboo of miscegenation but also defies the pressure of the town which would have lynched the man she refuses to name. In addition, he identifies her name with Rebecca, whose sons, Jacob and Esau, quarreled over the stolen birthright because of course Becky's sons have their birthrights stolen by the town (230 and 408).

29. I am indebted to Laura Dawkins for pointing out this passage in Wells, 270–71.

30. Gregory Howard Williams describes the racechange he and his brother were supposed to undergo when his father (who had passed as Italian) explained that his marriage to their white mother was over: "In Virginia you were white boys. In Indiana you're going to be colored boys" (33). Warned that "crackers . . . [will] beat the hell out of you," Williams and his brother are also told that "Colored don't like half-breeds either." And the author admits that "Nobody liked the half-breeds" (38) because of TV Westerns but also because the "'white nigger' baby" was "a daily reminder . . . of the forbidden and unforgivable star-crossed union between black and white" (62).

31. See also Hacker's use of Harriet Tubman as a poetic mask in "Part of a True Story" and "Inheritances," where she compares the slavery of race (experienced by her husband's family) to the slavery of class (experienced by her own), both in *Assumptions*, 25–28 and 33–34.

32. According to *Newsweek* (July 3, 1995), the story ends on an upbeat note when the white couple is "heartened" by the way in which the biological father of the dark child reacted to the news: "The first question he asked was, 'Do they love the child?'" (38).

33. See Rushdy and McDowell for more extended analyses of the novel.

34. Adrian Piper quotes Perry, *Another Present Era*: "She really thought everyone would be like her some day, neither black nor white, but something in between. It might take

decades or even centuries, but it would happen. And sooner than that, racism and the concept of race itself would become completely obsolete" (247).

35. On the very complicated relationship between Jews and blacks, see Rogin, *Blackface*, 251–68 as well as see Cornel West's foreword to Anna Deavere Smith, *Fires in the Mirror*, xvii-xxii and Takaki, 406–9.

36. See esp. pp. 115–22 of *Black Skin, White Masks*.

37. Elizabeth Bartholet explains in her chapter on "Adoption and Race" that "Racial matching policies represent a coming together of powerful and related ideologies—old-fashioned white racism, modern-day black nationalism, and what I will call 'biologism,' the idea that what is 'natural' in the context of the biological family is what is normal and desirable in the context of adoption" (93). She concludes about the large number of black children in need of homes (because the black adoptive families demanded by policies remain unavailable) that "the current racial matching regime, by barring and discouraging white parents from transracial adoption rather than welcoming them in the agency doors, denies adoptive homes to large numbers of minority children" (101). Finally, she argues that "Current racial matching policies are in conflict with the basic law of the land on race discrimination" (106).

38. Consider the popularity of a group of TV shows that presented the cute little black child adopted by white parent surrogates: *Webster, Diff' rent Strokes*, etc.

39. Such a devaluation is related to resistance to oppression. One thinks, for example, of Elizabeth Barrett Browning's dramatic monologue "The Runaway Slave at Pilgrim's Point" (1850) in which an infanticidal slave mother maddened by rape exclaims, "I am black, you see,—/ And the babe who lay on my bosom so, / Was far too white, too white for me" (I.113–15) so she retaliates by murdering the too-white infant.

40. Grounding her political disaffection from whiteness in a colonized past, Michelle Cliff in *Claiming an Identity They Taught Me to Despise* also views whiteness as a mistake, for she uses the same language Jean Rhys's heroine exploits in *Wide Sargasso Sea* (1966) to identify racial lightening with the degradation of sexual colonization:

> White cockroaches
> white niggers
> quadroons
> octoroons
> mulattos
> creoles
> white niggers. (44)

41. For an extensive reading of Dante's influence, see Catherine C. Ward.

42. As Henry Louis Gates, Jr., has explained in his response to Homan's "The Woman in the Cave," "the confusing phenomenon of the black bourgeois" in Naylor's novel may be modeled on white affluence without its citizens ever becoming integrated into white society; mimicry does not collapse into identity "(Linden Hills, the same as its white echelons of corporate success; Scarsdale in blackface)" (618–19).

All the characters in *Linden Hills* remain entrapped in structures that preexist their individual existences, enforcing identities upon them. To the extent that their thwarted lives demonstrate how different structures of domination operate to suppress difference differently, they exhibit the fear that keeps Naylor's closeted homosexual from risking a new life. Indeed, the speech composed of Whitman's lyrics about "the love of comrades" that marks the demise of the homosexual couple's union can be extended to encompass the leap of faith none of her characters dare to make:

The way is suspicious—the result uncertain, perhaps destructive;
You would have to give up all else—I alone would expect to be your God, sole and exclusive,
Your novitiate would even then be long and exhausting,
The whole past theory of your life, and all conformity to the lives around you, would have to be abandon'd;
Therefore release me now, before troubling yourself any further—(88; emphasis mine)

Although Naylor insists on the complex incongruence of the various binds imposed by color, class, gender, and sexual orientation, all her characters fear the uncertainty of leaving behind the comforting familiarity of the known, even though the known consists of systems of oppression damaging to body and soul. What "conformity to the lives around you" means in the racial terms that closet African Americans in *Linden Hills* is the double bind of trying to appear similar to or different from whites.

Chapter 7. The Edible Complex

Epigraphs: Montaigne, 185; Wright, 74; Whitman, *Song of Myself*, 16 ("I am of old and young, of the foolish as much as the wise"), lines 346, 349; Blanchot, 18.

1. *Newsweek*, Feb. 12, 1990, p. 52.
2. Indeed, what does it mean that racist dualisms seem more effectively challenged by racechanges in physiological rather than in cultural venues? Despite the efforts of many theorists to debiologize race so as to emphasize the possibility of socially reconstructing nonracist values, the most optimistic racechange scenarios seem to involve actual or electronically imagined physical (not social) transformations that are visible to the eye: the hybrid child, the morphed image. At the present moment, when magazines devote many words and pictures to illustrating the propositions that inter-racial marriages have escalated from 310,000 to more than 1.1 million in the past two decades and that the incidence of births of mixed-race babies has multiplied 26 times as fast as that of any other group (*Time*, 142, no. 21 (Fall 93): 64), we may find ideas about race forced to shift because of transformations situated more in the genetic than in the political realm. (Needless to say, however, "the simplistic antidote of More Miscegenation" cannot counter the past "pervasive anti-miscegenist horror of tainted bloodlines," as Patricia J. Williams has warned, at least in part because that horror was preceded by judicial justifications of miscegenation between white men and their "chattel" during slave times (190–91).)
3. Lest such a view appear happily fantastic or anachronistic—ensconced in a mythic past—consider the story told by the Mississippi bluesman Big Bill Broonzy about a man in his home town called Mister White whose property was surrounded by a white fence:

Trees, he painted them white, up as fur as he could git . . . And all the cattle . . . uh, and the sheeps, the goats, and the hogs, and the cows, mules, horses, and everything on his place was white. And any time that his cow, or his goat or whatsonever it was have a black colt, anything like that . . . he'd give it to the niggers. He didn't want nothing on his plantation black, see. . . .

When a state highway is run through his plantation, Mr. White builds a bypass and puts up a sign entitled *Negro Turn* so as to ensure the purity of his place. Though told as a hilarious tall tale to the folklorist Alan Lomax, Broonzy's account describes the psychology of separatism.

The CD *Blues in the Mississippi Night* (as told to and recorded by Alan Lomax) features Memphis Slim, Bill Broonzy, and Sonny Boy Williamson, who tell stories about African Americans led to refer to white mules as "Mister Mule" and asking for a can of Prince Albert tobacco (which had a picture of that white man on the can) with the sentence "Gimme can of Mister Prince Albert."

4. John Carlos Rowe argues that Nu-Nu's dead corpse functions as one aspect of "Poe's poetic mastery, his poetics of postmodern colonialism" in his reading of *Pym* (132).

5. Besides Freud's Oedipus complex, I am alluding to bell hooks's stimulating essay "Eating the Other" in *Black Looks*, 21–39.

6. It is interesting to juxtapose these passages with the novel written about Jefferson's slave mistress, Sally Hemings. In William Wells Brown's *Clotel; or, The President's Daughter* (1853), an abolitionist text centers on the child Jefferson fathered as a symbol of the injustice of slavery. See Sollors, *Ethnicity*, 225.

7. Diane Elam examines Derrida's claim that "This obligation to project the other's otherness is not merely a theoretical imperative" in the final chapter of *Feminism and Deconstruction*, 111.

8. See also Fuchs, 23–24.

9. See the useful comments of bell hooks on the film's conclusion and specifically her argument that the bored black woman has no need of Bernhard's performance and thus inscribes her ironic condemnation of her own efforts to perform blackness (esp. 38) and of Jean Walton, who points out that the black woman, filmed reading Harold Bloom's *Kabbalah and Criticism*, remains linked through Jewishness to the white star (in "Sandra Bernhard," esp. 254).

10. Phone conversation with the artist, March 18, 1996.

11. Another project undertaken by Udé, who clearly focuses on the importance of commercialized Hollywood images in his native Nigeria and elsewhere, involves an experiment in living art for which he constructed a magazine kiosk to display *Glamour, Mirabella*, and *Town & Country* magazines whose covers feature his own face transmuted through a series of costumes and cosmetics into multiple racial and sexual guises.

12. When during the 1980s and '90s an all-white New York theatrical troup called the Wooster Group used burnt cork—in reenactments of Pigmeat Markham's blacked-up vaudeville routines juxtaposed with a videotaped performance of Wilder's *Our Town* and in Eugene O'Neill's *The Emperor Jones* staged with a blackfaced actress playing the title role—they did so precisely to draw attention to the ironies of racial representation. I am indebted to Andrea Most for information on the Wooster Group. Shohat and Stam discuss what they call "the possibilities of epidermically incorrect casting in *Seeing Double* (1989), a San Francisco Mime Troupe play" about Israeli-Palestinian conflict (191).

13. In this regard, see Sollors's essay "A Critique of Pure Pluralism," in which he argues that "the ethnic perspective"—when taken exclusively as an emphasis on a writer's descent—"all but annihilates polyethnic art movements, moments of individual and cultural interaction, and the pervasiveness of cultural syncretism in America" (256).

14. Perhaps this is the reason why Charles Johnson's novels about slavery remain fascinated with what he calls "the theater of tattoes" in which his characters read "the profound mystery of the One and the Many" (*Oxherding Tale*, 195–6). Both *Oxherding Tale* (1982) and *Middle Passage* (1990) hinge on an "epiphany of skin," a vision of phantasmagoric images on epidermis that dramatize the boundaries and borders Americans perpetually race and erase (Gysin 289).

15. See the somewhat different reading of this tale in Ozick, 43.

16. For Malamud, as for Williams, the fact that cultural identities have been shaped by

lethal forms of racism—that anti-Semitism inflects Judaism with a self-subverting definition of Jewish-American identity and racism stamps blackness with a self-subverting definition of African-American identity—does not abrogate their persisting power over definitions of selfhood, though it does complicate their impact. Walter Benn Michaels asks in the last footnote of his book, "What exactly would be lost if everybody in Quebec stopped speaking French or if no one ever again thought of himself or herself as a Jew?" and answers that something of value might be lost "but that identity is never lost" (182); Malamud, like so many of the artists involved in racechanges, would have disagreed.

17. David Lloyd examines "the persistence of racism" as "an effect of ideological interpellation: approximation to the position of the Subject, theoretically available to all regardless of 'race or creed,' in fact requires the impossible negation of racial or cultural differences" (86).

18. I am indebted to the discussion of Wright and Wideman in Gysin, 293.

WORKS CITED

Abel, Elizabeth. "Black Writing, White Reading: Race and the Politics of Feminist Interpretation." *Critical Inquiry* 19, no. 3 (Spring 1993): 470–98.

Abrahams, Roger D. *Singing the Master: The Emergence of African-American Culture in the Plantation South*. New York: Penguin, 1992.

Ackroyd, Peter. *T. S. Eliot: A Life*. New York: Simon and Schuster, 1984.

Adams, Parveen. "Of Female Bondage." In *Between Feminism and Psychoanalysis*, ed. Teresa Brennan, 247–65. London and New York: Routledge, 1989.

Aiken, George L., and George C. Howard, *Uncle Tom's Cabin*. Ed. Thomas Riis. New York: Garland Publishing, 1994.

Alkire, Stephen Robert. "The Development and Treatment of the Negro Character as Presented in American Musical Theatre 1927–1968." Ph.D. diss., Michigan State University, 1972.

Allen, Don Cameron. *The Legend of Noah*. Urbana: Univ. of Illinois Press, 1949.

The Anchor Bible Dictionary. Vol. 3. Ed. David Noel Freedman. New York: Doubleday, 1992.

Anderson, Sherwood. "The Man Who Became a Woman." In *Horses and Men*, 185–228. New York: B. W. Huebsch, 1923.

Appiah, Anthony. "The Uncompleted Argument: Du Bois and the Illusion of Race." *Critical Inquiry* 12, no. 1 (Autumn 1985): 21–37.

Atlas, James. "Allan Bloom: Chicago's Grumpy Guru." *New York Times Magazine* (Jan. 3, 1988): 111.

Awkward, Michael. *Negotiating Difference: Race, Gender, and the Politics of Positionality*. Chicago: Univ. of Chicago Press, 1995.

Bailey, Randall C. "Africans in Old Testament Poetry and Narratives." In Felder, 165–86.

Baker, Houston A., Jr. *Long Black Song: Essays in Black American Literature and Culture*. Charlottesville: Univ. Press of Virginia, 1972.

———. *Modernism and the Harlem Renaissance*. Chicago: Univ. of Chicago Press, 1987.

———. *Singers of Daybreak: Studies in Black American Literature*. Washington, D.C.: Howard Univ. Press, 1974.

———. *Workings of the Spirit: The Poetics of Afro-American Women's Writing*. Chicago: Univ. of Chicago Press, 1991.

Bakhtin, M. M. *The Dialogic Imagination: Four Essays*. Ed. Michael Holquist, trans. Caryl Emerson and Michael Holquist. Austin: Univ. of Texas Press, 1992.

Baldwin, James. "The Black Boy Looks at the White Boy." In *Nobody Knows My Name: More Notes of a Native Son*, 169–90. New York: Dial Press, 1961.

———. *The Fire Next Time*. New York: Dial Press, 1963.

———. *Notes of A Native Son*. New York: Dial Press, 1972.

———. *The Price of the Ticket*. New York: St. Martin's, 1985.

Barth, John. *The Floating Opera and the End of the Road*. New York: Anchor, 1967.

Bartholet, Elizabeth. *Family Bonds: Adoption and the Politics of Parenting*. New York: Houghton Mifflin, 1993.

Beauvoir, Simone de. *The Second Sex*. Trans. H. M. Parshley. New York: Knopf, 1953.

Beemer, Suzy. "'Assay the Power You Have': Compromised Subjectivities and English Renaissance Literary Women." Ph.D. diss., University of Nebraska, 1996.

Bellow, Saul. *Mr. Sammler's Planet*. New York: Penguin, 1977.

Benjamin, Jessica. *The Bonds of Love: Psychoanalysis, Feminism, and the Problem of Domination*. New York: Pantheon, 1988.

Bergner, Gwen. "Who Is That Masked Woman? or, The Role of Gender in Fanon's *Black Skin, White Masks*." *PMLA* 110, no. 1 (Fall 1994): 75–88.

Berlant, Lauren. "National Brands/National Body: *Imitation of Life*." In *Comparative American Identities: Race, Sex, and Nationality in the Modern Text*, ed. Hortense J. Spillers, 110–40. New York: Routledge, 1991.

Bernstein, Leonard, and Alan Jay Lerner. "1600 Pennsylvania Avenue: A Musical Play about the Problems of Housekeeping." Typescript libretto from the Indiana University School of Music, 1976.

Berryman, John. *The Dream Songs*. New York: Farrar, Straus & Giroux, 1990.

Bersani, Leo, and Ulysse Dutoit. *The Forms of Violence*. New York: Schocken, 1985.

Berzon, Judith. *Neither White nor Black: The Mulatto Character in American Fiction*. New York: New York Univ. Press, 1978.

Bhabha, Homi. *The Location of Culture*. New York: Routledge, 1994.

Blackburn, Julia. *The Book of Colour*. London: Jonathan Cape, 1995.

Blake, William. *Poems of William Blake*. Ed. W. H. Stevenson. London: Longman, 1971.

Blanchot, Maurice. *The Writing of the Disaster*. Trans. Ann Smock. Lincoln and London: University of Nebraska Press, 1995.

Bogle, Donald. *Toms, Coons, Mulattoes, Mammies, and Bucks: An Interpretive History of Blacks in American Films*. New York: Continuum, 1989.

Boime, Albert. *The Art of Exclusion: Representing Blacks in the Nineteenth Century*. Washington and London: Smithsonian Institution Press, 1990.

Bonner, Marita. "One Boy's Story." In *Frye Street & Environs*, ed. Joyce Flynn and Joyce Occomy Stricklin, 78–91. Boston: Beacon Press, 1987.

Boone, Joseph A. "Vacation Cruises; or, The Homoerotics of Orientalism." *PMLA* 110, no. 1 (Fall 1995): 89–107.

Boose, Lynda E. "'The Getting of a Lawful Race': Racial Discourse in Early Modern England and the Unrepresentable Black Woman." In *Women, "Race," and Writing in the Early Modern Period*, ed. Margo Hendricks and Patricia Parker, 35–54. New York: Routledge, 1994.

Boskin, Joseph. *Sambo: The Rise and Demise of an American Jester*. New York: Oxford Univ. Press, 1986.

Brasch, Walter M. *Black English and the Mass Media*. Lanham, New York, London: Univ. Press of America, 1981.

Breines, Wini. *Young, White, and Miserable: Growing Up Female in the Fifties*. Boston: Beacon, 1992.

Brown, Ray B. "Shakespeare in American Vaudeville and Negro Minstrelsy." *American Quarterly* 12, no. 3 (Fall 1960): 374–91.

Browne, Thomas. *Pseudodoxia Epidemica; or, Enquiries into Very Many Received Tenents, and Commonly Presumed Truths*. 2nd ed. London: A. Miller, for Edw. Dod and Nath. Ekins, 1650.

Browning, Elizabeth. *The Poetical Works of Elizabeth Barrett Browning*. Ed. Ruth M. Adams. Boston: Houghton Mifflin, 1974.

Browning, Robert. *The Poetical Works of Robert Browning*. With an intro. by G. Robert Stange. Boston: Houghton Mifflin, 1974.

Burgin, Victor. "Paranoiac Space." *New Formations* 12 (Dec. 1990): 62–73.

Butler, Octavia E. *Kindred*. Intro. by Robert Crossley. Boston: Beacon Press, 1988.

Canarroe, Joel. *John Berryman*. New York: Columbia Univ. Press, 1977.

Carlyle, Thomas. *The French Revolution*. Centenary Edition. London: Chapman and Hall, 1937.

Carpenter, Edward. *Selected Writings*. Vol. 1: *Sex*. London: Gay Modern Classics, 1984.

Carringer, Robert L. *The Jazz Singer*. Madison: Univ. of Wisconsin Press, 1979.

Cartwright, Dr. Samuel A. "Unity of the Human Race Disproved by the Hebrew Bible," *De Bow's Review* 29 (vol. 4, no. 2): 129–36.

Cassuto, Umberto. *A Commentary on the Book of Genesis, Part II*. Trans. Israel Abrahams. Jerusalem: Magnes Press, Hebrew University, 1964.

Certeau, Michel de. *The Practice of Everyday Life*. Trans. Steven Rendeall. Berkeley: Univ. of California Press, 1984.

Chesnutt, Charles W. "Her Virginia Mammy." In *"The Wife of His Youth" and Other Stories of the Color Line*, 25–59. Ann Arbor: Univ. of Michigan Press, 1968.

———. *The House Behind the Cedars*. New York: Penguin, 1993.

———. *The Marrow of Tradition*. New York: Penguin, 1993.

———. "Mars Jeems's Nightmare." In *The Conjure Woman*, 54–102. Ridgewood, N.J.: Gregg Press, 1968.

———. "White Weeds." In *The Short Fiction of Charles W. Chesnutt*, ed. Sylvia Lyons Render, 391–404. Washington: Howard Univ. Press, 1981.

Chisholm, Anne. *Nancy Cunard*. New York: Alfred A. Knopf, 1979.

Chopin, Kate. "Désirée's Baby." In *The Awakening and Selected Stories*, 189–94. New York: Penguin, 1983.

Chow, Rey. *Writing Diaspora: Tactics of Intervention in Contemporary Cultural Studies*. Bloomington: Indiana Univ. Press, 1993.

Churchill, Caryl. *Cloud Nine*. New York: Routledge, 1987.

Cixous, Hélène. "The Laugh of the Medusa." In *New French Feminisms*, ed. Elaine Marks and Isabelle de Courtivron, 245–63. Amherst: Univ. of Massachusetts Press, 1980.

Cleaver. Eldridge. *Soul on Ice*. New York: McGraw-Hill, 1968.

Cliff, Michelle. *Bodies of Water*. New York: Dutton, 1990.

———. *Claiming an Identity They Taught Me to Despise*. Watertown, Mass.: Persephone Press, 1980.

Clifford, James. *The Predicament of Culture*. Cambridge, Mass.: Harvard Univ. Press, 1988.

Clifton, Lucille. "my dream about being white." In *Next New Poems*. Brocksport, N.Y.: BOA, 1987.

Clover, Carol J. "Dancin' in the Rain." *Critical Inquiry* 21, no. 4 (Summer 1995): 722–47.

Comley, Nancy R., and Robert Scholes. *Hemingway's Genders: Rereading the Hemingway Text*. New Haven: Yale Univ. Press, 1994.

Cone, James. *A Black Theology of Liberation*. Philadelphia and New York: J. B. Lippincott, 1970.

Connelly, Marc. *Voices Offstage: A Book of Memoirs*. New York: Holt, Rinehart and Winston, 1968.

Conrad, Peter. "The Devil's Disciple: The Art and Artifice of Robert Mapplethorpe." *The New Yorker* (June 5, 1995): 85–91.

Cooley, John. "White Writers and the Harlem Renaissance." In *The Harlem Renaissance: Revaluations*, ed. Amritjit Singh, William S. Shiver, and Stanley Brodwin, 13–22. New York: Garland, 1989.

Coon, Russell E. "Writing on Ancient Egypt: The Practices and Politics of Egyptomania." Ph.D. diss. proposal, Indiana University 1995.

Copher, Charles B. "Three Thousand Years of Biblical Interpretation with Reference to Black Peoples." *Journal of the Interdenominational Theological Center* 13 (Spring 1986): 225–46.

Corso, Gregory. "Bomb." In *The Penguin Book of the Beats*, ed. Ann Charters, 174–78. New York: Penguin, 1992.

Craft, William and Ellen. *Running a Thousand Miles for Freedom*. London: W. Tweedie, 1860.

Crane, Hart. *Letters of Hart Crane and His Family*. Ed. Thomas S. W. Lewis. New York: Columbia Univ. Press, 1974.

Crawford, Robert. *The Savage and the City in the Work of T. S. Eliot*. Oxford: Clarendon Press, 1987.

Cripps, Thomas. *Slow Fade to Black: The Negro in American Film, 1900–1942*. London: Oxford Univ. Press, 1977.

Croce, Arlene. *The Fred Astaire and Ginger Rogers Book*. New York: Galahad Books, 1972.

Cross, Amanda [Carolyn Heilbrun]. *A Trap for Fools*. New York: Ballantine, 1989.

Crouch, Stanley. *The All-American Skin Game; or, The Decoy of Race*. New York: Pantheon, 1995.

Crowder, Henry. *Henry-Music*. N.p.: Hours Press, 1930.

Cullen, Countee. *Color*. New York: Harper & Brothers, 1925.

cummings, e.e. *Complete Poems*. 2 vols. Great Britain: Macgibbon and Kee, 1968.

———. *The Enormous Room*. New York: Liveright, 1978.

———. *Him*. New York: Liveright, 1927.

———. *Tom*. In *Three Plays and a Ballet*, ed. George J. Firmage. New York: October House, 1967.

Cunard, Nancy. *Grand Man: Memoirs of Norman Douglas*. London: Secker and Warburg, 1954.

———. *Negro: An Anthology*. London: Wishart, 1934.

Cuney, Waring, "No Images." In *American Negro Poetry*, rev. ed., ed. Arna Bontemps, 98–99. New York: Hill and Wang, 1974.

Daniel, Bradford. "Why They Can't Wait: An Interview with a White Negro." *The Progressive* (July 1964): 15–19.

Davis, David Brion. *The Problem of Slavery in Western Culture*. Ithaca: Cornell Univ. Press, 1966.

Davis, F. James. *Who Is Black?: One Nation's Definition*. University Park: Pennsylvania State Univ. Press, 1991.

Davis, Kathe, "'Honey Dusk Do Sprawl': Does Black Minstrel Dialect Obscure *The Dream Songs?*" *Language and Style: An International Journal* 18, no. 1 (Winter 1985): 30–45.

DeBona, Guerric, O.S.B. "Into Africa: Orson Welles and *Heart of Darkness.*" *Cinema Journal* 33, no. 3 (Spring 1994): 16–34.

De Jongh, James. *Vicious Modernism: Black Harlem and the Literary Imagination.* Cambridge: Cambridge Univ. Press, 1990.

De Lauretis, Teresa. *The Practice of Love: Lesbian Sexuality and Perverse Desire.* Bloomington: Indiana Univ. Press, 1994.

Diamond, Stanley. *In Search of the Primitive: A Critique of Civilization.* New Brunswick: Transaction Books, 1974.

Dickens, Charles. *American Notes and Pictures from Italy.* Intro. Sacheverell Sitwell. London: Oxford Univ. Press, 1966.

Dickstein, Morris. *Gates of Eden: American Culture in the Sixties.* New York: Basic Books, 1977.

Dijkestra, Bram. *Idols of Perversity: Fantasies of Feminine Evil in Fin-de-Siècle Culture.* New York: Oxford Univ. Press, 1986.

Diop, Cheikh Anta. *The African Origin of Civilization.* Trans. Mercer Cook. New York: Lawrence Hill, 1974.

Dixon, Thomas. *The Clansman.* New York: Doubleday, Page, 1905.

Doane, Mary Ann. *Femmes Fatales: Feminism, Film Theory, Psychoanalysis.* New York: Routledge, 1991.

Douglas, Ann. *Terrible Honesty: Mongrel Manhattan in the 1920s.* New York: Farrar, Straus and Giroux, 1995.

Doyle, Laura. *Bordering on the Body: The Racial Matrix of Modern Fiction and Culture.* New York: Oxford Univ. Press, 1994.

Du Bois, W.E.B. *The Souls of Black Folk.* Millwood, N.Y.: Kraus-Thomson, 1973.

———. "The Souls of White Folk." *The Independent* 69, no. 3220 (Aug. 18, 1910): 339–42.

Dunbar, Paul Laurence. "We Wear the Mask." In *American Negro Poetry*, rev. ed., ed. Arna Bontemps, 14. New York: Hill and Wang, 1974.

Dyer, Richard. "White." *Screen* 29, no. 4 (1988): 44–64.

Elam, Diane. *Feminism and Deconstruction: Ms. en Abyme.* New York: Routledge, 1994.

Elfenbein, Anna Shannon. *Women on the Color Line: Evolving Stereotypes and the Writings of George Washington Cable, Grace King, Kate Chopin.* Charlottesville: Univ. of Virginia, 1989.

Eliot, T. S. "The Beating of a Drum." *Nation and the Athenaeum* 34 (Oct. 6, 1926): 12–13.

———. *Sweeney Agonistes.* London: Faber & Faber, 1932.

———. *The Waste Land, a Facsimile and Transcript.* Ed. Valerie Eliot. New York: Harcourt Brace Jovanovich, 1971.

Ellenzweig, Allen. *The Homoerotic Photograph: Male Images from Durieu/Delacroix to Mapplethorpe.* New York: Columbia Univ. Press, 1992.

Ellis, Trey. "The New Black Aesthetic." *Callaloo* 12 (Winter 1989): 233–43.

Ellison, Ralph. "Change the Joke and Slip the Yoke." In *Shadow and Act*, 45–59. New York: Random House, 1964.

———. *Going to the Territory.* New York: Random House, 1987.

———. *Invisible Man.* New York: Random House, 1952.

Ellmann, Richard. *Oscar Wilde.* New York: Alfred A. Knopf, 1988.

Ely, Melvin Patrick. *The Adventures of Amos 'n' Andy: A Social History of an American Phenomenon*. New York: Free Press, 1991.

Everett, Barbara. "The New Style of *Sweeney Agonistes*." *Yearbook of English Studies* 14 (1984): 243–63.

Fanon, Frantz. *Black Skin, White Masks*. Trans. Charles Lam Markmann. New York: Grove Weidenfeld, 1967.

Faulkner, William. *As I Lay Dying*. New York: Viking, 1990.

———. "The Bear," "Delta Autumn," and "Go Down, Moses." In *Go Down, Moses*, 183–315, 319–48, 351–65. New York: Vintage, 1970.

———. *Light in August*. New York: Vintage, 1987.

Fauset, Jessie Redmon. *Plum Bun: A Novel Without a Moral*. Boston: Pandora, 1985.

Felder, Cain Hope, ed. *Stony the Road We Trod: African American Biblical Interpretation*. Minneapolis: Fortress Press, 1991.

Fiedler, Leslie. "Come Back to the Raft Ag'in, Huck Honey!" In *An End to Innocence: Essays on Culture and Politics*, 142–51. Boston: Beacon Press, 1952.

———. *Waiting for the End*. New York: Stein and Day, 1964.

Fish, Jefferson M. "Mixed Blood." *Psychology Today* (Nov./Dec. 1995): 55–61, 76, 80.

Fisher, Rudolph. *The Walls of Jericho*. New York and London: A. A. Knopf, 1928.

Fishkin, Shelley Fisher. *Was Huck Black?: Mark Twain and African-American Voices*. New York: Oxford Univ. Press, 1993.

Fitzgerald, Zelda. *Save Me the Waltz*. Carbondale: South Illinois Univ. Press, 1967.

Flanner, Janet. *Paris Was Yesterday, 1925–1939*. Ed. Irving Drutman. New York: Viking, 1972.

Ford, George H. *Double Measure: A Study of the Novels and Stories of D. H. Lawrence*. New York: Holt, Rinehart and Winston, 1965.

Foster, Hal. *Recordings: Art, Spectacle, Cultural Politics*. Seattle: Bay Press, 1985.

France, Richard. *The Theatre of Orson Welles*. Lewisburg: Bucknell Univ. Press, 1977.

Franklin, John Hope. "'Birth of Nation'"—Propaganda as History." *Massachusetts Review* 20, no. 3 (Autumn 1979): 417–33.

Fredrickson, George. *The Black Image in the White Mind: The Debate on Afro-American Character and Destiny, 1817–1914*. New York: Harper, 1971.

Freud, Sigmund. "Family Romances" (1909). In *Collected Papers*, vol. 5, ed. James Strachey, 74–76. London: Hogarth Press and the Institute of Psycho-Analysis, 1950.

Friedman, John Block. *The Monstrous Races in Medieval Art and Thought*. Cambridge: Harvard Univ. Press, 1981.

Friedman, Lester D. *Unspeakable Images: Ethnicity and the American Cinema*. Urbana and Chicago: Univ. of Illinois Press, 1991.

Fuchs, Cynthia J. "Michael Jackson's Penis." In *Cruising the Performative: Interventions into the Representation of Ethnicity, Nationality, and Sexuality*, ed. Sue-Ellen Case, Philip Brett, and Susan Leigh Foster, 13–33. Bloomington: Indiana Univ. Press, 1995.

Funderburg, Lise. *Black, White, Other: Biracial Americans Talk about Race and Identity*. New York: William Morrow, 1994.

Fuss, Diana. *Essentially Speaking*. New York: Routledge, 1989.

———. *Identification Papers*. New York: Routledge, 1995.

Gallop, Jane. "Phallus/Penis: Same Difference." In *Thinking Through the Body*, 124–33. New York: Columbia Univ. Press, 1988.

Gates, Henry Louis, Jr. "'Authenticity' and the Lesson of *Little Tree*." *New York Times Book Review* (Nov. 24, 1991).

———. "The Black Man's Burden." In *Black Popular Culture, a Project by Michele Wallace*, ed. Gina Dent, 75–83. Seattle: Bay Press, 1992.

———. *Colored People, a Memoir*. New York: Random House, 1994.

———. *Figures in Black: Words, Signs, and the "Racial" Self*. New York: Oxford Univ. Press, 1987.

———. "Significant Others, a Response to Margaret Homans." *Contemporary Literature* 29, no. 4 (1988): 606–23.

———. "White Like Me," *The New Yorker* (June 17, 1996): 66–81.

Geduld, Harry M. *The Birth of the Talkies*. Bloomington: Indiana Univ. Press, 1975.

Genet, Jean. *The Blacks*. Trans. Bernard Frechtman. New York: Grove Press, 1960.

———. *Prisoner of Love*. Trans. Barbara Bray. London: Picador, 1989.

George, Nelson. *The Death of Rhythm and Blues*. New York: Pantheon, 1988.

Gilbert, D. *American Vaudeville, Its Life and Times*. New York: McGraw-Hill, 1940.

Gilbert, Sandra M., and Susan Gubar. *Letters from the Front*. New Haven: Yale Univ. Press, 1994.

———. *Sexchanges*. New Haven: Yale Univ. Press, 1989.

Gilman, Sander L. "Black Bodies, White Bodies: Toward an Iconography of Female Sexuality in Late Nineteenth-Century Art, Medicine, and Literature." *Critical Inquiry* 12, no. 1 (Autumn 1985): 204–42.

———. *Difference and Pathology: Stereotypes of Sexuality, Race, and Madness*. Ithaca: Cornell Univ. Press, 1986.

———. *The Jew's Body*. New York: Routledge, 1991.

Gilroy, Paul. *The Black Atlantis: Modernity and Double Consciousness*. Cambridge: Harvard Univ. Press, 1993.

Ginsberg, Allen. *Collected Poems, 1947–1980*. New York: Harper & Row, 1984.

Ginsberg, Elaine K. "Introduction: The Politics of Passing." In *Passing and the Fictions of Identity*, ed. Elaine K. Ginsberg, 1–18. Durham: Duke Univ. Press, 1996.

Golden, Thelma. "My Brother." In *Black: Representations of Masculinity in Contemporary American Art*, ed. Thelma Golden, 19–43. New York: Whitney Museum of American Art, distributed by Harry N. Abrams, 1994.

Goldenberg, David M. "The Curse of Ham: A Case of Rabbinic Racism?" In *Struggles in the Promised Land: Towards a History of Black-Jewish Relations in the United States*, ed. Jack Salzman and Cornel West. New York: Oxford Univ. Press, forthcoming.

Goldwater, Robert. *Primitivism in Modern Art*. New York: Vintage, 1967.

Gordimer, Nadine. "The Moment before the Gun Went Off." In *Jump and Other Stories*. New York: Penguin, 1992.

Gordon, Lyndall. *Eliot's New Life*. New York: Farrar, Straus and Giroux, 1988.

Gould, Lois. *A Sea-Change*. New York: Farrar, Straus and Giroux, 1976.

Graves, Robert, and Raphael Patai. *Hebrew Myths: The Book of Genesis*. New York: Greenwich House, 1983.

Gray, Donald J. "The Uses of Victorian Laughter." *Victorian Studies* 10, no. 2 (Dec. 1966): 145–76.

Gregory, Dick. *What's Happening?* Photographs by Jerry Yulsman. New York: E. P. Dutton: 1965.

Griffin, John Howard. *Black Like Me*. New York: Signet, 1976.

Grosz, Elizabeth A. "Lesbian Fetishism?" *differences* 3, no. 2 Special Issue on Queer Theory, ed. Teresa de Lauretis (1991): 39–54.

Gubar, Susan. "Feminist Misogyny: Mary Wollstonecraft and the Paradox of 'It Takes One to Know One.'" *Feminist Studies* 20, no. 3 (Fall 1994): 453–74.

Guillaumin, Colette. "The Idea of Race and Its Elevation to Autonomous, Scientific and Legal Status." In *Sociological Theories: Race and Colonialism*, 37–67. Paris: UNESCO, 1980.

Gysin, Fritz. "Predicaments of Skin: Boundaries in Recent African American Fiction." In *The Black Columbiad: Defining Moments in African American Literature and Culture*, ed. Werner Sollors and Maria Diedrich, 286–97. Cambridge: Harvard Univ. Press, 1994.

Hacker, Andrew. *Two Nations: Black and White, Separate, Hostile, Unequal*. New York: Charles Scribner's Sons, 1992.

Hacker, Marilyn. *Assumptions*. New York: Alfred A. Knopf, 1985.

Hackett, Francis. "Brotherly Love." In *The Birth of a Nation*, ed. Robert Lang, 161–63. New Brunswick: Rutgers Univ. Press, 1994.

Haggard, H. Rider. *She*. New York: Hart, 1976.

Haizlip, Shirlee Taylor. *The Sweeter the Juice*. New York: Simon & Schuster, 1994.

Hall, Stuart. "What Is This 'Black' in Black Popular Culture." In *Black Popular Culture, a Project by Michele Wallace*, ed. Gina Dent, 21–33. Seattle: Bay Press, 1992.

Halsell, Grace. *Soul Sister*. Greenwich, Conn.: Fawcett Crest, 1969.

Haraway, Donna J. "Universal Donors in a Vampire Culture: It's All in the Family: Biological Kinship Categories in the Twentieth-Century United States." In *Uncommon Ground*, ed. William Cronon, 321–66. New York: Norton 1995.

Hare, Nathan. *The Black Anglo-Saxons*. London. Collier-Macmillan, 1965.

Harper, Michael S. *Images of Kin: New and Selected Poems*. Urbana: Univ. of Illinois Press, 1977.

Harris, Trudier. *Exorcising Blackness: Historical and Literary Lynching and Burning Rituals*. Bloomington: Indiana Univ. Press, 1984.

Hathaway, Heather. "'Maybe Freedom Lies in Hating': Miscegenation and the Oedipal Conflict." In *Refiguring the Father: New Feminist Readings of Patriarchy*, ed. Patricia Yaeger and Beth Kowaleski-Wallace, 153–67. Carbondale: Southern Illinois Univ. Press, 1989.

Haywood, Charles. "Negro Minstrelsy and Shakespearean Burlesque." In *Folklore and Society: Essays in Honor of Benjamin A. Botkin*, ed. Bruce Jackson, 77–92. Hatboro, Pa.: Folklore Association, 1966.

Head, Bessie. *A Question of Power*. Portsmouth, N.H.: Heinemann, 1974.

Hebdige, Dick. *Subculture: The Meaning of Style*. London: Methuen, 1987.

Hemenway, Robert E. *Zora Neale Hurston*. Urbana: Univ. of Illinois Press, 1980.

Hemingway, Ernest. *The Garden of Eden*. New York: Collier Books, 1986.

———. "The Sea Change." In *The Complete Stories of Ernest Hemingway*, 302–5. New York: Charles Scribner's Sons, 1987.

Hernton, Calvin C. *Sex and Racism in America*. New York: Grove Weidenfeld, 1988.

Heyward, DuBois. *Porgy*. N.p. New York: Grosset & Dunlap with George H. Doran, 1925.

Hoch, Paul. *White Hero, Black Beast: Racism, Sexism and the Mask of Masculinity*. London: Pluto Press, 1979.

Holton, Sylvia Wallace. *Down Home and Uptown: The Representation of Black Speech in American Fiction*. Rutherford, N.J.: Fairleigh Dickinson Univ. Press, 1984.

Homans, Margaret. "The Woman in the Cave: Recent Feminist Fictions and the Classical Underworld." *Contemporary Literature* 29, no. 3 (1988): 369–402.

Honey, Maureen, ed. *Shadowed Dreams: Women's Poetry of the Harlem Renaissance*. New Brunswick: Rutgers Univ. Press, 1989.

hooks, bell. *Black Looks: Race and Representation*. Boston: South End Press, 1992.

———. "Feminism Inside: Toward a Black Body Politic." In *Black Male: Representations of Masculinity in Contemporary American Art*, ed. Thelma Golden, 127–40. New York: Whitney Museum of American Art, distributed by Harry N. Abrams, 1994.

Huggins, Nathan Irvin. *Harlem Renaissance*. New York: Oxford Univ. Press, 1971.

Hughes, Langston. *The Collected Poems*. Ed. Arnold Rampersad and David Roessel. New York: Alfred A. Knopf, 1994.

———. "Limitations of Life." In *Black Theatre U.S.A.*, ed. James V. Hatch, 656–57. New York: Free Press, 1974.

———. *Mulatto: A Tragedy of the Deep South*. In *Five Plays by Langston Hughes*, ed. Webster Smalley, 1–36. Bloomington: Indiana Univ. Press, 1968.

———. *Simple Takes a Wife*. 1953. Reprint. Mattituck, N.Y.: Aeonian Press, 1976.

———. "Who's Passing for Who?" in *Laughing to Keep From Crying*. Mattituck, N.Y.: Aeonian Press, 1976.

———, et al., eds. *Fire!!, Devoted to Younger Negro Artists* 1926. Reprint. Metuchen, N.J.: Fire!! Press, 1982.

Hurst, Fannie. "The Smudge." In *The Vertical City*. New York: P.F. Collier and Sons, 1922.

Hurston, Zora Neale. "Characteristics." In *The Gender of Modernism*, ed. Bonnie Kime Scott, 175–87. Bloomington: Indiana Univ. Press, 1990.

———. *Color Struck* and *The First One*. In *Black Female Playwrights: An Anthology of Plays before 1959*, ed. Kathy A. Perkins, 89–102, 80–88. Bloomington: Indiana Univ. Press, 1989.

———. *Dust Tracks on a Road*. 2nd ed. Ed. with an intro. by Robert E. Hemenway. Urbana: Univ. of Illinois Press, 1984.

———. "How It Feels to Be Colored Me" and "The 'Pet' Negro System." In *I Love Myself When I Am Laughing . . . and Then Again When I Am Looking Mean and Impressive*, ed. Alice Walker, 152–55, 156–62. Old Westbury, N.Y.: Feminist Press, 1979.

———. *Jonah's Gourd Vine*. Foreword by Rita Dove. New York: Perennial, 1990.

———. *Mules and Men*. Preface by Franz Boas and intro. by Robert E. Hemenway. Bloomington: Indiana Univ. Press, 1978.

———. *Their Eyes Were Watching God*. New York: Perennial, 1990.

Hutchinson, George. "Jean Toomer and the American Racial Discourse." *Texas Studies in Literature and Language* 35, no. 2 (Summer 1993): 226–50.

———. *The Harlem Renaissance in Black and White*. Cambridge: Harvard Univ. Press, 1995.

Huxley, Aldous. "Silence Is Golden." In *Do What You Will*. New York: Doubleday, Doran, 1929.

Irigaray, Luce. *This Sex Which Is Not One*. Trans. Catherine Porter with Carolyn Burke. Ithaca: Cornell Univ. Press, 1985.

Jacobs, Harriet. *Incidents in the Life of a Slave Girl*. New York: Oxford Univ. Press, 1988.

JanMohamed, Abdul R. "The Economy of Manichean Allegory: The Function of Racial Difference in Colonialist Literature." *Critical Inquiry* 12, no. 1 (1985): 59–87.

Jefferson, Thomas. *Notes on the State of Virginia*. Ed. William Peden. New York: W. W. Norton, 1954.

Johnson, Barbara. "Thresholds of Difference: Structures of Address in Zora Neale Hurston." *Critical Inquiry* 12, no. 1 (1985): 278–89.

———. "Response to Henry Louis Gates, Jr." In *Afro-American Literary Study in the 1990s*, ed. Houston A. Baker, Jr., and Patricia Redmond 39–44. Chicago: Univ. of Chicago Press, 1989.

Johnson, Charles. *Oxherding Tale*. Bloomington: Indiana Univ. Press, 1982.

Johnson, Charles R. *Black Humor*. Chicago: Johnson Publishing, 1970.

Johnson, James Weldon. *Autobiography of an Ex-Coloured Man*. New York: Vintage, 1989.

Johnson, Ken. "Colescott on Black & White." *Art in America* (June 1989): 148–53, 187.

Jones, Amelia, "Postfeminism, Feminist Pleasures, and Embodied Theories of Art." In *New Feminist Criticism*, ed. Joanna Frueh, Cassandra L. Langer, and Arlene Raven, 16–41. New York: Harper-Collins, 1991.

Jones, LeRoi (Amiri Baraka). *Home: Social Essays*. New York: William Morrow, 1966.

Jordan, June. "What Would I Do White." In *No More Masks*, ed. Florence Howe, 264–66. New York: HarperPerennial, 1993.

Jordan, Winthrop D. *White over Black: American Attitudes toward the Negro, 1550–1812*. Kingsport: Univ. of North Carolina Press, 1968.

Julien, Isaac. "Black Is, Black Ain't: Notes on De-Essentializing Black Identities." In *Black Popular Culture, a Project by Michele Wallace*, ed. Gina Dent, 255–63. Seattle: Bay Press, 1992.

Kahane, Claire. "The Artificial Niggers." *Massachusetts Review* (Spring 1978): 183–98.

Kalaidjian, Walter. *American Culture Between the Wars: Revisionary Modernism and Postmodern Critique*. New York: Columbia Univ. Press, 1993.

Kerouac, Jack. *On the Road*. New York: New American Library, 1957.

———. *The Subterraneans*. New York: Grove, 1958.

Kauffmann, Stanley. "Books & the Arts: Her Life and Times." *New Republic* 203, no. 1 (July 2, 1990): 26–27.

Kellner, Bruce. *Carl Van Vechten and the Irreverent Decades*. Norman: Univ. of Oklahoma Press, 1968.

———. *"Keep A-Inchin' Along": Selected Writings of Carl Van Vechten about Black Art and Letters*. Westport, Conn.: Greenwood Press, 1979.

Kennedy, Adrienne. *Funnyhouse of a Negro*. In *Adrienne Kennedy in One Act*. Minneapolis: Univ. of Minnesota Press, 1988.

Kristeva, Julia. *Revolution in Poetic Language*. Trans. Margaret Waller, intro. Leon S. Roudiez. New York: Columbia Univ. Press, 1984.

———. *Strangers to Ourselves*. Trans. Leon S. Roudiez. New York: Columbia Univ. Press, 1991.

Kuper, Adam. *The Invention of Primitive Society: Transformations of an Illusion*. London: Routledge, 1988.

Lacoue-Labarthe, Philippe. *Typography: Mimesis, Philosophy, Politics*. Ed. Christopher Fynsk, intro. Jacques Derrida. Cambridge, Mass.: Harvard Univ. Press, 1989.

Lang, Robert. *"The Birth of a Nation*: History, Ideology, Narrative Form." In *The Birth of a Nation*, 3–24. New Brunswick: Rutgers Univ. Press, 1994.

Larsen, Nella. *Quicksand and Passing*. Ed. Deborah E. McDowell. New Brunswick: Rutgers Univ. Press, 1986.

Lavin, Maud. *Cut with the Kitchen Knife: The Weimar Photomontages of Hannah Höch*. New Haven: Yale Univ. Press, 1993.

Lawrence, D. H. "Cypresses." In *The Complete Poems*, ed. Vivian de Sola Pinto and F. Warren Roberts, 296–98. New York: Penguin, 1984.

———. *Women in Love*. New York: Penguin, 1982.

Lazarre, Jane. *The Mother Knot*. New York: McGraw-Hill, 1976.

———. *Worlds Beyond My Control*. New York: Dutton, 1991.

Le Guin, Ursula K. *The Language of the Night: Essays on Fantasy and Science Fiction*. New York: G. P. Putnam's Sons, 1979.

Leonard, William Torbert. *Masquerade in Black*. Metuchen, N.J.: Scarecrow Press, 1986.

Lindsay, Vachel. *The Congo and Other Poems*. New York: Dover Thrift Editions, 1992.

Linebarger, J. M. *John Berryman*. New York: Twayne, 1974.

Lipton, Lawrence. *The Holy Barbarians*. New York: Julian Messner, 1959.

Lloyd, David. "Race under Representation." *Oxford Literary Review* 13, nos. 1–2 (1991): 62–94.

Locke, Alain. "The Legacy of the Ancestral Arts." In *The New Negro*, ed. Alain Locke, 254–67. New York: Atheneum, 1968.

Loomba, Ania. *Gender, Race, Renaissance Drama*. Manchester: Manchester Univ. Press, 1989.

Lott, Eric. *Love and Theft: Blackface Minstrelsy and the American Working Class*. New York: Oxford Univ. Press, 1993.

———. "White Like Me: Racial Cross-Dressing and the Construction of American Whiteness." In *Cultures of United States Imperialism*, ed. Amy Kaplan and Donald E. Pease, 474–95. Durham: Duke Univ. Press, 1993.

Low, Gail Ching-Liang. "White Skins/Black Masks: The Pleasures and Politics of Imperialism." *New Formations* 9 (Winter 1989): 83–104.

Lowell, Robert. "Benito Cereno." In *The Old Glory*, 135–214. New York: Farrar, Straus & Giroux, 1968.

McBride, James. *The Color of Water: A Black Man's Tribute to His White Mother*. New York. Riverhead, 1996.

McClintock, Anne. *Imperial Leather: Race, Gender and Sexuality in the Colonial Context*. New York: Routledge, 1995.

McCloskey, Susan. "Shakespeare, Orson Welles, and the 'Voodoo' *Macbeth*." *Shakespeare Quarterly* 36, no. 4 (Winter 1985): 406–16.

McDowell, Deborah E. "Negotiating Between Tenses: Witnessing Slavery after Freedom— *Dessa Rose*." In *Slavery and the Literary Imagination*, ed. Deborah E. McDowell and Arnold Rampersad, 144–63. Baltimore: Johns Hopkins Univ. Press, 1989.

McEvilley, Thomas. *Art and Otherness: Crisis in Cultural Identity*. New York: McPherson, 1992.

McKay, Claude. *Banjo*. New York: Harper and Brothers, 1929.

———. "Near-White." In *Gingertown*, 72–104. New York: Harper and Brothers, 1932.

———. *The Passion of Claude McKay: Selected Poetry and Prose, 1912–1948*. Ed. Wayne F. Cooper. New York: Schocken, 1973.

Mailer, Norman. *Advertisements for Myself*. New York: G. P. Putnam's Sons, 1959.

———. "Ten Thousand Words a Minute." *Esquire* 59 (Feb. 1963): 109–20.

———. "The White Negro." In *The Penguin Book of the Beats*, ed. Ann Charters, 581–605. New York: Penguin, 1993.

Mairs, Nancy. *Ordinary Time: Cycles in Marriage, Faith, and Renewal*. Boston: Beacon, 1994.

Malamud, Bernard. "Angel Levine." In *The Magic Barrel*. New York: Farrar, Straus & Cudahy, 1958.

———. *The Tenants*. New York: Pocket Books, 1972.

Manso, Peter. *Mailer: His Life and Times*. New York: Simon and Schuster, 1985.

Mapplethorpe, Robert. *Robert Mapplethorpe's Black Book*. New York: St. Martin's Press, 1986.

Marcus, Greil. *Lipstick Traces*. Cambridge: Harvard Univ. Press, 1989.

———. *Mystery Train: Images of America in Rock 'n' Roll Music*. New York: E. P. Dutton, 1975.

Marcus, Jane. "Bonding and Bondage: Nancy Cunard and the Making of the *Negro* Anthology." In *Borders, Boundaries, and Frames: Cultural Criticism and Cultural Studies*, ed. Mae Henderson, 33–63. New York: Routledge, 1995.

Mariani, Paul. *Dream Song: The Life of John Berryman*. New York: William Morrow, 1990.

———. "Williams' Black Novel." *Massachusetts Review* (Winter 1973): 67–75.

Massa, Ann. *Vachel Lindsay: Fieldworker for the American Dream*. Bloomington: Indiana Univ. Press, 1970.

Masters, Edgar Lee. *Vachel Lindsay: A Poet in America*. New York: Biblo and Tannen, 1969.

Maston, T. B. *The Bible and Race*. Nashville, Tenn.: Broadman Press, 1959.

May, Larry. *Screening Out the Past: The Birth of Mass Culture and the Motion Picture Industry*. New York: Oxford Univ. Press, 1980.

Mellinkoff, Ruth. *The Mark of Cain*. Berkeley: Univ. of California Press, 1981.

Melville, Herman. "Benito Cereno." In *Billy Budd and Other Stories*. New York: Houghton Mifflin, 1970.

———. *The Confidence-Man*. London: Penguin, 1990.

Mercer, Kobena. "Looking for Trouble." In *The Lesbian and Gay Studies Reader*, ed. Henry Abelove, Michele Aina Barale, and David M. Halperin, 344–59. New York: Routledge, 1993.

———. "Skin Head Sex Thing: Racial Difference and the Homoerotic Imaginary." *New Formations* 16 (Spring 1992): 1–23.

———. *Welcome to the Jungle: New Positions in Black Cultural Studies*. New York: Routledge: 1994.

Mercer, Kobena, and Isaac Julien. "Race, Sexual Politics and Black Masculinity." In *Male Order: Unwrapping Masculinity*, ed. Rowena Chapman and Jonathan Rutherford, 97–164. London: Lawrence and Wishart, 1988.

Messenger, Christian K. "Norman Mailer: Boxing and the Art of His Narrative." *Modern Fiction Studies* 33, no. 1 (Spring 1987): 85–104.

Mezzrow, Milton "Mezz," and Bernard Wolfe. *Really the Blues*. New York: Random House, 1946.

Michaels, Walter Benn. "Race into Culture: A Critical Genealogy of Cultural Identity." *Critical Inquiry* 18 (Summer 1992): 655–85.

———. *Our America: Nativism, Modernism, and Pluralism*. Durham: Duke Univ. Press, 1995.

———. "The Souls of White Folk." In *Literature and the Body: Essays on Populations and Persons*, ed. Elaine Scarry, 185–209. Baltimore: Johns Hopkins Univ. Press, 1988.

Miller, Alyce. "Color Struck." In *The Nature of Longing*, 106–29. Athens: Univ. of Georgia Press, 1994.

Miller, Nancy K. *Getting Personal: Feminist Occasions and Other Autobiographical Acts*. New York: Routledge, 1991.

Miller, Jonathan. "The Sick White Negro." *Partisan Review* 7.6 (Spring 1963): 149–55.

Modleski, Tania. *Feminism Without Women: Culture and Criticism in a "Postfeminist" Age*. New York: Routledge, 1991.

Montaigne, Michel de. "Of Cannibals." In *The Essays*, vol. 1, trans. Jacob Zeitlin. New York: Alfred A. Knopf, 1934.

Morrison, Toni. *Beloved*. New York: Plume, 1988.

———. *The Bluest Eye*. New York: Plume, 1994.

———. *Playing in the Dark: Whiteness and the Literary Imagination*. Cambridge, Mass.: Harvard Univ. Press, 1992.

————. "Recitatif." In *The Before Columbus Foundation Fiction Anthology: Selections from the American Book Award*, ed. Ishmael Reed, Kathryn Trueblood, and Shawn Wong, 445–64. New York: W. W. Norton, 1992.

————. *Sula*. New York: Plume, 1982.

Mosse, George L. *Nationalism and Sexuality: Middle-Class Morality and Sexual Norms in Modern Europe*. Madison: Univ. of Wisconsin Press, 1985.

Mukherjee, Bharati. "An Invisible Woman." *Saturday Night* (March 1981): 36–40.

Murray, Timothy. *Like a Film: Ideological Fantasy on Screen, Camera and Canvas*. London and New York: Routledge, 1993.

Naremore, James. *Acting in the Cinema*. Berkeley: Univ. of California Press, 1988.

Naylor, Gloria. *Linden Hills*. New York: Penguin, 1985.

Nicoll, Allardyce. *The World of Harlequin, a Critical Study of the Commedia dell'arte*. Cambridge: Cambridge Univ. Press, 1963.

Nielsen, Aldon Lynn. *Reading Race: White American Poets and the Racial Discourse in the Twentieth Century*. Athens: Univ. of Georgia Press, 1988.

Nixon, Cornelia. *Lawrence's Leadership Politics and the Turn Against Women*. Berkeley: Univ. of California Press, 1986.

Norman, Charles. *e.e. cummings: The Magic-Maker*. Indianapolis: Bobbs-Merrill, 1972.

North, Michael. *The Dialect of Modernism: Race, Language and Twentieth-Century Literature*. New York: Oxford Univ. Press, 1994.

Nugent, Richard Bruce. "Drawings for Mulattoes." In *Ebony and Topaz: A Collection*, ed. Charles S. Johnson, 103–6. Freeport, N.Y.: Books for Libraries Press, 1971.

————. "Smoke, Lilies and Jade." In Hughes, ed., *Fire!!*, and reprinted under the pseudonym Richard Bruce in Nathan Irvin Huggins, *Voices from the Harlem Renaissance*, 99–110. New York: Oxford Univ. Press, 1995.

Oates, Joyce Carol. "Negative." In *Skin Deep: Black Women and White Women Write about Race*, ed. Marita Golden and Susan Richards Shreve, 60–86. New York: Doubleday, 1995.

O'Connor, Flannery. "The Artificial Nigger" and "Judgement Day." In *Collected Short Stories of Flannery O'Connor*, 531–50. New York: Farrar, Straus and Giroux, 1972.

O'Connor, Patrick. *Josephine Baker*. Boston: Little, Brown, 1988.

O'Daniel, Therman B. *Jean Toomer: A Critical Evaluation*. Washington, D.C.: Howard Univ. Press, 1988.

O'Grady, Lorraine. "Olympia's Maid: Reclaiming Black Female Subjectivity." *Afterimage* (1992): 14–23.

Olivier, Laurence. *On Acting*. New York: Simon and Schuster, 1986.

Omi, Michael, and Howard Winant. *Racial Formation in the United States*. New York: Routledge & Kegan Paul, 1986.

Ostendorf, Berndt. *Black Literature in White America*. Sussex, Engl.: Harvester Press, 1982.

Ovid. *Metamorphoses*. Vol. 1. Trans. Frank Justus Miller. Cambridge, Mass.: Loeb Classical Library, 1984.

Ozick, Cynthia. "Literary Blacks and Jews." In *Blacks and Jews: Alliances and Arguments*, ed. Paul Berman, 42–75. New York: Dell, 1994.

Paley, Grace. "At That Time, or The History of a Joke" and "Zagrowsky Tells." In *Later the Same Day*. New York: Farrar, Straus and Giroux, 1985.

Parks, Suzan-Lori. *The Death of the Last Black Man in the Whole Entire World*. In *The American Play, and Other Works*, 99–131. New York: Theatre Communications Group, 1995.

Peel, Ellen. "Semiotic Subversion in "Désirée's Baby." *American Literature* 62, no. 2 (June 1990): 223–37.

Phillips, Christopher. "'To Imagine That I Am Another.'" *Art in America* 80 (July 1992): 92–93.

Pickering, Michael. "Mock Blacks and Racial Mockery: The 'Nigger' Minstrel and British Imperialism." In *Acts of Supremacy: The British Empire and the Stage, 1790–1930*, ed. J. S. Bratton, Richard Allen Cave, Breandan Gregory, Heidi J. Holder and Michael Pickering, 179–236. Manchester: Manchester Univ. Press, 1991.

Pieterse, Jan Nederveen. *White on Black: Images of Africa and Blacks in Western Popular Culture*. New Haven: Yale Univ. Press, 1992.

Pifer, Ellen. "'Two Different Speeches': Mystery and Knowledge in *Mr. Sammler's Planet.*" *Mosaic: A Journal for the Interdisciplinary Study of Literature* 18, no. 2 (Spring 1985): 17–32.

Piper, Adrian. "Passing for White, Passing for Black." In *New Feminist Criticism: Art Identity Action*, ed. Joanna Frueh, Cassandra L. Langer, and Arlene Raven, 216–47. New York: Harper Collins, 1991.

Plath, Sylvia. *The Collected Poems*. New York: Harper Colophon, 1981.

Podhoretz, Norman. "The Know-Nothing Bohemians." *Partisan Review* 25, no. 2 (Spring 1958): 305–18.

———. "My Negro Problem—And Ours." *Commentary* 35 (1963): 93–101.

Poe, Edgar Allan. *The Narrative of Arthur Gordon Pym*. New York: Hill and Wang, 1977.

Price, Sally. *Primitive Art in Civilized Places*. Chicago: Univ. of Chicago Press, 1989.

Priest, Josiah. *Slavery as It Relates to the Negro, or African Race*. New York: Arnow, 1977.

Ray, Man. *Man Ray Photographs*. Intro. Jean-Hubert Martin. New York: Thames and Hudson, 1991.

Reddy, Maureen T. *Crossing the Colorline: Race, Parenting, and Culture*. New Brunswick, N.J.: Rutgers Univ. Press, 1994.

Reff, Theodore. *Manet: Olympia*. New York: Viking Press, 1977.

Reid, Mark A. *Redefining Black Film*. Berkeley: Univ. of California Press, 1993.

Rice, Gene. "The Curse that Never Was (Genesis 9:18–27)." *Journal of Religious Thought* 24 (1972): 6–27.

Rich, Adrienne. "Compulsory Heterosexuality and Lesbian Existence." In *Women: Sex and Sexuality*, ed. Catharine R. Stimpson and Ethel Spector Person, 62–91. Chicago: Univ. of Chicago Press, 1980.

———. "Turning the Wheel." In *The Fact of a Doorframe: Poems Selected and New, 1950–1984*, 305–10. New York: W. W. Norton, 1984.

Riggs, Marlon T. "Unleash the Queen." In *Black Popular Culture, a Project by Michele Wallace*, ed. Gina Dent, 99–105. Seattle: Bay Press, 1992.

Rivière, Joan. "Womanliness as a Masquerade." In *Formations of Fantasy*, ed. Victor Burgin, James Donald, and Cora Kaplan, 45–61. London: Methuen, 1986.

Robert Colescott: The One Two Punch. Written and directed by David Irving, created and produced by Linda Freeman. Chappaqua, N.Y.: L&S Video, 1993.

Roediger, David R. *The Wages of Whiteness: Race and the Making of the American Working Class*. London: Verson, 1991.

Rogers, J. A. *Sex and Race: Negro-Caucasian Mixing in All Ages and All Lands*. 3 vols. St. Petersburg, Fla.: Helga M. Rogers, 1952, 1967.

Rogin, Michael. "Blackface, White Noise: The Jewish Jazz Singer Finds His Voice." *Critical Inquiry* 18, no. 4 (Spring 1992): 417–53.

————. *Blackface, White Noise: Jewish Immigrants in the Hollywood Melting Pot.* Berkeley: Univ. of California Press, 1996.

————. "'Democracy and Burnt Cork': The End of Blackface, the Beginning of Civil Rights." *Representations* 46 (Spring 1994): 1–34.

————. "'The Sword Became a Flashing Vision': D.W. Griffith's *The Birth of a Nation.*" In Lang, ed., *Birth of a Nation,* 250–93.

Rollins, Bryant. "Does '*The Wiz*' Say Something Extra to Blacks?" *New York Times* (Dec. 28, 1975).

Roof, Judith. *Come as You Are: Sexuality and Narrative.* New York: Columbia Univ. Press, 1996.

————. *A Lure of Knowledge: Lesbian Sexuality and Theory.* New York: Columbia Univ. Press, 1991.

Rosaldo, Renato. *Culture and Truth: The Remaking of Social Analysis.* Boston: Beacon Press, 1989.

Rose, Phyllis. *Jazz Cleopatra: Josephine Baker in Her Time.* New York: Vintage, 1991.

Ross, Andrew. *No Respect: Intellectuals and Popular Culture.* New York: Routledge, 1989.

Rowe, John Carlos. "Poe, Antebellum Slavery, and Modern Criticism." In *Poe's Pym: Critical Explorations,* ed. Richard Kopley, 117–38. Durham: Duke Univ. Press, 1992.

Rubenstein, Roberta. "Intersexions: Gender Metamorphosis in Angela Carter's *The Passion of New Eve* and Lois Gould's *A Sea-Change.*" *Tulsa Studies in Women's Literature* 12, no. 1 (Spring 1993): 103–18.

Rubin, William, Helene Seckel, and Judith Cousins. *Les Demoiselles d'Avignon.* New York: Museum of Modern Art, distributed by Harry N. Abrams, 1994.

Rubin, William, ed. *"Primitivism" in 20th-Century Art.* 2 vols. New York: Museum of Modern Art, 1984.

Ruggles, Eleanor. *The West-Going Heart: A Life of Vachel Lindsay.* New York: W. W. Norton, 1959.

Rushdy, Ashraf H. A. "Reading Mammy: The Subject of Relation in Sherley Anne Williams' *Dessa Rose.*" *African American Review* 27, no. 3 (1993): 365–89.

Sacks, Howard and Judith. *Way Up North in Dixie, a Black Family's Claim to the Confederate Anthem.* Washington, D.C.: Smithsonian Press, 1993.

Said, Edward. *Culture and Imperialism.* New York: Vintage, 1994.

Salter, Elizabeth. *Edith Sitwell.* London: Oresko Books, 1979.

Sampson, Henry T. *Blacks in Blackface: A Source Book on Early Black Musical Shows.* Metuchen, N.J.: Scarecrow Press, 1980.

Sandburg, Carl. *Complete Poems.* New York: Harcourt, Brace & World, 1950.

Sante, Luc. "The Unexamined Life." *New York Review of Books* 42, no. 18 (Nov. 15, 1995): 42–47.

Saxton, Alexander, "Blackface Minstrelsy and Jacksonian Ideology." *American Quarterly* 27 (1975): 3–21.

Scales-Trent, Judy. *Notes of a White Black Woman: Race, Color, Community.* University Park: Pennsylvania State Univ. Press, 1995.

Scarry, Elaine. *The Body in Pain.* New York: Oxford Univ. Press, 1985.

Schor, Mira. "Representations of the Penis." *M/E/A/N/I/N/G* 4 (Nov. 1988): 3–17.

Schor, Naomi. "Female Fetishism." In *Bad Objects: Essays Popular and Unpopular,* 93–100. Durham: Duke Univ. Press, 1995.

Schickel, Richard. *D. W. Griffith.* London: Pavilion Books, 1984.

Schofield, Carey. *Jagger.* New York: Beaufort Books, 1985.

Schuyler, George. *Black No More*. With a new foreword by James A. Miller. Boston: North-eastern Univ. Press, 1989.

Sedgwick, Eve Kosofsky. *Epistemology of the Closet*. Berkeley: Univ. of California Press, 1990.

Shakespeare, William. *The Tempest*. In *William Shakespeare, the Complete Works*, ed. Alfred Harbage, 1373–95. Baltimore, Md.: Penguin, 1972.

Shohat, Ellan, and Robert Stam. *Unthinking Eurocentrism: Multiculturalism and the Media*. London and New York: Routledge, 1994.

Showalter, Elaine. "Rethinking the Seventies: Women Writers and Violence." In *Women and Violence in Literature*, ed. Katherine Anne Ackley, 237–54. New York: Garland, 1990.

———. *Sexual Anarchy: Gender and Culture at the Fin de Siècle*. New York: Viking, 1990.

Silverman, Kaja. *The Threshold of the Visible World*. New York: Routledge, 1996.

Sims, Lowery S., and Mitchell D. Kahan. *Robert Colescott: A Retrospective, 1975–1986*. San Jose: San Jose Museum of Art, 1987.

Singleton, Geoffrey. *Edith Sitwell: The Hymn to Life*. London: Fortune Press, 1961.

Sitwell, Edith. "Gold Coast Customs." In *Gold Coast Customs*. London: Duckworth, 1929.

Smith, Anna Deavere. *Fires in the Mirror: Crown Heights, Brooklyn, and Other Identities*. New York: Anchor, 1993.

———. *Twilight: Los Angeles, 1992*. New York: Anchor, 1994.

Smith, H. Seldon. *In His Image, But . . . : Racism in Southern Religion, 1780–1910*. Durham, N.C.: Duke Univ. Press, 1972.

Smith, Joseph. *The Pearl of Great Price (as Revealed to J. Smith, June 1830–February 1831)*. Salt Lake City: Church of Jesus Christ of Latter-Day Saints, 1985.

Smith, Lillian. *Killers of the Dream*. New York: W. W. Norton, 1949.

Snowden, Frank M., Jr. *Before Color Prejudice: The Ancient View of Blacks*. Cambridge: Harvard Univ. Press, 1983.

Solano, Solita. *Nancy Cunard: Brave Past, Indomitable Rebel, 1896–1965*. Ed. Hugh Ford. Philadelphia: Chilton, 1968.

Sollors, Werner. *Beyond Ethnicity: Consent and Descent in American Culture*. New York: Oxford Univ. Press, 1986.

———. "A Critique of Pure Pluralism." In *Reconstructing American Literary History*, ed. Sacvan Bercovitch, 250–69. Cambridge: Harvard Univ. Press, 1986.

———. *Neither Black Nor White Yet Both*. New York: Oxford Univ. Press, 1997.

———. "'Never Was Born': The Mulatto, an American Tragedy." *Ethnicity and Literature* 27, no. 2 (Summer 1986): 293–316.

Sontag, Susan. *On Photography*. New York: Farrar, Straus and Giroux, 1977.

Southern, Terry. *Blue Movie*. London: Calder & Boyars, 1973.

Soyinka, Wole. *Myth, Literature and the African World*. Cambridge: Cambridge Univ. Press, 1976.

———. "This Past Must Address Its Present" (the 1986 Nobel Lecture). *Statement: Occasional Papers of the Phelps-Stokes Fund*, no. 3 (March 1988).

Spark, Muriel. "The Black Madonna." In *The Go-Away Bird and Other Stories*, 1–27. Philadelphia and New York: J. B. Lippincott, 1960.

Spencer, Anne. "White Things." In the *Norton Anthology of Literature by Women*, ed. Sandra M. Gilbert and Susan Gubar, 1367. New York: W. W. Norton, 1996.

Spilka, Mark. "Hemingway's Barbershop Quintet: The *Garden of Eden* Manuscript." *Novel* 21, no. 1 (Fall 1987): 29–55.

Spillers, Hortense. "Mama's Baby, Papa's Maybe." *diacritics* 17, no. 2 (Summer 1987): 65–81.

Spivak, Gayatri. "Imperialism and Sexual Difference." *Oxford Literary Review* 8, nos. 1–2 (1986): 225–40.

Stafford, Barbara Maria. *Body Criticism: Imaging the Unseen in Enlightenment Art and Medicine.* Cambridge, Mass.: MIT Press, 1991.

Staples, Brent. *Parallel Time: Growing Up in Black and White.* New York: Pantheon, 1994.

Steele, Shelby. *The Content of Our Character.* New York: HarperPerennial, 1990.

Stein, Gertrude. *The Autobiography of Alice B. Toklas,* "Melanctha," and *Tender Buttons.* In *Selected Writings of Gertrude Stein,* ed. Carl Van Vechten. New York: Vintage Books, 1974.

Stevens, Holly. *Souvenirs and Prophecies: The Young Wallace Stevens.* New York: Alfred A. Knopf, 1977.

Stevens, Wallace. *The Collected Poems.* New York: Vintage, 1982.

———. *Opus Posthumous.* Ed. Samuel French Morse. New York: Alfred A. Knopf, 1957.

Stowe, William F., and David Grimsted. "White-Black Humor." *The Journal of Ethnic Studies* 3, no. 2 (Summer 1975): 78–96.

Street, Brain V. *The Savage in Literature: Representations of "Primitive" Society in English Fiction 1858–1920.* London: Routledge & Kegan Paul, 1975.

Styron, William. "This Quiet Dusk." *Harper's* 230, no. 1379 (April 1965): 135–46.

Sundquist, Eric J. *To Wake the Nations: Race in the Making of American Literature.* Cambridge, Mass.: Harvard Univ. Press, 1993.

Takaki, Ronald. *A Different Mirror: A History of Multicultural America.* Boston: Little, Brown, 1993.

Talalay, Kathryn. *Composition in Black and White: The Tragic Saga of Harlem's Biracial Prodigy.* New York: Oxford Univ. Press, 1995.

Tidey, Ashley. "Reflections Across the Color Line: White Double Consciousness and the Heritage of Slavery." Ph.D. diss., Indiana Univ., 1996.

Tischler, Barbara L. "Europa Jazz in the 1920s and the Musical Discovery of Harlem." In *The Harlem Renaissance: Revaluations,* ed. Amritjit Singh, William S. Shiver, and Stanley Brodwin, 185–94. New York: Garland, 1989.

Toll, Robert C. *Blacking Up: The Minstrel Show in Nineteenth-Century America.* New York: Oxford Univ. Press, 1974.

Toomer, Jean. *Cane.* Ed. Darwin T. Turner. New York: W. W. Norton, 1988.

Torgovnick, Marianna. *Gone Primitive: Savage Intellects, Modern Lives.* Chicago: Univ. of Chicago Press, 1990.

Toth, Emily. *Kate Chopin.* New York: William Morrow, 1990.

Turner, Darwin. "Introduction" to Toomer, *Cane,* ix–xxv. New York: Liveright, 1975.

Turner, Victor. "Comments and Conclusions." In *The Reversible World: Symbolic Inversion in Art and Society,* ed. Barbara A. Babcock, 276–95. Ithaca: Cornell University Press, 1978.

Twain, Mark. *Autobiography.* Ed. Charles Neider. New York: Harper, 1959.

———. *Pudd'nhead Wilson and Those Extraordinary Twins.* Ed. Sidney E. Berger. New York: W. W. Norton Critical Edition, 1980.

Udé, Iké. "The Unknown Norma Jean: Monroe's Darker Roots." *aRUDE* 2, no. 1 (1996): 32–35.

Unterecker, John. *Voyager: A Life of Hart Crane.* London: Anthony Blond, 1970.

Van Vechten, Carl. *Nigger Heaven.* New York: Alfred A. Knopf, 1926.

Vendler, Helen. *The Given and the Made: Strategies of Poetic Redefinition*. Cambridge: Harvard Univ. Press, 1995.

Wald, Gayle. "'A Most Disagreeable Mirror': Reflections on White Identity in *Black Like Me*." In Ginsberg, ed., *Passing and the Fictions of Identity*, 151–77.

Walker, Alice. "One Child of One's Own: A Meaningful Digression Within the Work(s)." In *In Search of Our Mothers' Gardens*, 361–83. New York: Harcourt Brace, Jovanovich, 1983.

———. *Meridian*. New York: Pocket Books, 1976.

Wallace, Michele. *Black Macho and the Myth of the Superwoman*. New York: Verso, 1990.

Walton, Jean. "Re-Placing Race in (White) Psychoanalytic Discourse: Founding Narratives of Feminism." *Critical Inquiry* 21, no. 4 (Summer 1995): 775–804.

———. "Sandra Bernhard: Lesbian Postmodern or Modern Postlesbian?" In *The Lesbian Postmodern*, ed. Laura Doan, 244–61. New York: Columbia Univ. Press, 1994.

Ward, Catherine C. Ward. "Gloria Naylor's *Linden Hills*: A Modern *Inferno*." *Contemporary Literature* 28, no. 1 (1987): 67–81.

Ward, Douglas Turner. *Happy Ending and Day of Absence*. New York: Dramatists Play Service, 1966.

Warren, Robert Penn. *Band of Angels*. New York: Random House, 1955.

Washington, Booker T. *Up from Slavery*. New York: Penguin, 1986.

Washington, Joseph R., Jr. *Anti-Blackness in English Religion 1500–1800*. New York: Edwin Mellen, 1984.

Wasserstrom, William. "Cagey John: Berryman as Medicine Man." *Centennial Review* 12(1968): 334–54.

Watkins, Glenn. *Pyramids at the Louvre: Music, Culture, and Collage from Stravinsky to the Postmodernists*. Cambridge: Harvard Univ. Press, 1994.

Watkins, Mel. *On the Real Side: Laughing, Lying, and Signifying—The Underground Tradition of African-American Humor That Transformed American Culture, from Slavery to Richard Pryor*. New York: Touchstone, 1995.

Weinauer, Ellen M. "'A Most Respectable Looking Gentleman': Passing, Possession, and Transgression in *Running a Thousand Miles for Freedom*." In Ginsberg, ed., *Passing and the Fictions of Identity*, 37–56.

Wells, Ida B. *Crusade for Justice: The Autobiography of Ida B. Wells*. Ed. Alfreda Duster. Chicago: Univ. of Chicago Press, 1970.

Weinberg, Jonathan. "'Boy Crazy': Carl Van Vechten's Queer Collection." *Yale Journal of Criticism* 7, no. 2 (1994): 25–51.

West, Cornel. *Race Matters*. New York: Vintage, 1994.

Wheatley, Phillis. *The Collected Works*. Ed. John Shields. New York: Oxford Univ. Press, 1988.

Wheeler, David L. "Helping Mixed-Race People Declare Their Heritage: Portrait of Terry P. Wilson." *Chronicle of Higher Education* (Sept. 7, 1994): A8.

Whitman, Walt. *Leaves of Grass*. Ed. Jerome Loving. New York: Oxford Univ. Press, 1990.

White, Mimi. "*The Birth of a Nation*: History as Pretext." In Lang, ed., *The Birth of a Nation*, 214–24.

White, Walter. "Has Science Conquered the Color Line?" Reprinted from *Look* in *Negro Digest* (Dec. 1949): 37–40.

———. *A Man Called White: The Autobiography of Walter White*. New York: Arno Press and the New York Times, 1969.

Wideman, John Edgar. "Charles Chesnutt and the WPA Narratives: The Oral and Literate Roots of Afro-American Literature." In *The Slave's Narrative*, ed. Charles T. Davis and Henry Louis Gates, Jr., 59–77. New York: Oxford Univ. Press, 1985.

———. *Sent for You Yesterday*. London: Allison & Busby, 1984.

Wiegman, Robyn. *American Anatomies: Theorizing Race and Gender*. Durham: Duke Univ. Press, 1995.

Williams, Delores S. *Sisters in the Wilderness: The Challenge of Womanist God-Talk*. Maryknoll, N.Y.: Orbis Books, 1993.

Williams, Gregory Howard. *Life on the Color Line: The True Story of a White Boy Who Discovered He Was Black*. New York: Dutton, 1995.

Williams, Patricia J. *The Alchemy of Race and Rights: Diary of a Law Professor*. Cambridge, Mass.: Harvard Univ. Press, 1991.

———. *The Rooster's Egg: On the Resistance of Prejudice*. Cambridge: Harvard Univ. Press, 1995.

Williams, Raymond. *The Politics of Modernism: Against the New Conformists*. London: Verso, 1989.

Williams, Sherley Anne. *Dessa Rose*. New York: Berkeley, 1987.

Williams, William Carlos. *The Collected Poems*. Vols. 1 and 2. Ed. A. Walton Litz and Christopher MacGowan. New York: New Directions, 1986, 1988.

———. *In the American Grain*. New York: New Directions, 1956.

———. "Man Orchid." *Massachusetts Review* (Winter 1973): 77–117.

———. *Paterson*. New York: New Directions, 1963.

Williamson, Joel. *The Crucible of Race*. New York: Oxford Univ. Press, 1984.

———. *New People: Miscegenation and Mulattoes in the United States*. New York: Free Press, 1980.

Willis, Susan. "I Shop Therefore I Am: Is There a Place for Afro-American Culture in Commodity Culture?" In *Changing Our Own Words: Essays on Criticism, Theory, and Writing by Black Women*, ed. Cheryl A. Wall, 173–95. New Brunswick: Rutgers Univ. Press, 1991.

Wilson, Judith. "Scenes of War." In *I Tell My Heart: The Art of Horace Pippin*, 56–69. Philadelphia: Pennsylvania Academy of the Fine Arts, 1993.

Wirth, Thomas H. "Richard Bruce Nugent." *Black American Literature Forum* 19 (Spring 1985): 16.

Wittke, Carl. *Tambo and Bones: A History of the American Minstrel Stage*. New York: Greenwood Press, 1968.

Woll, Allen. *Black Musical Theatre: From Coontown to Dreamgirls*. Baton Rouge: Louisiana State Univ. Press, 1989.

Woolf, Virginia. "Professions for Women." In *The Death of the Moth and Other Essays*, 235–42. Orlando, Fla.: Harcourt Brace, 1942.

Wright, Richard. *White Man, Listen!* Garden City, N.Y.: Anchor Books, 1964.

X, Malcolm. *The Autobiography of Malcolm X*. With the assistance of Alex Haley. New York: Ballantine Books, 1992.

Yaeger, Patricia. "The Poetics of Birth." In *Discourses of Sexuality: From Aristotle to AIDS*, ed. Domna C. Stanton, 262–96. Ann Arbor: Univ. of Michigan Press, 1992.

Yatron, Michael. *America's Literary Revolt*. New York: Philosophical Library, 1959.

Yeomans, W. E. "T. S. Eliot, Ragtime, and the Blues." *University Review—Kansas City* 34 (1968): 267–75.

Zack, Naomi. *Race and Mixed Race*. Philadelphia: Temple Univ. Press, 1993.

Žižek, Slavoj. *Looking Awry: An Introduction to Jacques Lacan Through Popular Culture*. Cambridge, Mass.: MIT Press, 1992.

INDEX